Life and Times of James Abram Garfield

LIFE AND TIMES

OF

JAMES ABRAM GARFIELD,

TWENTIETH PRESIDENT OF THE UNITED STATES.

BY A. D. HOSTERMAN,

AUTHOR OF "NOBLE AND HEROIC DEEDS OF MEN AND WOMEN."

FARM AND FIRESIDE LIBRARY.

NUMBER 15. [illegible] SUBSCRIPTION PRICE, PER YEAR, [illegible]

PUBLISHED BY FARM AND FIRESIDE CO., SPRINGFIELD, OHIO.

Entered at the Post Office at Springfield, [illegible] mail matter.

J. A. Garfield

Lucretia R. Garfield

LIFE AND TIMES

OF

JAMES ABRAM GARFIELD,

TWENTIETH PRESIDENT OF THE UNITED STATES.

PRESENTING A GRAPHIC AND COMPLETE HISTORY OF HIS CAREER; EMBRACING NUMEROUS AND INTERESTING INCIDENTS OF HIS EARLY STRUGGLES AND TRIUMPHS; PORTRAYING HIS STEADY RISE TO PRE-EMINENCE; RELATING THE SAD AND TRAGIC STORY OF HIS DEATH; INCLUDING NUMEROUS SELECTIONS FROM HIS BEST AND MOST MASTERLY SPEECHES, AND CONCLUDING WITH A CHOICE SELECTION OF POETRY AND SONG.

ILLUSTRATED WITH SPIRITED ENGRAVINGS.

"Statesman, yet friend to truth? Of soul sincere,
In action faithful and in honor clear!
Who broke no promise, served no private end;
Who gained no title, who lost no friend;
Ennobled by himself, by all approved.
Praised, wept and honored by the muse he loved."
—POPE.

BY A. D. HOSTERMAN,
AUTHOR OF "NOBLE AND HEROIC DEEDS OF MEN AND WOMEN."

PUBLISHED BY
FARM AND FIRESIDE PUBLISHING COMPANY,
SPRINGFIELD, OHIO.
1882.

M. Sw.

TO

THE BOYS AND GIRLS OF AMERICA:

IN THE HOPE

THAT IT MAY ENCOURAGE, STIMULATE AND REGULATE THEIR LIVES AND PURPOSES FOR THE ACCOMPLISHMENT OF HIGH AND NOBLE ENDS,

THIS VOLUME IS AFFECTIONATELY DEDICATED

BY THE AUTHOR.

TABLE OF CONTENTS.

LIST OF ILLUSTRATIONS.

GARFIELD—THE BOY AND MAN.

PROPHECY.

I look forward with joy and hope to the day when our brave people, one in heart, one in their aspirations for freedom and peace, shall see that the darkness through which we have traveled, was but a part of that stern but beneficent discipline, by which the Great Dispenser of Events has been leading us on to a higher and nobler national life.—JAMES A. GARFIELD.

FULFILLMENT.

The resolutions drafted at New Orleans upon Garfield's death recite, "That in his death, we mourn the demise of a man of high and exalted attainments, of lofty purpose, of majestic strength; of a Chief Magistrate, whose serene self-respect, gentle dignity and deep patriotism seem, like a magician's wand, to have spread the bond of universal confidence and accord around a people divided by fears and prejudices, and the dissensions of statesmen; whose comprehensive grasp of heart and mind, enlightened by experience and study, responded as by intuition to the demands of his high office, through which he promised to raise our country to a height of dignity, peace and happiness unparalleled in the history of nations."

A combination, and a form, indeed,
Where every god did seem to set his seal,
To give the world assurance of a man.
—Shakespeare's "Hamlet," Act iii., Scene 4.

CHAPTER I.

GENEALOGY AND BIRTH.

If honest fame awaits the truly good, if setting aside the ultimate success, excellence alone is to be considered, then was his fortune as proud as any to be found in the records of our ancestry.—LUCAN.

JAMES ABRAM GARFIELD, TWENTIETH PRESIDENT OF THE UNITED STATES, died September 19th, 1881, at Elberon, Long Branch. His demise was the result of a pistol shot, which he had received on the second of July previous, from the hand of an assassin. The hopes and prayers of his countrymen had gone out for his restoration, but death came at last, and triumphantly he met it. Garfield had repaired to the sea-shore, accompanied by members of his family, his friends, and officers of state, hoping that the change from Washington air and surroundings would be beneficial to his wasted strength. But Providence, in his wise ministerings, called him from earth. His last hours comported well with the calm dignity and the imposing grandeur of his character and his life. The summons of death was heard with the same serenity, and obeyed with the same prompt submission, with which every call of duty during his life had been answered and met. When Garfield died, the most illustrious career, the most sublime character, which has ever yet graced the civil history of our republic, ended. Garfield was in every sense of that term a pure and Christian statesman. His life is one of which his countrymen may feel proud. He lived the embodiment of the highest principles of civilization. To trace the life of this illustrious American is the object of the following pages.

A good name is rather to be chosen than rubies; and a good character is the best passport to win success and respect in society and the world. It arrests the gaze of our fellowmen, and by it we are made to stand or fall. As grand and imposing architecture finds admirers among all its beholders; as the mammoth pile in which grace and proportion are harmoniously blended, invariably attracts the passer-by; and as the huge mountain, lifting its snow-crested summit above the surrounding heights, piercing the very sky, is a delight to every lover of the beautiful: so is dignity of character the delight of the historian as he sweeps his wand over the broad field of biography. The first sight of St. Peter's at Rome, is sufficient to fill every soul with admiration and delight. In this structure arch upon arch, pillar upon pillar, stand a monument of human greatness and capacity. But there was a time when St. Peter's Cathedral existed only in crude and unattractive material. Before the artisan's hammer and the artist's chisel gave shape, and carved statues all but animate, there was little to foretell the grand architectural wonder of to-day. In this respect man much resembles crude materials. The possibilities of a boy are greater than the man, because the boy is father to the man.

But little over fifty years ago the subject of this volume was an infant in the backwoods. There was nothing unusual in the appearance of the boy baby—nothing certainly to indicate the great man of the future; and yet a character grander than the architecture of St. Peter's stands out before the world to-day, the direct result of influences about him, as we shall see, and more than all, of his own well directed efforts in the line of improvement and success.

When history first becomes acquainted with James Abram Garfield he is scarcely more than an ordinary country lad, unusually attractive only because he was broad shouldered, sinewy and muscular. The history of Garfield is already indelibly written in the memory of his countrymen and the world. James A. Garfield accomplished nothing that every American youth cannot accomplish, for he did nothing more than polish, shape and beautify the talents and attain the possibilities within his reach. He may have reached a higher station, but his greatness, like all true greatness, consists in having done good. At his birth he was endowed with several hardy elements, which, ripened and augmented as manhood advanced, by culture, study, privations and lessons of hardship, secured for him a character than which none is more noble.

Individual history or biography is earliest interested in what elements of greatness are implanted in the individual at birth. What endowments of superiority the parents have bequeathed, becomes a most important and interesting investigation for every biographer. Everything has a beginning and a history. The smallest pebble by the roadside, the tree, the leaf, the firmament, and greatest of all, MAN, began existence at some time, was connected in some manner with the world's drama, and hence proved the existence of a purpose. Small beginnings should not be despised, for the diamond hidden in the most out-of-the-way place, when burnished, often becomes the most beautiful and valuable. Great men are seldom born with silver spoons in their mouths—more often surrounded by want and penury. Especially in America is this true. This is the talisman of our greatness; for the greater part of those who are and have been great in our history, are those whose birth, if not in a manger, was at least in a log cabin surrounded by forest wilds. James Abram Garfield was born on the 19th day of November, 1831. His first outlook upon things was from a cabin door in Cuyahoga county, Ohio.

I have said that at birth James A. Garfield was endowed with several hardy elements of character; and these, like two principal sources of a mighty river, only needed the increase of other tributary streams to make a Mississippi or an Amazon. We shall see what these elements were. To do this it will only be necessary to trace the genealogy of our subject and understand the race peculiarities which assisted in giving him being. The name seems to be broadly English enough in spite of the fact that it is a corruption of Garfelder or Garbefelder, of Anglo-Saxon origin.

The first root of the Garfield family of which there is any tangible knowledge was a James Garfield (or Gearfeldt), who, in 1587, was given a tract of land on the border of Wales, near Chester, England, through the influence of Robert Dudley, Earl of Leicester. A natural inference would be that he had performed some military service on the continent under that celebrated favorite of royalty, or was of some special service to Robert at Kenilworth or London. The estate thus conferred is said to be situated near Osvestry, and not far from the most beautiful and celebrated vale of Tlangollen, on the border of Wales. What was the nationality of this James Garfield—whether Welsh or English, German or Dutch—does not appear. The most probable conjecture is that he was Welsh, and was a warrior of some note—perhaps a descendant of the old knights of Gairfili castle. The estate conferred upon him was either released by him, or for some reason his children did not inherit it, and no mention of them appears, so far as is now known, in any record of the Garfield family until 1630, when Edward Garfield, of Chester, England, came to America in a company of colonists, having embarked with his family under the auspices of Governor John Winthrop. The name appears again at Watertown, Massachusetts, in 1635, and is probably the same man. Of this individual quite full accounts are handed down, and curious investigators into the family history claim to have discovered his coat of arms, and, if the description of it is correct, it goes far to confirm the previous conclusion that the Garfields were a martial family of wealth and influence in the days of Queen Elizabeth, if not in the crusades. It had three horizontal bars of red on a field, or background, of gold in the centre of the shield, and a red Maltese cross on an ermine canton or corner piece. The crest consisted of a helmet with the visor raised, and an uplifted arm holding a drawn sword. For a motto were the words: "*In cruce vinco*" (I conquer by the cross). This Edward Garfield, from whom the present large Garfield family in America has descended, appears to have taken no great pride in his lineage or lordly titles, for he took a personal and laborious share in the manual labor connected with the clearing of his land in Watertown, and left but a meager trace of his armorial badge. His house was built on a beautiful spot in Watertown, overlooking the Charles river, and the site is still pointed out to visitors, near the railroad station of the Fitchburg railroad. In this house he lived but a few years until he was able to purchase a much larger estate in the western part of Watertown, near the present location of the Waltham town line. On this land he erected a capacious mansion, and surrounded himself with all the comforts and elegance of the "gentleman" of that period, and the estate now known as the "Governor Gore place" still holds its position as one of the most beautiful and valuable estates in the vicinity of Boston. This Edward Garfield had a son, Edward, Jr., and he in turn had a son, Benjamin, who became a distinguished citizen of Watertown, and was given a captain's commission, by the governor, in the colonial militia. He held numerous town offices, and was elected nine times to the colonial legislature. He was a stout, broad shouldered man, with an open, cheerful countenance, and most affable and kind in his manners. His light complexion, and especially the light hair, appear to have descended to the present generation. The next ancestor in line was Lieutenant Thomas Garfield, who had offspring numbering an even dozen. Thomas, Jr., the third in order, was the one who should be written among the ancient grandfathers of the late President, and the next one down the scale was Solomon Garfield, the oldest son of the junior Thomas. He was married in 1766 to Sarah Stimpson, a widow with children by her first husband, and went to live in the town of Weston, Massachusetts. Solomon's brother Abraham was an earnest devotee of American independence, and lived in the town of Lincoln when the Revolutionary war began. He was one of the first volunteers enlisted in the defense of the colonies, and was in the fight at Concord, and side by side with many illustrious Americans, including Judge E. Rockwood Hoar, whose descendant and namesake has become noted in the councils of the nation in later years. The signatures of Judge Hoar's great-grandfather, John Hoar, and Abraham Garfield are still preserved, and the curious document they signed was an important matter in its time. The affidavits they sent to the Continental Congress at Philadelphia were to prove that the British were the aggressors in that affair, and fired twice before the patriots replied. It seems that the skirmish was regarded somewhat as if it had been a case of assault and battery, and the patriots were desirous of justifying themselves by showing who were the aggressors. At the beginning of the Revolution, separation from England was not generally meditated; and it was deemed important to fix the responsibility for the beginning of the conflict, showing which side struck the first blow, in the event of a settlement of the troubles. Therefore the affidavits of many persons concerned were secured and preserved.

Solomon's eldest son, Thomas Garfield, was born in 1775, and lived a farmer's life at Worcester, Otsego county, New York, and married Asenatte Hill, of Sharon, New York. Their children were Polly, Betsy, Abram and Thomas. When his youngest son was but two years old, and he thirty-two, he died of small-pox, which he contracted while taking a load of produce to Albany. Abram, named after his patriotic uncle, who fought at Concord, was the father of the late President. He was born December 28, 1799, at Worcester, New York. He was kept hard at work on a farm, with little opportunity for an education, being bound out to James Stone, a relative on his mother's side. Of his boyhood and early experiences there remain but meager accounts. He was a tall, robust young fellow, of very much the same type as his famous son, but a handsomer man, according to the verdict of his wife. He had a sunny, genial temper, like most men of great physical strength. He was a great favorite with his associates, and was a natural leader and master of the rude characters with whom he came in contact in his forest clearing work, and his later labors in building the Ohio Canal. His education was confined to a few terms in the Worcester district school, and the only two specimens of his writing extant show that it was not thorough enough to give him much knowledge of the science of orthography. He was fond of reading, but the hard life of a poor man in a new country gave him little time to read books, if he had had the money to buy them. The weekly newspapers and a few volumes borrowed from neighbors formed his intellectual diet. As a boy, rugged and sun-tanned, he had made the acquaintance of a prim little girl, born in a New England town, Eliza Ballou by name, who interested him not a little, and who occupied such of his moments as were given over to heart hopes and heart troubles. But Eliza Ballou moved west, and left Abram Garfield alone in his eastern home. He was not long following where his heart prompted, and in the autumn of 1819, being eighteen years of age, he journeyed westward, to meet and win his bride. His leisure hours were agreeably filled in with the courtship of Eliza Ballou, whom he in due course married. His contractor work over, the canal built, with a fair profit in his pocket, he moved to Orange, Cuyahoga county, and bought a piece of land. He moved practically into the wilderness, for there was but one house within seven miles.

A word about the wife. At her marriage she was only eighteen years of age, and her husband not yet twenty-one. Eliza Ballou's father was a cousin of Hosea Ballou, the founder of Universalism in this country. Eliza was born in 1801. The Ballous are of Huguenot origin, and are directly descended from Maturin Ballou, who fled from France on the revocation of the Edict of Nantes, and with other French Protestants, joined Roger Williams' colony in Rhode Island, the only American colony founded on the basis of full religious liberty. Upon the principle, "In civil matters, law; in religious matters, liberty," he built a queer old church, from the pulpit of which he thundered forth his philippics against religious intolerance. The building still stands, and is a curiosity of architecture. Not a nail was used in its construction. For generation after generation the descendants of this man were eloquent preachers, occupying the very pulpit of their ancestors. Their names are famous. They were men of powerful intellects, thorough culture and splendid characters. Many have been the distinguished legislators, orators, divines and soldiers which this family has given the country. The Ballou family has always been a superior one, and its characteristics have ever been, sterling integrity, spotless demeanor, high bearing, and the burning, eloquent gifts of the orator. These facts are all important and suggestive. They prove whence some of the most important and salient elements of Garfield's power came.

We have, then, from this cursory review of the genealogy of Garfield's parentage, the hereditary preparations for a great man. "From these two sources, the English-Puritan and the French-Huguenot, came the late President—his father, Abram Garfield, being descended from the one, and his mother, Eliza Ballou, from the other. It was good stock on both sides—none better, none braver, none truer. There was in it an inheritance of courage, of manliness, of imperishable love of liberty, of undying adherence to principle. Garfield was proud of his blood; and, with as much satisfaction as if he were a British nobleman reading his stately ancestral record in Burke's Peerage, he spoke of himself as ninth in descent from those who would not endure the oppression of the Stuarts, and seventh in descent from the brave French Protestants who refused to submit to tyranny even from the Grand Monarque. General Garfield delighted to dwell on these traits, and, during his only visit to England, he busied himself in discovering every trace of his forefathers in parish registries and on ancient army rolls. Sitting with a friend in the gallery of the House of Commons one night after a long day's labor in this field of research, he said, with evident elation, that in every war in which for three centuries patriots of English blood had struck sturdy blows for constitutional government and human liberty, his family had been represented. They were at Marston Moor, at Naseby and at Preston; they were at Bunker

Hill, at Saratoga, and at Monmouth, and in his own person he had battled for the same great cause in the war which preserved the Union of the States."*

From his father's side came immense muscular development and a constitution of iron, which was destined, ere the sands of life had run, to be severely tried and taxed. From this source also came an immense brain, though crude and uncultured. Heroism and devotion to duty were also indelibly imprinted in all of the Garfield lineage. Courage to do and dare, to defend principle though death result, courage, the more highly developed because striving after liberty of conscience, liberty of thought, and liberty in matters of religion, was his patrimony. From the other channel of hereditary descent came culture, faculties of imagination, and fine development in general. The Ballou's were small of stature, of energetic temperaments, and of the finest grain both physically and mentally. They were, and have for centuries been scholars and thinkers. The faculty of imparting knowledge, and hence eloquence, was also distinctively characteristic. To his father Garfield owed his large brain and robust and manly frame; but to his mother he was indebted for the untiring energy, unyielding pluck and patient courage which enabled him to overcome obstacles that would have altogether daunted any common man. In the drawing-room of General Garfield's house in Washington hung an exquisite painting, which the casual observer would take for a portrait of Mary, the mother of Washington. It has the same fine, regular features; the same high, full forehead; and the same serene, spiritual eyes: but the firm lines about the mouth, and the intense look in the deep, clear eyes, reveal a depth and energy of nature that is not seen in the face of the revered mother of Washington. The face of this woman shows that she has hoped and feared and struggled; that life to her has been a stern conflict; but that in the conflict she has at last come off grandly victorious. This is written all over her features; but is most clearly seen in the placid smile which encircles the firmly closed mouth, and irradiates the whole of the noble countenance. This is the mother of Garfield. She has made him what he is. Her personality and her principles have molded his character and shaped his whole career; and the deference which he always showed her is the same he felt for her when, a friendless boy, he was struggling in poverty and privation to acquire the means for an education. And when we look into the private lives of great men, do we not see it to be true that all their real greatness is traceable to the influence of some such woman, who was either their wife or their mother? To the earnest solidity and love of liberty of the Welshman, Edward Garfield, mixed with the reflective thought of a fair-haired German wife, was added the characteristic charms and vivacity of the French mind. In Garfield's parentage these noble traits unite, and Garfield's future history is the history of the development of these gifts.

This is the law of heredity! Nor could the thoughtful and investigating student examine this part of our subject other than in this manner. The law is already well recognized that all creation produces after its kind. And just as truly as the oak tree produces an oak in every way like the parent, so are the characteristics and mental and physical powers of man bequeathed to his offspring.

*Blaine's Eulogy.

"Every American State has its own story of the brave and adventurous spirits who were its early settlers: the men who build commonwealths, the men of whom commonwealths are builded. The history of the settlement of Massachusetts, of central New York, and of Ohio, is the history of the Garfield race. They were, to borrow a felicitous phrase, 'hungry for the horizon.' They were natural frontiersmen. Of the seven generations born in America, including the late President, not one was born in other than a frontiersman's dwelling. Each of the six generations who dwelt in Massachusetts has left an honorable record, still preserved. Five in succession bore an honorable military title. Some were fighters in the Indian wars. At the breaking out of the Revolution the male representatives of the family were two young brothers; one, whose name descended to the President, was in arms at Concord Bridge at sunrise on the 19th of April; the other, the President's great-grandfather, dwelling thirty miles off, was on his way to the scene of action before noon. These men knew how to build themselves log-houses in the wilderness. They were more skilful still to build constitutions and statutes. Slow, cautious, conservative, sluggish, unready in ordinary life, their brains move quick and sure as their rifles flash, when great controversies that determine the fate of states are to be decided, when great interests that brook no delay are at stake, and great battles that admit no indecision are to be fought. There never was a race of men on earth more capable of seeing clearly, of grasping, and of holding fast the great truths and great principles which are permanent, sure and safe for the government of the conduct of life, alike in private and in public concerns."*

It is not surprising then that Garfield's predominant characteristics were just such as we find them. That he should be eloquent, logical, studious, courageous and deeply religious are just the direction we should expect his mind and talents to take, once knowing his ancestry. But in finding these characteristics already a part of his nature at birth, we do not perceive anything that would subtract one iota from Garfield's greatness. While a man may be well endowed, yet the one who makes the best of his gifts is always the one who does the most good and becomes the greatest. It is a well known fact that of two boys, one, perhaps, who is well endowed mentally, who grasps all subjects easily but is deficient in application; and another who, while he has pluck, application and probity, but little quickness of thought, the latter, nine cases out of ten, will surpass the former. But when the happy combination of superior mental and physical endowments and intense application is secured, then the best and grandest results will be sure to follow. Such a one was Garfield. It was his own personal devotion to culture—the spirit of knowing everything—that made him superior. There are hundreds of men fully as well endowed as was Garfield, who have never risen above mediocrity. No man knows what are his powers, whether he is capable of great or only of little things, till he has tested himself by actual trial. Let every one starting out in life put forth his whole strength, without troubling himself with the question whether he has genius or not; then, as Sir Joshua Reynolds says: "If he has great talents, industry will improve them; if he has but moderate abilities, industry will supply their deficiency."

*Senator Hoar's eulogy.

It was on the third of February, 1820, that Abram Garfield and Eliza Ballou were married in the village of Zanesville. The newly married couple began life in a log-hut on a new farm of eighty acres, in Cuyahoga county, about fifteen miles south-east of Cleveland. Life here flowed quietly on, just as in many other Western log-cabins. The father managed his farm and added an acre or two of clearing to it every year. In January, 1821, their first child, Mehitabel, was born. In October, 1822, Thomas was born, and Mary in October, 1824. In 1826 the family removed to New Philadelphia, Tuscarawas county. In 1827 the fourth child, James B., was born. This was the only one of the children that the parents lost. He died in 1830, after the family returned to the lake country.

HOME OF GARFIELD'S CHILDHOOD.

In January, 1830, Abram went to Orange township, Cuyahoga county, where lived Amos Boynton, his half-brother—the son of his mother by her second husband—and bought eighty acres of land at two dollars an acre. The country was nearly all wild, and the new farm had to be carved out of the forest. Boynton purchased at the same time a tract of the same size adjoining, and the two families lived together for a few weeks in a log-house built by the joint labors of the men. Soon a second cabin was reared near by. The dwelling of the Garfields was built after the standard pattern of the houses of poor Ohio farmers in that day. Its walls were of logs, its roof was of clapboards, and its floor of rude puncheons split out of tree-trunks with a wedge and maul. It had only a single room, at one end of which was the big, cavernous chimney, where the cooking was done, and at the other a bed. The younger children slept in a trundle-bed, which was pushed under the bedstead of their parents in the daytime to get it out of the way, for their was no room to spare; the older ones climbed a ladder to the loft and slept under the steep roof. In this house James A. Garfield was born. At the time of his birth his only brother was nine years of age, and his two sisters respectively seven and eleven years. The mother looked after the cabin comforts, and did what she could to make her children fit for the struggle of existence. The father prospered fairly. For two years after the birth of their youngest child, James, the lives of Abram and Eliza Garfield flowed on peacefully and hopefully enough. The children were growing; the little farm improving; new settlers were coming in daily. It was a happy family. Though poor, they were content, and the distance which divided them from the world, bound them more closely together, like different spires in a sheaf of wheat, with separate individualities, but with only one life. With this much of hope and encouragement before them they looked forward to the future with buoyant hearts. But in the midst of life we are in death. What a day or an hour may bring forth we know not. The sky clear and bright, now auguring continued sunshine, may darken and grow threatening before an hour has passed; and from out the black folds, the lightning's flash and roaring thunder may be seen and heard. What before was bright and hopeful is now dark and foreboding.

Every fireside has its tragedy. In one short hour this happy, peaceful home of the Garfield's had gone, and darkness worse than the fabled Cimmerian, settled on the heads of the mother and her family. Without warning and with the swiftness of the wind, the fire-fiend and his destruction devotees coursed their way through the dry forests of north-western Ohio. In an instant, the evening sky was red with flame. It was a moment of horror. Sweeping on through the blazing tree tops with the speed of the wind came the tornado of fire. Laughing at the havoc and ruin, at the crying and wailings of those stung to the heart core, rushed the fiends. Everything in the course must perish. Houses, fences, crops, everything that the self-sacrificing frontiersmen possessed, in one short hour, wasted! In this emergency the neighbors, for miles around, gathered under the lead of Abram Garfield to battle for all that was near and dear. A plan for operations was speedily formed. Hour after hour this little band struggled and fought, and fought with all the advantages against them—a foe more destructive than an armed host. Suffocated, blinded, bleeding, with scarred hands and singed brows, they held their ground until the foe weakened and was turned aside. Abram Garfield, worn out with a night of bitter toil, bead-drops of perspiration standing upon his forehead and coursing down his heated, cinder-stained cheeks, walked to his home with a weary step. The trunks of unburnt trees stood out against the sky, blackened witnesses of destruction, and the wind was scattering the ashes hither and thither, as the farmers, knowing their scanty crops were saved, turned homeward. Abram Garfield, honest, hard-working farmer that he was, naturally had taken pride in his grain, a pride he could not afford to see humbled by the agency of a vagrant fire in the woods. When it approached the edge of his fields, he had gone forth to the fight, and after hours of exhausting work, succeeded in getting the better of his enemy. Reaching his cabin, he sank wearily on a three-legged stool that stood by the open door, and raised his hat that he might wipe away the perspiration beading his forehead. With no thought but that of rest, he allowed the breezes that blew over his saved wheat fields to cool his face with their grateful breath. In this most natural act he contracted a severe cold and sore throat, the over-tension of his system laying it open to influences that his otherwise hardy nature would have easily withstood. Chill followed chill, and inflammation set in, becoming rapidly so intense that his good wife Eliza determined to send for the only doctor the county boasted, a semi-quack, who lived several miles away. The leech responded promptly, came, and with many a profound gesture that illustrated nothing so well as his profound ignorance, ordered a blister for the sick man's throat—it was applied with all the instant virulence of quack practice in an unsettled country. The treatment was in faith so heroic that Abram Garfield, shortly after the blister was applied, choked to death. Feeling that the last great act of his life had come, he motioned his wife to his side, and said, with thick, broken utterance: "I am going to leave you, Eliza. I have planted four saplings in these woods, and I must now leave them to your care." One last embrace from the grief-stricken wife and children, a last long look upon his little farm as it stretched beyond the window toward the rising sun, he called his oxen by name, turned upon his side and expired.

A few days before the death of the father, he was reading a volume of Plutarch's Lives, and holding the boy on one knee. James had just begun to say "papa" and "mamma," and a very few words were his whole vocabulary. Stopping his reading a moment to listen to the child's prattle, the father said: "Say Plutarch, James." The boy pronounced the word plainly, and repeated it several times. "Eliza," said the father, "this boy will be a great scholar some day."

The poor widow was stunned by the suddenness of her great misfortune. It had come upon her so quickly it was impossible to realize at the moment of her husband's passing away, the full extent of her loss. Gradually the iron entered her soul, she became aware of her loneliness. Bowing her head she wept bitterly. "Do not cry, my mother, I will take care of you," said her son Thomas a mere slip of a boy, who stood by her side, scarce comprehending what he said or why he said it. "God bless you, my son; I will try to be brave for your sweet sakes," said the stricken woman, as she wound her arms convulsively about the boy. Rising, she called the two little girls to her side, and explained to them their loss—the death of their father. Tenderly she lifted them in her arms and bade them kiss the cold, calm face, for the last time. Then from the cradle she lifted the youngest, her baby-boy, James, almost two years old, the pride of her hearthstone. The boy looked down, wonderingly, out of his great blue eyes at his father's face so still upon the pillow. With a childish, questioning look, he lisped, "Papa sleep?" The mother's tears, flowing rapidly, was the only answer. Two days later, Abram Garfield was laid to rest, and the baby-boy was carried to the funeral in the arms of his uncle, William Letcher. The child, as was natural in one so young, paid no attention to the sad ceremonies until he was brought beside the coffin to take a last look at the dead. Recognizing his father, he called aloud for him, the tears following each other rapidly down his face. When the earth was thrown upon the coffin the child continued his cries until the whole company burst into tears. Who of us that have passed through such a scene can ever forget it? The agony of a few brief moments then, often lives forever. They are to the mind what scars are to the body, and remain upon us while life lasts, teaching always, however, their lesson, just as the rock, when rent, discloses the gem, or the little obstacle that impedes the onward progress of the brook serves to make music and keep pure its water. So with Eliza Garfield. The influence of her chastening is upon her; it will be to her a softening thought, and one to nerve her arm, for her's is a heroic soul—she comes from no common mold; she will come forth from the death-chamber well armed for the battle of life. In her veins runs the blood of the Puritans, and all the energy, intelligence and perseverance of that grand old race lies mingled in her frame. No danger it will fail her now; no danger but that such a woman will succeed; no danger but that such a mother is a fit woman to raise a President.

Though stunned by this appalling calamity, Mrs. Garfield, true to the heroic ancestry from which she sprang, took up the burden of life with invincible courage. The prospect was a hard one. With four children to support, the oldest of whom was only ten years old, with a farm only begun, and the resources very scanty, she knew all too well what it meant. Nothing now remained to bind up these broken lives but the weak, puny arms of the mother; but she threw them about the little household, and set her face bravely to meet the wintry storms that were coming; and it was a cold, hard winter, and they were alone in the wilderness. The snow lay deep all over the hills; and often, when lying awake in their narrow beds, the little ones would hear the wolves howling hungrily around the lonely cabin, and the panthers crying and moaning before the door, like children who had lost their way in a forest.

CHAPTER II.

BOYHOOD AND EARLY EXPERIENCES.

"Youth with swift feet walks onward in the way;
The land of joy lies all before his eyes."
FRANCES ANNE KEMBLE BUTLER.

"Youth is to all the glad season of life, but often only by what it hopes, not by what it attains, or what it escapes."—CARLYLE.

In a new settlement the wealth of the family is in the right arm of the father. To say that the father, who had himself been left an orphan when he was an infant, left his children fatherless in infancy, is to say that the family was reduced to extremest poverty. But the poverty was not mean and ignoble.

"The early life of Garfield was one of privation, but its poverty has unjustly been made prominent. Thousands of readers have imagined him as the ragged, starving child whose reality too often greets the eye in the squalid sections of our large cities. General Garfield's infancy and youth had none of their destitution, none of their pitiful features appealing to the tender heart and to the open hand of charity. He was a poor boy in the same sense in which Henry Clay was a poor boy; in which Andrew Jackson, Daniel Webster and a large majority of the eminent men of America in all generations have been poor boys. Before a great multitude of men, in a public speech, Mr. Webster bore this testimony: 'It did not happen to me to be born in a log cabin, but my elder brothers and sisters were born in a log cabin raised amid the snowdrifts of New Hampshire at a period so early that when the smoke rose first from its rude chimney and curled over the frozen hills, there was no similar evidence of a white man's habitation between it and the settlements on the rivers of Canada. Its remains still exist. I make to it an annual visit. I carry my children to it to teach them the hardships endured by the generations which have gone before them. I love to dwell on the tender recollections, the kindred ties, the early affections, and the touching narratives and incidents which mingle with all I know of this primitive family abode.' With the requisite change of scene, the same words would aptly portray the early days of Garfield. The poverty of the frontier, where all are engaged in a common struggle, and where a common sympathy and hearty co-operation lighten the burdens of each, is a very different poverty; different in kind, different in influence and effect, from that conscious and humiliating indigence which is every day forced to contrast itself with neighboring wealth on which it feels a sense of grinding dependence. The poverty of the frontier is indeed no poverty. It is but the beginning of wealth, and has the boundless possibilities of the future always opening before it. No man ever grew up in the agricultural regions of the West, where a house-raising, or even a corn-husking, is matter of common interest and helpfulness, with any other feeling than that of broad-minded, generous independence. This honorable independence marked the youth of Garfield as it marks the youth of millions of the best blood and brain now training for the future citizenship and future government of the Republic. Garfield was born heir to land, to the title of freeholder, which has been the patent and passport of self-respect with the Anglo-Saxon race ever since Hengist and Horsa landed on the shores of England. His adventure on the canal—an alternative between that and the deck of a Lake Erie schooner—was a farmer boy's device for earning money, just as the New-England lad begins a possibly great career by sailing before the mast on a coasting vessel or on a merchantman bound to the farther India or to the China Seas. No manly man feels anything of shame in looking back to early struggles with adverse circumstances, and no man feels a worthier pride than when he has conquered the obstacles to his progress. But no one of noble mold desires to be looked upon as having occupied a menial position, as having been repressed by a feeling of inferiority, or as having suffered the evils of poverty until relief was found at the hand of charity. General Garfield's youth presented no hardships which family love and family energy did not overcome, subjected him to no privations which he did not cheerfully accept, and left no memories save those which were recalled with delight, and transmitted with profit and with pride." * He was born not in the the lap of luxury, but in the abode of poverty that has a hopeful future. He came into the world, not the possessor of broad acres and massive walls, but to an inheritance of care, and a life of struggle. He opened his eyes, not the heir of the ages, but the son of toil. His only patrimony were the elements of a sublime life. His fidelity to duty was the amalgam that joined his early home of obscurity yonder upon the lake shore, to the loftiest pinnacle of American greatness.

The winter following the father's death was truly an uncomfortable one. It wore away at last, but spring brought no fair weather to the little household. They were not only poor, but in debt. The debt must be paid, and the future, ah! that stared darkly in their faces. But this brave mother went to work bravely. Fifty acres of the little farm of eighty acres was sold, and she and the older children went to work upon the remainder. Thomas, the older boy, who now was ten, hired a horse, and ploughed and sowed the small plat of cleared land; and the mother split the rails, and fenced in the little house-lot. The maul was so heavy that she could only just lift it to her shoulder, and with about every blow she herself came down to the ground; but she struggled on with the work, and soon the lot was fenced, and the little farm in tolerable order.

The little clearing of twenty acres, with the imperfect cultivation which one weak woman, unaided, could give it, had to be depended on, not only to furnish food for herself and the four children, but to pay the taxes and interest on the mortgage, and gradually to lessen the principal of the debt itself. So fearful were the odds against the dauntless mother, that her friends pointed out the overwhelming difficulties of the situation, and advised her to give her children

* Blaine's Eulogy.

out to the neighbors to be brought up. This mistaken, but well-meant advice, she put aside, and with an invincible courage, she said, "My family must not be separated. It is my wish and duty to raise these children myself. No one can care for them like a mother." The force of such a decision can scarcely be estimated. Every mother who has seen the advantages resulting from raising her own children, will understand the nobility of this hero mother. Hunger, poverty, privation and uncompromising obstacles were not sufficient to turn her from her noble maternal desire. And who can say but that this act of the mother, as much as anything else, contributed to her noble and illustrious son's advantage? Had she, in this dark hour, listened to the voice of friends, and given up the charge of her children, there might possibly have been no occasion for this volume. How all-important then is the watchfulness and direction of a mother. Advisers yielded to her will, and she had her way. She took up the mantle of head of the family, and with that brevet rank which widowhood never fails to confer upon deserving women, she made herself thoroughly respected by her sterling force of character, and high resolve to dare and do for the weal of her children. Though small of stature, and thirty years of age, she had the ability and energy of a larger and older woman. The farm was to be kept up, the home continued as it had been since 1830, the "four saplings" cared for until they were ready to be transplanted. Then, and not till then, would she give up the farm. This was a resolve that boded a harvest in its fruition. For there was nothing strikingly beautiful in the country where she dwelt, there was nothing remarkably attractive. The soil was not noticeably excellent. There were a thousand farms that surpassed it, and she had nothing to work with but energy and willingness. She rose early and retired late. Her work never sought her, she sought it. The homestead assumed a more homelike appearance each year, as new comforts were added by the thrifty woman who managed it. The young orchard which Abram Garfield had planted grew amazingly, and the trees fulfilled the promise of their planting. Cherries, apples, and plums, other fruits, proved quite an addition to the frugal fare of the family, and the gathering of these was always a delight to the children.

With the opening of spring the corn was running low in the bin, and it was a long time till harvest. So the mother measured out the corn, reckoned how much her children would eat, and went to bed without her supper. For weeks she did this. But the children were young and growing; their little mouths were larger than she had measured, and after awhile she omitted to eat her dinner also. One meal a day, and she a weak and fragile woman! Is it to be wondered at that she is loved and revered by her children? But the harvest came at last, and then want was driven away, and it never again looked in with gaunt jaws upon the lonely widow. Neighbors, too, soon gathered round the little log cottage in the wilderness. The nearest was a mile away; but a mile in a new country is not near so far as a mile in an old one, and they came often to visit the lonely household. They had sewing to do, and the widow did it; ploughing to do, and Thomas did that; and after a time one of them hired the boy to work on his farm, paying him twelve dollars a month for fourteen hours daily labor. Thomas worked away like a man; and—while I do not state it as an historical fact—I verily believe that no man ever felt himself so much of a man as he did when he came home and counted out into his mother's lap his first fortnight's wages—all in silver half-dollars. Reader, picture to yourself this scene. Call the mother by the right name, and she is a heroine. The sudden flash of the meteor across the heavens strikes us as a wonderful phenomenon. We watch it and admire its swiftness, its magnificent sweep; but when it vanishes, it is soon forgotten. But how different are our feelings concerning the great source of light. His regular course is run day by day. Each revolution brings us light, warmth and sunshine—therefore, pleasure. This we do not forget, for it gives us new joys, new hopes each day. And so does the analogy hold good here. The highest heroism is not that which manifests itself in some single, great and splendid crisis. It is seldom seen when regiments dash forward upon blazing batteries, and in ten minutes are either conquerors or conquered. It is not always seen in the martyr. It is not found in the courtly tournaments of the past, where knights, in glittering armor, flung the furious lance of defiance into the face of their foe. Splendid, heroic, are these all. But this is in the similitude of the shooting-star. It dazzles, but is not the most abiding. There is a heroism grander than these all; it is the heroism which endures, not merely for a moment, but through the hard and bitter toils of a lifetime; which, when the inspiration of the crisis has passed away, and weary years of hardship stretch their stony path before tired feet, cheerfully takes up the burden of life, undaunted and undismayed. In all the annals of the brave, who, in all times, have suffered, and endured, there is no scene more touching than the picture of this widow toiling for her children. To no nobler matron did ever Roman hero trace his origin.

From the first the Garfield children performed tasks beyond their years. After the first winter of desolation, the bitter edge of poverty wore off. The high executive ability of the little widow began to tell on the family affairs. Having now surveyed the Garfield estate from without, let us enter the little cabin and read the inner history. Every household has two distinct histories. The one is the outward, and read at a glance by the world. The other, the inner or fireside history, which few are permitted to read. Of the two, the latter is the more important to the historian. It is undoubtedly true, that, as the fireside history is, so will be that which the world reads. There never was a fireside at which love ruled, where the Penites of Self-sacrifice, Devotion and Conjugal Affection were worshiped, that did not also write a similar history in society. We have already seen that the Garfield family at this period, whose only head was a mother, had developed the highest traits of nobility and courage. Knowing, then, the relation existing between these facts and those of inner history, we are able to conjecture a supplementary history of thought and love, as well as economy and work. Mrs. Garfield loved books, and mastered those that came into her possession as successfully as she did the business of managing the little homestead. Her husband and herself had been members of the Church of the Disciples, followers of Alexander Campbell. Every Sunday morning, in company with all her children, this widow-mother could be seen on her way to the little church. And, we are told, that for years she and her children never missed a Sabbath. If Christianity ever meant anything to a mother, it certainly did to Eliza Garfield. No sacrifice or duty was too arduous to perform, and with such a mother's influence, the children grew up to youth, and then to manhood and womanhood. A short, cheerful prayer each morning, no matter how early she and the children rose; a word of thankfulness at the beginning of every meal, no matter how meager, and a thoughtful Bible-reading and prayer at night, formed part of that cabin life. Sensible of the few advantages for education, she daily gathered her little flock about her, and told them of history, recounted incidents in the lives of the great, and pointed out the simple beauties of the Bible. What a fire-side scene. The children—and would we be surmising too much in believing that little James, the most eagerly drinking in the savory feast of truth and reason, from an honest mother's lips—had through Providence found an instructor better than any which any school could furnish. O mothers! do you realize what are your possibilities? Do you not realize that your early teaching is worth to every child more than the richest diamond-field?

"As the twig is bent, the tree inclines," and as the child is influenced, so will be the man. Realize then you Cornelias, you Aspasias, you Mary Washingtons, you Eliza Garfields, you mothers *all*, that every child intrusted to your care and keeping is a "sapling' planted in the garden of life. As you nurture, protect, and above all, intellectualize them, will you rejoice in the beauty of the tree. Every mother owes it to her offspring to guard carefully the early years, when impressions are so easily made. Your children will honor you the more, and you will win a brighter crown by doing only your unmistakable DUTY in this respect.

Eliza Garfield plainly understood this, and the truth of our words is certainly apparent in the history of her son, and the respect the world pays her to-day. True, every mother cannot raise up and rejoice in seeing her son crowned as the President of his country, but every mother can do much towards making her children honorable, respected and worthy of high places in state and in society. Let the fact then be taken home to every mother, and let the late President's mother stand as a proof of the truth.

When James was five years old, his older sister for some time carried him on her back to the log school-house, a mile and a half distant. The distance was a great drawback to the little student's attendance. Mrs. Garfield thoughtfully considered the matter, and finally decided that her children should not be compelled to plod through all kinds of weather to attend the school. If there was not another luxury or privilege her children could have, there was one they should enjoy, and that was a good education. The school was too far away. A donation of a part of her farm was made to secure the location of a school-house on it. It would be as far away from the homes of most of the neighbors as the other was, but they caught her spirit, and in the course of the autumn built a new school-house. It was of logs, only twenty feet square, and had a puncheon floor, a slab roof, and log benches without backs or a soft spot to sit on; but it was to turn out men and women for the nation. Nowhere is her enterprise and far-sightedness shown more conclusively than in this one act. She was determined on her children having the best education the wilderness afforded, and they had it.

Among the Garfield children there was a wide difference. Their tastes and inclinations diverged from childhood. True, their ancestry was the same, as also were the surroundings. The girls were cheerful, contented, industrious and

MRS. ELIZA BALLOU GARFIELD.

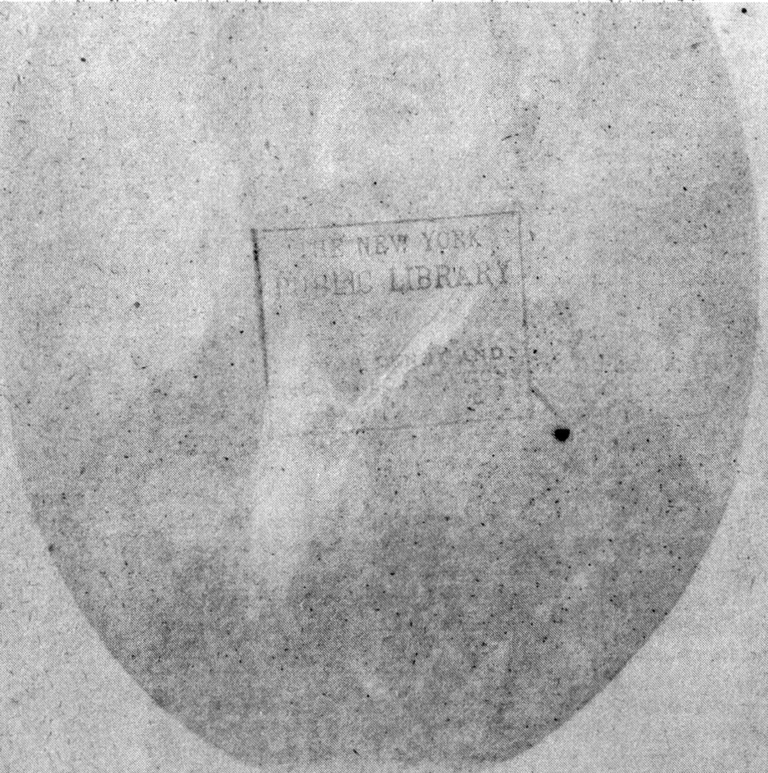

loving. At the district school they were fair scholars, and always were regarded as superior children. In the little household they labored early and late, and did much to lighten the burden resting on their mother's shoulders. The rude home was beautified by their handiwork. They spun, mended the boys clothes, and assisted in performing the household work of the farm. At the gatherings in the neighborhood they were always to be found. In these frolics young James was in his element. The apple-butter boilings were hardly forgotten before the corn-huskings lightened the cool autumn days, and gave to labor wings of pleasure. Garfield's sisters were happy in spite of their adversity, and were ambitious only to be good and pure women. Thomas, the elder brother, was a Garfield out and out. The girls, too, followed more prominently the father's traits. James partook of both his father's and mother's characteristics; and here is the secret of the greater success of the latter. Thomas was great because he was noble. If he is not known to-day in history it is only because he was more anxious for the success and advancement of others than he was for himself. Thomas had little ambition for anything more than to become a good, honest farmer. He wanted the other children to attend the school; so he worked away with a will to earn money enough to keep the family through the winter. He stayed at home to finish the barn, thresh the wheat, shell the corn, and help his mother force a scanty living for them all from the little farm of thirty acres. Nowhere is nobility of purpose seen more clearly than in this self-sacrificing spirit of Thomas Garfield. Had he been as ambitious as he was noble, the world would have known scarcely less of him to-day than it does of his younger brother. He never sought notoriety, being content to occupy a humble position in life, and is therefore known only by a limited circle of friends and near neighbors. Ambition, rightly tempered, and energy of purpose, are the forces young men must court if great success is desired. He chose a life of toil and humbleness, that he might help his brother become educated and great; and if there is not greatness in this, then the world has no greatness.

It is said that there were two things with which his mother was specially familiar—the Bible and the rude ballads of the war of 1812. The children learned the Bible at their mother's knee, and the love of country from the cradle-hymns. James was a mere scrap of a boy, not five years old, and only able to spell through his words, when one day he came across a little poem about the rain. After patient effort he made out this line:

"The rain came pattering on the roof."

"Why, mother," he shouted, "I've heard the rain do that myself!" All at once it broke upon him that words stand for thoughts; and all at once a new world opened to him—a world in which poor boys are of quite as much consequence as rich men, and it may be of a trifle more; for nearly all the work and thinking of the world has been done by poor boys. This new world opened to him; and the boy set himself zealously to work to open the door which leads into it. Before he was out of bed in the morning he had a book in his hand; and after dark he would stretch himself upon the naked hearth, and by the light of the fire spell out the big words in "The English Reader," until he had much of the book in his memory. Before the winter set in the school-master came—an awkward, slab-sided young man, rough as the bark and green as the leaves of the pine-trees which grew about his home in New Hampshire; but, like the pine-trees, he had a wonderful deal of sap in him—a head crammed with knowledge, and a heart full of good feeling. He was to "board round" among the neighbors, and at first was quartered at the little cottage, to eat the widow's corn-bread, and sleep in the loft with James and Thomas. He took at once a fancy to James, and as the little fellow trotted along by his side on the first day of school, he put his hand upon his head, and said to him, "If you learn, my boy, you may grow up yet, and be a general." The boy did not know exactly what it was to be a general, but his mother had told him about the red and blue coats of the Revolution, and of their brass buttons and gilded epaulets; so he fancied it must be some very grand thing; and he answered, "Oh, yes, sir; I'll learn—I'll be a general!" It was, as is common, one of the rules of the school that the scholars should sit still, and not gaze about the school-room. But James never sat still in all his life. The restless activity of his brain made it impossible for him to observe this rule. He tried to do it, and he tried so hard that he minded nothing else, and entirely neglected to study. The result was that his lessons were not learned, and after a few days the teacher said to his mother, "I don't want to grieve you, ma'am; but I fear I can make nothing of James. He won't sit still, and he does not learn his lessons." But he did grieve the poor woman; nothing had grieved her so much since the death of her husband. She looked at the boy and said, "Oh, James!" This was all she said; but it went to the heart of the five-year-old boy. He thought that he was very wicked, that he had done very wrong, and, burying his face in her lap, he sobbed out that he would be a good boy, he would sit still, he would learn. The victory was a triumph of love. That term James made a success of his studies. He was still restless and difficult to manage, but, withal, obedient and studious. Numerous incidents are related of the restless disposition of Garfield even during his later years. When a boy, and sleeping with his brother, he would often kick the covers off at night, and then disturb his bed-fellow by saying: "Thomas, cover me up." A military friend relates that one time during the war, when Garfield was lying with a distinguished officer, both of whom had been engaged in a hard encounter the day previous, the cover came off in the old way, and in sleep he murmured, "Thomas, cover me up." His own words awakened him, and memories of his old cabin home, of his mother and her tenderness, came to him. At this he burst into tears, and wept himself to sleep.

The sorrow manifested by James touched the heart of the teacher; and he tried him again, and tried him now in the right way. He let him move about as much as he liked, calling to mind that he came to school to become a scholar, and not a block of wood. At the end of a fortnight he said to the widow: "James is perpetual motion; but he learns—not a scholar in the school learns so fast as he." This healed the mother's sorrow; for she had set her heart upon this boy becoming a man of learning. Day by day Garfield's avidity for books, and especially for those of adventure and romance, increased. Among the books were two of greatest interest to young James, Weems' "Life of Marion," and Grimshaw's "Napoleon." "Mother, read to me about that great soldier," he says almost every night; and as the martial deeds of the first man of France are recited, the boy's eyes dilate, his breast swells, and once he exclaims, enthusiastically, "Mother, when I get to be a man, I am going to be a soldier." At this the girls laugh heartily, and James, chagrined, says, "Well, you will see that I will be a soldier, and whip people as Napoleon did." The good-natured and matter-of-fact Thomas reminds him that it is far better to be a farmer, and so the matter drops. The little school that he attends is not far from the house, and within its walls on due effort, he easily leads the boys and girls who are his classmates. One day he and his brother are caught whispering, and the teacher sends them home. Thomas stays around the school house, hoping that somehow he will be forgiven. Jim runs right home and then right back again. When he comes into the room the teacher says: "James, I thought I sent you home. Didn't I?" "Yes, ma'am," says Jim. "Well, why didn't you go?" "I did go; I just got back," and, with a laugh, the teacher allows him to stay. He was very clever at this age, and not infrequently he would go to Sunday-school with the teacher, and would sit on the desk and ask the boys Bible questions, such as these: "Who was the wisest man?" "Who was the meekest man?" "Who was in the whale's belly?" The boys did not know, and then Jim's superior knowledge would come into play, and he would gravely inform them, and always with accuracy. Thus the winter passes away, and the summer comes on all too soon.

At the district school James had some reputation as a fighting boy. He found that the larger boys were disposed to insult and abuse a little fellow who had no father or big brother to protect him, and he resented such imposition with all the force of a sensitive nature backed by a hot temper, great physical courage, and a strength unusual for his age. Many stories are told in Orange of the pluck shown by the future major-general in his encounters with the rough country lads in defense of his boyish rights and honor. They say he never began a fight and never cherished malice, but when enraged by taunts or insults would attack boys of twice his size with the fury and tenacity of a bull-dog.

The high sense of honor which characterized Garfield at this period cannot be better illustrated than by the following incident. It shows us at the same time the spirit of heroism and moral courage that he had, and that it would be well for every boy to imitate. Upon one occasion a companion of his proposed to visit a mutual acquaintance in a distant part of the vicinity from where they lived, on the Sabbath. "Not on Sunday," said James. "Why?" "Because it is not right." "If you and I do nothing worse than that, Jim, we shall be pretty good fellows." "We should not be any better, certainly, for doing that." "Nor any worse, in my opinion," rejoined David. "My mother would not consent to it," continued James. "I don't know whether mine would, and I don't care; I sha'n't ask her," said David. "I never should go anywhere against my mother's advice," continued James. "I know what she thinks of the Sabbath, and I respect her feelings. I sha'n't go on Sunday." "And you can't go on any other day, because you have so much to do," added David. "Rather than go on Sunday, I shall not go at all," was James' emphatic reply. "If I had no scruples of my own about it, I would take no comfort, feeling that I went against mother's wishes." This emphatic refusal ended the matter. It was an illustration of the noble character of James. Boys, respect the Sabbath and your mothers, and like this heroic boy, frankly and openly resist all temptations to wrong doing, and never consent to anything that would be displeasing to your parents.

So things went on—Thomas tilling the farm or working for the neighbors, and James going to school, and helping his brother mornings and evenings, until one was twelve and the other twenty-one years old. Then, wanting to make more money than he could at home, Thomas went to Michigan, and engaged in clearing land for a farmer. In a few months he returned with seventy-five dollars, all in gold. Counting it out on the little table, he said, "Now, mother, you shall have a framed house." All these years they had lived in the little log cottage, but Thomas had been gradually cutting the timber, getting out the boards, and gathering together the other material for a new dwelling; and now it was to go up, and his mother have a comfortable home for the rest of her days. Soon a carpenter was hired, and they set to work upon it. James took so handily to the business that the joiner told him he was born to be a carpenter. This gave the boy an idea. He would set up for a carpenter, and, like Thomas, do something to help his mother. James now began to grasp with thoughts of great moment. "To do something," and "be somebody" were forces which energized him. The care and skill requisite to putting a house together, fitting the rafters and beams into place, and joining part to part with mathematical precision, gave him an idea that these things were of a higher order than farm labor. A variety of tools now began accumulating about the young workman. He had a corner where he kept his tools, in imitation of the great carpenter who built the house, which he called his "shop." Such offices in the way of mending and repairing as he was able to perform were in constant demand, and hence he was always employed. The skill thus acquired soon brought him work from the neighbors. The first money ever earned by Garfield in this manner was one dollar, which the carpenter of the village paid him for planing one hundred boards at a cent each. His active and diligent performance of every duty brought him plenty of offers, and between the age of twelve and fifteen years he helped erect a number of buildings in the neighborhood, many of which are still standing. During the next two years he worked on four or five barns, going to school only at intervals; but he then had learned all that is to be learned from "Kirkham's Grammar," "Pike's" and "Adam's Arithmetics," and "Morse's (old) Geography"—that wonderful book, which describes Albany as a city with a great many houses, and a great many people, "all standing with their gable ends to the street." With this immensity of knowledge he thought he would begin the world. Not having got above a barn, he naturally concluded he was *not* "born to be a carpenter," and so cast about for some occupation better suited to his genius. One—about its suitableness I will not venture an opinion—was not long in presenting itself.

About ten miles from his mother's house, and not far away from Cleveland, lived a man who did a thriving business as a black-salter. He had a large establishment, and it was growing. It was growing, for James had just helped to add a woodshed to the log shanties of which it was composed; and so it came about that he met its proprietor, and the current of his life was changed—diverted into one of those sterile by-ways in which currents will now and then run without being able to give any good reason for so useless a proceeding.

"You kin read, you kin write, and you are death on figgers," said the man to the boy one day, as he watched the energetic way in which he did his work; "so stay with me, keep my 'counts, and 'tend to the saltery. I'll find you, and give you fourteen dollars a month." Fourteen dollars a month was an immense sum for a boy of his years; so that night he trudged off through the woods to consult his mother. She was naturally pleased that the services of her son were so highly valued; but she had misgivings about the proposed occupation—a world of wickedness, she thought, lurked between buying and selling. But the boy overcame her scruples, and thus our future President became prime-minister to a black-salter. To this useful pursuit he applied the rules of arithmetic and the principles of grammar. And he did it well—so well that the black-salter would occasionally say to him, in his rough but hearty fashion, "You're a good boy; keep on, and one of these days you'll have a saltery of your own; and maybe as big a one as our'n."

And so he might, had not good or bad fortune thrown in his way the few choice works which comprised the black-salter's library. These books, selected by the daughter of the village—who wrote "poetry" for a Cleveland newspaper, and therefore had some literary taste—were such standard productions as "Sinbad the Sailor," "The Lives of Eminent Criminals," "The Pirate's Own Book," and Marryat's novels. Totally different from the dry but wholesome reading on which he had been nurtured, they roused the imagination and fostered the love of adventure which was born in the backwoods boy. But soon he was thrown upon the world these books tell about, and taught that "all is not gold that glitters," and life not a gorgeous romance, "full of sound and fury, signifying nothing." One day a female member of the family, in his hearing, spoke of him as a "servant," and that he could not tolerate. He a servant! He who had read all about the battle of Bunker Hill, whose great-grandfather had been a signer of a Declaration of Independence in Massachusetts! *He* a servant! The blood boiled in his veins, rushed to his face, and tingled way down to the tips of his toes! Oh, that a man had said it! But it was a woman, so his hands and feet were tied. With the latter, however, he managed to climb up the rickety ladder which led to his lodgings, and tying his few garments together he announced to the black-salter that a boy and a bundle of clothes were about to be subtracted from the population of his vicinity. The worthy man saw the main prop of his fortunes falling, and demeaned himself accordingly. But entreaties and remonstrances were alike unavailing. Outraged dignity could not be appeased; so in half an hour James, with his little bundle of clothes thrown over his shoulder, was on his way homeward. His mother received him with open arms and a blessing. "Providence," she said, "will open some better way for you, my son." And Providence did; but it took its own time and way about it.

Books of adventure, tales of daring, lives of freebooters, seemed to fascinate his mind the most. The air of wild freedom, the nonchalance and absence of care with which pirates lived, was a great attraction to the boy's spirit, already equal in its boldness to the most daring freebooter the sea ever knew. "The Pirate's Own Book," was a treasure-house of stories in which Garfield took an extreme, ever vivified delight. No matter how many times he pored over the book; no matter how often he absorbed its wild life and seemed to breathe the very atmosphere in which his heroes lived and moved, it was ever a well-spring of pleasure to him. He shared in all the dangers of the pirates, he made the bivouac with them on the lonely beach among the shadows, he drank their coffee, he ate their biscuits and fruit, he stole with them on stealthy foot over the difficult paths to where the gold was buried from the last great prize—a Spanish treasure galleon—he boarded the stranger ship, he carried a torch that set her on fire with the best of them, and he joined with all a boy's ardor in the lusty cheer as the prize went down. He lived their lives over again, he was every brave chief in turn, and he loved the salt waves with the most enthusiastic of them all. It was perhaps fortunate at this juncture that there were no opportunities to gratify the wild fancies thus born within the boy's heart—fancies the black shadows of which he hardly saw. As it was, the "Pirate's Own Book" only fired his ambition to be something, and so did no harm. He saw, too, that his ambition could only be gratified with money, and upon a larger field of life than opened to him in the Cuyahoga wilderness or was contained within the bounds of Orange. One day he came to his mother and said, "Mother, I have engaged to chop twenty-five cords of wood for seven dollars." "But are you sure you are quite strong enough for such an undertaking?" inquired the careful woman. "Oh, yes," replied James, laughingly, "I shall get through with it somehow." The place where this was done was near Newburg, a small town close to Cleveland. During this time his mother hoped and prayed that the previous intention of her son, to go to the lake and become a sailor, would weaken, and that he would be led to remain at home; but fate decreed otherwise. He went bravely to work, but soon found he had indeed undertaken a formidable task. His pride forbid him to give up. He had said he could do it, and do it he would, let it cost what it might. The task was that of a man, and his boy's strength began to fail him before it was half over; but he toiled on day after day. At every stroke of the axe he could look up and catch the sun's glimmer on the slaty-blue waves of Lake Erie. The excitement within him, as each sail went out beyond the horizon, never ceased. The story never grew old. The pirate had not died, but still plotted for plunder, and hungered for black flags, cutlasses and blood. No doubt Garfield would have been a good hearted corsair—one of the generous fellows who plundered Spanish galleons just because their gain had been ill-gotten; who spared the lives and restored the money of the innocent, and gave no quarter to the real villains, and never let a fair woman go unrescued. It prompted all the imaginings of his young heart so deeply stirred by the "Pirate's Own Book." He thought the lake to be the sea, and already he saw himself a bold rover with a gallant crew, commanding a staunch, black ship that proudly carried the black flag at the peak, flowing out upon its restless bosom. And when he would lie down at night his day thoughts turned into dreams of the sea and its life of wild attractiveness. In his dreams he was ever a sailor. When his wood-chopping was done he went to the Newburg farmer for whom he had worked, received his seven dollars, and carried it straight to his mother. Mrs. Garfield looked at the pale boy, and though proud of his manly achievement, she saw, with some apprehension, that he had overtasked himself. She softly remonstrated with his ardor, urging it as a caution for the future. It was precisely this future that was on the boy's mind, and still strong in his sailor fancies, it was this that he had come to speak about. Harvest time would soon approach, and his services were needed on the farm. Of course, he stayed; helped them through the season, and even spent some extra time working for a neighbor. But the fate of a boy's future, sometimes cannot be changed by circumstances. A firm, set resolve may be hindered long, but not forever. James Garfield had set his head to be a sailor, and a sailor he would be. Farming was a very good business, no doubt, and just the thing for the brother Thomas, but by no means suited to a young salt like himself.

We are now prepared to close this chapter. The stories which have come down to us show, after all, that Garfield was different from the other boys around him. His mind was grasping. Every hint of the outside world fascinated him. His zeal for work is already prominent; and anything that would "help mother" was done with the lightest heart and cheerfulness. The scenes are now to change, for James is to leave his mother's home and go out into the world.

CHAPTER III.

SECURES A POSITION AS CANAL HAND.

The talent of success is nothing more than doing what you can do well, without a thought of fame.—HENRY W. LONGFELLOW.

There's a divinity shapes our ends,
Rough-hew them how we will.
—SHAKESPEARE.

I cannot repeat too often that no man struggles perpetually and victoriously against his own character; and one of the first principles of success in life is so to regulate our career as rather to turn our physical constitution and natural inclinations to good account, than to endeavor to counteract the one or oppose the other.—SIR H. L. BULWER.

Thus the saplings planted in the wilderness grew. But we must follow the thread of our story less generally, and trace more particularly the history of the son whose life we are writing. The ideas already planted in his fertile brain, of the great world around and about his humble home, began taking more decided shape and form. He longed to see and know. The reading that he had done while in the employ of the black-salter satisfied him that the acme of greatness and happiness was in a life on the sea. Here the free and easy spirit, the liberty of the surroundings, only increased his desire to be a seaman. White sails began to spread themselves in his brain. The story of Nelson and Trafalgar, and the like men and things, began to take shape in his thoughts as the central facts of history; and a life on the ocean wave hung aloft before him as the summit of every aspiration worth a moment's entertainment. Thus again we see the importance of early influences. It has been truthfully said that if you give a child its first look at the world through blue spectacles, the world will be blue to the child. Give a boy his first ideas of the world beyond his neighborhood, by means of soldiers and navies, and he will be soldier and sailor at once. James was now approaching sixteen years of age. He began to think himself a man, and consequently able to take care of himself. He had already spent some time away from home, and this only tended to increase his faith in his own wisdom and prudence.

James A. Garfield in this respect was no different from every other boy. Every boy has more or less of a roving disposition, and between the ages of fourteen and eighteen they will generally be found to be the most restless. At this age boys long to be free from all restraint. They have enlarged ideas of everything pertaining to life; and the more restraint put upon them the greater will be the probabilities of their ignoring bounds put about them. But James, like most boys, was not disobedient. If there was any one for whom he had respect it was his mother. Her wishes ever guided him. Whenever an idea became fixed in his mind he would invariably approach his mother on the subject; and if by his arguments and importunings he generally carried his point, he was never satisfied in doing anything until her consent had been secured.

The affections of family and the many forces which were about Garfield had hitherto kept him near home; the outward tending movements now became powerful, and struggled for supremacy. The passion for the sea had only been heightened by his nearness to Lake Erie while engaged in chopping wood.

By day he thought of the project, and at night it was in his dreams. Finally he came to his mother, and said: "Mother, I want to be a sailor, and I am going to sea.' Mrs. Garfield turned pale, for she knew too well, alas! this meant a separation for years, and, perhaps forever, from her son. "Nay, James," she replied, gently; "why not be content with us at home? the sea is a hard life, and I fear I could not part with you just yet. The haying season is at hand, and your brother will need your assistance on the farm. I pray you give up this sea faring idea for the present." James said not a word, but went about the work on the farm. He assisted in the hay-fields and the gathering of the harvest, but when it was all over he came again to his mother, and announced to her that he could no longer restrain his desire.

The struggle between home and the sea was a hard one. At home was the dear mother, with her great longing that he should love books, go to school, and become a great man. And how could he leave her? The struggle for life had not yet become an easy one on the little farm, and his absence would be felt. "Leave us not," pleads the home. "The sea, land-lubber, the wild, free ocean," says the buccaneer within. Seldom can a boy's future be changed by circumstances. A deep-rooted resolve may be delayed, hindered, and brushed aside for a time, but not forever. James Garfield had set his head on being a sailor, and a sailor he would be. His mother seeing he had set his heart upon it, forbore to oppose him; for she felt sure that God would, in his own time and way, turn him back from such a life. At last she consented to his going to Cleveland; but she stipulated that he should try to procure some other respectable employment. Then the boy, with a small bundle of clothes upon his back, and a few dollars in his pocket, departed, amidst his mother's prayers and God's blessings. How eagerly the anxious mother must have watched that boy, as he left the threshold. See her eyes fastened on him, as he trudges onward. As the distance increases, his form becomes more and more indistinct, but she still watches; and then, as he disappears beyond the hill and vanishes from her vision, with a heavy heart, she returns to her work. What an hour that must have been to her! Mothers who have had similar experiences can only know the grief, the heaviness of heart, and, above all, the longings for the return of the dear one. But young James hurried along with cheer and hope, bound for the harbor at Cleveland. The distance was not great, and, so far as we know, the way was void of noteworthy incidents.

He walked the whole way—seventeen miles—and, weary and footsore, arrived at Cleveland just at dark. But a good night's sleep and a warm breakfast refreshed him greatly, and in the morning he strolled out to view the great city. It was scarcely a fourth of its present size, but to the boy it was an immensity of houses. He had never seen buildings half so large, nor steeples half so high; in fact, he had never seen steeples at all, for the simple people among whom he had lived did not put cocked hats and cockades upon their meeting-houses. He wandered about all day, stepping now and then, as he had promised his mother, into the business places to enquire for employment; but no one wanted an honest lad who could read, write, and was "death on figgers." Everybody could

GARFIELD AT SIXTEEN.

read and write, and there was no end to their figuring—so said a good-natured gentleman, who advised him to go home and do honest work for a living.

Night found him, weary and footsore, down upon the docks among the shipping. "These," said he to himself, as he looked around upon the little fleet of sloops and schooners, "are the ships that Captain Marryat tells about," and visions of the free life of which he had dreamed came again, even more vividly, before him. He sat down upon the head of a pier and looked out on the great lake, heaving, and foaming, and rolling in broken waves all about him. He watched it creeping up the white beach, and gliding back, singing a low hymn among the shining stones, or muttering hoarse cries to the black rocks along the shore; and then looked out on the white sails that were dancing about all over its bosom. His mother's little cottage, and the lonely woman herself—even then, it may be, seated in the open door-way, looking up the road for his coming—faded from his sight as he gazed, and he stepped down upon one of the tossing vessels. It was an evening in July, of 1848. He strolled about the deck waiting for the appearance of the glorious captain. He inquired of a sailor on the deck for the captain. He was told that he would soon come up, and soon he did, a half-drunken wretch, with bloated features and filth-besmeared clothes, swearing like a pirate. Stepping modestly forward, the boy asked if a hand was wanted; when, turning upon him, the reeling brute poured forth a volley of oaths and invectives that made him shudder.

The experience of that hour was never forgotten. This was the first lesson Garfield had of the realities of life and the sea. It was not a lesson calculated to inspire him above measure. But it did one thing, which was of great advantage to him—it made him think. Garfield was informed that his services were not needed, and he was compelled to retire from the dirty fore-and-aft schooner, with mildewed sails, a greasy deck, and a low-sunken cabin, in confusion; amid the continued curses of the drunken commander, and the uncouth hilarity of a half dozen men, with reeking clothes and sooty faces, who were commanded.

Here, again, is another turning point in young Garfield's life. Trivial circumstances often turn aside wrong purposes and aims. Garfield's future history is written all over with the results of that day's experience. "What to do now," was the next thought that came to his mind. The sea had been found to be different in all respects from what fancy had pictured it. The sails were not near so white, the ships all but glorious, and the captain and crew far from magnanimous, chivalric, and noble. But his disposition for a seaman's life was far from conquered yet. He imagined his treatment at the hands of the captain had probably arisen principally from his rustic appearance; and he predicted a similar rebuff should he try again. Go home he would not, until he had conquered defeat. Work, in the city, he could not find, and again reiterating the determination to be a sailor, he solved the problem by the following argument: The ocean is too far away, and I must make my way there by lake, meanwhile learning what I can about the business. But I can't go to the lake now. As the lake is a step to the ocean, so the canal is a step to the lake, and he would begin with the canal.

To the canal he now went. Armed with this new resolve, his step became lighter and quicker, and hope once more cheered him on. If the sea could not be won just then, the canal could; and the latter was only a preparation for the former. A determination, such as Garfield showed in this emergency, is always commendable. While the objects for which he was striving were not in keeping with his powers and possibilities, yet at this period he conceived the greatest good to lie in his success on the water. And now that he is denied a place on the larger waters, he is willing to accept the lowest position in the canal service. This is for preparation, and he is determined some day to be capable of filling the highest office on the finest vessel that floats the waters. But how fortunate it is that his plans were frustrated. He, no doubt, would have made a good seaman and an excellent captain, but the country would have lost a hero, a President whom we love to honor and respect, and a character which, to-day, is doing more to shape the destinies of the youth of the land for uprightness than any other of history. How infinite, then, and past finding out, are the ways of Providence! How inscrutible his dealings with men! He guides the destinies of men, and had a grander work for James A. Garfield to perform than commanding a "barge of the waters."

It was the old Ohio and Pennsylvania canal which he sought; and he found, by rare good fortune, a boat called the *Evening Star*, tied to the moorings, and ready to start. The captain was found to be rather a genial, good natured man, full of sympathy; his name was Amos Letcher, and he was Garfield's cousin. The experiences of the day were recounted by Garfield, and, Letcher becoming interested in him, gave him employment. He was to drive the mules, the wages being ten dollars a month and found. Letcher is still living, and recalls his boy-driver to-day in the following fashion:

"There was nothing prepossessing about him at that time, any more than he had a free, open countenance. He had no bad habits, was truthful, and a boy that every one would trust on becoming acquainted with him. He came to me in the summer of 1848, when I was captain of the *Evening Star*, and half owner —B. H. Fisher, now Judge Fisher, of Wichita, Kansas, being my partner. Early one morning, while discharging a cargo, Jim Garfield tapped me on the shoulder and said: 'Hello, Ame, what are you doing here?' 'You see what I'm doing. What are you doing here?' 'Hunting work.' 'What kind of work do you want?' 'Anything to make a living. I came here to ship on the lake, but they bluffed me off, and called me a country greenhorn.' 'You'd better try your hand on smaller waters first; you'd better get so you can drive a horse and tie a tow-line. I should like to have you work for me, but I've nothing better than a driver's berth, and suppose you would not like to work for twelve dollars a month?' 'I've got to do something, and, if that is the best you can do, I will take the team.' 'All right, I will give you a better position as soon as a vacancy occurs.' I called my other driver, and said, 'Ikey, go and show Jim his team.' Just as they were going to start, Jim asked, 'Is it a good team?' 'As good as is on the canal.' 'What are their names?' 'Kit and Nance.' Soon after we were in the 'eleven-mile lock,' and I thought I'd sound Jim on education—in the rudiments of geography, arithmetic and grammar. For I was just green enough those days to imagine that I knew it all. I had been teaching school for three winters in the backwoods of Steuben County, Indiana. So I asked him several questions, and he answered them all; and then he asked me several that I could not answer. 'Jim,' I said, 'you have too good a head on you to be a wood-chopper or a canal-driver. You go to school one term more, and you will be qualified to teach a common school, and then you can make anything you have a mind to out of yourself.' 'Do you think so, captain?' And it set him to a-thinking, I know. Soon we met a boat, and the two drivers had some trouble about their lines—they got sort of tangled. The impetus of our boat had carried her up even with the horses, and as there was a waste-way a few rods ahead, my steersman called out, 'Hurrah Jim, whip up that team, or your line will catch on the bridge.'" So Jim he cracks his whip, and his team was soon on the trot; but, just as the team was at the middle of the bridge, the line tightened, and jerked horses, driver and all into the canal. It came very nearly drowning the whole pile, and my opinion is, if it had, we would have lost a good President. But 'all is well that ends well.'. So, after everything was all right, I asked Jim, 'What were you doing in the canal?' 'Oh, I was just taking my morning bath,' he answered.'

"As we were approaching the twenty-one locks of Akron, I sent my bowsman to make the first lock ready. Just as he got there, the bowsman from a boat above made his appearance, and said: 'Don't turn this lock, our boat is just round the bend, ready to enter.' My man objected, and began turning the gate. By this time, both boats were near the lock, and their head-lights made it almost as bright as day. Every man from both boats was on hand ready for a field fight. I motioned my bowsman to come to me. Said I, 'Were we here first?' 'It's hard telling, but we'll have the lock anyhow.' 'All right, just as you say.' Jim Garfield tapped me on the shoulder, and asked: 'Does that lock belong to us?' 'I suppose, according to law, it does not. But we will have it anyhow.' 'No, we will not.' 'Why?' said I. 'Why?' with a look of indignation I shall never forget, 'why, because it don't belong to us.' Said I, 'Boys, let them have it.'

"Next morning, one of the hands accused Jim of being a coward, because he would not fight for his rights. Said I: 'Boys, don't be hard on Jim. I was mad last night, but I have got over it. Jim may be a coward, for aught I know, but if he is, he is the first one of the name that I ever knew that was. His father was no coward. He helped dig this canal, and weighed over two hundred pounds, and could take a barrel of whisky by the chime and drink out of the bung-hole, and no man dared call him a coward. You'll alter your mind about Jim before fall.'"

The trip to Pittsburg, for that was the destination of the *Evening Star*, was a long one. The boat was freighted with copper ore, which had come to Cleveland in schooners from Lake Superior, where those great treasuries of ore, which still seem inexhaustible, were at that time just beginning to become important interests. The canal-boats carried this ore to Pittsburg, and returned loaded with coal. The first return trip of the boat brought with it a load of coal from Brier Hill, on the Mahoning River. It was received from the mines owned by David Tod, afterwards Governor of Ohio, and a warm friend of Garfield's in after life. These cargoes, no doubt, did much to inform Garfield of the immense riches of the country, and prove to him the boundless possibilities lying all about him. The forges, furnaces and mines in and about the great manufacturing centre of Pennsylvania, the forces at work supplying them with ore and material, the advantages of the canal, the millions of capital, and thousands of skilled workmen employed, all indicated activity and enterprise; and the greatest advantage Garfield received from this trip, was the mental stimulus imparted.

The life of the average child is monotonous indeed. Hundreds are the children all about us, who, until manhood's morning begins to dawn upon them, have scarcely been without the limits of the city or county in which they live. They are shut in and surrounded by a higher wall than ever protected China. The daily routine of early life is associated only with home affairs. Parents owe it to their children to counteract this tendency. From the very beginning of reason, the child should constantly be introduced to new sights. This is the age of seeing, and nothing interests a child more than looking for the first time at some common-place object, a city perchance, with towering steeples and lofty roofs, a beautiful sweep of country, a body of water, anything, in fact, that will serve as subjects of thought to their youthful minds. And this is a plain duty of parents. It is the best education children can have. Parents should strive to make their offspring think early for themselves, and in the long-run, the advantages will be great. We have found that Garfield, at sixteen years of age, began to see the world, and naturally thoughtful and meditative, he also began to think upon subjects far beyond his years. We would urge, then, that parents heed this advice, and gratify the child's desire to see whatever is to its advantage.

This was the boy's first trip, and now again he did his work well; so well that before its close he was promoted to the more responsible position of bowman. But, to tell the exact truth, this may have been quite as much owing to the admiration which the honest captain had conceived for the boy's courage, as to any regard he had for his close attention to his duties as driver; for he soon showed that he was not a coward, and it was on this first trip that he fought his first battle, and won his first victory. It was in this wise:

The *Evening Star* was at Beaver, and a steamboat was ready to tow her up to Pittsburg. The boy was standing on deck, with the setting pole against his shoulders, and some feet away stood Murphy, one of the boat hands, a big burly fellow of thirty-five, when the steamboat threw the line, and, owing to a sudden lurch of the boat, it whirled over the boy's shoulders and flew in the direction of the boatman. "Look out, Murphy!" cried the boy; but the rope had anticipated him, and knocked Murphy's hat off into the river. The boy expressed his regret, but it was of no avail. In a towering rage the man rushed upon him, with his head down, like a maddened animal; but stepping nimbly aside, the boy dealt him a powerful blow behind the ear, and he tumbled to the bottom of the boat among the copper ore. Before he could rise the boy was upon him, one hand upon his throat, the other raised for another blow upon his frontispiece. "Pound the cussed fool, Jim!" cried Captain Letcher, who was looking on, appreciatingly. "If he hain't no more sense 'n to get mad at accidents, giv it ter him! Why don't you strike?" But the boy did not strike, for the man was down and in his power. Murphy expressed regret for his rage, and then Garfield gave him his hand, and they became better friends than before. This victory of a boy of sixteen over a man of thirty-five, obliterated the notion of young Garfield's character for cowardice, and gave him a great reputation with his associates. The incident is still well remembered among the boatmen of the Ohio and Pennsylvania Canal.

The monotonous life of a canal hand was led until November, of 1848. Then came a change. The devoted mother at home was still watching and anxiously waiting for the return of her wandering boy. Her prayers made mention of his name, and she still longed for the fulfillment of her early dreams and hopes, that James might become a great and good man. An accident brought him home.

GARFIELD ON THE TOW PATH.

Young Garfield remained on the canal four months, and during this period, by actual count, fell into the water fourteen times. His last immersion made a deep impression upon him, and was the turning point in his history. It changed the whole current of his life, gave him a purpose, and made him a man.

One rainy midnight, as the boat on which he was employed was leaving one of those long reaches of slack-water, which abound in the Ohio and Pennsylvania Canal, he was called up to take his turn at the bow. Tumbling out of bed, his eyes heavy with sleep, he took his stand on the narrow platform below the bow-deck, and began uncoiling a rope to steady the boat through a lock it was approaching. Slowly and sleepily he unwound it, till it knotted and caught in a narrow cleft in the edge of the deck. He gave it a sudden pull, but it held fast; then another and a stronger pull, and it gave way, but sent him over the bow into the water. Down he went into the dark night and the still darker river; and the boat glided on to bury him among the fishes. No human help was near, and he could not swim a stroke. God only could save him, and he only by a miracle. So the boy thought, as he went down, saying the prayer his mother had taught him. Instinctively clutching the rope, he sank below the surface; but then it tightened in his grasp and held firmly. Seizing it hand-over-hand, he drew himself up on deck, and was again a live boy among the living. Another kink had caught in another crevice, and saved him! Was it that prayer, or the love of his praying mother, which wrought this miracle? He did not know; but, long after the boat had passed the lock, he stood there, in his dripping clothes, pondering the question.

Coiling the rope, he tried to throw it again into the crevice; but it had lost the knack of kinking. Many times he tried—a hundred says my informant—and then sat down and reflected. "I have thrown this rope," he thought, "one hundred times; I might throw it ten times as many without its catching. Ten times one hundred are one thousand—so, there were a thousand chances against my life! Against such odds Providence only could have saved it. Providence, therefore, thinks it worth saving; and if that's so, I won't throw it away on a canal boat. I'll go home, get an education, and be a man."

Upon this determination he acted. He was convinced that a life on the sea was not his portion; and he was satisfied that he had been saved for some better fortune than his present life promised him. Before they got back to Cleveland, he had the ague. He left the boat at the eleven-mile lock, and struck across the country to his home.

The romantic element of his character was not yet gone. That could not be destroyed; and it took the long months of sickness that were before him, to entirely subdue his marine aspirations. Arriving at his mother's home one night while the stars were shining brightly, he entered the yard and saw his mother kneeling before an open book which lay on a chair in the corner. She was reading; but her eyes were off the page, looking up to the Invisible. "Oh, turn unto me," she said, "and have mercy upon me! give thy strength unto thy servant, and save the son of thine handmaid!" More she read, which sounded like a prayer; but this is all that the boy remembers. He opened the door, put his arm about her neck, and his head upon her bosom. What words he said I do not know; but there, by her side, he devoted to God the life which God had given. So the mother's prayer was answered. So sprang up the seed which in toil and tears she had planted.

Mrs. Garfield felt that her triumph was now at hand; and set herself about to secure it. For a short time he remained at home, comforting his mother and endeavoring to reconcile her to his hopes of a sea-faring life. This he more than accomplished, and was just about to take his second departure, when the malaria took hold of him, and he was seized in the vice-like grip of fever and ague. For four or five months his strong frame was shaken. He lay upon the bed, the "ague-cake" by his side. Tenderly, indefatigably, his mother nursed him during his days of suffering, which her care and his iron constitution, at last permitted him to overcome. Mrs. Garfield added the beauty of song and conversation to her tender care. She knew a marvelous number of songs, and hourly could have been heard singing to her sick boy. Strength and renewed health at last returned: and new plans for the future were unfolding.

CHAPTER IV.

SEEKING AN EDUCATION.

Take him to develop, if you can
And hew the block off, and get out the man.
—POPE

He (the upright student) keeps his purpose—and whatever he has resolved to do, that he does, were it only because he has resolved to do it.—FICHTE.

It is told of Hercules, god of real force, that "whether he stood, or walked, or sat, or whatever thing he did, he conquered."—REV. F. D HUNTINGTON, D. D.

Young Garfield is now approaching eighteen years of age. The days of boyhood are fast passing away. He is withal, one who has had experiences far above his years. His education thus far, has mainly been that of experience, and he found this a hard, but a very useful school. Garfield arose from his bed of sickness a more thoughtful boy, and cognizant of the great expectations and possibilities surrounding him. He had been led to see, through the kindly ministerings of his faithful mother, the result of the two courses—one in following the towpath, the other through education. His mother used all the eloquence of her nature to induce him to embrace the latter. She stimulated in her son a renewed, and subsequent events prove, a lasting desire for study.

She brought to her help the district school-teacher, a young man, not many years older than James, an excellent, thoughtful man, named Samuel D. Bates, now a distinguished minister of the gospel in Ohio, who fired the boy's mind with a desire for a good education, and doubtless changed the course of his life. He had attended what was then a high school, and known as the Geauga Seminary, and he and Garfield became firm friends. Bates was full of his school experiences, and finding his new acquaintance so intelligent, with true proselyting spirit, as was so common among men in the backwoods who were beginning to taste the pleasures of education, he was very anxious to take back several new students with him. Garfield listened to the representations of his eloquent friend, and decided to accompany him.

Just here permit a few words relative to Garfield's political and religious impressions, at this period. Up to this time politics had not at all interested our hero. He was able to remember having attended a political meeting during the ever-memorable and never-to-be-forgotten Harrison campaign. But in this he was nothing interested more than as a looker-on and spectator.

He had been a regular and faithful attendant upon the Disciples' meetings, first at Bentleyville, and later at the school-house near his home, where his uncle Boynton had organized a congregation. He repulsed all efforts to persuade him to join the church, and when pressed hard stayed away from the meetings for several Sundays. Apparently he wanted full freedom to reach conclusions about religion by his own mental processes. It was not until he was eighteen and had been two terms at the Chester school that he joined his uncle's congregation. Previous to this time, however, he had showed himself a formidable disputant on matters pertaining to the Bible. One day, when about fifteen, he was digging potatoes for Mr. Patrick, in Orange, and carrying them in a basket from the field to the cellar. Near the cellar-door sat a neighbor talking to the farmer's grown-up daughter, about the merits of the sprinkling and immersion controversy, and arguing that sprinkling was baptism within the meaning of the Scriptures. James overheard him say that a drop was as good as a fountain. He stopped on his way to the field, and began to quote this text from Hebrews: "Let us draw near with a true heart in full assurance of faith, having our hearts sprinkled from an evil conscience." "Ah, you see," said the man, "it says 'sprinkled.'" "Wait for the rest of the text," replied James—"'and our bodies washed with pure water?' Now, how can you wash your body in a drop of water?" and, without waiting for a reply, he hastened off to the potato field.

Geauga Seminary was a Free-will Baptist institution in the village of Chester, ten miles away from the home of the Garfields in Orange. This school Samuel D. Bates had attended during the spring previous, and in the winter had taken the school on the Garfield farm, expecting to save some money with which to continue his studies at Geauga. He was an enthusiast in the matter of education, and eloquent were the words with which he endeavored to induce James to return to Geauga with him. The arguments which this young man used took a practical and economical turn. He showed Garfield how he might be able to attend school part of the year, and then would be fitted to teach during the winter. When the time came for the next term to open at Geauga, James had fully made up his mind to attend. Before doing so, however, he took one more precautionary step and did a characteristically sensible thing. There resided in Bedford a physician named Dr. J. P. Robinson, a man of good judgment and skill. To him the awkward country lad went, and asking an expression of opinion upon the matter of an education, the physician sounded him well, as to both body and mind. And this was his opinion: "You are well fitted to follow your ambition as far as you are pleased to go. Your brain is large and good; your physique is adapted to hard work. Go ahead, and you are sure to succeed." These words fixed the lad's wavering resolution, and gave him a definite purpose, from which he never afterward swerved. "It is a great point gained," he wrote in after-life, "when a young man makes up his mind to devote several years to the accomplishment of a definite work." He had gained this point, and thenceforward, for nine years, amidst innumerable difficulties, this homespun lad of sixteen pursued his end till he was graduated at twenty-five with the highest honors of an eastern institution.

Accordingly he joined two other young men, Wm. Boynton (his cousin), and Orrin H. Judd, of Orange, and they reached Chester March 6, 1849, and rented a room in an unpainted frame house nearly west from the seminary and across the street from it, and went to work. Garfield bought the second algebra he had ever seen, and began it. English grammar, natural philosophy and arithmetic made up the list of his studies. Garfield had seventeen dollars in his pocket, scraped together by his mother and his brother Thomas. They took provisions along, and a cooking stove, and a poor widow prepared their meals and did their washing for an absurdly small sum. The academy was a two-story building, and the school, with about a hundred pupils of both sexes, drawn from the farming country around Chester, was in a flourishing condition. It had a library of perhaps one hundred and fifty volumes—more books than young Garfield had ever seen before. A venerable gentleman named Daniel Branch was principal of the school, and his wife was his chief assistant. Then there were Mr. and Mrs. Coffin, Mr. Bigelow, and Miss Abigail Curtis. In the second year of Garfield's attendance, Mr. and Mrs. Branch retired, and were succeeded by Mr. Fowler and Mr. Beach.

The frugal method of living adopted by the boys was even subsequently thought to be extravagant by Garfield. He had read the autobiography of Henry C. Wright, who related a tale about supporting life on bread and crackers. From that time all unnecessary expense was curtailed. The cook was dismissed, and they did the work themselves. We are compelled to add, however, that this method of living was short lived, for they soon abandoned it. And who that has considered the matter does not know that in the majority of cases, the boys who acquire an education under difficulties, requiring the exercise of something of self-sacrifice, are the ones who use their attainments to the best advantage? Academic life under these circumstances may lack polish and finish, but always contains power. There has never yet been found a royal road to education. In these days of luxury and wealth, the average youth is buoyed up with the props of ease, money and luxury, regarding honest poverty as the lot of a menial. And this is the reason, young man, young woman, you boys and girls who some day will be expected to fill the high positions of honor and trust, why so few students after graduation from college are, figuratively speaking, unable to walk. College education is an excellent attainment, but when the tendency is to make out of the young men and women only abnormalities, then the time is ripe for reform. In the present college educational system we have nothing of which to complain, but it were far better were the students taught more fully than at present, the value of their mental and moral training. The average young man having just left the portals of his Alma Mater, and casting about for his position in the scale of life, is apt to be disappointed and chagrined that he must begin so low and work up to prominence. In his mind, a diploma is recommendation sufficient to obtain for him any position he may choose to occupy. And this feeling arises in great part from the fact that he has been induced to believe that a high position of honor awaits him after graduation. The men who are the leaders of thought to-day are those who obtained their education similarly to James A. Garfield. Work and study, study and work, calling into play the exercise of self and self's powers, depending for whatever is desirable upon one's own exertions, this is the routine of nine tenths of the most successful men and students. "It is the misfortune," as Matthews says, "of many young persons to-day that they begin life with too many advantages.

Every possible want of their many-sided nature is supplied before it is consciously felt. Books, teachers, mental and religious training, lectures, amusements, clothes and food, all of the best quality and without stint in quantity—in short, the pick of the world's good things, and helps of every kind, are lavished upon them, till satiety results, and all ambition is extinguished. What motive has a young man, for whom life is thus "thrice winnowed," to exert himself? Having supped full of life's sweets, he finds them palling on his taste; having done nothing to earn its good things, he cannot appreciate their value. Mere hardships, of course, will not make a man strong, but it is important aid in the development of greatness."

In illustration of what we are saying, let us look again at Garfield's life at the seminary. "The labors which he performed at this academy, in one term, from his arrival on March 6, 1849, to the end, were probably more than equal to the four years' studies of many a college graduate. He never forgot for a moment the purpose for which he was there. Every recitation found his work well done; every meeting of the literary society knew his presence and heard his voice. The library was his favorite corner of the building. A new world was to be conquered in every science, a new country in every language. Thus a yea passed, and Garfield's first term at Geauga was ended." With this as matter of fact, who can say that this prodigious amount of study, the immense amount of work accomplished by Garfield, was not done with a purpose in view? 'Tis true that man owes certain duties to society, but a student's duties lie first in the channel of study and mental discipline. Let our colleges remember this, and encourage such a spirit, and better results will follow—there will be more students and MEN like Garfield. Lord Macauley has well said of our country: "Here, society is not fixed in horizontal layers, like the crust of the earth, but, as a great New England man said, years ago, it is rather like the ocean—broad, deep, grand, open, and so free in all its parts that every drop that mingles with the yellow sand at the bottom may rise through all the waters, till it gleams in the sunshine on the crest of the highest wave. So it is here in our free society, permeated with the light of American freedom. There is no American boy, however poor, however humble, orphan though he may be, that, if he have a clear head, a true heart, a strong arm, he may not rise through all the grades of society, and become the crown, the glory, the pillar of the state."

Mornings and evenings, and Saturdays, Garfield worked in the carpenters' shops in the village, and thus managed to earn enough to pay for his living when his mother's seventeen dollars were expended. After this he paid his own way, never calling on Thomas or his mother for further assistance; he worked hard, but he had most excellent health, a robust frame, and he acquired knowledge easily; so that this combined mental and physical toil, which has broken down many an ambitious youth, did not tell on his splendid constitution.

When the school closed for the summer vacation, Garfield returned to his home. But he was kept constantly busy. Part of the time he assisted his brother in building a barn on the home estate, and then he closed a second contract for chopping wood, assisting also during harvesting in the harvest field. About the latter a good story remains to us. With two well grown, but young, school-fellows, James applied to a farmer who needed hands, asking employment. Their youthful appearances were thought by the farmer to be against them, but finally he decided to hire them, upon their offering to work for "whatever he thought right." But this kind of work was not new to them, and by their dexterous swinging of the scythe, soon made it a warm task for the other men to keep even with them. The farmer looked on admiringly for a while, and then said to his men: "You fellows had better look to your laurels; them boys are a-beatin' ye all holler." This spurred the men on somewhat, but already the advantage was against them. When settling-up time came, it is worth while to remark that the boys were paid the same as the men.

These money-making schemes had given James somewhat of a fund, with which to start at the opening of the next term at Geauga. It was now decided to abandon the self-cooking method of living, and he concluded to board with one of the families living near the school. The same method of study and work was pursued. Although he had become more or less independent, having some money, and being able to live better, his method of study was unchanged. The price he paid for board, washing and lodging was one dollar and six cents per week. His landlady was a Mrs. Stiles, and after Garfield had become somewhat distinguished, she was fond of relating an incident connected with his residence in her family. The young man was without overcoat or underclothing, and had only one suit of clothes, and those were of cheap Kentucky jean. Toward the close of the term his trousers had worn exceedingly thin at the knees, and on one occasion when he was bending forward, they tore half way around the leg, exposing his bare knee to view. The mortified young man pinned the rent garment together as well as he could, and to the family that night bewailed his poverty, and his inability to remedy the misfortune to his only pair of trousers. "Why, that is easy enough," said the good Mrs. Stiles. "You go to bed, and one of the boys will bring down your trousers, and I will darn the hole so it will be better than new. You shouldn't care for such small matters. You will forget all about them when you get to be President."

The amount necessary to pay his board and incidental expenses he expected to earn by helping the carpenter on Saturdays and at odd hours on school days. The carpenter was building a two-story house, and James' first work was to get out siding at two cents a board. The first Saturday he planed fifty-one boards, and so earned over a dollar, the most money he had ever got for a day's work. That term he paid his way, bought a few books, and returned home with eight dollars in his pocket.

The idea of teaching now confronted him. He had studied in the academy long enough to give him confidence in his abilities. Consequently, about the first of November he was examined and received a creditable certificate to teach. The school directors in the vicinity were already employing teachers, and he started out to find a school. Two whole days he tramped about Cuyahoga county, but failed to find employment. Dispirited and discouraged, humiliated by the many refusals of his service, he returned home worse than discouraged. But it was only to find the boon he wished; for an offer to teach the Ledge school, near by, for twelve dollars a month and board, was waiting him, and he accepted.

While still in the depths of despondency, he heard a man call to his mother from the road, "Widow Gaffield" (a local corruption of the name Garfield), "where's your boy Jim? I wonder if he wouldn't like to teach our school at the Ledge." James went out and found a neighbor from a district a mile away, where the school had been broken up for two winters by the rowdyism of the big boys. He said he would like to try the school, but before deciding must consult his uncle, Amos Boynton. That evening there was a family council. Uncle Amos pondered over the matter, and finally said, "You go and try it. You will go into that school as the boy, 'Jim Gaffield;' see that you come out as Mr. Garfield, the schoolmaster." The young man mastered the school, after a hard tussle in the school-room with the bully of the district, who resented a flogging and tried to brain the teacher with a billet of wood.

Only a short time before Garfield left Mentor for Washington, to be inaugurated President of the United States, he referred to this incident while in conversation with several of his friends. The subject under discussion, at the time, was "office seeking" in general, and the "second term" in particular.

"The fall that I was eighteen years old, I traveled a considerable circuit round about Orange in quest of a district school to teach. I was refused in one place after another, for different reasons; so that at last I came home tired and discouraged. I had made up my mind that seeking positions was not in harmony with my nature; that I never should succeed in life if I hunted places; and that I would make no further effort in that direction, but would wait and see what would come to me. An hour or two after reaching home, with these conclusions fully wrought out in my mind, a man from an adjoining neighborhood called at my mother's house, and said he was 'huntin' widow Gaffield's Jimmie.' He wanted a teacher for his district, and he 'lowed that Jimmie would do.' "I was called in," said the President-elect, "and a bargain was soon concluded. The coming of this man confirmed me in the opinion that place-seeking was not in my line; and I have never asked anybody for a place from that day to this."

Years after Garfield had ceased to teach, and when he had already acquired a national reputation as a statesman, he one day gave a lecture to the teachers' class in Hiram College. It was in this lecture that he related the following anecdote:

"When I first taught a district school, I formed and carried out this plan: After I had gone to bed at night, I threw back the bed-clothes from one side of the bed. Then I smoothed out the sheet with my hand. Next, I mentally constructed on this smooth surface my school-room. First I drew the aisles; here I put the stove; there the teacher's desk; in this place, the water-pail and cup, in that, the open space at the head of the room. Then I put in the seats, and placed the scholars upon them in their proper order. Here is John, with Samuel by his side; there Jane and Eliza; and so on, until they were all placed. Then I took them up in order, beginning next my desk, in this manner: This is Johnny Smith; what kind of a boy is he? What is his mind, and what his temper? How is he doing? What is he now, as compared with a week ago? Can I do anything more for him? And so I went on from seat to seat, and from pupil to pupil, until I had made the circuit of the room. I found this study and review of my pupils of great benefit to them and to me. Besides, my ideal construction, made on the bed-sheet in the dark, aided me materially in the work."

The reader can reflect upon this narrative at leisure. Here it suffices to say, that, a young man who had the ingenuity, patience, and thoughtfulness to carry on such work as this, night after night, could not but succeed as a teacher, not to speak of higher capacities.

Once more Garfield returned to Geauga after closing his school. It is said that in 1851 he took his first ride on a railway-train. With his mother, he this year went to Columbus. The road was the Cleveland and Columbus, and was then new. At the capital, Gamaliel Kent, the representative from Geauga county, became their guide, and showed them the sights of the city. From Columbus, the mother and son went to Zanesville, and afterwards down the Muskingum, some eighteen miles, to visit relatives. While there James taught a short term of school; the coal used in heating the school-room, he dug from a bank just behind the building. After this came the renewal of school days at Chester.

Biography interests itself in minutiae. The little acts are often the best precursors of greater ones. As the little flitting clouds often augur and indicate the character of the weather, so do seemingly unimportant incidents foretell something of the future. We now know of what metal our hero must have been composed. During the first term he had renewed the rusty recollections of his early acquirements, and pursued arithmetic, algebra, grammar, and natural philosophy; afterwards came more of the regular academic studies, including the rudiments of Latin and Greek; he also studied botany, and collected a good herbarium. Every step had been carefully taken, and his mind was becoming accustomed to close thinking.

At the end of the first term in Chester, the literary society gave a public entertainment; on that occasion James made a speech, which is referred to in the diary he kept at that time, with this comment: "I was very much scared, and very glad of a short curtain across the platform that hid my shaking legs from the audience."

We have already mentioned the fact of Garfield's joining his uncle's church at the age of eighteen. While he was teaching the Ledge school, the old log school-house on the Garfield farm was regularly used as a meeting place for the "Disciples." He was a constant attendant, and soon became deeply interested in matters pertaining to religion. Some of his early wayward and restless disposition was leaving him, and as manhood stood ready to clothe him with her mantle, he again returned to the simple faith of his childhood. The preaching of the Gospel made a deep and effective impression upon him. The sect to which his family belonged was a new one. Alexander Campbell was its head and leader. This man had been a Presbyterian, but rejecting the Confession of Faith, had founded a new church, called the "Disciples of Christ," whose only written creed was the Bible.

In March of this year, after having exercised his full freedom in reaching conclusions, Garfield joined church, and was baptized in a little stream that flows into the Chagrin River. His conversion was brought about by a quiet, sweet-tempered man, who held a series of meetings in the school-house near the Garfield homestead, and told in the plainest manner, and with the most straightforward earnestness, the story of the Gospel. The creed of the Disciples is one of largeness of view, and allows great latitude in ecclesiastical matters. When Garfield accepted its tenets, but few were the believers, but now it has over half a million followers. Of the influence on Garfield's life of his "Disciple" training we shall learn presently.

During this fall he entered a school of book-keeping, penmanship and elocution, kept by Dr. Alonzo Harlow, located at Chagrin Falls, Cuyahoga county, Ohio. Garfield was the doctor's janitor, paying his tuition in that manner, and at the same time earning his board of a neighboring farmer by doing chores about the place. It was here that he took his first lessons in elocution, and received the first real encouragement to fit himself for public life.

In the winter he taught a village school in Warrensville, receiving sixteen dollars a month and board. One of the boys under his charge at this school desired to study advanced mathematics. Garfield had never got so far in mathematics, but he bought a text-book, studied nights, kept ahead of his pupil, and took him through without his once suspecting that the master was not an expert in the science. This is the last of Garfield in Chester or its neighborhood. Writing many years afterward, on the time spent here, he said: "I remember with great satisfaction the work which was accomplished for me at Chester. It marked the most decisive change in my life. While there I formed a definite purpose and plan to complete a college course. With the educational facilities now afforded in our country, no young man, who has good health and is master of his own actions, can be excused for not obtaining a good education. Poverty is very inconvenient, but it is a fine spur to activity, and may be made a rich blessing."

Hiram college is located in Hiram, Portage county, then a cross-road village, twelve miles from any town or railroad. The settlement was mostly composed of the new religious sect, and in 1850 the college was built. In that day the Disciples of the Western Reserve were mostly rural people, sharing the old-fashioned prejudices against towns and cities. Thought in Northern Ohio was narrowly provincial in 1850. There were only two or three railroads in the State. No one dreamed of our present railroad system, or foresaw the centralization of wealth and population that the steam locomotive has wrought. Traveling was done in wheeled vehicles, or on horseback. People owned their own conveyances and horses, so the fathers asked, "Why can they not turn their horses heads towards Hiram as well as towards any other place?" Hiram, then, offered the desired seclusion. The aims of the school were both general and specific. More narrowly they were these: 1. To provide a sound scientific and literary education. 2. To temper and sweeten such education with moral and Scriptural knowledge. 3. To educate young men for the ministry. One peculiar tenet of the religious movement in which it originated, was impressed upon the Eclectic Institute at its organization. Disciples believed that the Bible had been in a degree obscured by theological speculations and ecclesiastical systems. They believed, also, that to the Holy Writings belonged a larger place in general education than had yet been accorded to them. This may be called the distinctive feature of their school.

His religious feeling naturally called him to the young institution of his own denomination. In August, 1851, he arrived at Hiram, and found a plain brick building standing in the midst of a corn-field, with, perhaps, a dozen farm-houses near enough for boarding places for the students. It was a lonely, isolated place, remote from any main thoroughfare or center of population. No stage-coach wheels even rolled within five miles of the place. Probably twenty farm-houses lay within a radius of a mile, on a high ridge dividing the waters flowing into Lake Erie from those running southward to the Ohio. The "Centre" was a cross-roads, with a post-office, one or two shops, two white churches, and three or four dwelling-houses. The Rev. A. S. Hayden was the principal; Thomas Munnell and Norman Dunshee were teachers; the latter teaching mathematics and Greek.

HIRAM COLLEGE.

When Garfield went to Hiram, everything was new and crude. In after years Garfield himself said: "The Eclectic was compelled to form its own scholarship and culture. Very few of its early students had gone beyond the ordinary studies of the district school; and a large majority of them needed thorough discipline in the common English branches." President Hinsdale has well said: "The opening of this new school was coincident with three things important in this history: 1. With a general educational awakening in the State of Ohio. In an important sense, the present school system of the State dates from the year 1853. The population of the State had grown marvelously. The homes of the people were full of youth; and wealth had so grown, that men, in great part freed from the burden of sweeping away the forests, were enabled to pay greatly increased attention to the education of their children. 2. With an important epoch in the history of the Disciples of the Reserve. They had now a school of their own, in which they took pride. 3. With the young manhood of James A. Garfield." His first presentation of himself to the Board of Trustees, as related by Mr. Frederick Williams, one of the number, is characteristic, and therefore worth repeating. "The Board was in session with closed doors," says Mr. Williams, "when the door-keeper entered and said there was a young man at the door, very desirous of seeing the Board without delay. No objections being made, the young man entered, and addressing the Board, said, "Gentlemen, I want an education, and would like the privilege of making the fires and sweeping the floors of the building to pay part of my expenses." Mr. Williams, seeing in his bearing and countenance an earnestness and intelligence that was more than common, said to the Board, "Gentlemen, I think we had better try this young man." Another member said to him, "How do we know, young man, that the work will be done as we may want?" "Try me," was the answer; "try me two weeks, and if it is not done to your entire satisfaction, I will retire without a word." The offer was accepted, and James A. Garfield again found himself a rich man; rich in opportunities, rich in health, rich in having *some* way, though a humble one, to support himself through another period of magnificent mental growth. An obvious and interesting analogy between the school and the pupil could be readily traced; both were full of strength and enthusiasm; both needed growth and ripeness. Having lost his father in his infancy, his sense of responsibility, his judgment, and his self-helpfulness were developed beyond the average. He was full of animal spirits and young joviality. Two terms he made fires, swept the floors and rang the bell. Scores of men and women can now be found who well remember seeing the future President of the United States at the end of the Hiram bell-rope.

Garfield, at the age of nineteen, was duly installed as janitor and bell-ringer of the institution, over which he was afterward to preside, and whose prosperity he was to be largely instrumental in advancing. In the morning he could be seen with his hand on the bell-rope, ready to give the signal calling teachers and scholars to engage in the duties of the day. He had a cheerful word for every one. He was probably the most popular person in the institution. He was always good-natured, fond of conversation, and very entertaining. He was witty, and quick at repartee, but his jokes, though brilliant and striking, were always harmless, and he never would willingly hurt another's feelings.

"Whatever he undertook to do, it was always his purpose to do it well. He soon became popular, not only with the other students, but, also, with the instructors, who at once recognized his determined purposes of study. At one time the teacher of Science and English became sick, and young Garfield was asked to fill the vacancy. So successful was he, in this undertaking, that other classes were given him, and it will reflect no discredit upon any one to say that they were never taught better. He was particularly adapted to impart instruction; and hence his classes never flagged in interest. He was not given much to amusements or the sports of the play-ground. He was too industrious, and too anxious to make the utmost of his opportunities to study. He was a constant attendant at the regular meetings for prayer, and his vigorous exhortations and apt remarks upon the Bible lesson were impressive and interesting. There was a cordiality in his disposition which won quickly the favor and esteem of others. He had a happy habit of shaking hands, and would give a hearty grip which betokened a kind-hearted feeling for all. He was always ready to turn his mind and hands in any direction whereby he might add to his meager store of money. One of his gifts was that of mezzotint drawing, and he gave instructions in this branch. In those days the faculty and pupils were in the habit of calling him 'the second Webster,' and the remark was common, 'He will fill the White House yet.' In the lyceum he early took rank far above the others as a speaker and debater. He was frequently asked to address the people, and this becoming a habit, rapidly improved, and he came to be called 'the most eloquent young man in the county.' That the first interest in politics was shown at this period is evident. Father Bentley, the pastor of the church at Hiram, one time invited Garfield to occupy a seat in the pulpit with him, it being understood, of course, that the young orator should address the congregation. Unnoticed by the pastor, a young man approached Garfield, and called him away. The young man had been sent to bring him to address a political meeting. Noticing, at length, his departure, Bentley was about to call him back, when, suddenly stopping, he said, 'Well, I suppose we must let him go. Very likely he will be President of the United States some day!' When he went to Hiram he had studied Latin only six weeks and had just begun Greek; but he was, in fact, the finest Latin and Greek scholar that the school ever saw, and was, therefore, just in a condition to fairly begin the four years' preparatory course ordinarily taken by students before entering college in the freshman class. Yet in three years' time he fitted himself to enter the junior class, thus crowding six years' study into three, and teaching for his support at the same time. To accomplish this, he shut the whole world out from his mind, save that little portion of it within the range of his studies; knowing nothing of politics or the news of the day, reading no light literature, and engaging in no social recreations that took his time from his books.

"During the month of June, the entire school went in carriages to their annual grove meeting at Randolph, some twenty-five miles away. On this trip he was the life of the party, occasionally bursting out in an eloquent strain at the sight of a bird, or a trailing vine, or a venerable giant of the forest. He would repeat poetry by the hour, having a very retentive memory. At the Institute the members were like a band of brothers and sisters, all struggling to advance in knowledge. They all dressed plainly, and there was no attempt or pretence at dressing fashionably or stylishly. Hiram was a little country place, with no fascinations or worldly attractions to draw off the minds of the students from their work."

Garfield's general progress at Hiram was intimately connected with that of the people about him; and the best possible view of him must come from a knowledge of his friends, and the work they did together. In an address to the

Alumni of Hiram, Garfield furnished a good sketch of the kind of human material that made up the Eclectic Institute:

"In 1850 it was a green field, with a solid, plain brick building in the centre of it, and almost all the rest has been done by the institution itself. Without a dollar of endowment, without a powerful friend anywhere, a corps of teachers were told to go on the ground and see what they could make of it, and to find their pay out of the tuitions that should be received; who invited students of their own spirit to come here on the ground, and find out by trial what they could make of it. The chief response has been their work, and the chief part of the response I see in the faces gathered before me to-day. It was a simple question of sinking or swimming, and I do not know of any institution that has accomplished more, with little means, than this school on Hiram hill. I know of no place where the doctrine of self-help has had a fuller development. As I said a great many years ago, the theory of Hiram was to throw its young men and women overboard, and let them try for themselves. All that were fit to get ashore got there, and we had few cases of drowning. Now, when I look over these faces, and mark the several geologic ages, I find the geologic analogy does not hold—there are no fossils. Some are dead and glorified in our memories, but those who are alive are ALIVE. I believe there was a stronger pressure of work to the square inch in the boilers that ran this establishment than any other I know of. Young men and women—rough, crude and untutored farmer boys and girls—came here to try themselves, and find out what manner of people they were. They came here to go on a voyage of discovery, to discover themselves, and in many cases I hope the discovery was fortunate."

Before continuing the chronological order of events in Garfield's life further, we must stop to be introduced to a few of the leading characters at Hiram; those with whom Garfield was most intimate. And to do so, we will employ Garfield's own language:

"A few days after the beginning of the term, I saw a class of three reciting in mathematics—geometry, I think. I had never seen a geometry, and, regarding both teacher and class with a feeling of reverential awe for the intellectual height to which they had climbed, I studied their faces so closely that I seem to see them now as distinctly as I saw them then. And it has been my good fortune since that time to claim them all as intimate friends. The teacher was Thomas Munnell, and the members of his class were William B. Hazen, George A. Baker and Almeda A. Booth."

All scholars, who have few books and other educational advantages in youth, can take in this picture at once—teacher, class, and the honest, open-eyed youth of twenty, full of wonder, appreciation and reverence.

Subsequently he met here, for the second time, a young lady whom he had met before at Geauga Academy. Her name was Lucretia Rudolph, and she was the daughter of a farmer in the neighborhood—"a quiet, thoughtful girl," says one who knew her, "of singularly sweet and refined disposition, fond of study and reading, and possessing a warm heart, and a mind capable of steady growth." It was years before the lives of the two young people were united; but from this time forward she exerted a marked influence upon the boy-student, inspiring him to even harder work, and a firmer resolve to act a manly part in the world's struggle. The father of this young woman was from Maryland, his uncle had been a brave soldier of the Revolution. It is also related that he afterwards went to France, enlisted under the banner of Napoleon, and was soon known to the world as Marshal Ney. Lucretia's mother had come from Vermont, her name having been Arabella Mason. The family were poor, but honest and very industrious. Lucretia had been sent to Hiram, and during Garfield's early tutorship became one of his pupils. Often, therefore, did the two meet. Few advances were made at first, and they continued simply to be good, staunch friends. With her sweet, modest and unassuming demeanor the awkward James was attracted. She, a sensible and intelligent girl, saw a noble heart and promising future in Garfield, although his clothes were coarse and home-spun. His leadership in everything pertaining to study and thought, his great popularity among all his college acquaintances, naturally won the admiration of the maiden. The old friendship ripened into affection, and then love, and before Garfield left Hiram they were engaged to marry.

He lived in a room with four other pupils, studied harder than ever, having now his college project fully anchored in his mind, got through his six books of Cæsar that term, and made good progress in Greek. He met, on entering the institute, a woman who exercised a strong influence on his intellectual life, Miss Almeda Booth—the Margaret Fuller of the West—a teacher in the school. This woman, perhaps, had more influence upon his life at this time than any other person. Miss Almeda A. Booth was a woman of wonderful force of mind and character. She was only nine years his senior; but she concentrated upon him all the impassioned force of a strong maternal soul, and she led him to intellectual heights seldom trod by any but the highest intellects. "I never met the man," he once said, "whose mind I feared to grapple with; but this woman could lead where I found it hard to follow." She not only guided his studies, but she shared in them as a comrade and co-worker; and a friend relates how she sat with him after school one night, talking up a thesis he was preparing for an exhibition day, both so supremely absorbed in the work that neither realized the night had worn away till the morning light came breaking through the window. This woman had more influence in forming his intellectual character than any one he ever met, except that great and good man, President Hopkins. She had taught her first school at the age of seventeen. The one to whom she had been engaged to marry, died, and she ever afterwards devoted herself to teaching and kindred pursuits. Thus the quiet current of life was not wrecked, but went smoothly on, clear and beautiful. The shadow of death resting over her only made her mind the more thoughtful, serious and meditative. Her mind gloried in strength, and the opportunity for a career of usefulness helped to make her happy. She died in 1875, and the tribute which Garfield paid to her memory is one of the most eloquent things he has ever spoken or written. In this he gives us an insight into their friendship and colabors. "In mathematics and the physical sciences I was far behind her; but we were nearly at the same place in Greek and Latin. She had made her home at President Hayden's almost from the first, and I became a member of his family at the beginning of the winter term of 1852-53. Thereafter, for nearly two years, she and I studied together in the same classes (frequently without other associates) till we had nearly completed the classical course."

The summer vacation of 1853 only brought harder work. In company with eleven students he formed a class, and hired Professor Dunshee to give them private lessons for one month. He was also a member of an active literary society during this month. When the fall term was fairly under way, Garfield went at it again, to hasten his preparation for college. He, with some other students, formed a Translation Society, that met at Miss Booth's rooms two evenings a week, and made a joint translation with her of the Book of Romans. The work done was more thorough than rapid. An entry in Garfield's diary for December 15, 1853, reads: "Translation Society sat three hours in Miss Booth's rooms, and agreed upon the translation of nine verses." To this class Professor Dunshee contributed some essays on the German commentators, DeWette and Tholock. During the winter (1853–54), Garfield read the whole of "Demosthenes on the Crown."

No one who is thoroughly familiar with President Garfield's history can doubt that his connection with Hiram and the Disciple habits and methods had a most important influence upon his mind, his whole life and character. At the same time, he was farthest removed from a sectarian or denominationalist. His religious thoughts were ever broad, his spirit ever catholic. By alternating work with study, he had laid by about half enough to carry him through a two years' collegiate course, and, it was an interesting question how he should provide for the remainder. And now the reputation he had established for integrity, industry, and persistency of purpose stood him in good stead. The sum needed was several hundred dollars, but a kind-hearted gentleman, who had watched his course, volunteered to loan him the required amount, to be advanced from time to time, when it was needed. To secure the advance, Garfield took out a policy of insurance on his life; and as he placed it in the hands of the worthy gentleman, he said, "If I live I shall pay you; and if I die, you will suffer no loss."

The college question was before him. But where should he go? He had recently read some lectures by President Hopkins, of Williams, that had made him think favorably of that institution. But he had originally intended to enter Bethany College, the institution sustained by the church of which he was a member, and presided over by Alexander Campbell, the man above all others he had been taught to admire and revere. A familiar letter shall tell us how he reasoned and acted:

There are three reasons why I have decided not to go to Bethany: 1. The course of study is not so extensive or thorough as in Eastern colleges. 2. Bethany leans too heavily toward slavery. 3. I am the son of Disciple parents, am one myself, and have had but little acquaintance with people of other views, and, having always lived in the West, I think it will make me more liberal, both in my religious and general views and sentiments, to go into a new circle, where I shall be under new influences. These considerations led me to conclude to go to some New England college. I therefore wrote to the presidents of Brown University, Yale and Williams, setting forth the amount of study I had done, and asking how long it would take me to finish their course.

Their answers are now before me. All tell me I can graduate in two years.

They are all brief, business notes, but President Hopkins concludes with this sentence: "If you come here we shall be glad to do what we can for you." Other things being so nearly equal, this sentence, which seems to be a kind of friendly grasp of the hand, has settled the question for me. I shall start for Williams next week.

Some points in this letter of a young man about to start away from home to college will strike the reader as remarkable. Nothing could show more mature judgment about the matter in hand than the wise anxiety to get out from the Disciples' influence and see something of other men and other opinions. It was notable that one trained to look upon Alexander Campbell as the master intellect of the churches of the day, should revolt against studying in his college because it leaned too strongly to slavery. And in the final turning of the decision upon the little friendly commonplace remark that closed one of the letters, we catch a glimpse of the warm, sympathetic nature of the man, which much and wide experience of the world in after years never hardened.

So, in the fall of 1854, the pupil of the Geauga Seminary and of the Hiram Institute applied for admission at the venerable doors of Williams College. He knew no graduate of the College, and no student attending it; and of the President he only knew that he had published a volume of lectures which he liked, and that he had said a kindly word to him when he spoke of coming. Our carpenter and tow-path boy had gone as far as the high-schools and academies of his native region could carry him. Garfield was now a man of twenty-three. Boyhood had passed away, and with it his nautical desires. When he became a man he put away the ambitions and air-castles of youth. Before him were as yet marvelous growth, and possibilities, the attainment of which now became his daily thought. The struggling, hard-working boy had developed into a self-reliant man. He was the neighborhood wonder for scholarship, and a general favorite for the hearty, genial ways that never deserted him. Garfield goes to Williams, and leaves behind the friends of boyhood, all the attachments dear to him, and casts his lot among new and untried friends.

CHAPTER V.

STUDENT AT WILLIAMS COLLEGE.

His body thus adorn'd, he next designed,
With lib'ral acts to cultivate his mind.
-DRYDEN.

Him for the studious shade, kind nature form'd.—SHAKESPEARE.

And with unwearied fingers drawing out
The lines of life from living knowledge hid.
—SPENSER.

As might well be expected, Garfield's new life and experiences at Williams College were very much different from those at Hiram. The latter could scarcely claim the lofty sobriquet of college. It aimed merely at preparation for the higher education of its students. Its prospective point was Bethany; but Garfield, as we have already seen, chose an Eastern college of more prominence.

The Western carpenter and village school-teacher received many a shock in the new sphere in which he now entered. On every hand he felt the social superiority of his fellow-students. Their ways were free from the little awkward habits of the untrained laboring youth. Their speech was free from the uncouth phrases of the provincial circles in which he had moved. Their toilets made the handiwork of his village tailor look sadly shabby. Their free-handed expenditures contrasted strikingly with his enforced parsimony. To some tough-fibred hearts these would have been only petty annoyances; to the warm, social, generous mind of young Garfield they seem, from more than one indication of his college life that we can gather, to have been a source of positive anguish. No storm of merciless ridicule, however, greeted the shy, awkward, ungainly backwoodsman. The pupils of Williams understood what some of our colleges seem never to know—that reverence for the republican life of which they form a part is honorable.

When Garfield went to Williams he was over six feet high. Society culture had never rounded off the sharp angles of awkwardness, and he looked every inch a backwoodsman. By those who knew Garfield at this time he is described as a tall, awkward youth, with a great shock of light hair rising nearly erect from a broad, high forehead, and an open, kindly and thoughtful face, which showed no traces of his long struggle with poverty and privation. He was strong-framed, deep-chested, and had a quick blue eye. Physically, he was the Garfield of twenty years later, only he had the pulpy adolescence of twenty. Time had not yet rounded out his figure, browned his hair, and put into his face the lines of thought. His great success at Hiram in mastering his studies permitted him easily to pass the examination for admittance into the junior class. Garfield's three years at Hiram had been successful to an extraordinary degree. He had gotten out of the school all that he could get; he left much of himself behind. He might have finished his studies at Williams in one year; but, feeling the need of longer and more thorough training, he wisely determined to take two years.

At the college there was a student named Wilbur, a cripple, who had come from Ohio, and in him Garfield became interested. His kindness to his lame chum was a matter of common remark and respect. About him were the sons of wealthy Eastern gentlemen, and his position in the college, entering as he did one of the advanced classes, brought him into close contact with them, but he bore bravely up, maintained the advance standing in the junior class to which he had been admitted on his arrival, and at the end of his two-years' course bore off the metaphysical honor of his class, reckoned at Williams among the highest within the gift of the institution to her graduating members.

When Garfield reached Williams College, in June, 1854, he had about three hundred dollars, which he had saved while teaching in the Hiram school. With this money he hoped to manage to get through a year. A few weeks remained of the closing school-year, and he attended the recitations of the sophomore class in order to get familiar with the methods of the professors before testing his ability to pass the examinations for the junior year. During the summer vacation, while the other students were seeking pleasure and recreation, Garfield, although his year's work had been of the most severe and trying kind, remained at Williams. He realized as soon as he came to Williams that his reading and general fund of information was somewhat small. This was owing to the fact that but few opportunities had been afforded him in this direction. His time had been occupied in the double occupation of teaching and preparing for college, and hence but little time was left him for general reading, had he had the opportunity. He had never seen a copy of Shakespeare, and had never read a novel written by any of the great authors. His knowledge of literature, hence, was small. Shakespeare was known only to him by having seen one or two quotations from that author in the readers. The tenets and beliefs of the church of which he was a member, were opposed to novel reading, and he had ever conscientiously observed its creed. Here now was a golden opportunity. The large library of which the college was possessed was at his disposal. Several months in which to improve the opportunity lay before him; and, at once, he plunged in. The best books of which literature can boast were to be found on the shelves of the library. He read poetry, history, metaphysics, science, scarcely pausing long enough for meals. This powerful mind, like an engine, was at work; it had been aroused to activity as never before, and the vacation's work became a mine of wealth to him. Garfield's work was done with all the more keenness and relish, because he realized that poverty and privation had kept him back, and he was but making up the time he had lost. His mental and physical powers seemed to know no fatigue; and he was but proving the truth of Dr. Robinson's predictions, made years before, that hard work would not hurt him. Weaker minds would have foundered on the diet our hero was living on; but not so with him. With note book in hand, ready to set down any fact not clear in his mind, he worked along day after day. These memoranda he afterwards would take the time to look up, fixing all references, mythologic, historical or literary, in his mind by separate investigation. The work was done well, notwithstanding the terrific speed. It is worth while to remark that this outside reading was kept up during his entire stay at Williams. God gave him a big brain and a great heart, and he did not misuse or neglect the one nor suffer the other to grow cold or corrupt. He reached manhood in an age of great opportunities, and he was equal to them. He was ever heaping up knowledge and gleaning wisdom. Ideas were brighter to him than dollars.

Concerning this period of Garfield's life an eminent gentleman, Hon. Clement H. Hill, of Boston, who was a classmate, says: "I think at that time he was paying great attention to German, and devoted all his leisure time to that language. In his studies, his taste was rather for metaphysical and philosophical studies than for history and biography, which were the studies most to my liking; but he read besides a good deal of poetry and general literature."

His classmates still speak of his prodigious industry, his cordial, hearty, and social ways, and the great zest with which he entered into all the physical exercises of the students. He soon became distinguished as the most ready and effective debater in the college, and one occasion on which he displayed these peculiar abilities is specially mentioned. Charles Sumner had been stricken down in the Senate-chamber by Brooks of South Carolina, and the news reaching the college, caused great excitement among the students. An indignation meeting was that evening held among them, and, mounting the platform, Garfield—so says my informant, who was himself one of the students—delivered "one of the most impassioned and eloquent speeches that was ever heard in old Williams."

Garfield had been raised in a region of country where mountains were unknown. The beauty of the scenery in and about Williamstown made a strong impression on his mind. The contrast between the level and unbroken country of the Western Reserve, and the mountainous region about Williams College was striking. The spurs of the Green Hills which reach down from Vermont and enclose the little college town in their arms, were to the young man a wonderful revelation of grandeur and beauty. All the valleys and retreats of the neighborhood were eagerly explored by Garfield, and his unusually imaginative mind received many impressions which gave coloring to his oratory in later days.

Whole poems which he committed to memory were recited during his solitary rambles through the mountains. After he had been six or eight months at college, and had devoured an immense amount of serious reading, he began to suffer from intellectual dyspepsia. He found his mind was not assimilating what he read, and would often refuse to be held down to the printed page. Then he revised his notions about books of fiction, and concluded that romance is as valuable a part of intellectual food as salad is of dinner. He prescribed for himself one novel a month, and on this medicine his mind speedily recuperated and got back all its old elasticity. Cooper's Leatherstocking Tales were the first novels he read, and afterward Walter Scott. An English classmate introduced him to the works of Dickens and Thackeray. Garfield studied Latin and Greek and took up German as an elective study. One year at Williams completed his classical studies, on which he was far advanced before he went there. In a short time he had mastered German so thoroughly that he could read Goethe and Schiller without difficulty.

The fact that there are so few stories concerning Garfield's college life which have found their way into print, may have been a matter of some surprise to many readers. But there is a reason for it. Every student who passes through college, casts a different picture of his career on the mind of each of his fellow students. The college "yarn" is generally a tradition of some shrewd trick, some insubordination to discipline, or some famous practical joke. But Garfield is not remembered in this way. The picture he left on the mind of his fellow-students was far different. There were no hen-roosts that were disturbed through his instrumentality, no pilfered orchards, no plundered melon patches. His mind was far differently occupied than in planning mock processions, sham class battles, editing bogus newspapers, tarring the banisters of the college stairs, and such other evidences of insubordination. There are stories extant in almost every college of how recitation rooms were broken into, and specimens removed, of how the class hats or canes were confiscated, but we are acquainted with no such incidents in which Garfield was a participant while at Williams. He was here under great pecuniary pressure, and for a high and solemn purpose. Work was his purpose, not play. Nothing was sufficient inducement to turn him from his high and noble purpose. At one time he became a chess player. He enjoyed the game to the utmost, but perceiving that its playing carried him to late hours, he denied himself even the pleasure of this game.

At the end of the fall term of 1854, Garfield enjoyed a winter vacation of two months which he spent in North Pownal, Bennington county, Vermont, teaching a writing class. He did this to obtain funds to defray his expenses while pursuing his studies. Garfield wrote a broad, handsome hand, a hand that was strongly individual, and the envy of the boys and girls who tried to imitate it. North Pownal was formerly known as Whiffles Corner, and is situated in the south-west corner of the state; and by the usually traveled road, one passes in an hour's ride from New York through the corner of Vermont by way of this place into the state of Massachusetts. In 1851 Chester A. Arthur, fresh from Union College, came to North Pownal, and for one summer taught the village school. About two years afterward Garfield taught his writing school in the same building. Thus from a common starting point in early life, after the lapse of more than a quarter of a century, after years of manly toil, these distinguished gentlemen were by the action of the Chicago Convention brought into a close relationship.

At the end of the College year in June, Garfield returned home to see his mother, who was then living with a daughter at Solon. His money was exhausted, and he had to adopt one of two plans, either to borrow enough to take him through to graduation at the end of the next year, or set to work as a teacher until he earned the requisite amount, and so break the continuity of his college course. Dr. Robinson came to his aid and advanced the money, which in due time Garfield was able to return. Garfield chose not to be an object of charity, even in the matter of receiving his education. President Chadbourne, of Williams College, said recently: "The college life of General Garfield was so perfect, so rounded, so pure, so in accordance with what it ought to be in all respects, that I can add nothing to it by eulogizing him. Everything about him was high and noble and manly; the man in college gave promise of what the man was to become. And so, when some charges were made against him some years ago, I wrote to General Garfield, and have said in speeches since that time, that when a young man goes through a college course without exhibiting a mean or dishonest trait, and then goes out and lives so as impress upon other men the idea that he has been true at all times and in all places, it will take a great deal of proof to convince me that that man has forsaken the path he trod so long."

But it was in the debating society that Garfield excelled. He was a member of the Philologian Literary Society. Here he was a power, and his towering intellect won for him many a signal victory. His breadth of statement, his grasp of fact, his quick repartee, combined to make him the leading orator of the college. In the matter of preparation he showed himself to be a master. The subject of debate would always be placed under divisions, and his colleagues were given such parts of the subject as best suited their particular minds and methods of thought. By this means the library would be examined, and every volume bearing in the least on the subject-matter was gleaned, annotations made, notes compared, and a "campaign" planned. After this thorough review of the subject, the method of presenting the subject to produce the best effect was studied. Garfield's mind was always clear and logical. Scraps of information gathered in his cursory reading were often introduced with striking effect. By presuming and affecting to be fully acquainted with a new subject, he would often throw his antagonist off his guard and thus gain an important point. A notable instance of this occurred in a public debate during his junior year. The preceding speaker had used a lengthy and somewhat irrelevant illustration from Don Quixote. When Garfield's turn for reply came, he brought down the house by saying: "The gentleman is correct in drawing analogies between his side of this question and certain passages in the life of Don Quixote. There is a marked resemblance, which I perceive myself, between his argument and the scene of the Knight attacking the windmill; or, rather it would be more appropriate to say that he resembles *the windmill attacking the Knight.*" At the college supper, which followed the public entertainment, Garfield's extensive acquaintance with standard literature was being talked about, when he laughingly told his admiring friends that he had never read Don Quixote, and had only heard a mention of the tournament between the crazy Knight and the windmill.

Garfield's morals were as spotless as the stars. A classmate who knew him well, writes: "I never heard an angry word, or a hasty expression, or a sentence which needed to be recalled. He possessed equanimity of temper, self-possession, and self-control in the highest degree. What is more, I never heard a profane or improper word, or an indelicate allusion from his lips. He was in habits, speech, and example, a pure man."

The impression made upon Garfield's mind by the character of the country's topography has already been mentioned. An incident will not be out of place here concerning one of the memorable "Mountain Days," which were annually celebrated at old Williams. On these days some picturesque place in the mountains near by would be visited, and the boys, free from all thoughts of study, would enjoy the day to the utmost. On one of these occasions, an incident revealed the courage and piety of "Old Gar," as the boys lovingly called their leader. They were at the summit of "Old Greylock," seven miles from the college. The air was cool, notwithstanding the fact that it was summer. The little group of collegians were gathered about a camp-fire that blazed up briskly in the darkening air of the evening. Some were sitting, some were standing, but all were silent. The splendor and solemnity of the scene, the dark winding valley, the circling range of mountains, the over-bending sky, the distant villages, with the picturesque old college towers, the glories of the sunset, filled every heart with religious awe. Just as the silence became oppressive, it was broken by the voice of Garfield: "Boys, it is my habit to read a chapter in the Bible every evening with my absent mother. Shall I read aloud?" At once the little company gave their assent, and drawing from his pocket a well-worn Testament, he read, in soft, rich tones, the chapter which his mother in Ohio was reading at the same time, and then called on a classmate in that mountain top to pray.

While studying at Williams College, he preached regularly for one church, and frequently for others. He was frequently paid for these services, and hence, he sought such opportunities to preach, that he might add to his means in his struggle for an education.

At the commencement of his senior year, and after having returned from his visit to Ohio, Garfield was chosen one of the editors of the *Williams Quarterly*, the paper published at the college. Associated with him in this work were W. R. Baxter, Henry E. Knox, E. Clarence Smith and John Tatlock. Many were the productions which found their way into the columns of the *Quarterly* from Garfield's pen. He was considered an easy and rapid writer, and his connection with this publication gave polish and strength to his writing. Garfield proved himself to be equal to all emergencies in his college work, as he ever did in his public career. He had brains and splendid powers, and these gave him prominence. Nowhere in the world does ability rise to the top, and mediocrity sink to the bottom, so surely and swiftly, as at college.

We shall now pause to examine some of Garfield's productions contained in the *Quarterly* during his editorship. We discover at once a vein of poetry, which, had it been developed and cultured, might have made him a tolerable poet. The first contribution we shall reproduce is entitled "Memory." The subject is visionary, metaphysical and abstract, but the poet-author has handled it in a manner pleasing and highly creditable. "At this time his intended profession was teaching, and it is possible that the presidency of a Christian college was 'the summit where the sunbeams fell,' but in the light of events the last lines seem almost prophetic."

MEMORY.

'Tis beauteous night; the stars look brightly down
Upon the earth, decked in her robe of snow.
No light gleams at the window save my own,
Which gives its cheer to midnight and to me.
And now with noiseless step sweet Memory comes,
And leads me gently through her twilight realms.
What poet's tuneful lyre has ever sung,
Or most delicate pencil ere portrayed
The enchanted shadowy land where Memory dwells?
It has valleys, cheerless, lone and drear,
Dark-shaded by the mournful cypress tree.
And yet its sunlit mountain tops are bathed
In heaven's own blue. Upon its craggy cliffs,
Robed in the dreamy light of distant years,
Are clustered joys serene of other days;
Upon its gently sloping hillsides bend
The weeping willows o'er the sacred dust
Of dear departed ones; and yet in that land,
Where'er our footsteps fall upon the shore,
They that were sleeping rise from out the dust
Of death's long, silent years, and round us stand,
As erst they did before the prison tomb
Received their clay within its voiceless halls.
The heavens that bend above that land are hung
With clouds of various hues; some dark and chill,
Surcharged with sorrow, cast their sombre shade
Upon the sunny, joyous land below;
Others are floating through the dreamy air;
White as the falling snow their margins tinged
With gold and crimson hues; their shadows fall
Upon the flowery meads and sunny slopes,
Soft as the shadows of an angel's wing.
When the rough battle of the day is done,
And evening's peace falls gently on the heart,
I bound away across the noisy years,
Unto the utmost verge of Memory's land,
Where earth and sky in dreamy distance meet,
And Memory dim with dark oblivion joins;
Where woke the first remembered sounds that fell
Upon the ear in childhood's early morn;
And wandering thence, along the rolling years,
I see the shadow of my former self
Gliding from childhood up to man's estate.
The path of youth winds down through many a vale
And on the brink of many a dread abyss,
From out whose darkness comes no ray of light,
Save that a phantom dances o'er the gulf,
And beckons toward the verge. Again the path
Leads o'er a summit where the sunbeams fall;
And thus in light and shade, sunshine and gloom,
Sorrow and joy, this life-path leads along.

Another poem which appeared during his senior year is equally suggestive. It might have passed for a very creditable production of a much more renowned writer. In it there is much of poetic power. The description of the scene, Nature pictured as "wearing her shroud of snow," is very fine. In all of Garfield's writings we distinguish a strong sympathy with nature.

AUTUMN.

Old Autumn, thou art here! Upon the earth
And in the heavens the signs of death are hung;
For o'er the earth's brown breast stalks pale decay,
And 'mong the lowering clouds the wild winds wail,
And sighing sadly, shouts the solemn dirge,
O'er Summer's fairest flowers, all faded now.
The Winter god, descending from the skies,
Has reached the mountain tops and decked their brows
With glittering frosty crowns, and breathed his breath
Among the trumpet pines, that herald forth
His coming.
Before the driving blast
The mountain oak bows down his hoary head,
And flings his withered locks to the rough gales
That fiercely roar among his branches bare,
Uplifted to the dark, unpitying heavens.
The skies have put their mourning garments on,
And hung their funeral drapery on the clouds.
Dead Nature soon will wear her shroud of snow
And lie entombed in Winter's icy grave.
Thus passes life. As heavy age comes on
The joys of youth—bright beauties of the Spring—
Grow dim and faded, and the long, dark night
Of death's chill winter comes. But as the Spring
Rebuilds the ruined wreck of Winter's waste,
And cheers the gloomy earth with joyous light,
So o'er the tomb the star of hope shall rise
And usher in an ever-during day.

From these we turn to scan a production of an entirely different nature. In another more jovial and lighter frame of mind the following parody on Tennyson's "Light Brigade" must have been composed. It was called the "Charge of the Tight Brigade."

Bottles to right of them,
Bottles to left of them,
Bottles in front of them,
Fizzled and sundered.
Ent'ring with shout and yell,
Boldly they drank and well,
They caught the Tartar then;
Oh, what a perfect sell!
Sold—the half hundred.
Grinned all the dentals bare,
Swung all their caps in air,
Uncorking bottles there,
Watching the Freshmen while
Every one wondered;
Plunged in tobacco smoke,
With many a desperate stroke,
Dozens of bottles broke,
Then they came back, but not,
But not the half hundred.

Of his college prose writings there are many excellent selections that we might make, but these few must suffice. In a strong editorial in which he speaks of the purposes of the *Quarterly* he says:

"It proposes a kind of intellectual tournament where we may learn to hurl the lance and wield the sword, and thus prepare for the conflict of life. It shall be our aim to keep the lists still open and the arena clear, that the knights of the quill may learn to hurl the lance and wield the sword of thought, and thus be ready for sterner duties. We shall also endeavor to decorate the arena with all the flowers that our *own gardens* afford, and thus render the place more pleasant and inviting. We should remember, however, that it is no honor or profit merely to *appear* in the arena, but the wreath is for those who *contend.*"

From a brilliant review of the life and writings of the unfortunate Karl Theodor Korner, that appeared in the number for March, 1856, we cut a single paragraph:

"The greater part of our modern literature bears evident marks of the haste which characterizes all the movements of this age; but, in reading these older authors, we are impressed with the idea that they enjoyed the most comfortable leisure. Many books we can read in a railroad car, and feel a harmony between the rushing of the train and the haste of the author; but to enjoy the older authors, we need the quiet of a winter evening—an easy chair before a cheerful fire, and all the equanimity of spirits we can command. Then the genial good nature, the rich fullness, the persuasive eloquence of those old masters will fall upon us like the warm, glad sunshine, and afford those hours of calm contemplation in which the spirit may expand with generous growth, and gain deep and comprehensive views. The pages of friendly old Goldsmith come to us like a golden autumn day, when every object which meets the eye bears all the impress of the completed year, and the beauties of an autumnal forest."

Garfield defines the historian's duty in the following terse and well chosen language:

"There are two points which the historian should ever have before him:

"First—The valuation of facts to each other and the whole body of history; and,

"Second—The tendency of the whole toward some great end.

* * * * * * * * * *

"For every village, State and nation there is an aggregate of native talent which God has given, and by which, together with his Providence, he leads that nation on, and thus leads the world. In the light of these truths we affirm that no man can understand the history of any nation, or of the world, who does not recognize in it the power of God, and behold his stately goings forth as he walks among the nations. It is his hand that is moving the vast superstructure of human history, and, though but one of the windows were unfurnished, like that of the Arabian palace, yet all the powers of earth could never complete it without the aid of the Divine Architect.

"To employ another figure—the world's history is a divine poem, of which the history of every nation is a canto, and of every man a word. Its strains have been pealing along down the centuries, and, though there have been mingled the discord of roaring cannon and dying men, yet to the Christian philosopher and historian—the humble listener—there has been a divine melody running through the song, which speaks of hope and halcyon days to come. The record of every orphan's sigh, of every widow's prayer, of every noble deed, of every honest heart-throb for the right, is swelling that gentle strain; and when, at last, the great end is attained—when the lost image of God is restored to the human soul; when the church anthem can be pealed forth without a discordant note, then will angels join in the chorus, and all the sons of God again 'shout for joy.'"

In this production there is nothing sophomorical and visionary. It rather shows the highest oratorical art. There is more about it than the calm, quiet flow of the essay style; it is that of an orator before an audience. It is a production that would move an audience and make them feel the weight of their truth. As another has it, "The boldness of the figure which would captivate an audience, is a little palling to the quiet and receptive state of the reader. The mental attitude of Garfield when he wrote that passage was not that of the writer in his study, but of the orator on the platform with a hushed assemblage before him. It will be noticed that this characteristic of style only became more marked with Garfield after he had left the mimic arena of the college. But the idea embodied in this article is as significant and characteristic as is its expression. In some form or other most of the world's great leaders have believed in some outside and controlling influence, which really shaped and directed events. To this they attributed their own fortune. Napoleon called and believed himself to be "The Child of Destiny." Buddha believed in fatalism. So did Calvin. Julius Cæsar ascribed his own career to an overwhelming and superimposed destiny. The same spirit which prompted Garfield to write these sentiments, was an all-controlling one during life. Superstitious beliefs in something kindred to fate, destiny and predestination belonged to Garfield. We shall see more of this before the life we are now tracing is closed.

We are now nearing the end of Garfield's college life as a student. The holiday vacation of his senior year he spent at Poestenkill, a country neighborhood, near Troy, New York. While teaching a writing school there he became acquainted with some of the members of the Christian church, and afterwards with some of the officers of the schools at Troy. The Rev. T. Brooks, a respected minister of the Disciples' church, for whom Garfield frequently preached, relates meeting Garfield at this time at Poestenkill: "I formed an intimate acquaintance with him," he writes, "and admired his genial, manly and pleasant ways. Shortly afterward, there being a vacancy in the High School in Troy, and having an influence by which I could secure it for a friend, I offered it to Garfield, at a salary of fifteen hundred dollars a year, well knowing his financial needs. After listening to my enumeration of the advantages of taking the position, he rose, and, with a flush of animation and decision, said, 'Brother Brooks, this is exceedingly tempting, and I thank you; but it has been the ambition and struggle of my life to win an honorable diploma from some Eastern college, for then I can hold it in the face of the world and win honor and distinction. I cannot accept the alluring offer.'" The salary offered was far above what he knew he could earn after graduation in Ohio. It was a turning point in his life. If he accepted he could soon pay his debts, marry, and live a life of comfort in an attractive Eastern city; but he could not finish his college course, and he would have to sever the ties with friends in Ohio, and with the struggling school at Hiram, to which he was so deeply attached. Had he taken the position his whole subsequent career would, no doubt, have been different.

While attending church in Chicago, just previous to his nomination to the Presidency, he recognized in the congregation the man who made him the offer in Troy. The two had not met since that time. "Do you remember what you said on that occasion?" asked his old friend. "No, I cannot recall the conversation." "We were walking on a hill called Mount Olympus, when I made you my proposition. After a few moments silence you said: 'You are not Satan, and I am not Jesus, but we are upon a mountain and you have tempted me powerfully. I think I must say, get thee behind me. I am poor, and the salary would soon pay my debts and place me in a position of independence; but there are two objections: I could not accomplish my resolution to complete a college course, and should be crippled intellectually for life. Then my roots are all fixed in Ohio, where people know me and I know them, and this transplanting might not succeed as well in the long run as to go back home and work for smaller pay.'"

Study at Williams was easy for Garfield. He had been used to much harder work at Hiram, where he had crowded a six years' course into three, and taught at the same time. Now he had the stimulus of a large class, an advantage he had never enjoyed before. His lessons were always perfectly learned. Professor Chadbourne says he was "the boy who never flunked," and he found a good deal of time for courses of reading that involved as much brainwork as the college text-books. He graduated August, 1856, with a class honor established by President Hopkins, and highly esteemed in the college—that of Metaphysics—reading an essay on "The Seen and the Unseen." It is singular how at different times in the course of his education he was thought to have a special aptitude for some single line of intellectual work, and how at a later period his talents seemed to lay just as strongly in some other line. At one time it was mathematics, at another the classics, at another rhetoric, and finally he excelled in metaphysics. The truth was that he had a remarkably vigorous and well-rounded brain, capable of doing effective work in any direction his will might dictate. The class of 1856 contained among its forty-two members a number of men who have since won distinction. Three became general officers in the volunteer army during the rebellion—Garfield, Daviess and Thompson. Two, Bolter and Shattuc, were captains, and were killed in battle; Eldridge, who now lives in Chicago, was a colonel; so was Ferris Jacobs, of Delhi, N. Y.; Rockwell is a quartermaster in the regular army; Gilfillan is Treasurer of the United States. Hill was Assistant Attorney-General, and is now a lawyer in Boston. Knox is a leading lawyer in New York. Newcombe is a professor in the New York University, of New York.

In the class ahead of Garfield was Hitchcock, lately Senator from Nebraska, and Ingalls, now a Senator from Kansas. To furnish two United States Senators from one class, and a Senator-elect and President from the next following class, is an honor which has probably never before fallen to any college.

Ingalls was the poet of the school in his days, and many of his associates believed him destined to take rank in the future close up to Tennyson. Many years after, when he was in the Senate, Garfield met him at a dinner party, and brought the blushes to the Kansas statesman's face by reciting from memory two or three of his college productions.

Garfield's mind had become interested in another subject since he had left his Western home, and that was politics. The East then was the very centre of political thought and action, and, naturally he became more or less interested. We have already seen that in the ancestry of Garfield there were strong traits and tendencies for liberty, and hence politics. The early life of our subject in the wilderness of Ohio had only kept back the growth of these faculties. But his life in the East changed all this. During his entire stay at Williams he was more or less interested in all political questions, but it was not until during his last term there that he made his first political speech. It was an address before a meeting gathered in one of the class-rooms to support the nomination of John C. Fremont. Although he had passed his majority nearly four years before, he had never voted. The old parties did not interest him; he believed them both corrupted with the sin of slavery; but when a new party arose to combat the designs of the slave power it enlisted his earnest sympathies. His mind was free from all bias concerning the parties and statesmen of the past, and he could equally admire Clay or Jackson, Webster or Benton.

The smouldering flames which for years before had been ready to blaze, in 1855 began to burn brightly. Slavery was the objective point. In the West anarchy reigned. Kansas was a hot-house of dissension. Murder, rapine, bloodshed and destruction were coursing their way through the land. The Slavery and Free-Soil adherents were in bloody contest. The country was full of dead bodies, mostly of Free-Soilers and Anti-Slavery men, lying here, there and everywhere. Their dead bodies exposed to the sun and the elements, with knives sticking in their hearts, presented a sickening scene indeed. Kansas became at once a subject of universal interest. Societies were formed for throwing into her borders, with the utmost expedition, settlers who could be relied upon to mold her government in the interests of freedom. At the same time there was set in train all the political machinery that could be used to agitate the question, until the cry of "Bleeding Kansas" was heard throughout the land.

In this state of universal excitement there can be but little wonder that any young man of Garfield's promise and abilities should become interested. The rupture between the North and South was drawing nearer and nearer, and already the dark, threatening cloud of rebellion was beginning to rise above the horizon. But in all this discord there was destined to be a great arm that should quell the storm and once more re-unite the country in one bond of brotherhood. Here Garfield enters politics, and the ship of state feels his power. We who know the sequel, the years of bloody and unrelentless war, the heart-breakings, the destruction, the sad separations, the brother pitched against brother, and, more than all, the long years of reconciliation, which was only accomplished finally in the shedding of Garfield's blood, know full well his influence and greatness.

In 1855 old parties were breaking up, and the lines reformed upon the slavery question. In the fall of this year, John Z. Goodrich, a member of Congress from the Western district of Massachusetts, delivered a political speech in Williamstown. In company, with a classmate, Garfield attended. The Kansas-Nebraska struggle was the matter under discussion. Says the classmate, Mr. Lavallette Wilson, of New York: "As Mr. Goodrich spoke I sat at Garfield's side, and saw him drink in every word. He said as we passed out, 'This subject is new to me. I am going to know all about it.'" And this was not an idle resolve, for he at once sent away for documents relating to the subject; and before many days had passed had carefully reviewed the subject, and was thoroughly posted. But there were other subjects of the day, such as the dangers from foreign immigration, the Roman Catholic power, the Crimean war, and the advantages of an elective judiciary, in the investigation of which he was particularly interested. More especially upon the subject of slavery did his mind dwell. His views were broad and liberal; and when the new-fledged Republican party started on its race to power on June 17, 1856, claiming as its pivotal point, opposition to slavery and protection for Kansas, he was ready for the party as the party was ready for him.

Before we are ready to follow Garfield into public life, we must stop to speak of the great influence exerted upon Garfield by one of the greatest metaphysicians of the age, ex-President Hopkins, of Williams College. He formed a strong attachment for Garfield, and concerning him once wrote: "One point in General Garfield's course of study, worthy of remark, was its evenness. There was nothing startling at any one time, and no special preference for any one study. There was a large general capacity applicable to any subject, and sound sense. As he was more mature than most, he naturally had a readier and firmer grasp of the higher studies. Hence his appointment to the metaphysical oration, then one of the high honors of the class. What he did was done with facility, but by honest and avowed work. There was no pretence of genius, or alternation of spasmodic effort and rest, but a satisfactory accomplishment in all directions of what was undertaken. Hence, there was a steady, healthful, onward and upward progress."

Fortunate, indeed, is that man who has influences surrounding him through life which spur him on to greatness. The tired traveler hastens on again with willing steps when the brow of some fatiguing hill is reached, and in the distance and all about him the beauties of the scene are stretched before him. The animus which the traveler most needs is grandeur beyond. Just so in the life of man an analogy obtains. Life, study, and toil would become dreary, indeed, were we not frequently permitted to look beyond into expectancy—were we not urged onward by those about us who are near and dear. "Man never is, but always to be blest." It has almost become to be an undeniable fact, that the man who accomplishes the most, and does the most good, is that one who has had these silent influences ever present about him. Study the matter and look further into the mystery and you will find the great men of history, and those to-day who occupy the positions of honor and trust, are those who have aimed to fulfill the hopes of a mother, a wife, or friend. Can there be any question of this? Look to the lives of Washington, Lincoln, Wesley, Adams, and above all, Garfield.

These facts have become so incontrovertible that the historian and biographer must consider their power, must look for this influence somewhere in all their dealings with great men. But the application of this truth in the life of Garfield is all the more potent. We see a boy, merging into a young man; the young man of the backwoods finally grappling with matters of education, predictions concerning his probable future greatness already made; the young man rounded and polished into beautiful manhood, until finally he has reached the highest citadel of government. And what say ye, was it nothing but the immature, crude and unambitious boy, with reachings out after the great future which he attained, that accomplished all this? Impossible. And it does not deteriorate one iota from Garfield's greatness in ascribing the animus of his life to their proper places. In giving his now aged mother the great part of the credit for directing her son to the fountain from which greatness flowed; in saying that Miss Almeda A. Booth left an indelible impression on his mental life, supplying it with new nourishment and stimulant; and that an overpowering personal influence was exercised upon him by Mark Hopkins, as well as others, only shows how susceptible to right influences Garfield was, and to what high purposes he put hem. In some shape or other these influences are exerted over every man; and because so few are able to understand their benefit and live up to their teaching, gives only the more credit to such men as Garfield.

Garfield went to Williams with strong, but uncultured thoughts. He had his mental eye-sight, but he saw men as trees, walking. But under the influence of Hopkins the scales fell from his eyes. In after years Garfield always said that whatever perceptions he had of general ideas, came from this great man. The venerable President rose before him like a sun, and enlightened his whole mental and moral nature. His preaching and teaching were a constant inspiration to the young Ohio student, and he became the centre of his college life—the object of his reverence and hero-worship.

One winter in Washington the National Teachers' Association was in session, and Garfield frequently dropped in to take a share in the discussion. One day he said: "You are making a grand mistake in education in this country. You put too much money in brick and mortar, and not enough into brains. You build palatial school-houses with domes and towers; supply them with everything beautiful and luxuriant, and then put putty men inside. The important thing is not what is taught, but the teacher. It is the teacher's personality which is the educator. I had rather dwell six months in a tent with Mark Hopkins, and live on bread and water, than to take a six-year's course in the grandest brick and mortar university on the continent."

CHAPTER VI.

THE MORNING OF POWER—PRESIDENT OF HIRAM.

I came up stairs unto the world for I was born in a cellar.—CONGREVE.

To climb steep hills requires slow pace at first.—SHAKESPEARE.

Every person has two educations,—one which he receives from others, and one, more important, which he gives himself.—GIBBON.

Graduation over, then came separation. Separation from all the fond associations which two happy years had formed. Responsibility, with all its attendant duties, now confronted him as never before. He had been living, studying and working, for a purpose. He had been dealing with students; and the stage upon which he had acted and the drama in which he had been an actor were but as a preface to the higher and more responsible one of life. Duty stood ready for his powers. You that have crossed the college threshold for the last time as a student know full well Garfield's feelings as his partings were said. The last shake of the hand with classmates, who had been dearer if possible than brothers, who had feasted at the same fountains of learning, drinking in draughts as sweet nectar, must be given. The paths of their several lives now began to diverge as widely as when they were brought together in college associations. All this over, Garfield returned to his Ohio home. And with what pride did that fond mother welcome her son's return! His separation had always been a source of sorrow to her. But how much more bearable while he was at college than when a boy he followed the canal path. That home was a happy one when James again returned. But how different is both the external and internal appearance from what it was when we first saw it! The forests had been cleared, and beautiful fields of grain surrounded the house on all sides. Along the roadsides many new and neat houses were erected. The frontier aspect had disappeared. The house and barn, though not pretentious, were neat and altogether respectable. The fences were in good repair and everything gave evidence of thrift and prosperity. Thus had Thomas worked and labored during the absence of James.

Our hero was now nearing twenty-five years of age. He had the advantage of beginning life with a much more mature mind than the majority of young men. He was mature in manhood and fully able to rely upon his judgment in all emergencies. Then, his mental developement had always been far beyond his years, which now was all the more in his favor. As the result of his constant, self-denying toil of nearly twenty years, he had a collegiate education, a few threadbare clothes, a score or more of college text-books, his diploma, and a debt of four hundred and fifty dollars. But, being in excellent health, and strong and active, mentally and physically, he was splendidly accoutred for the work of life, and not long in finding a field for his activities. But now on his return to his home, the young man who had gone so far East as to old Williams, and had come back decorated with her honors, was thought good enough for anything. He was at once elected teacher of Latin and Greek in the Hiram Eclectic Institute, in which two years before he had been a pupil, and so he began to work for money to pay his debts. The academy was poor and in debt, but Garfield threw all his energies into the work of building it up on a solid foundation.

At the end of the school-year, Principal Hayden, after seven years of service, resigned. Subsequently the minutes of the Board have the following action recorded:

"It was resolved that the present teachers of the institution be constituted a Board of Education, to conduct the educational concerns of the school, subject to the counsel and advice of the Board." So high a position did Garfield at once take, and so popular had he become, that he was thereupon chosen as chairman and made principal, when four hundred students were in attendance. The position of principal and teacher of Ancient Languages he held until he went into the army in 1861. Hoping that he might return—unwilling to part even with his name—the board kept him nominally at the head two years longer. Then he fell out of the catalogue, to reappear as a trustee and as advisory principal and lecturer in 1864 and 1865. Then his name finally disappears from the faculty page of the catalogue. His last service as an instructor was an admirable series of ten lectures on "Social Science," given in the spring of 1871.

Consider, doubting young man, what things may be in store for you. Garfield probably had at times no brighter prospects ahead than you have, and yet see how soon the reward for his toil and labor came. The secret of much of Garfield's success, I think, will be found in his uncompromising devotion to duty and study. This is what makes men. In nine cases out of ten will a young man show in college what wealth of powers he has, and what he can make of himself. Success in life depends in great part upon success in college or youth. As the boy is, so can we rightly expect the man to be. True there are many exceptions to this statement—boys who gave little promise of greatness have surprised all by a face about and met with great success, and on the other hand those with splendid opportunities and something of promise have fallen in the back ground—but still these are only exceptions and the general fact remains undisturbed. Activity, thought and enterprise are the levers which to-day are moving the world—these compose the philosopher's touch-stone. Carlyle says the race of life is becoming wonderfully interesting and intense. Even at the very heels of those in the front ranks others are pressing onward; and the first falling back only brings another to the front. Garfield realized this, and with his splendid powers he began the race to pre-eminence as soon as graduation was over. So, young man, it must be with you if you wish to become an ornament to society and your country.

Hiram, when he returned to it, had not much improved since two years before. It was a lonesome country village, three miles from a railroad, built upon a high hill, overlooking twenty miles of cheese-making country to the southward. It contained fifty or sixty houses clustered around the green, in the centre of which stood the homely red-brick college structure. Plain living and high thinking was the order of things in those days; and there was a great deal of hard, faithful study done, and many courageous plans formed. The young principal was ambitious for the success of the institution under his charge. There probably never was a younger college president, but he carried his new position remarkably well, and brought to it energy, vigor and good sense, which are the mainsprings of his character. While it was true that all the teachers of the Institute were compelled to teach often outside their regular branches; still, each teacher generally worked within certain lines, though the lines were not very straight or rigid. Accordingly it must not be thought that Principal Garfield taught all Latin and Greek, or that he taught nothing else. Classes in all the higher branches of study received the benefit of his instruction. The standard had been greatly raised since the day that young Garfield looked with such wonder upon a class in geometry. In English analysis he was a specialist. The study was a special favorite with him, and nowhere else did he shine more as a teacher. Through this class most of the better scholars at some time passed, even if they considered themselves thorough in it before. Then his geology class, that recited at five o'clock in the morning, cannot be forgotten by a single surviving member. He strove to awaken the student's faculties. He sought to energize or vitalize him. He revealed the world to the student, and the student to himself. He stimulated thought, created the habit of observation and reflection, aroused courage, widened the field of mental vision, and furnished inspiration in unlimited measure.

Everything connected with the college soon felt his influence. It soon entered upon a career of prosperity, and won a high rank among western educational institutions. He was full of animal spirits, and used to run out on the green almost every day and play cricket with his scholars. He was a tall, strong man, but dreadfully awkward. Every now and then he would get a hit, and he muffed his ball and lost his hat as a regular thing. He was left-handed, too, and that made him seem all the clumsier. In the class-room Garfield was a strict disciplinarian. If he wanted to speak to a pupil, either for reproof or approbation, he would generally manage to get one arm around him and draw him close up to him. This sympathetic manner has helped him to advancement. One who was janitor at that time of Hiram says he used sometimes to stop him and ask his opinion about this and that, as if seriously advising with him. Once when asked what was the best way to pursue a certain study, Garfield said, "Use several text-books. Get the views of different authors as you advance. In that way you can plow a broader furrow. I always study in that way." He tried hard to teach his scholars to observe carefully and accurately. He broke out one day in the midst of a lesson with, "Henry, how many posts are there under the building down-stairs?" Henry expressed his opinion, and the question went around the class, hardly any one getting it right. Then it was, "How many boot-scrapers are there at the door?" "How many windows in the building?" "How many trees in the field?' What were the colors of different rooms, and the peculiarities of any familiar objects? He was the keenest of observers. A friend was walking with him through Cleveland one day, when Garfield stopped and darted down a cellar-way, asking his companion to follow only briefly pausing to explain himself. The sign "Saws and Files" was over the door, and in the depths was heard a regular clicking sound. "I think this fellow is cutting files," said he, "and I have never seen a file cut." Down they went and, sure enough, there was a man recutting an old file, and they stayed ten minutes, and found out all about the process. Garfield would never go by anything without understanding it. Mr. Garfield was very fond of lecturing to the school. He spoke two or three times a week, on all manner of topics, generally scientific, though sometimes literary or historical. He spoke with great freedom, never writing out what he had to say, and his lectures were generally a rapid compilation of his current reading. He probably threw it into this form partly for the purpose of impressing it on his own mind. His facility of speech was learned when he was a pupil at Hiram. The societies had a rule that every student should take his stand on the platform and speak for five minutes on any topic suggested at the moment by the audience. It was a very trying ordeal. Garfield broke down badly the first two times he tried to speak, but persisted, and was at last, when he went to Williams, one of the best of the five-minute speakers. When he returned as principal his readiness was striking and remarkable.

President Hinsdale, Garfield's successor in the college at Hiram, and one of his former pupils, has the following to say: "My real acquaintance with Garfield," he writes, "did not begin until the fall of 1856, when he returned from Williams College. He then found me out, drew near to me, and entered into all my troubles and difficulties pertaining to questions of the future. In a greater or less degree this was true of his relations to his pupils generally. There are hundreds of these men and women scattered over the world to-day who cannot find language strong enough to express their feeling in contemplating Garfield as their old instructor, adviser, and friend. Since 1856 my relations with him have been as close and confidential as they could be with any man, and much closer and more confidential than they have been with any other man. I know that he possessed all the great elements of character in an extraordinary degree. His interest in humanity was always as broad as humanity itself, while his lively interest in young men and women, especially if they were struggling in narrow circumstances to obtain an education, was a characteristic known as widely over the world as the footsteps of Hiram boys and girls have wandered. The help that he furnished hundreds in the way of suggestions, teaching, encouragement, inspiration and stimulus, was most valuable. I have repeatedly said that, as respects myself, I am more indebted to him for all that I am, and for what I have done in the intellectual field, than to any other man that ever lived. His power over students was not so much that of a drill-master or disciplinarian as that of one who was able to inspire and energize young people by his own intellectual and moral force."

In the course of a lecture delivered at the college on the day following Garfield's nomination, this same gentleman read a letter from his former preceptor, dated as far back as 1857, which should be read and pondered by every young man in the country. He said that in the fall of 1856 he had left the Eclectic Institute, now Hiram College, in great distress of mind, growing out of his own life-questions. He had passed his nineteenth birthday, and the question of the future weighed heavily upon his mind. That winter he taught a district school. He had already won a friend in Mr. Garfield, then twenty-five years old, and just out of Williams College. Garfield was then teaching at Hiram as Professor of Ancient Languages. In his distress of mind Hinsdale wrote Garfield a letter, in which he fully opened his mind. In reply, he received a letter that gave him great help. This letter, which had been religiously preserved, might give help to some of the young men before him, the president thought. Besides, there was peculiar propriety in his producing it, on account of what had taken place the day before in Chicago. He then proceeded to read from the original, yellow with age, and worn from repeated foldings and unfoldings, the following beautiful letter:

HIRAM, January 15, 1857.

MY DEAR BROTHER BURKE:—I was made very glad a few days since by the receipt of your letter. It was a very acceptable New Year's present, and I take great pleasure in responding. You have given a vivid picture of a community in which intelligence and morality have been neglected, and I am glad you are disseminating the light. Certainly, men must have some knowledge in order to do right. God first said, "Let there be light." Afterward he said, "It is very good." I am glad to hear of your success in teaching; but I approach with much more interest the consideration of the question you have proposed. Brother mine, it is not a question to be discussed in the spirit of debate, but to be thought over and prayed over as a question out of which are the issues of life. You will agree with me that every one must decide and direct his own course in life—and the only service friends can afford is to give us the data from which we must draw our own conclusion and decide our course. Allow me, then, to sit beside you and look over the field of life and see what are its aspects. I am not one of those who advise every one to undertake the work of a liberal education. Indeed, I believe that in two thirds of the cases such advice would be unwise. The great body of the people will be and ought to be intelligent farmers and mechanics, and in many respects these pass the most independent and happy lives. But God has endowed some of his children with desires and capabilities for a more extended field of labor and influence, and so every life should be shaped according to what the man hath. Now, in reference to yourself, I know you have capabilities for occupying positions of high and important trust in the scenes of active life, and I am sure you will not call it flattery in me nor egotism in yourself to say so. Tell me, Burke, do you not feel a spirit stirring within you that longs to know, to do, and to dare—to hold converse with the great world of thought, and hold before you some high and noble object to which the vigor of your mind and the strength of your arm may be given? Do you not have longings such as these, which you breathe to no one, and which you feel must be heeded, or you will pass through life unsatisfied and regretful? I am sure you have these, and they will forever cling around your heart until you obey their mandate. They are the voices of that nature which God has given you, and which, when obeyed, will bless you and your fellow-men. Now, all this might be true, and yet it might be your duty not to follow that course. If your duty to your father or your mother demands that you take another, I shall rejoice to see you taking that other course. The path of duty is where we all ought to walk, be that where it may; but I sincerely hope that you will not, without an earnest struggle, give up a course of liberal study. Suppose you could not begin your study again until after your majority. It will not be too late then, but you will gain in many respects. You will have more maturity of mind to appreciate whatever you may study. You may say you will be too old to begin the course, but how could you better spend the earlier days of life? We should not measure life by the days and moments that we pass on earth.

> "The life is measured by the soul's advance,
> The enlargement of its powers, the expanded field
> Wherein it ranges, till it burns and glows with heavenly joy,
> With high and heavenly hope."

It need be no discouragement that you be obliged to hew your own way and pay your own charges. You can go to school two terms of every year and pay your own way. I know this, for I did so when teachers' wages were much lower than they are now. It is a great truth, that "Where there is a will there is a way." It may be that by and by your father could assist you. It may be that even now he could let you commence on your resources, so that you could begin immediately. Of this you know, and I do not. I need not tell you how glad I should be to assist you in your work. But if you cannot come to Hiram while I am here, I shall still hope to hear that you are determined to go on as soon as the time will permit. Will you not write me your thoughts on this whole subject, and tell me your prospects? We are having a very good time in the school this winter. Give my love to Rolden and Louisa, and believe me always your friend and brother. J. A. GARFIELD.

P. S.—Miss Booth and Mr. Rhodes send their love to you. Henry James was here, and made me a good visit a few days ago. He is doing well. He and I have talked of going to see you this winter. I fear we cannot do it. How far is it from here? Burke, was it prophetic that my last word to you ended on the picture of the Capitol of Congress? J. A. G.

The last question in the postscript refers to the little picture of the Capitol which, in those days, was so common in the upper left-hand corner of the Congress note-paper. The letter was written on one of these sheets, and filled it completely, and was written crosswise at the end, the last word coming exactly across the picture of the Capitol. The General was quick to perceive this, and referred to it in that neat question.

Before he went to college, Garfield had begun to preach a little in the country churches around Hiram, and when he returned he began to fill the pulpit in the Disciples' church in Hiram with considerable regularity. In his denomination no ordination is required to become a minister. Any brother having the ability to discourse on religious topics to a congregation is welcomed to the pulpit. His fame as a lay preacher extended throughout the counties of Portage, Summit, Trumbull and Geauga, and he was often invited to preach in the towns of that region.

He engaged in public debates on theologic and scientific questions; and took the stump for the Republican party. He began the study of the law, having entered his name as a student-at-law with a Cleveland firm, and after only two years' preparation, with all his other work on hand, in 1860 he was admitted to practice at the Cleveland bar. He carried on his legal studies at home, and with such thoroughness and zeal, that he fitted for the Ohio bar in the time usually required by students who have nothing else to do. Yet with all this load on him, he impressed himself on each pupil in Hiram College as a personal friend. Often these boys had troubles peculiarly their own. Some were poor; some were tethered to home; some wanted courage and self-reliance; some tended to despondency. Mr. Garfield found them out. He remembered his own experience. He seemed to read by intuition a mind that teemed with new facts, ideas and impressions, that was stirred by a new spirit and power, that sighed for wider and higher activity. These students he aided with his counsel and encouragement.

But a better idea of Garfield as an educator, and of his work at Hiram, can be obtained from the following remarks he made to a friend, than from anything that any other person has written on the subject. It was in 1877, after he had made one of his masterly speeches, in that hard-fought campaign, and as he lay upon his back under one of the famous old elms of Guernsey County, Ohio, that he thus unbosomed himself to one of his former college companions. He said: "I have taken more solid comfort in the thing itself, and received more moral recompense and stimulus in after-life, from capturing young men for an education than from anything else in the world. As I look back over my life thus far," he continued, "I think of nothing that so fills me with pleasure as the planning of these sieges, the revolving in my mind of plans for scaling the walls of the fortress; of gaining access to the inner soul-life, and at last seeing the besieged party won to a fuller appreciation of himself, to a higher conception of life, and of the part he is to bear in it. The principal guards which I have found it necessary to overcome in gaining these victories, are the parents or guardians of the young men themselves. I particularly remember two such instances of capturing young men from their parents. Both of those boys are, to-day, educators of wide reputation—one president of a college, the other high in the ranks of graded school managers. Neither, in my opinion, would to-day have been above the commonest walks of life, unless I or some one else had captured him. There is a period in every young man's life when a very small thing will turn him one way or the other. He is distrustful of himself, and uncertain as to what he should do. His parents are poor, perhaps, and argue that he has more education than they ever obtained, and that it is enough. These parents are sometimes a little too anxious in regard to what their boys are going to do when they get through with their college course. They talk to the young man too much, and I have noticed that the boy who will make the best man is sometimes most ready to doubt himself. I always remember the turning period in my own life, and pity a young man at this stage from the bottom of my heart. One of the young men I refer to, came to me on the closing day of the spring term, and bade me good-by at my study. I noticed that he awkwardly lingered after I expected him to go, and had turned to my writing again. 'I suppose you will be back again in the fall, Henry,' I said, to fill in the vacuum. He did not answer, and, turning toward him, I noticed that his eyes were filled with tears, and that his countenance was undergoing contortions of pain. He at length managed to stammer out, 'No, I am not coming back to Hiram any more. Father says I have got education enough, and that he needs me to work on the farm; that education don't help along a farmer any.' 'Is your father here?' I asked, almost as much affected by the statement as the boy himself. He was a peculiarly bright boy—one of those strong, awkward, bashful, blonde, large-headed fellows, such as make men. He was not a prodigy by any means. But he knew what work meant, and when he had won a thing by the true endeavor, he knew its value. 'Yes, father is here, and is taking my things home for good,' said the boy, more affected than ever. 'Well, don't feel badly,' I said. 'Please tell him Mr. Garfield would like to see him at his study before he leaves the village. Don't tell him that it is about you, but simply that I want to see him.' In the course of half an hour the old gentleman, a robust specimen of a Western Reserve Yankee, came into the room, and awkwardly sat down. I knew something of the man before, and I thought I knew how to begin. I shot right at the bulls-eye immediately. 'So you have come up to take Henry home with you, have you?' The old gentleman answered 'Yes.' 'I sent for you because I wanted to have a little talk with you about Henry's future. He is coming back again in the fall, I hope?' 'Wal, I think not. I don't reckon I can afford to send him any more. He's got eddication enough for a farmer already, and I notice that when they git too much they sorter git lazy. Yer eddicated farmers are humbugs. Henry's got so far 'long now that he'd rother hev his head in a book than be workin'. He don't take no interest in the stock nor in the farm improvements. Everybody else is dependent in this world on the farmer, and I think that we've got too many eddicated fellows setting around now for the farmers to support.' 'I am sorry to hear you talk so,' I said; 'for really I consider Henry one of the brightest and most faithful students I have ever had. I have taken a very deep interest in him. What I wanted to say to you was, that the matter of educating him has largely been a constant outgo thus far, but if he is permitted to come next fall term, he will be far enough advanced so that he can teach school in the winter, and begin to help himself and you along. He can earn very little on the farm in the winter, and he can get very good wages teaching. How does that strike you?' The idea was a new and good one to him. He simply remarked, 'Do you really think he can teach next winter?' 'I should think so, certainly,' I replied. 'But if he cannot do so then, he can in a short time, anyhow.' 'Wal, I will think on it. He wants to come back bad enough, and I guess I'll have to let him. I never thought of it that way afore.' I knew I was safe. It was the financial question that troubled the old gentleman, and I knew that would be overcome when Henry got to teaching, and could earn his money himself. He would then be so far along, too, that he could fight his own battles. He came all right the next fall, and, after finishing at Hiram, graduated at an Eastern college."

His friend asked General Garfield how he managed the campaign for capturing the other young man. "Well, that was a different case. I knew that this youth was going to leave mainly for financial reasons also, but I understood his father well enough to know that the matter must be managed with exceeding delicacy. He was a man of very strong religious convictions, and I thought he might be approached from that side of his character; so when I got the letter of the son telling me, in the saddest language that he could master, that he could not come back to school any more, but must be content to be simply a farmer, much as it was against his inclination, I revolved the matter in my mind, and decided to send an appointment to preach in the little country church where the old gentleman attended. I took for a subject the parable of the talents, and in the course of my discourse dwelt specially upon the fact that children were the talents which had been intrusted to parents, and if these talents were not increased and developed there was a fearful trust neglected. After church I called upon the parents of the boy I was besieging, and I saw that something was weighing upon their minds. At length the subject of the discourse was taken up and gone over again, and in due course the young man himself was discussed, and I gave my opinion that he should, by all means, be encouraged and assisted in taking a thorough course of study. I gave my opinion that there was nothing more important to the parent than to do all in his power for the child. The next term the young man again appeared upon Hiram Hill, and remained pretty continuously till graduation."

Knowing now something of Garfield as a teacher, we would be surprised did we find him anything else than a good disciplinarian. He had nothing of the regulation school-master about him, and he put red tape to small use. He never spent his force on little things. He understood what was and what was *not* essential to discipline and good order, and he secured the first all the more readily because he was indifferent to the second. He always had a code of printed rules that he expounded each term; he exacted weekly reports of conduct, but his own personality was worth far more than both rules and reports. His management of disciplinary cases was skillful. On one occasion, after morning prayers, he read impressively selections from the seventh chapter of Proverbs. He added, " * * * (naming three boys) are expelled from this school." Not another word was said, but the whole made a profound impression.

As president of an institute, it was natural that Garfield should appear upon the platform on every public occasion. The Church of the Disciples, as before stated, like the Society of Friends, is accustomed to accord large privileges of speaking to its laity; and so it came to be expected that President Garfield should address his pupils on Sundays—briefly even when ministers of the gospel were to preach—more at length when no one else was present to conduct the services. The remarks of the young president were always forcible, generally eloquent, and the community presently began to regard him as its foremost public speaker, to be put forward on every occasion, to be heard with attention on every subject. His pupils also helped to swell his reputation and the admiration for his talents. His large brain was stored with information always at his command; he was fluent without being verbose; and he had in an unusual degree the happy quality of clearness. This, added to his commanding appearance and effective delivery, made him sought for on all public occasions. Meantime he had begun to attract attention through wider circles than a mere academy teacher would have been expected to reach. He had the temperament of an orator—the warm feelings, the fervid imagination, the intensity of purpose. He was gifted with a copious flow of language, to which his thorough study of the ancient classics had given strength and purity. He was still a student, but he was already a comprehensive scholar, versed in an unusually wide range of subjects. His sincerity, his unblemished character, and his eloquence were well known, not only all about the region where he lived, but throughout the State, and the fact that Mr. Garfield was to appear in the pulpit anywhere always drew a great crowd. In 1859 or 1860 this was a common day's work for him: A chapel lecture in the morning; five solid hours of teaching, perhaps six; attention to administrative details; a speech ten miles away in the evening; home to bed at midnight. If the next day was Sunday, he would give two sermons, perhaps fifteen miles off; of course no man who covers such a field as this can be called a specialist. Still, he always kept abreast of his school work. The range of his ability, and the great strength that he put into whatever he undertook, attracted public attention, gave prominence to the school, and increased the pride that his pupils felt in him.

He remained, as we have said, at Hiram, until the war called him away, and steadily refused all efforts made to induce him to desert the institution for whose welfare he had done so much. In March, 1861, he was offered the place of vice-principal of the Cleveland Institute, at a salary of fifteen hundred dollars a year. To the offer he returned this reply:

I am very much obliged to you for your kind offer, but you would not want to employ me for a short time, and I feel it my duty to say that some of my friends have got the insane notion in their heads that I ought to go to Congress. I know I am not fit for the position, and I have fought against it all I could. I know nothing about political wire-pulling, and I have told my friends plainly that I would have nothing to do with that kind of business, but I am sure that I can be nominated and elected without my resorting to any unlawful means, and I have lately given authority to allow my name to be used. I don't know that anything will come of it; if there does not, I will gladly accept your offer.

Garfield read everywhere and almost everything. He read "hard reading," but poetry and fiction as well. He naturalized Tennyson, of whom he became a profound student. He read on the cars, in the omnibus, and after retiring at night. He rarely, or never, went away from home, even for a few hours, but he took his book. He made special efforts to procure out-of-the-way reading. If he was leaving Washington only for a few days, in after life, and had nothing requiring immediate attention on hand, he would go to the great library of Congress, and say to the librarian, "Mr. Spofford, give me something that I don't know anything about." A stray book coming to him in this way would often lead to a special study of the subject. In this way he kept his mind full and fresh. In his studies he strove to get hold of the underlying principle, and was never satisfied until he could reduce facts to order. Once he said, "I could not stay in politics unless I found some philosophy." Hence, the breadth of his views on all subjects. Here is also the explanation of Judge Cooley's remark in his Ann Arbor oration. "He always discussed large subjects in a large way."

We have already seen that years before he had wooed and won a maiden, whose image ever occupied his heart, and whose virtues and charms had been a spur to activity and success on his part. Two years of teaching left him even with the world. It was, therefore, in November, 1858, that the sweet romance of their youth reached its fruition in the marriage of Garfield and Lucretia Rudolph, whose mental gifts, both native and acquired, well fitted her for his wife and companion. Ever since the painful separation had taken place between Garfield and his future bride, when he left for Williams College, they had remained true to the vows and pledges of love. When Garfield went to Williams, Miss Rudolph started for Cleveland to teach in the public schools, and patiently to wait the realization of their hopes, which was agreed to be as soon as he should graduate and become established in life. This he considered accomplished when he succeeded to the head of the Hiram Institute, and accordingly, in 1858, they were married. The match was a love-match and has turned out very happily. Garfield attributes much of his success in life to his wise selection. His wife has grown with his growth, and has been, during all his career, the appreciative companion of his studies, the loving mother of his children, the graceful, hospitable hostess of his friends and guests, and the wise and faithful friend in the trials, vicissitudes and successes of his busy life.

After the war, Grandma Garfield, now known so pleasantly to the world as "the little white-haired mother," was generally a member of the family, and it was a happy trio. At first Garfield and his wife did not set up housekeeping but boarded. Their Hiram life was perfectly simple and natural, as became their estate, their nature and their surroundings. Save the constantly used and ever growing library, nothing in or about Garfield's home stood in contrast to the homes of his neighbors. His house was a place for "plain living and high thinking." If the old wall could speak, what thoughts would they not voice, what emotions utter, what joyousness describe! He never kept a carriage, and save for two short intervals—one just before and one just after the war—never a horse and buggy.

Garfield remained in the school five years. During this time he preached regularly, rarely missing a Lord's-day. He averaged more than two sermons per week during all these years. He preached regularly part of the time, sometimes one half, sometimes one fourth, for churches in Solon, Chagrin Falls, Hiram, and other places. He was paid for such services, and was regarded by the Disciples of the Western Reserve as one of their regular preachers, as much as any other man in Ohio. He held protracted meetings, baptized persons, performed the marriage ceremony, had charge of congregations, and preached as regularly as any man in the ranks.

Rev. R. H. Leonard, of Cincinnati, is authority for the following little incident, certainly characteristic of Garfield: He says: "My first acquaintance with Professor Garfield was in the winter of 1858-9, and was in this wise. I had delivered a discourse in the chapel of the Institute at Hiram, on the relation and bearing of seamen on our commercial, social, and religious institutions, with a view of establishing a Sailors' Home and Library in the city of Cleveland. The next day I met him in the road, with his pocket-book in hand. 'Yes, sir,' said he, 'the seamen have claims upon the American people which can never be cancelled until the home shelters Jack Tar in every port.' And then he led me to the shelter of his own pleasant home, where the bride of the cottage presided with the early grace which ripened to adorn the White House at last."

Ordinarily such ceaseless activities as we have seen occupied Garfield's attention during this period, would seem to be more than scope for one man's powers; but not so with Garfield. His reserve force was yet immeasurable; and the exciting political times, again brought into play at Hiram the same desires for political questions which he had at Williams. It is now my purpose to look at these times and the questions which made them so stirring, more in detail. His labors upon the stump, beginning in 1856, with perhaps a score of speeches for Fremont and Dayton in country school-houses and town-halls in the region around Hiram, were extended in 1857 and 1858 over a wider area of territory, and in 1859 he began to speak at county mass meetings. The opinions which he had formed at Williams now began to bear fruit. The seed had been planted in fruitful soil, and his public position gave him considerable prominence, so that from the first he exerted no small influence. His study of the law and investigation of the causes which were instrumental in producing that era of political discord, only the more enlivened his interest and activity on the stump. Those were memorable years. They were times when public sentiment was forming all over the land on the issues of slavery and States rights. The times of arousing public sentiment on any new and live issue, especially where rights have been invaded, and liberty in any form is sought, are always exciting ones. Old parties were breaking up and dissolving, because of the two forms of opinion held by members on the issues just mentioned. In the South there were harsh mutterings of discord, and through the sky of union flitted clouds of darkness, foreboding and threatening. These were the years just preceding the recent rebellion—the "years when the grasping power of slavery was seizing the virgin territories of the West, and dragging them into the den of eternal bondage;" the years of the underground railroad and of the fugitive slave law. The barracoon and auction-block were objects familiar to the public gaze, and domiciled as among the recognized, if not cherished, fixtures of Southern society; these were the years of John Brown's heroic attempt to incite an insurrection of the slaves themselves. The Anti-Slavery and Free Soil journals entered earnestly upon the work of indoctrinating and impressing the popular mind and heart. In arousing the people, they had endeavored to convince them that so long as a national party had a wing in the South, it could never be trusted on any point in which the interests of slavery were involved. The objects sought to be obtained foretokened a fearful contest, fierce encounters and bloody strifes. No summer clouds ever met in mid-heaven more heavily surcharged with elements of storm and danger. Disunion, threatenings and defiance were heard on all sides. The instincts of resistance to oppression, and of sympathy for the oppressed, which Garfield inherited from his dauntless ancestry, began to stir within him.

Each month only witnessed more excitement. The Missouri Compromise, the

Kansas-Nebraska trouble, the Dred-Scott trial, the famous "war of words" between Abraham Lincoln and Stephen A. Douglass, and the increase of the slave power, only made the times more and more stormy. Garfield's spirit rose with the emergency, and into his political speeches he threw his entire strength. In this emergency the people of all sections were naturally casting about for leaders. Garfield was looked upon as the rising man in his section of the State, and readily the people looked to him for leadership.

Garfield being a man known for his ability, sterling integrity and his fervid eloquence, there is reason why he should be looked to as a leader in the stirring times that now were approaching. Up to 1856 he had taken but little interest in public affairs. He had been engrossed in his work as an educator; but with the Kansas-Nebraska legislation his political pulses began to stir. He saw that freedom was about to engage in a hand-to-hand struggle with slavery, and, attempered as he was, he was irresistibly drawn into the conflict. It was the birthday of the Republican party. He enrolled himself at once among its speakers, and soon became one of its most effective advocates. In a speech at a later time he thus alludes to this stirring period: "Long familiarity with traffic in the bodies and souls of men had paralyzed the consciences of a majority of our people. The baleful doctrine of State sovereignty had shaken and weakened the noblest and most beneficent powers of the National Government; and the grasping power of slavery was seizing the virgin territories of the West, and dragging them into the den of eternal bondage. At that crisis the Republican party was born. It drew its first inspiration from that fire of liberty which God has lighted in every human heart, and which all the powers of ignorance and tyranny can never wholly extinguish. The Republican party came to deliver and save the Republic. It entered the arena where the beleaguered and assailed territories were struggling for freedom, and drew around it the sacred circle of liberty, which the demon of slavery has never dared to cross. It made them free forever." It was quite natural that the strong anti-slavery people of Portage and Summit counties should select him as a representative, so in 1859 he was nominated for the State Senate. During that campaign he appeared in Akron on the same platform with Mr. Chase, then candidate for Governor; and one good judge said the senatorial candidate made the better speech. He was elected by a large majority, and though yet scarcely twenty-eight, at once took high rank as a man unusually well-informed on the subjects of legislation.

Some who were acquainted with the facts related in the early part of this chapter concerning his preaching and ecclesiastical labors, have been inclined to equivocate and conceal them, for fear he might have been charged with abandoning the ministry for politics. That the pulpit took a strong hold of his mind, cannot be questioned. Once he was called to the pulpit of what is now the Central Church of Cincinnati. No doubt he would have achieved high distinction as a preacher but he did not feel that he had been called for the work. His genius drew him to the State by its very bent, as any one who has followed his history can see. Concerning this matter, one who knew Garfield well during this period, Clark Braden, says: "On the other hand, it is equally true that he never intended to make preaching his life work. Neither did he intend to follow teaching. Still he was for years a regular professional teacher, as much so as any one in Ohio. He was as fully a regular preacher. The earnest desire of the people and churches, his desire to do good, to earn a livelihood in these noble callings, and to cultivate his powers in them, led him to preach for years, as he taught for years. During this time I know by his statements to me that he was reading law and intending to enter that profession as his life work, with thoughts of political life." In the winter of 1858–9 he engaged in a public discussion in Chagrin Falls, with William Denton, a noted lecturer on geology and defender of the atheistic theories of materialistic evolution and development. Prof. Denton gave a series of lectures at Chagrin Falls, and attempted to prove by scientific discoveries that the Bible could not be true. In the course of his discussion he had been able to convince quite a number of people, and it began to be boldly asserted on the streets and in the factories that the Bible was only an ingenious fable. The professor was a critical scholar, and had a very plausible way of stating his theories, and there was no one found to withstand his arguments. Ministers attacked him, but only with invectives, which did more harm than good. Teachers and public speakers often ridiculed him, but such things only avail against a shallow reasoner, or one manifestly unpopular. Prof. Denton was gaining the thinking men and women, and felt sure, as his adherents boasted, "of shutting up the churches and abolishing the Bible from Chagrin Falls." It was one of those strange, almost unaccountable freaks of public opinion, and men were drawn into it, who, all their lives, had been the most orthodox believers in the Holy Bible. The churches of the Disciples viewed the success of Prof. Denton with the deepest dismay. The church at Chagrin Falls seemed in danger of annihilation, and the whole denomination viewed its tottering condition with great alarm. It happened that the noted professor had one weak point illustrating the truth of that book he was endeavoring to overturn, wherein it says that "great men are not always wise." He had a habit of boasting, and one evening he went so far as to challenge any and every believer of the Bible in Ohio to refute his statements. He offered the use of the hall and ample time to any person who dared to undertake the task. At once, the listeners who adhered to the Bible thought of Mr. Garfield. They had heard him preach at Chagrin Falls and in the surrounding country towns, and they felt that if any man could cope with the learned professor it would be he. They felt that some one must champion their cause or all would be lost. In a distress of mind not easily realized by people living in other portions of the religious world, these sincere and sorrowful Christians turned to Mr. Garfield for help. At first he declined to meet the professor, thinking it unbecoming a Christian man to debate such questions in a public hall. But the continued petition of his friends, and the alarm of the churches, caused him at last to consent, and a committee of citizens was appointed to arrange for the public discussion. It was a great day at Chagrin Falls, and one which will not soon be forgotten, when these two champions met in the arena of serious, earnest religious debate. Mr. Garfield had never heard Prof. Denton, and was consequently supposed to be ignorant of just the position the professor would take. But Mr. Garfield had been too wise to risk a cause which he believed so holy to the impulses and guesses of an impromptu speech; and, as soon as he knew that he was to meet the professor, he had taken steps to find out the arguments which the infidel used. Having ascertained privately that the professor was to lecture on the same topic in a distant part of the State before the date of the discussion, Mr. Garfield had sent a friend to hear these lectures, and write them out for his use. Of course the professor knew nothing of this, and had no doubt of his ability to silence a man who had not made science a special study. When, however, Mr. Garfield had received the copies of the lectures, he had at once sent in various directions and procured the latest scientific books, together with those the professor had quoted as being against the Bible. He had also obtained learned opinions of distinguished scholars, and before the day of the discussion, was thoroughly armed with arguments and authorities. When the hour came for the discussion, the hall was crowded to suffocation by an eager, and, on the part of the Disciples, an almost breathless audience. But they did not lose faith in Mr. Garfield. They thought that if any one could overcome the learned professor, then they had secured the right man. The professor, amid the smiles of his followers, and with a perfect confidence in his ability, opened the debate with his statement of scientific facts and their bearing on the accounts of creation and the miracles in the Bible. The professor did not try to be precise and accurate in all his statements, for he was sure Mr. Garfield would not attack him on scientific ground, and, when he stated any difficult question, he explained it very kindly in "simple language" for Mr. Garfield's better understanding. He repeated, however, almost verbatim, the lecture of which Mr. Garfield had a copy. Mr. Garfield said nothing until his turn came, and when he arose, it was apparent to all that the professor had predisposed the audience in favor of infidelity. When, however, Mr. Garfield coolly, and with a readiness and knowledge which really astounded his hearers, took up the professor's arguments, one by one, and quoting voluminously from books and history, using the professor's own authorities against him, and piled up unanswerable names above them, there was such a sudden overturning as an earthquake might make. It seemed miraculous to the people, who, very reasonably, supposed that Mr. Garfield had not heard the professor's arguments before. The professor had the closing speech to make, but he saw that he had lost the battle, and that his forces were too thoroughly routed to be rallied again. So, while he claimed that with further research he could yet establish his theories, he manfully admitted that he was surprised and defeated for the time by the apparently inexhaustible learning of his opponent. He said it was the first time he had met so gifted and learned an adversary. Of course, the tide of unbelief in the Scriptures was stayed.

There are facts connected with his first nomination to office that explain his entrance into political life. Portage county, Ohio, was then a close county. In the "off years" the Democrats often carried the election by small majorities. A State Senator was to be elected in 1859, an "off year." In the Republican Convention, held in Ravenna, in August of that year, a prominent Republican said to the convention: "Gentlemen, I can name a man whose standing, character, ability and industry will carry the county. It is President Garfield, of the Hiram school." The nomination was made by acclamation. Whether Garfield would accept the new and high honor, no one knew. The leading Disciples vehemently opposed his further entering into politics. Should he do so it would be at a loss of his character, they argued. At the various places where Garfield frequently preached, there was no little alarm at the prospect of the popular and successful young professor and minister going off into the vain struggle of worldly ambition. The nomination fell on the Disciple churches of the Reserve like a clap of thunder out of a clear sky. It raised great excitement. He did not accept the nomination for several days. He was nominated on Tuesday, and on Friday following the Cuyahoga annual county meeting of the Disciple churches began in Solon, and continued till noon the ensuing Monday. Almost the sole topic of conversation was the nomination of "Brother Garfield," as he was called. A large majority were earnest in their opposition to his abandoning the ministry for politics, for so they regarded an acceptance of the nomination. Some were very loud and severe in their condemnation.

Garfield was preaching for the church in Solon and attended the meeting. He did not come to Solon till Friday evening, and entered the meeting when the evening session was about half through. As soon as the audience was dismissed he was surrounded by men and women, all deprecating his acceptance of the nomination, and some were severe in their denunciation. There was much entreaty that he would then and there say that he would not accept it. To all he replied pleasantly that he had not accepted the nomination, and would not till satisfied that duty required him to do so. He remarked to Mr. Braden, who was quietly regarding the scene, amused at the earnestness of the throng surrounding him: "Clark, I want to walk down the road with you." Mr. Braden says: "As soon as he could get out of the crowd we started. Throwing an arm around me, as those who were intimate with him remember he would when earnest and confidential, he asked if I had been in the meeting during the day. I replied that I had. 'Have you noticed what has been said, and can you tell me how the brethren and sisters feel about my accepting this nomination?' I replied that I had listened attentively and that a majority were opposed to it, and some were very severe in their condemnation of such an act—what they termed abandonment of the ministry for politics. They had been very much gratified with his career and success, and had great expectations of him as a preacher, and would be sorely disappointed if he accepted the nomination. Stopping and facing me, with his hand still on my shoulder, he asked very earnestly: 'Clark, what do you advise me to do? What would you do?' I replied: 'Brother Garfield, I advise you to follow your own convictions of right and duty. You have achieved great success as a preacher. You have a most promising future before you as a preacher. But, if you believe you can take with you into political life your integrity and Christian manhood, and retain them, there is a far higher and more useful career open before you there. We need Christian statesmen. It is the crying want of the hour. If you can be one, there is your place. We can get a thousand to fill your place as a preacher far more easily than we can get one to fill the place waiting for a Christian statesman.' Now, after the lapse of twenty-two years, I am confirmed in the views I then expressed. The career he chose was far higher and nobler than any success as a preacher could have been. After a moment's silence he replied earnestly and slowly: 'I believe I can enter political life and retain my integrity, manhood and religion. I believe, with you, that there is vastly more need of such men than of preachers. You know I never deliberately decided to follow preaching as a life work any more than teaching. Circumstances have led me into both callings. The desire of brethren to have me preach and teach for them, a desire to do good in all ways that I could, and to earn, in noble callings, something to pay my way through a course of study, and to discharge debts, and the discipline and cultivation of mind in preaching and teaching, and the exalted topics for investigation in teaching and preaching, have led me into both callings. I have never intended to devote my life to either, or both; although lately, Providence seemed to be hedging my way, and crowding me into the ministry. I have always intended to be a lawyer, and perhaps to enter political life. Such has been my secret ambition ever since I thought of such things. I have been reading law for some time. This nomination opens the way, I believe, for me to enter into the life work I have always preferred. I have made up my mind. Mother is at Jason Robbins'. I will go there and talk with her. She has had a hope and desire that I would devote my life to preaching ever since I joined the church. My success as a preacher has been a great satisfaction to her. She regarded it as the fulfillment of her wishes, and has of late regarded the matter as settled. If she will give her consent I will accept the nomination.' I saw him the next day. He told me his mother said, in substance: 'James, I have had a hope and a desire, ever since you joined the church, that you would preach. I have been happy in your success as a preacher, and regarded it as an answer to my prayers. But I do not want my wishes to lead you into a life work that you do not prefer to all others—much less into the ministry, unless your heart is in it. If you can retain your manhood and religion, in political life, and believe you can do the most good there, you have my full consent and prayers for your success. A mother's prayers and blessing will be yours.' He concluded: 'I have written and accepted the nomination.' Who, in view of his subsequent career, can, for a moment, doubt that he followed the path of duty in so doing?"

The question solved, his mind settled, he thereupon placed his foot on the first round in the aspiring ladder. Garfield has now left the shores and harbors of private life, and in the sea of public turmoil, strife and ambition, his sails are spread. He is twenty-eight years of age; in body and mind a Titan, and of whose spotless honor, tireless industry and integrity there are the most satisfying evidences. All this being his heritage before the Capitol of Ohio was reached, is there any wonder that a high place in the State Senate should soon be his? It would be hard to find in this country a man so well equipped by nature, by experience and by training, as was Garfield when he entered the Ohio Senate in 1860. He was in his own person the representative of the plainest life of the backwoods and the best culture of the oldest eastern community. He had been accustomed in his youth to various forms of manual labor. The years which he devoted to the profession of teaching and of presiding, were years of great industry, in which he disciplined his powers of public speaking and original investigation. His first winter in the Senate was all that his most admiring friends could wish. Before the session had closed he had conquered many an opponent in debate, had clearly demonstrated his marvelous faculty of statement and research, and throughout the state Garfield became well and favorably known. Among the legislative works which remain to attest his greatness is a committee report, drawn by his hand, upon the geological survey of Ohio. It is a document of high order, revealing a scientific knowledge and power to group statistics and render them effective, which would be looked at with wide-eyed wonder by the modern state legislator. Another report on the care of pauper children, and still another, on the legal regulation of weights and measures, presenting a succint sketch of the attempts at the thing, both in Europe and America, are equally notable as entirely out of the ordinary rut of such papers. While in Columbus, much of the time, including evenings, when the legislature was not in session, his passion for literature was satisfied to a large extent, for at these times he could almost always be found in the state library.

But Garfield was destined to use his great powers to the best advantage not so much in time of peace as in time "when war walked with heavy tread through the land." The times became electric. Sparks, indicating intense heat, began flying in all directions. On all sides it was felt that a terrible crisis upon the slavery and states' rights questions was approaching. At this time the memorable national campaign of 1860, when Abraham Lincoln became the cynosure of all eyes, was in progress. The "Great Unknown" was elected as President of the United States. The South claimed that he was a sectional candidate, and became all the more obdurate than before. The dissolution of the Union appeared not far off, but Garfield's faith in its perpetuity was unshaken. What a striking similarity obtains between the hope of the country's future as expressed by Lincoln and by Garfield! While en route to Washington to deliver his inaugural, Lincoln addressed the citizens at Indianapolis. On this occasion he said: "All we want is time, patience, and a reliance on that God who has never forsaken his people."

Garfield spoke as follows at Ravenna, Ohio, on July 4, 1860:

"Our nation's future—shall it be perpetual? * * Shall its sun rise higher and higher, and shine with ever brightening luster? Or, has it passed the zenith of its glory, and left us to sit in the lengthening shadows of its coming night? * * *Shall civil dissension or intestine strife rend the fair fabric of the Union?* The rulers of the old world have long and impatiently looked to see fulfilled the prophecy of its downfall. * * The granite hills are not so changeless and abiding as the restless sea. Quiet is no certain pledge of permanence and safety. Trees may flourish and flowers may bloom upon the quiet mountain side, while silently the trickling rain-drops are filling the deep cavern behind the rocky barriers, which, by and by, in a single moment, shall hurl to wild ruin its treacherous peace. It is true, that in our land there is no such outer quiet, no such deceitful repose. Here society is a restless and surging sea. The roar of the billows, the dash of the wave, is forever in our ears. Even the angry hoarseness of breakers is not unheard. But there is an understratum of deep, calm sea, which the breath of the wildest tempest can never reach. There is, deep down in the hearts of the American people, a strong and abiding love of our country and its liberty, which no surface-storms of passion can ever shake. That kind of instability which arises from a free movement and interchange of position among the members of society, which brings one drop to glisten for a time on the crest of the highest wave, and then gives place to another, while it goes down to mingle again with the millions below; such instability is the surest pledge of permanence. On such instability the eternal fixedness of the universe is based. Each planet, in its circling orbit, returns to the goal of its departure, and on the balance of these wildly rolling spheres God has planted the broad base of his mighty works. So the hope of our national perpetuity rests upon that perfect individual freedom, which shall forever keep up the circuit of perpetual change. God forbid that the waters of our national life should ever settle to the dead level of a waveless calm. It would be the stagnation of death—the ocean grave of individual liberty."

GARFIELD—THE SOLDIER AND GENERAL.

OUR HERO.

Alas! for Columbia, her chieftain low lying,
  No more wields the scepter, her tower and her pride,
No solace but this for our heart's heavy sighing—
  A hero he lived and a hero he died!

At first, through the dark and mazy jungle of learning,
  He crept or he leaped to the sunlight of truth,
All barriers dispelling, discouragement spurning—
  The Garfield we mourn was a hero in youth!

When wrong and oppression held sway in our borders,
  And the wild, southern war-cloud ensanguined the sky,
Obedient he sprang to his dear country's orders,
  His strong heart determined to conquer or die!

At the semblance of peace, in the hush of war-clamor,
  His genius and courage his countrymen claimed;
His keen eye detected the perilous glamour—
  To dispel it, heroic the efforts he aimed.

On field and on forum, in peace and in riot,
  His learning, discretion and valor rose high;
But grander the hero in Elberon quiet,
  Who showed how a patriot and Christian can die!

So thin is the veil at the portal Elysian,
  So pure was the man, with the angels who trod,
Transfigured he lived in the light of a vision,
  And felt the heart-throbs of the Infinite God!

Oh, bright be the bloom by the summer-wind shaken,
  And green be the sod where his ashes repose;
For the name of our hero forever shall waken
  The homage of friends and the honor of foes!

his grave be the Mecca through myriad ages,
  Where pilgrims shall gather with reverent feet!
his life be a star upon history's pages,
  Where the glory of power and gentleness meet!

—MINNIE WARD PATTERSON.

CHAPTER VII.

THE EVE OF A NATIONAL STRIFE.

Heroes cannot die, but their clay.
The grief throbs of the Nation's heart bespeak
His many virtues, and their lustrious beams
O'erspread the political heav'ns, ere while
The reflection of their brightness, athwart
The Republic portends the birth of
Ennobled civil life, of purer aims
In State, and of a holi'r destiny.

—PAX ARMI.

But time moves on apace, and with it comes more certain evidence of the approaching storm. The horizon grows darker and darker. Frequently from out the black darkness of the storm-cloud, flashes the lightning, for near by are the hostile elements in combat. The muttering thunders of war and discord are heard in the distance. Yet even then, few men thought of war. It was difficult to understand how two sections of our land of liberty could stand in hostile array against one another. Never before were the times so stirring, for never before had "the house been divided against itself." These were the times when good, true and conscientious men were needed in official positions, and the high place in the State Senate held by Garfield, in a commonwealth around which the interests of the North centred, made it possible for his powers of leadership to assert themselves. He seemed always prepared to speak; he always spoke fluently and to the point; and his genial, warm-hearted nature served to increase the kindness with which both political friends and opponents regarded him. Three Western Reserve Senators formed the Radical triumvirate in that able and patriotic legislature, which was to place Ohio in line for the war. One was a highly-rated professor of Oberlin College; another, a lawyer already noted for force and learning, the son-in-law of the president of Oberlin; the third was our village carpenter and village teacher from Hiram. He was the youngest of the three, but he speedily became the first. The trials of the next six years were to confirm the verdict of the little group about the State capital that soon placed Garfield before both Cox and Monroe. The college professor was abundantly satisfied with the success in life which made him a consul at a South American port. The adroit, polished, able lawyer became a painstaking general, who, perhaps, oftener deserved success than won it, and who at last, profiting by the gratitude of the people to their soldiers, rose to be Governor of the State, but there (for the time, at least) ended. The village carpenter started lower in the race of the war, and rose higher, became one of the leaders in our national councils, and confessedly one of the ablest among the younger of our Statesmen.

Garfield saw in the distance the emergency which was to result in the black and horrible fate of civil war. In letters to his friend, President B. A. Hinsdale, he uses the following language:

COLUMBUS, January 15th, 1861.

My heart and thoughts are full almost every moment with the terrible reality of our country's condition. We have learned so long to look upon the convulsions of European States as things wholly impossible here, that the people are slow in coming to the belief that there may be any breaking up of our institutions; but stern, awful certainty is fastening upon the hearts of men. I do not see any way, outside a miracle of God, which can avoid civil war with all its attendant horrors. Peaceable dissolution is utterly impossible. Indeed, I cannot say that I would wish it possible. To make the concessions demanded by the South would be hypocritical and sinful; they would neither be obeyed nor respected. I am inclined to believe that the sin of slavery is one of which, it may be said, that without the shedding of blood there is no remission. All that is left us as a State, or say as a company of Northern States, is to arm and prepare to defend ourselves and the Federal Government. I believe the doom of slavery is drawing near. Let war come, and the slaves will get the vague notion that it is waged for them, and a magazine will be lighted whose explosion will shake the whole fabric of slavery. Even if all this happen, I cannot yet abandon the belief that one government will rule this continent, and its people will be one people.

Meantime, what will be the influence of the times on individuals? Your question is very interesting and suggestive. The doubt that hangs over the whole issue bears touching also. It may be the duty of our young men to join the army, or they may be drafted without their own consent. If neither of these things happen, there will be a period when old men and young will be electrified by the spirit of the times, and one result will be to make every individuality more marked and their opinions more decisive. I believe the times will be even more favorable than calm ones for the formation of strong and forcible characters.

Just at this time (have you observed the fact?) we have no man who has power to ride upon the storm and direct it. The hour has come, but not the man. The crisis will make many such. But I do not love to speculate on so painful a theme. * * * I am chosen to respond to a toast on the Union at the State Printers' festival here next Thursday evening. It is a sad and difficult theme at this time.

COLUMBUS, February 16th, 1861.

Mr. Lincoln has come and gone. The rush of people to see him at every point on the route is astonishing. The reception here was plain and republican, but very impressive. He has been raising a respectable pair of dark-brown whiskers, which decidedly improve his looks, but no appendage can ever render him remarkable for beauty. On the whole, I am greatly pleased with him. He clearly shows his want of culture, and the marks of Western life, but there is no touch of affectation in him, and he has a peculiar power of impressing you that he is frank, direct and thoroughly honest. His remarkable good sense, simple and condensed style of expression, and evident marks of indomitable will, give me great hopes for the country. And, after the long, dreary period of Buchanan's weakness and cowardly imbecility, the people will hail a strong and vigorous leader. I have never brought my mind to consent to the dissolution peaceably. I know it may be asked: Is it not better to dissolve before war than after? But I ask: Is it not better to fight before dissolution than after? If the North and South cannot live in the Union without war, how can they live and expand as dissevered nations without it? May it not be an economy of bloodshed to tell the South that disunion is war, and that the United States Government will protect its property and execute its laws at all hazards.

On the 24th of January, 1861, Garfield championed a bill to raise and equip six thousand State militia. With his colleagues, he worked day and night to prepare them for the result which his wisdom and foresight saw at a glance. Blinded, and unwilling to believe that the emergency was to result in war, it was no easy task to secure the passage of the measure. He saw in one glance, not only the enemies in front, but traitors in the rear. He thereupon drew up and put through to its passage, a bill defining treason—"providing that, when Ohio's soldiers go forth to maintain the Union, there shall be no treacherous fire in the rear."

The Radical triumvirate were busy wheeling their State into line for the approaching war. Even when the news of the firing of Sumter had flashed across the country, the Ohio Senate, over the desperate protests of the men, there being only six, Garfield leading, who for months had forseen the war, passed the famous Corwin Constitutional Amendment, stipulating that Congress should have no power to legislate in the future on the question of slavery! Yet, notwithstanding all this, Garfield's State was the first in the North to reach a war footing.

To write the career of James A. Garfield during the trying hours of rebellion, is to write at once a history of intrepid bravery, exquisite coolness in danger and sure success in action. His career has been rarely equalled by any American who entered the war as a civilian and laid down his sword with the rank of a major-general. His record, while bearing testimony to the marvelous spirit that always pervades a great people in a great crisis, and brings to the front a leader for every emergency, is a strangely complete illustration of how perfectly a man of brains and determination may succeed in some difficult walk in life, for which special and particular training have been always considered necessary. When the South chose to inaugurate the return of the flowers, the budding of the leaves, in 1861, by tearing from the old flag some of its sacred stars, the country paused a moment, waiting, as it were, actors for the tragedy about to begin, leaders for the now inevitable armies. The guns that had opened upon Sumter on the memorable 12th of April, had not merely crumbled the walls of that

Southern fortress, but they shattered also all hopes of a peaceful solution of the problems then before the country. Civil war had become a necessity; a bitter fact to write upon the pages of a nation's history begun so gloriously in 1776. The President's proclamation of the 15th called forth the militia for objects entirely lawful and constitutional, and it was responded to with a patriotic fervor which melted down all previously existing party lines. This "uprising of a great people," as it was well termed by a foreign writer, was a kindling and noble spectacle. The hearts of a whole land throbbed as one. But we cannot glance back upon the brilliant and burning enthusiasm that lighted our beloved country like a torch without a touch of sadness. For there was commingled with it so much ignorance, not merely of the magnitude of the contest before us, but of the nature of war itself. The high-spirited young men who thronged to swell the ranks of the volunteer force at the call of duty, marched off as gayly as if they were participants in a holiday turnout, a party of picnickers rather than devoted patriots upon a high percentage of whom the death seal was already set. The rebellion was to be put down at once, and by little more than the mere show of the preponderating force of the loyal States; and the task of putting it down was to be attended with no more danger than was sufficient to give the enterprise a due flavor of excitement. War was unknown to us except by report; the men of the Revolution were but spectres of a jeweled past; the veterans of 1812 were some of them still alive, but even they were gray with years and the memories of events.

"All of which they saw, and part of which they were,"

could be but dimly, disjointedly recalled. We had read of battles; we had seen something of the pomp of holiday soldiers; but of the grim realities of war we were absolutely ignorant. Indeed, not a few had come to the conclusion that war was a relic of barbarism, which civilization had so outgrown that modern times had forever dispensed with the soldier and his sword. It need hardly be said that the call to conflict found us totally unprepared for the great storm about to break. Our regular army was insignificant in numbers and scattered over our vast terrtory or along our Western frontier, so that it was impossible to collect any considerable force anywhere together. Our militia system had everywhere fallen into neglect, allowed to die for want of interest, and in some States had almost ceased to have any existence whatever. The wits laughed at it; it was a common subject of newspaper criticism; it was christened "the cornstalk militia;" platform orators declaimed against it. Indeed, so low had it fallen in public estimation, that it required some moral courage to march through the streets at the head of a company.

The South had been wiser, or at least more provident, in this respect. The military spirit had never been discouraged there. Many of the political leaders had long been looking forward to the time when the unhappy sectional contests which were distracting the country would blaze into a civil war and were preparing for it. They watched the smouldering fire of discontent, and waited the great conflagration of blood. In some of the States there had been military academies where a military education had been obtained, so that they had a greater number of trained officers to put into their regiments. This gave them a considerable advantage at the start, an advantage more real than seeming, and one they were not slow to turn to its fullest promise. At the North the people paused a moment to ask themselves where were they to get the needed officers. Graduates of West Point were scattered over the country; to them the civil authorities turned for assistance. This they rendered freely and ably, but it was, of necessity, limited in its scope. In most States the militia elected their own officers, and there was no other resource than to continue the system until time and the fire of the enemy's guns should level the abilities of the civilians, and bring to the front those who had the best title to be there. This produced a result of which we have no reason to be the least ashamed. A race of civilian officers, proving their right to command by deeds, not diplomas, winning experience at the point of the bayonet and testing bravery beneath the bullets of the foe, sprang everywhere into sight in the great upholding of the stars and stripes. To this class, now occupying a place in our history, that is to us a crowning wreath of credit, James A. Garfield belonged, and of those who were his comrades few show a better, braver record than he. When the secession of the Southern States began, National considerations were of paramount importance in Ohio as elsewhere. Indeed, the early signs of the dissolution between the North and South had attracted earnest attention and severe comment in that State. In its Senate and House of Representatives many a debate had been held, wherein the seeds of secessionists' doctrines had been sought to be planted by men who saw amiss. Garfield, as it will be remembered, was a member of the Senate, having been elected to represent Portage and Summit counties two years before. The spring of 1861 found the Senate, of which he was a member, earnestly occupying its time with those questions that had so much interest within as well as beyond the borders of Ohio. Garfield's course on all these questions was manly and outspoken. He was among the foremost in maintaining the right of the National Government to coerce seceded States. "Would you give up the forts and other government property in those States, or would you fight to maintain your right to them?" was his adroit way of putting the question to a conservative Republican who deplored his incendiary views. Ohio, when the great call came, was as unprepared as were other States. There was a small force of militia nominally organized, but the constitution and laws of the State provided that all its officers should be elected by the men, and the governor was limited in his selection of officers, in case the militia was called out, to the parties so chosen. Everywhere, however, there was enthusiasm for the cause and a wild willingness to help the government by every possible sacrifice that a great people could make. When the President's call for seventy-five thousand men was announced to the Ohio Senate, Senator Garfield was instantly on his feet, and amid the tumultuous cheers, moved that twenty thousand men and three million dollars be voted as Ohio's quota.

What a valuable acquisition to literature and history would that volume be which should faithfully recount the history of these times. Without law or precedent, a few determined men broke down the obstacles with which treason hedged the path of patriotism. All that is necessary for us to know is that when the storm cloud of treason broke, every Northern State stepped to the front for battle; and that is enough.

"When the time came for appointing officers for the troops so hastily got together, Garfield displayed," says Whitelaw Reid, in his "Ohio in the War," "his signal want of tact and skill in advancing his own interests. Of the three leading Radical senators, Garfield had the most personal popularity. Cox was at that time, perhaps, a more compact and pointed speaker; he had matured earlier as, to change the figure, he was to culminate sooner. But he had never aroused the warm regard which Garfield's whole-hearted, generous disposition always excited; yet Cox had the sagacity to see how his interests were to be advanced. He abandoned the senate chamber, installed himself as assistant in the governor's office, made his skill felt in the rush of business, and soon convinced the appointing power of his special aptitude for military affairs. In natural sequence he was presently appointed a brigadier-general." On the 14th of August, 1861, some months after the adjournment of the legislature, Governor Dennison offered Garfield the lieutenant-colonelcy of the Forty-second Ohio, a regiment not yet formed, and one which Garfield was instrumental in bringing into existence, with the active aid of Judge Sheldon, of Illinois, Don A. Pardee, of Medina, Ralph Plumb, of Oberlin, and other patriotic citizens of his district.

General Garfield decided to accept the appointment tendered him by Governor Dennison, and resigning the presidency of the college at Hiram, he placed himself and his abilities wholly at the service of the national government. Before doing so, however, he went to his home, opened the Bible his mother had given him, and pondered long and earnestly upon the subject. What a night of thought that was! He began to think of the sacrifices that must be made. He had fine prospects ahead of him in the literary world; and how hard it was to abandon this! He had a wife, a child, and about three thousand dollars. If his life should be sacrificed for his country, would God and the three thousand dollars provide for his wife and child? He consulted the Book about it. It seemed to him to give an affirmative answer; and before the morning he wrote to a friend as follows:

"I have had a curious interest in watching the process in my own mind, by which the fabric of my life is being demolished and reconstructed, to meet the new condition of affairs. One by one my old plans and aims, modes of thought and feeling, are found to be inconsistent with present duty, and are set aside to give place to the new structure of military life. It is not without a regret, almost tearful at times, that I look upon the ruins. But if, as the result of the broken plans and shattered individual lives of thousands of American citizens, we can see on the ruins of our national errors a new and enduring fabric arise, based on larger freedom and higher justice, it will be a small sacrifice indeed. For myself I am contented with such a prospect, and, regarding my life as given to the country, am only anxious to make as much of it as possible before the mortgage upon it is foreclosed." It is remarkable with what facility the American mind adapts itself to new situations, and this has never been so strikingly illustrated as in the great movements of 1861, which transformed in so short a time so great a multitude of young men from the unlimited independence of American citizens to the willing but severe restraints of military discipline. With Garfield, however, it was not merely the temporary adoption of a new profession—it was the overturning of all his life plans; and to his mother it was the demolition of all her ambitious hopes—hopes which had sustained her through long years of poverty and privation—that this son would pursue a scholarly career which would be worthy of her distinguished family. But, after the first shock of mingled surprise and disappointment was over, she quietly said, "Go, my son; your life belongs to your country."

Before Garfield was given a command, he made a trip to the Illinois arsenal to secure a large quantity of muskets. Immediately after Sumter was fired men crowded at the State capital ready to go to war. But soldiers without arms were useless, and, thereupon, with a requisition, Garfield left for the west. By swift diplomacy he secured and shipped to Columbus five thousand stand of arms, a prize valued at that time more than an equal number of troops. These incidents of the opening of the war are still fresh in the minds of many of my readers. The opening of the muster-rolls, the incessant music of martial bands, the waving of banners, the shouts of the drill-sergeant, the departure of crowded trains carrying the brave and true to awful fields of blood and glory—these cannot be effaced from our memory; and when years that are yet unborn are rolled into the past, our children's children will know of them by tradition and history. It was something of a task for Garfield to decide just where the line of duty for him was. As already stated, Governor Dennison had offered him a command—a lieutenant-colonelcy. For him duty seemed to have many calls. In a letter to his friend, Hinsdale, he said: "I hardly knew myself, till the trial came, how much of a struggle it would cost me to give up going into the army. I found I had so fully interested myself in the war that I hardly felt it possible for me not to be a part of the movement. But there were so many who could fill the place tendered to me, and would covet the place, more than could do my work here, perhaps, that I could not but feel it would be to some extent a reckless disregard of the good of others to accept. If there had been a scarcity of volunteers I should have accepted. The time may yet come when I shall feel it right and necessary to go." And that time did come, and Garfield went. The offer made by Governor Dennison was accepted with the condition that the colonel of the regiment should be a West Point graduate. The condition was complied with; and on the 16th of August, Garfield reported for duty and received his commission. He went to Brigadier-General Hill, at Camp Chase, near Columbus, for instruction in camp-duty and discipline. Here he staid during the next four months, studying the art of war; being absent only at short periods when in the recruiting service. In the business of raising troops he was very successful. The Forty-second Ohio Volunteer Infantry was about to be organized, and Garfield raised the first company. It was in this wise: Late in August he returned to Hiram and announced that at a certain time he would speak on the subject of the war and its needs, especially of men. A full house greeted him at the appointed hour. He made an eloquent appeal, at the close of which a large enrollment took place, including sixty Hiram students. In a few days the company was full, and he took them to Camp Chase, where they were named Company A, and assigned to the right of the still unformed regiment. On September 5th, Garfield was made colonel, and pushed forward the work, so that in November the requisite number was secured.

Five weeks were spent in drilling. Companies A, B, C and D were mustered into service September 25th, 1861; Company E, October 30th; Company F, November 12th, and Companies G, H, I and K November 26th, at which time the organization was completed. Garfield at once set vigorously to work to master the art and mystery of war, and to give his men such a degree of discipline as would fit them for effective service in the field. Bringing his saw and jack-plane again into play, he fashioned companies, officers, and non-commissioned officers out of maple blocks, and with these wooden-headed troops he thoroughly mastered the infantry tactics in his quarters. Then he organized a school for the officers of his regiment, requiring thorough recitation in the tactics, and illustrating the manœuvres by the blocks he had prepared for his own instruction. This done, he instituted regimental, company, squad, skirmish and bayonet drill, and kept his men at these exercises from six to eight hours a day, until it was universally admitted that no better drilled or disciplined regiment could be found in Ohio. The regiment saw three years of service; the last of the men were mustered out December 2d, 1864.

It was not until the 14th of December that orders for the field were received at Camp Chase for Colonel Garfield's command. Yet to this date no active operations had been attempted in the great department that lay south of the Ohio river. The spell of Bull Run still hung over our armies. Save the campaign in Western Virginia and the attack by General Grant at Belmont, not a single engagement had occurred over all the region between the Alleghanies and the Mississippi. General Buell was preparing to advance upon Bowling Green, when he suddenly found himself hampered by two co-operating forces skillfully planted within striking distance of his flank. General Zollicoffer was advancing from Cumberland Gap toward Mill Spring; and Humphrey Marshall, moving down the Sandy Valley from Virginia, was threatening to overrun Eastern Kentucky. Till these could be driven back, an advance upon Bowling Green would be perilous, if not actually impossible. To General George H. Thomas, then just raised from his coloneley of regulars to a brigadiership of volunteers, was committed the task of repulsing Zollicoffer; to the untried colonel of the raw Forty-second Ohio the task of repulsing Humphrey Marshall. And on their success the whole army of the department waited. Colonel Garfield's orders directed him to move his command to Catlettsburg, Kentucky, a town at the junction of the Big Sandy and the Ohio, and to report immediately, in person, to the department headquarters at Louisville. The regiment went by rail to Cincinnati, and thence by boat to Catlettsburg, where it arrived on the morning of December 17th. By sunset of the 19th, Colonel Garfield reported to General Buell, at Louisville. In his interview with that officer, he was informed that he was to be sent against Humphrey Marshall, who had in his advance reached as far north as Prestonburg, driving the Union forces before him.

To this man, who thus went into the war with a life not his own, was given, on the 20th of December, 1861, command of the little army which held Kentucky to her moorings in the Union. He knew nothing of war beyond its fundamental principles—which are, I believe, that a big boy can whip a little boy, and that one big boy can whip two little boys, if he take them singly, one after the other. He knew no more about it; yet he was selected by General Buell—one of the most scientific military men of his time—to solve a military problem which has puzzled the heads of the greatest generals; namely, how two small bodies of men, stationed widely apart, can unite in the presence of an enemy and beat him, when he is of twice their united strength, and strongly posted behind entrenchments. With the help of many "good men and true," he solved this problem; and in telling how he solved it, I shall give the history of the most remarkable campaign that occurred during the war of the rebellion. Don Carlos Buell was, at this time, forty-three years of age; a man accomplished in military science and experienced in war. He had graduated at West Point in 1842; and had won proud honor in the Mexican war; besides performing signal other services. Look at the two men! Garfield was only thirty years of age, and just five years out of college. His only knowledge of the unknown duty before him, had been gathered from books. Taking a map of Kentucky, Buell briefly showed Garfield the problem, and told him to solve it. The problem has been stated. In a word, it was, How shall the Confederates be driven out of Kentucky? The rebels badly needed the State, and so did the Unionists. Having made known the business, the great commander told Garfield to retire to his quarters, and at nine o'clock the next morning report his plan for conducting the campaign.

Garfield immediately shut himself up in a room, with no company but his map. The situation was as follows: Humphrey Marshall, with a large body of Confederates, was rapidly taking possession of eastern Kentucky. Entering Kentucky at Pound Gap, Marshall had fortified a strong natural position near Paintville, and with small bands, was overrunning the whole Piedmont region. This region, containing an area larger than the whole of Massachusetts, was occupied by about four thousand blacks and one hundred thousand whites — a brave, hardy, rural population, with few schools, scarcely any churches, and only one newspaper, but with that sort of patriotism which grows among mountains and clings to its barren hill-sides as if they were the greenest spots in the universe. Among this simple people Marshall was scattering firebrands. Stump orators were blazing away at every cross-road, lighting a fire which threatened to sweep Kentucky from the Union. Marshall's present position was at the head of the Big Sandy River. Catlettsburg, where the Forty-second had gone, is at the river's mouth. How many men Marshall had, was not known, but he was rapidly gathering an army, and, if unmolested, would soon have a large force with which he could hang on Buell's flank, and so prevent his advance into Tennessee; or, if he did advance, cut off his communications, and, falling on his rear, while Beauregard encountered him in front, crush him, as it were, between the upper and nether mill-stones. This done, Kentucky was lost; and that occurring so early in the war, the dissolution of the Union might have followed. Garfield studied the subject with tireless attention. All night long he thought and pondered, and when daylight broke he was ready to report.

The plan he recommended was, in substance, that a regiment be left, first some distance in the interior, say at Paris or Lexington, this mainly for effect on the people of that section. The next thing was to proceed up the Big Sandy River against Marshall, and run him back into Virginia; after which it would be in order to move westward, and, in conjunction with other forces, keep the State from falling into hostile hands. Meanwhile, Zollicoffer would have to be taken off by a separate expedition. His interview with the commanding general, on the following morning, was, as may be imagined, one of peculiar interest. Few army officers ever possessed more reticence, terse logic, and severe military habits than General Buell; and as the young man laid his rude map and roughly outlined plan on his table, and, with a curious and anxious face, watched his features to detect some indication of his thought, the scene was one for a painter. But no word or look indicated the commander's opinion of the feasibility of the plan, or the good sense of the suggestions. He spoke, now and then, in a quiet, sententious manner; but said nothing of approval or disapproval; only at the close of the conference he did make the single remark, "Your orders will be sent to you at six o'clock this evening." Promptly at that hour the order came, organizing the Eighteenth Brigade of the Army of the Ohio, Colonel Garfield commanding; and with the order came a letter of instructions, in Buell's own hand, giving general directions for the campaign, and recapitulating, with very slight modifications, the plan submitted by Garfield. On the following morning he took leave of his general, and the latter said to him, at parting, "Colonel, you will be at so great a distance from me, and communication will be so slow and difficult, that I must commit all matters of detail, and much of the fate of the campaign to your discretion. I shall hope to hear a good account of you."

To check this dangerous advance, meet Marshall—a thoroughly educated military man—and the uncounted hordes whom his reputation would draw about him, the inexperienced Ohio colonel was offered—what? Twenty-five hundred men—eleven hundred of whom, under Colonel Cranor, were at Paris, Kentucky; the remainder—his own regiment, and the half-formed Fourteenth Kentucky, under Colonel Moore, at Catlettsburg; a hundred miles of mountain country, infested with guerillas, and occupied by a disloyal people, being between them. To the Ohio canal-boy was committed the task of extinguishing this conflagration. It was a difficult task; one which, with the means at command, would have appalled any man not made equal to it by early struggles with hardship and poverty, and entire trust in the Providence that guards his country. Garfield set out at once for Catlettsburg, and, arriving there on the 22d of December, found his regiment had already proceeded to Louisa—twenty-eight miles up the Big Sandy. A state of general alarm existed throughout the district. The Fourteenth Kentucky—the only force of Union troops left in the Big Sandy region—had been stationed at Louisa; but had hastily retreated to the mouth of the river during the night of the 19th, under the impression that Marshall, with his whole force, was following to drive them into the Ohio. Union citizens and their families were preparing to cross the river for safety; but with the appearance of Garfield's regiment, a feeling of security returned, and this was increased when it was seen that the Union troops boldly pushed on to Louisa, without even waiting for their colonel. This, however, was only in pursuance of orders he had telegraphed on the morning after he had formed the plan for the campaign by midnight, in his dingy quarters at the hotel in Louisville. Waiting at Catlettsburg only long enough to forward supplies to his forces, Garfield appeared at Louisa on the morning of the 24th of December, and thenceforward he became the chief actor in a drama which, all its circumstances considered, is one of the most wonderful to be read of in history.

CHAPTER VIII.

THE BIG SANDY CAMPAIGN.

"A soldier of the camp, we knew him thus:
No saintly champion high above his kind,
To follow with devotion mad and blind—
He fought and feared.
And so, half hearted, went we where he led;
And, following whither beckoned his bright blade,
Learned his high will and purpose undismayed;
And brought him all our faith."

Garfield, now a soldier of the Union, was beginning to experience the real and trying exigencies of war. As we have seen, almost within the twinkling of an eye, he had been transferred from the pleasant associations of Hiram life and the public duties of a State Senator, not only to the sphere of army tactics, but to the more trying duties of actual war. Without experience in commanding bodies of men drawn up for battle, without anything more than theory upon which to base his judgments and plan his campaigns, he is at once given the responsible task of conducting if not one of the greatest, certainly at that time one of the most important, campaigns. How few men there are who, under all these circumstances, would have proven themselves equal to the task in hand. Success with him now meant everything. An unsuccessful issue, a wrong movement, would have imperiled, not only his men, but the cause for which war became a necessity. But Garfield never faltered. With a firm trust in the guidance of Providence, he grew strong, and was successful, as we shall presently see. The question may well be asked, and, no doubt, has already occurred to many readers, What were General Buell's thoughts as he bent over Garfield, the morning when the young colonel reported his plans for the Big Sandy campaign? And what was there about Garfield to give the great and experienced officer so much confidence in Garfield's known inexperience? But the answer to those questions must remain in great part a mystery. The enthusiasm of Garfield's manner and speech; the perfection of the plan as it developed before him; the carefulness with which he saw the subject had been handled, and the valor with which he must have believed it would be successfully carried out, certainly were some of the reasons that satisfied Buell of Garfield's fitness. But we shall not dwell upon these conjectures. To recount the history of the Big Sandy campaign, the following out ot Garfield's plans, must be taken up.

Garfield had two very difficult things to accomplish. He had to open communication with Colonel Cranor, while the intervening country, as has been said, was infested with roving bands of guerillas, and filled with a disloyal people. He had also to form a junction with the force under that officer, in the face of a superior enemy, who would, doubtless, be apprised of his every movement, and would be likely to fall upon his separate columns the moment that either was set in motion, in the hope of crushing them in detail. Either operation was hazardous, if not well-nigh impossible. Garfield now went to Paris, where Colonel Cranor's regiment was stationed, to see that he was well established. This done he returned and hastened to overtake his own regiment, reaching Catlettsburg on the 20th of December. Supplies were sent from here up the river to Louisa, an old half-decayed village built after the Southern style, where his men were waiting for him. The march up the river from Catlettsburg to Louisa was a difficult one; and the Forty-second Ohio began, for the first time, the process of seasoning which soon made veterans out of raw civilians. Old and tried soldiers would, undoubtedly, have considered the march a very hard one; but to the men, who only five days before had left Columbus without any experience whatever in the hardships of a march, it was rough and tiresome in the extreme. Early on the morning of the eighteenth the first division started, twenty-five mounted on horses, and one hundred going by boat. The cavalry made good progress; but those in the boat found their way hedged in. The circuitous course of the river, and the channel being shallow on account of low water, gave the boat much trouble, and, after a few miles of bumping, it finally stuck fast. There was no alternative now but to abandon it and continue the trip on foot. The wildness of the country was striking. Spurs of mountains, hills, narrow and torturous paths, up hill and down, only the more increased the unpleasantness of their situation. Eight miles was all that the tired men traveled that day. The next day, however, sufficed to bring them to Louisa, their destination, where the horsemen had already arrived and held the town. The other companies were still en route. It commenced raining, the winds blew from the north, and it soon became very cold. These were their first experiences, and it is useless to say that not a man was over-enthusiastic at the prospects ahead. The steep, rocky paths scarcely afforded room for the wagon train, whose conveyances were lightened of their load by throwing off many articles of comfort which these soldiers, with their unwarlike notions of life, hated to lose. But their only business now was to advance; and this they must do, if only the guns and knapsacks could be carried. On the twenty-first all were together again.

Paintville, where it was intended to attack Marshall, is located on Painter Creek, near the west fork of the Big Sandy, about thirty miles from Louisa. The first thing necessary to be done was to cross the intervening country immediately, and attack the enemy without delay. Tardy movements now would be sure disaster. While the advance was being made it would also be of the utmost importance to see to the matter of re-enforcements; for it was learned that Marshall had upwards of five thousand men, and Garfield less than two thousand. The only thing possible to be done was to open communications with Colonel Cranor, of the Fortieth Ohio, stationed at Paris, one hundred miles distant. That hundred miles was accessible to Marshall, and full of rebel sympathizers. The man who should carry the message would do so at the risk of his life, with all the odds against him. To find such a one who was able and willing to perform the hazardous undertaking, would be like "stumbling over a diamond in an Illinois cornfield." To this end the Union commander applied to Colonel Moore, of the Fourteenth Kentucky, and said to him: "I must communicate with Cranor; some of your men know this section of country well; have you a man who will die rather than fail or betray us?" The Kentuckian reflected a moment, then answered, "I think I have—John Jordan, from the head of Baine." What kind of a man he was has been well told by a writer in the *Atlantic Monthly*, for October, 1865. Jordan was sent for. He was a tall, gaunt, sallow man of about thirty, with small gray eyes, a fine falsetto voice, pitched in the minor key, and his speech was the rude dialect of the mountains. His face had as many expressions as could be found in a regiment, and he seemed a strange combination of cunning, simplicity, undaunted courage, and undoubting faith; yet, though he might pass for a simpleton, he had a rude sort of wisdom, which, cultivated, might have given his name to history.

The young colonel sounded him thoroughly, for the fate of the little army might depend upon his fidelity. The man's soul was as clear as crystal, and in ten minutes Garfield saw through it. His history is stereotyped in that region. Born among the hills, where the crops are stones, and sheep's noses are sharpened before they can nibble the thin grass between them, his life had been one of the hardest toil and privation. He knew nothing but what Nature, the Bible, the "Course of Time," and two or three of Shakespeare's plays, had taught him; but somehow in the mountain air he had grown to be a man—a man, as civilized nations account manhood.

"Why did you come into the war?" at last asked the colonel.

"To do my sheer fur the kentry, gin'ral," answered the man. "And I didn't druv no barg'in wi' th' Lord. I guv him my life squar' out; and ef he's a mind ter tuck it on this tramp, why, it's a his'n; I've nothin' ter say agin it."

"You mean that you've come into the war not expecting to get out of it?"

"That's so Gin'ral."

"Will you die rather than let the dispatch be taken?"

"I wull."

The colonel recalled what had passed in his own mind when poring over his mother's Bible that night at his home in Ohio, and it decided him. "Very well," he said; "I will trust you." The despatch was written on tissue-paper, rolled into the form of a bullet, coated with warm lead, and put into the hand of the Kentuckian. He was given a carbine, a brace of revolvers, and the fleetest horse in his regiment, and, when the moon was down, started on his perilous journey. He was to ride at night, and hide in the woods or in the houses of loyal men in the daytime. Space will not permit me to detail the incidents of this perilous ride over nearly a hundred miles of disaffected country. On his first day out the scout was waylaid by a band of guerillas, who were apprised of the object of his journey through the treachery of one of his own comrades in the Fourteenth Kentucky. They surrounded the house of a loyal man at which he was sleeping, and he had barely time to intrust the despatch to the worthy housewife, and to enjoin her, in case he was killed, to convey it safely to Colonel Cranor at Paris, when the door was burst open, and they were upon him. He fled to the woods. Two horsemen were guarding the door. Thinking to get a moment's advantage of his pursuers, as the door opened, he brandished a red garment before the horses, which made them for a moment unmanageable. In a second he had leaped over the fence, but the race was an uneven one, and the riders were gaining. Turning on them, Jordan discharged his revolver, and one less pursuer rode behind, for the bullet had entered a vital part, and death was instantaneous. Another discharge, and the other man's horse fell. Ere the others of the squad could reach him, he had found a secure retreat in the timber. There he lay concealed until night, when he stole again to the loyal man's dwelling, recovered the dispatch, and with it again set out on his hazardous journey. After a ride of forty miles more, with several other encounters and escapes, he at last, at midnight of the following day, reached the camp of Colonel Cranor, having ridden nearly a hundred miles with a rope round his neck, for thirteen dollars a month, hard-tack, and a shoddy uniform. Colonel Cranor opened the dispatch. It was dated Louisa, Kentucky, December 24th, midnight; and directed him to move at once with his regiment (the Fortieth Ohio, eight hundred strong), by the way of Mt. Sterling and McCormick's Gap, to Prestonburg. He would encumber his men with as few rations and as little luggage as possible, bearing in mind that the safety of his command depended on his expedition. He would also convey the dispatch to Lieutenant-colonel Woodford at Stamford, and direct him to join the march with his three hundred cavalry. Hours now were worth months of common time, and on the following morning Cranor's column began to move. The scout lay by till night, then set out on his return, and at last rejoined his regiment in safety, although the faithful animal that carried him had fallen, pierced by a rebel ball.

The contents of the bullet which Jordan conveyed to Colonel Cranor indicated that it was the intention of the Union commander to move at once upon the enemy. Of Marshall's real strength he was ignorant; but his scouts and the country people reported that the main body of the Confederates—which was intrenched in an almost impregnable position near Paintville—was from four to seven thousand strong, and that an outlying force of eight hundred occupied West Liberty, a town directly on the route by which Cranor was to march to effect a junction with the main Union army. Cranor's column, as has been said, was eleven hundred strong, and the main body under Garfield now numbered about fifteen hundred; namely, the Forty-Second Ohio Infantry, ten hundred and thirteen strong, and the Fourteenth Kentucky Infantry, numbering five hundred rank and file, but imperfectly armed and equipped. All told, therefore, Garfield had a force of twenty-six hundred in a strange district, and cut off from re-enforcements, with which to meet and crush an army of at least five thousand, familiar with the country, and daily receiving recruits from the disaffected Southern counties.

Having followed Jordan to the successful accomplishment of his daring exploit, we will now return to inquire what was doing in Garfield's camp during his absence. The days were full of activity. On the morning of December 23d, the march toward Paintville commenced. Evidently a forward movement was hazardous; but the Union commander did not waste time in considering the obstacles and dangers of the expedition. The heavy rains which had fallen for several days had been stopped by the increasing coldness of the weather, and, as a result, the hills and road were icy and slippery. The night previous to the first day's march was a memorable one. Most of the men scarcely slept at all, but remained around the camp-fire the entire night to keep from freezing. During the first day they advanced but ten miles, and tired indeed were they when that distance was accomplished. During half the distance, one crooked little creek, which wound around in a labyrinth of coils, was crossed no less than twenty-six times. The second day's experience was even more trying than the first, for progress was much slower, and provisions became very scarce. A large part of the wagon train and equipments had been taken up the river by boats, and the close proximity of the enemy rendered it unsafe to make so wide a detour from the river as would be required to send supplies by the table-lands to the westward. In these circumstances, Garfield decided to depend mainly upon water navigation for the transport of his supplies, and to use the army train only when his troops were obliged, by absolutely impassable roads, to move away from the river. Those supplies that had started with them had been left far in the rear. Their hunger became so great, that pigs and poultry belonging to a certain farmer were captured by the soldiers and eaten. For this act Garfield severely reprimanded the offenders and repaid the farmer.

On the 27th, a squad of Marshall's men were encountered, and two men captured. On the following day, three Union soldiers fell into the hands of the Confederates, thus paying for all that had been gained. The slowness with which the advance was necessarily made, gave rise to numerous skirmishes with the enemy each day, as the opposing forces neared each other. On the 6th of January, 1862, the Eighteenth Brigade, except that portion which was coming from Paris, was encamped within seven miles of Paintville; and at last it had become possible to bring things to a crisis, and determine, by the awful arbitrament of war, who should possess that part of Kentucky. Garfield's movements had been made entirely in the dark. He had not heard what had become of his dispatch to Cranor, and he was uncertain as to the exact position and strength of the enemy.

The Big Sandy is a narrow, fickle stream, and finds its way to the Ohio through the roughest and wildest spurs of the Cumberland Mountains. At low water it is not navigable above Louisa, except for small flat-boats pushed by hand; but these ascend as high as Piketon, one hundred and twenty miles from the mouth of the river. In time of high water small steamers can reach Piketon; but heavy freshets render navigation impracticable, owing to the swift current, filled with floating timber, and to the overhanging trees, which almost touch one another from the opposite banks. At this time the river was of only moderate height; but, as will be readily seen, the supply of a brigade at mid-winter by such an uncertain stream, and in the presence of a powerful enemy, was a thing of great difficulty. However, the obstacles did not intimidate Garfield. Gathering together ten days' rations, he chartered two small steamers, and impressed all the flat-boats he could lay hands on, and then, taking his army wagons apart, he loaded them, with his forage and provisions, upon the flat-boats. This was on the first of January, 1862, and the day before Garfield received an unexpected re-enforcement, that cannot be omitted in a full statement of the progress of the expedition. Next morning Captain Bent, of the Fourteenth Kentucky, entering Garfield's tent, says to him: "Colonel, there's a man outside who says he knows you—Bradley Brown, a rebel thief and a scoundrel." "Brown," says Garfield, raising half-dressed from his blanket. "Bradley Brown. I don't know any one of that name." "He has lived near the head of the Baine, been a boatman on the river, says he knew you on the canal in Ohio." "Oh, yes," answered Garfield, "bring him in; now I remember him." In a moment Brown is ushered into the colonel's quarters. He is clad in country homespun, and spattered from head to foot with the mud of a long journey, but, without any regard for the sanctity of rank, he advances at once upon the Union commander, and grasping him warmly by the hand, exclaims, "Jim, ole feller, how ar' ye!" The colonel received him cordially, but noticing his ruddy face, says: "Fifteen years haven't changed you, Brown; you will take a glass of whiskey? But what's this I hear? Are you a rebel?" "Yes," answers Brown, "I belong to Marshall's force, and"—and this he prefaces with a burst of laughter, "I've come stret from his camp to spy out yer army." The colonel looks surprised, but says, coolly: "Well, you go about it queerly." "Yes, quar, but honest, Jim—when yer alone I'll tell yer about it." As Bent was leaving the tent he said to his commander, in an undertone: "Don't trust him, colonel; I know him—he's a thief and a rebel." Brown proved to be rather a camp-follower, and was but little trusted by his officers. The region of country in which the operations were being made was thoroughly familiar to him, and when he heard that his old comrade was commander, he hastened to offer his services as a scout. Brown's disclosures, in a few words, are these: Hearing, a short time before, at the rebel camp, that James A. Garfield, of Ohio, had taken command of the Union forces, it at once occurred to him that it was his old canal companion, for whom, as a boy, he had felt a strong affection. This supposition was confirmed a few days later by his hearing from a renegade northern man something of the antecedents of the colonel. Remembering their former friendship, and being indifferent as to which side was successful in the campaign, he at once determined to do an important service to the Union commander. With this object he sought an interview with Humphrey Marshall, stated to him his former acquaintance with Garfield, and proposed that he should take advantage of it to enter the Union camp, and learn for the rebel general all about his enemy's strength and intended movements. Marshall at once fell into the trap, and the same night Brown set out for the Union camp, ostensibly to spy for the rebels, but really to tell the Union commander all that he knew of the rebel strength and position. He did not know Marshall's exact force, but he gave Garfield such facts as enabled him to make, within half an hour, a tolerably accurate map of the rebel position. When this was done, the Union colonel said to him: "Did Bent blindfold you when he brought you into camp?" "Yes, colonel, I couldn't see my hand afore me." "Well, then, you had better go back directly to Marshall." "Go back to him! Why, colonel, he'll hang me to the first tree!" "No he won't—not if you tell him all about my strength and intended movements." "But how kin I? I don't know a thing. I tell ye I was blindfolded." "Yes, but that don't prevent your guessing at our numbers, and about our movements. You may say that I shall march to-morrow straight for his camp, and in ten days be upon him." Brown sat for a moment musing, then he said: "Wal, colon'l, ye'd be a durned fool, and if ye's thet ye must hev growed to it since we were on the canal—ef ye went upon Marshall, trenched as he is, with a man short on twenty thousand. I kin 'guess' ye's that many." "Guess again. I haven't that number." "Then, ten thousand." "Well, that will do for a Kentuckian. Now, to-day, I will keep you under lock and key, and to-night you can go back to Marshall." At nightfall, Brown set out for the rebel camp. About midnight, Garfield was roused from his sleep by a man who said his business was urgent. The colonel rubbed his eyes, and raised himself on his elbow. "Back safe?" he asked. "Have you seen Cranor?" "Yes, colonel; he can't be any more than two days behind me." "God bless you, Jordan! You have done us a great service," said Garfield, warmly. "I thank you, colonel," answered Jordan, his face trembling, "that is more pay than I expected." He had returned safely, but the Providence which so wonderfully guarded his way out, seemed to leave him to find his way back, for, as he expressed it, "The Lord cared more for the dispatch than he cared for me, and it was natural he should, because my life counts only one, but the dispatch, it stood for the whole of Kentucky."

Next morning, another horseman rode up to the Union headquarters. He was a messenger direct from General Buell, who had followed Garfield up the Big Sandy with dispatches. They contained only a few hurried sentences, from a man to a woman, but their value was not be estimated in money. It was a letter from Humphrey Marshall to his wife, which Buell had intercepted, and it revealed the important fact that the rebel general had five thousand men—four thousand four hundred infantry and six hundred cavalry—with twelve pieces of artillery, and was daily expecting an attack from a Union force of ten thousand.

Garfield put the letter in his pocket, and then called a council of his officers. They assembled in the rude log shanty, and the question was put to them: "Shall we march at once, or wait the coming of Cranor?" All but one said, "Wait!" He said, "Move at once; our fourteen hundred can whip ten thousand rebels." Garfield reflected awhile, then closed the council with the laconic remark: "Well, forward it is. Give the order." Three roads led to the rebel position—one at the east, bearing down to the river and along its western bank; another, a circuitous one, to the west, coming in on Painter creek at the mouth of Jenny creek, on the right three miles from the village; and a third between the two others, a more direct route but climbing a succession of almost impassable ridges. These three roads were held by strong rebel pickets, and a regiment was outlying at the village of Paintville. To deceive Marshall as to his real strength and designs, Garfield orders a small force of infantry and cavalry to advance along the river road, drive in the rebel pickets, and move rapidly after them as if to attack Paintville. Two hours after this small force goes off, a similar one with the same orders sets off on the road to the westward, and two hours later still another small party takes the middle road. The effect is that the pickets on the first route being vigorously attacked and driven, retired in confusion to Paintville, and dispatched word to Marshall that the Union army is advancing along the river. He hurries off a thousand infantry and a battery to resist the advance of this imaginary column. When this detachment had been gone an hour and a half, Marshall hears from the routed pickets on his left that the Union forces are advancing along the western road. Countermanding his first order, he now directs the thousand men and the battery to check he new danger, and hurries off the troops at Paintville to the mouth of Jenny creek, to make a stand at that point. Two hours later the pickets on the central route are driven in, and finding Paintville abandoned, they flee precipitately to the fortified camp with the story that the whole Union army is close at their heels, and already occupying the town. Conceiving that he has thus lost Paintville, Marshall hastily withdraws the detachment of a thousand to his camp, and then, Garfield moving rapidly over the ridges of the central route, occupies the abandoned position, having with him the Forty-second Ohio, Fourteenth Kentucky, and four hundred Virginia cavalry.

Some of the cavalrymen were chasing the rebel horse, whom they followed five miles, killing three and wounding several. Two killed and one wounded was the only loss sustained by the Union army. The day following, January 8th, a short period of rest was taken, while preparations were making for a renewal of the fight. In the afternoon the order to advance was given. Painter creek was impassable; but going to a saw-mill near by, the soldiers soon constructed a raft with which they might cross. The ubiquitous Marshall, having been thoroughly posted as to these movements, was meditating what next to do.

So affairs stand when a spy enters the camp of Marshall with tidings that Cranor, with thirty-three hundred men, is within twelve hours' march to the westward. On receipt of these tidings, the "big boy"—he weighed three hundred pounds by the Louisville hay-scales—conceiving himself outnumbered, breaks up his camp, and retreats precipitately toward Petersburg, abandoning or burning a large portion of his supplies. Seeing the fires, Garfield mounts his horse, and, with a thousand men, enters the deserted camp at nine in the evening, while the blazing stores are yet unconsumed. He sends off a detachment to harass the retreat, and waits the arrival of Cranor, with whom he means to follow and bring Marshall to battle in the morning. An appearance of hasty flight and confusion was seen on every hand. Meat was still cooking before the fire, and all preparations for the evening meal were abandoned. This location was at the top of a hill, three hundred feet high, covering about two acres, and would soon have been a strong fortification. In the morning Cranor comes, but his men are footsore, without rations, and completely exhausted. They cannot move one leg after the other. But the canal-boy is bound to have a fight; so every man who has strength to march is ordered to come forward. Eleven hundred—among them four hundred of Cranor's tired heroes—step from the ranks, and with them, at noon on the 9th, Garfield sets out for Prestonburg, sending all his available cavalry to follow the line of the enemy's retreat, and harass and delay him.

CHAPTER IX.

OPERATIONS IN MIDDLE CREEK VALLEY.

Hark to that roar whose swift and deafening peals
In countless echoes through the mountains ring,
Startling pale midnight on her starry throne;
Now swells the intermingling din—the jar,
Frequent and frightful, of the bursting bomb,
The falling brave, the shriek, the groan, the shout,
The ceaseless clangor, and the rush of men.

—SHELLEY.

The contest is now becoming interesting. It is plain that Marshall is waging an unequal contest—unequal, not because a superior number is against him, but only because the superior tactics of his opposing leader made it seem so. Every inch of ground abandoned by the Confederates, was soon occupied by Garfield's forces. The Ohio "boys" had seen several weeks of hardship, such as they had never anticipated, and were, on that account, all the more ready to enjoy the victory and rejoice at Marshall's discomfiture. In an hour the tables had turned. Then the snug quarters of the enemy contrasted painfully with the unpleasantness surrounding Garfield's regiment. Now the warrior is out-warriored, and around the camp-fires, which shortly before the Confederates had gathered, are now seen the hungry and tired boys in blue.

But the fighting had not ended yet. The action which followed is known as the battle of Middle Creek. Marching eighteen miles further up the west fork, he reached, at 9 o'clock that night, the mouth of Abbott's Creek, three miles below Prestonburg, he and the eleven hundred. Two parallel creeks flow in between the hills; the northermost one is Abbott's Creek, the next Middle Creek. It was evident that Marshall would place himself behind this double barrier and make a stand there, if he should endeavor to turn the tide of defeat at all. Garfield hears that Marshall is encamped on the stream, three miles higher up; and throwing his men into bivouac, in the midst of a sleety rain, he sends an order back to Lieutenant-colonel Sheldon, who is left in command at Paintville, to bring up every available man with all possible dispatch, for he shall force the enemy to battle in the morning. Garfield spends the night in learning the character of the surrounding country, and the disposition of Marshall's forces. He makes a hasty meal off a stewed rabbit, eaten out of a tin-cup—he sharing the single spoon and the stew with one of his officers; and now again John Jordan comes into action.

A dozen Confederates are grinding at a mill, and a dozen Union men come upon them, capture their corn and make them prisoners. The miller is a tall, gaunt man, and his clothes fit the scout as if they were made for him. He is a dis-unionist, too, and his very raiment should bear witness against this feeding of his enemies. It does. It goes back to the Confederate camp, and—the scout goes in it. That chameleon face of his is smeared with meal, and looks the miller so well that the miller's own wife might not detect the difference. The night is dark and rainy, and that lessens the danger; but still he is picking his teeth in the very jaws of the lion. Space will not permit me to detail this midnight ramble; but it gave Garfield the exact position of the enemy. They had made a stand, and laid an ambuscade for him. Strongly posted on a semicircular hill, at the forks of Middle Creek, on both sides of the road, with cannon commanding its whole length, and hidden by the trees and underbrush, they were waiting his coming. Deeming it unsafe to proceed farther in the darkness, Garfield, as has been said, had ordered his army into bivouac at nine in the evening, and climbing a steep ridge, called Abbott's Hill, his tired men threw themselves upon the wet ground to wait for the morning. It was a terrible night, a fit prelude to the terrible day that followed. A dense fog shut out the moon and stars, and shrouded the lonely mountain in Cimmerian darkness. A cold wind swept from the north, driving the rain in blinding gusts into the faces of the shivering men, and stirring the dark pines into a mournful music. But the slow and cheerless night wore away at last, and at four in the morning the tired and hungry men, their icy clothing clinging to their half-frozen limbs, were roused from their cold beds, and ordered to move forward. Slowly and cautiously they descended into the valley, feeling at every step for the enemy. The enemy was waiting them, they were waiting him. The necessity for still additional re-enforcements was evident, and Colonel Garfield dispatched Colonel Cranor to send all his available men at once. The last bivouac has ended, and nothing now remains but to advance and measure their lives against the foe. Morning dawned, and the little Federal army, stiff almost with cold and tired from loss of sleep, but heroic and brave, proceeded cautiously down into the valley, then over the hills again, until a mile beyond, they were ready to descend into the valley of Middle Creek, and charge against the enemy on the opposite heights. About daybreak, while rounding a hill which jutted out into the valley, the advance-guard was charged upon by a body of Confederate horsemen. Forming his men in a hollow square, Garfield gave the Confederates a volley that sent them reeling up the valley—all but one; and he, with his horse, plunged into the stream, and was captured. Knowing full well that it was injudicious to open a general engagement until the re-enforcements from Cranor had arrived, skirmishing was all that was done from eight till one o'clock. By this means a better knowledge of the situation was gained.

The main body of the enemy, it was now evident, was not far distant; but whether he had changed his position since the visit of Jordan was uncertain. To dertermine this, Garfield sent forward a strong corps of skirmishers, who swept the cavalry from a ridge which they had occupied, and, moving forward, soon drew the fire of the hidden Confederates. Suddenly a puff of smoke rose from beyond the hill, and a twelve-pound shell whistled above the trees, then ploughed up the hill, and buried itself in the ground at the very feet of the adventurous little band of skirmishers. Now the action must come, and throwing his whole force upon the ridge whence the Confederate cavalry had been driven, Garfield prepared for the impending battle. It was a trying and perilous moment. He was in the presence of a greatly superior enemy, and how to dispose his little force, and where first to attack, where things not easy to determine. But he lost no time in idle indecision. Looking in the faces of his eleven hundred, he went at once into the terrible struggle. His mounted escort of twelve men he sent forward to make a charge, and, if possible, to draw the fire of the enemy. The ruse worked admirably. As the little squad swept round a curve in the road, another shell whistled through the valley, and the long roll of nearly five thousand muskets chimed in with a fierce salutation. Then began the battle. In the centre of the strip of meadow-land, lying between Middle Creek and the opposite hills, was a high point of land, upon which was a little log church, and a small grave-yard. That a base for operations might be secured, the first ruse was to occupy that point. Both the rebel cavalry and artillery had stationed themselves in such a manner as to control the church. But the guns were badly manned and were ineffective; the cavalry made a charge; but were soon withdrawn. A glance at the ground will best show the real nature of the conflict. It was on the margin of Middle Creek, a narrow, rapid stream, and three miles from where it finds its way into the Big Sandy, through the sharp spurs of the Cumberland Mountains. A rocky road, not ten feet in width, winds along this stream, and on its two banks abrupt ridges, with steep and rocky sides, overgrown with trees and underbrush, shut closely down upon the road and the little streamlet. At twelve o'clock Garfield had gained the crest of the ridge at the right of the road, and the charge of his handful of horsemen had drawn Marshall's fire, and disclosed his actual position. The main force of the Confederates occupied the crests of the two ridges at the left of the stream, but a strong detachment was posted on the right, and a battery of twelve pieces held the forks of the creek and commanded the approach of the Union army. It was Marshall's plan to lure Garfield along the road, and then, taking him between two enfilading fires, to surround and utterly destroy him. But his hasty fire betrayed his design, and unmasked his entire position. The dauntless riders returned safely, and then the battle began. Four hundred men of the Fortieth and Forty-second Ohio, under Major Pardee, quickly advanced up the hill in front, while two hundred of the Fourteenth Kentucky, under Lieutenant-colonel Monroe, went down the road some distance, and endeavored by a flank movement to so engage a portion of the rebels that not all of them could be turned against Pardee. Garfield acted with promptness and decision. A hundred undergraduates, recruited from his own college, in the Forty-second Ohio, under Pardee, were ordered to cross the stream, climb the ridge whence the fire had been hottest, and bring on the battle. Boldly the little band, altogether inferior in numbers, plunged into the creek, the icy water up to their waists, and, clinging to the trees and underbrush, ascended the rocky path. They are determined to reach the summit some way. Half-way up the ridge, the fire of at least two thousand rifles open upon them, but springing from tree to tree, they press on, and at last reach the summit. Then suddenly the hill is gray with Confederates, who, rising from ambush, poured their deadly volleys into the little band of only one hundred. In a moment they waver, but their leader calls out, "Every man to a tree! Give them as good as they send, my boys!" And after the Indian fashion they fight. For the brave Union boys there are some advantages. Their opponents prove to be raw recruits and aim too high, while the Federals do much better execution. The Confederates, behind rocks and a rude intrenchment, are obliged to expose their heads to take aim at the advancing column; but the Union troops, posted behind the huge oaks and maples, can stand erect and load and fire, fully protected. Though they are outnumbered ten to one, the contest is, therefore, for a time, not so very unequal. The rebel general was desperate, and now hastens his reserve force forward to swell the number. But soon the Confederates, exasperated with the obstinate resistance, rush from cover, and charge upon the little handful with the bayonet. Slowly they are driven down the hill, and two of them fall to the ground wounded. One never rises; the other—a lad of only eighteen—is shot through the thigh, and one of his comrades turns back to bear him to a place of safety. The advancing Confederates are within thirty feet, when one of them fires, and his bullet strikes a tree directly above the head of the Union soldier. He turns, levels his musket, and the Confederate is in eternity. Then the rest are upon him; but zigzaging from tree to tree, he is soon with his driven column. But not far are the brave boys driven. A few rods lower down they hear again the voice of the brave Captain Williams, their leader, "To the trees again, my boys!" he cries. "We may as well die here as in Ohio!" The fight grows hotter and whistling death is in the air. The critical moment has arrived. The jubilant rebels rush down in swelling numbers; and the prey is about to be seized. To the trees the Federals go, and in a moment the advancing horde is checked, and then rolled backward. Up the hill they turn, firing as they go, and the little band follows. Soon the Confederates reach the spot where the Hiram boy lies wounded; and one of them said to him, "Boy, guv me yer musket." "Not the gun, but its contents," cries the boy; and the Confederate falls, mortally wounded. Another raises his weapon to brain the prostrate lad; but he, too, falls, killed with his comrade's own rifle. And all this is done while the hero-boy is on the ground bleeding. An hour afterward his comrades bear the boy to a sheltered spot on the other side of the streamlet, and then the first word of complaint escapes him. As they are taking off his leg, he says, in his agony, "Oh, what will mother do?" A fortnight later his words, repeated in the Senate of Ohio, aroused the noble State to at once make provision for the widows and mothers of its soldiers. I do not know if he be dead or living, but his name should not be forgotten. It was Charles Carlton, of Franklin, Ohio. Meanwhile the Union commander is standing upon a rocky height on the other side of the narrow valley, and his quick eye has discerned, through the densely curling smoke, the real state of the unequal contest. "They are being driven," he says. "They will lose the hill if they are not supported." Instantly five hundred of the Ohio Fortieth and Forty-second, under Major Pardee and Colonel Cranor, are ordered to the rescue. Holding their cartridge-boxes above their heads, they dashed into the stream, up the hill, and into the fight, shouting, "Hurrah for Williams and the Hiram boys!" But shot and shell and canister, and the fire of four thousand muskets, are now concentrated upon the few hundred heroes. "This will never do?" cries Garfield. "Who will volunteer to carry the other mountain?" "We will?" shouts Colonel Monroe, of the Twenty-second Kentucky. "We know every inch of the ground." "Go in, then," cries Garfield, "and give them Hail Columbia!" Fording the stream lower down, they climb the ridge at the left, and in ten minutes are upon the enemy. Like the others, these Confederates are posted behind rocks, and, as they uncover their heads, become ghastly targets for the unerring Kentucky rifles. "Take good aim, and don't shoot till you see the eyes of your enemy," shouts the brave colonel. The men have never been under fire, but in a few moments are as cool as if shooting at a turkey match. "Do you see that Reb?" says one to a comrade, as a head appears above a rock. "Hit him while I'm loading." Another is bringing his cartridge to his mouth, when a bullet cuts away the powder and leaves the lead in his fingers. Shielding his arm with his body, he says, as he turns from the foe and rams home another cartridge, "There; see if you can hit that!" Another takes out a piece of hard-tack, and a ball shivers it in his hand. He swallows the remnant, and then cooly fires away again. One is brought down by a ball in the knee, and lying on the ground, rifle in hand, watches for the man who shot him. Soon the man's head rises above the rock, and the two fire at the same instant. The loyal man is struck in the mouth; but as he is borne down the hill, he splutters out, "never mind, that secesh is done for!" The next morning the Confederate is found with the whole upper part of his head shot away by the other's bullet.

The brave Kentuckians climb or leap up along the side of the mountain. Now they are hidden in the underbrush, now sheltered by the great trees, and now fully exposed in some narrow opening; but gradually they near the crest of the ridge, and at last are at its very summit. Then comes a terrible hand-to-hand struggle, and the little band of less than six hundred, overpowered by numbers, are driven far down the mountain. Soon the men rally, and as they turn, a bullet grazes the colonel's side, and buries itself in the breast of a man whom he has seen send five Confederates to the great accounting. Blood will have blood, and so he, too, goes to the judgment. Meanwhile, another cannon has opened on the hill, and round shot and canister fall thickly among the weary eleven hundred. Seeing his advance about to waver, the Union commander sends volley after volley from his entire reserve, at the central point, between his two detachments, and for a time the enemy's fire is silenced in that quarter. But soon it opens again, and then Garfield orders all but a hundred reserves upon the mountain. Then the battle grows terrible. Thicker and thicker swarm the enemy on the crest; sharp and sharper rolls the musketry along the valley, and, as volley after volley echoes among the hills, and the white smoke curls up in long wreaths from the gleaming rifles, a dense cloud gathers overhead, as if to shut out this scene of carnage from the very eye of heaven. For five hours the contest rages. Now the Union forces are driven back; then, charging up the hill, they regain the lost ground, and from behind rocks and trees, pour in their murderous volleys. Then again they are driven back, and again they charge up the hill, strewing the ground with corpses. So the bloody work goes on; so the battle wavers, till the setting sun, wheeling below the hills, glances along the dense lines of rebel steel moving down to envelop the weary eleven hundred. It is an awful moment, big with the fate of Kentucky. At its very crisis two figures stand out against the fading sky, boldly defined in the foreground. One is in the Union blue. With a little band of heroes about him, he is posted on a projecting rock, which is scarred with bullets, and in full view of both armies. His head is uncovered, his hair streaming in the wind, his face upturned in the darkening daylight, and from his soul is going up a prayer—a prayer for Sheldon and his forces. He turns his eyes to the northward, and his lip tightens as he throws off his outer coat, and, as it catches in the limb of a tree, says to his hundred men, "Come on, boys; *we* must give them Hail Columbia!"

The other is in Confederate gray. Moving out to the brow of the opposite hill, and placing a glass to his eye, he, too, takes a long look to the northward. He starts, for he sees something which the other, on lower ground, does not distinguish. He listens, and he hears a cheerful shout ring across the narrow valley; then louder it grows, while the echoes clatter back from hillside to hillside like the tumult of ten thousand voices. He, with his Confederate horde, peers out through the branches and views the opposite road. The faces just flushed with hopes of victory, now turn pale at the sight. The force from Paintville has come in sight at last. The hard-pressed men with Pardee can see nothing, but they catch new inspiration from the music of the shout; and back they answer. While the thousand voices and ten thousand echoes on the Union side are heard, only one word of reply is given from the rebel commanders' mouth. Soon he wheels his horse, and the word "Retreat!" echoes along the valley between them. It is his last word; for six rifles crack, and the Confederate major lies on the ground quivering. This is the close of the struggle. The commander in blue looks to the north again, and now, floating proudly among the trees, he sees the starry banner. It is Sheldon and re-enforcements! They are seven hundred strong. On they come like the rushing wind, filling the air with their shouting. The weary eleven hundred take up the strain, and then, above the swift pursuit, above the lessening conflict, above the last boom of the wheeling cannon, goes up the wild huzza of victory! The gallant Garfield has won the day, and rolled back the tide of disaster which has been sweeping on ever since Big Bethel. Garfield and his men are already occupying the hill-top, and a detachment are following the fleeing troops of the enemy. It was decided, however, not to pursue the enemy far, as it was not known in how bad a condition they were. As they come back from the short pursuit the young commander grasps man after man by the hand, and says, "God bless you boys, you have saved Kentucky!"

Of this battle, the genial Edmund Kirke says: "It was a wonderful battle. In the history of the late war there is not another like it. Measured by the forces engaged, the valor displayed, and the results that followed, it throws into the shade the achievements of even the mighty hosts which saved the nation. Eleven hundred foot-sore and weary men, without cannon, charge up a rocky hill, over stumps, over stones, over fallen trees, over high intrenchments, right in the face of five thousand fresh troops, with twelve pieces of artillery."

To the reader, the action may seem insignificant, but it was of considerable importance to the Federal armies at this juncture. Captain F. H. Mason, in his history of the Forty-Second Ohio Infantry, defines its place in history: "The battle of Middle Creek, trifling though it may be considered in comparison with later contests, was the first substantial victory won for the Union cause. The people of the North, giving freely of their men and their substance in response to each successive call of the government, had long and anxiously watched and waited for a little gleam of victory to show that northern valor was a match for southern impetuosity in the field. They had waited in vain since the disaster at Bull Run, during the previous summer, and hope had almost yielded to despair. The story of Garfield's success at Middle Creek came, therefore, like a benediction to the Union cause. The victory at Mill Creek proved the first wave of a returning tide."

And what was the cost of this victory? The loss to the Union army was but two killed and twenty-five wounded. The Confederates left twenty-seven dead on the field, and carried off about thirty-five more. Twenty-five men, ten horses and a quantity of army supplies were also captured. At about eight o'clock that night, at a gathering of his officers, Garfield showed them the intercepted letter of Marshall, and for the first time they knew that the valiant eleven hundred had routed an intrenched force of five thousand, strongly supported with artillery; and that their leader was fully conscious of his enemy's strength when he moved to attack him.

Towards midnight a bright light appeared in the sky in the direction Marshall had taken. The wagons and camp equipments were burning at Marshall's instigaton. The field had been won; and Buell's commission to Garfield had been faithfully executed. While war is the greatest of earthly enormities, it is strange the interest a battle-field always awakens. "We go over the ground, marking the spot where occurred some fearful struggle, or where some noble regiment went down to a swift destruction, and we do not see the pallid faces of the dead, or hear the moans of the wounded. But this is when the grass has grown green, and the smoke has cleared away, letting in the light of heaven. But when the ground is red, when the unburied dead lie in heaps, and the wounded are stretched on the trodden grass, rending the air with cries for succor, then it is we realize the real horror of the battle-field." It was thus that an informant saw it, when, with a water-bucket on his arm, he walked slowly along the mountain-side on the evening of this fearful conflict. Leaning against a tree, he saw a fair-haired youth, his hands clasped across his knees, and his head bent slightly forward. His face was flushed, and his eyes gleamed bright in the moonlight. Baring his breast to check the still-flowing blood, he spoke to him gently. The eyes looked out in a mute appeal, but the still lips gave no answer. With him the battle of life was over forever. A little farther on five dead and one wounded lay behind a rock, two of the dead fallen across the living. The living man's leg was shattered, but his wound was not mortal. "You must be in great pain; can I do anything for you?" "There are others worse off," said the man; "tend to them; then you may look after me." Moving the dead from his crushed limb, our informant went forward. One had received a ball through the neck, which destroyed the power of speech, and he made frantic signs for water; another, a dark-hued man, was lying under a tree, his thigh broken. He was stern and morose, asking only for one thing—to be put out of his misery. The other said kindly, "you will soon be taken to a surgeon; he will relieve you." Then the man faltered out, "I thank you." An old man sat at the foot of a stump, with a ball directly through the base of his brain. A ghastly smile was on his face, his eyes looked wildly out upon the night, and his breath was rapid and heavy. He was a breathing corpse—dead, and yet living. The atmosphere of death was on the earth; it was a scene on which one needs look but once to remember it forever. Thus ended this remarkable battle. It was the first wave in the tide of victory, which, with now and then an ebbing flow, swept on to the capture of Richmond. President Lincoln, when he heard of it, said to a distinguished army officer who happened to be with him, "Why did Garfield, in two weeks, do what would have taken one of you regular folks two months to accomplish?" "Because he was not educated at West Point," answered the West-Pointer, laughing. "No," replied Mr. Lincoln; "that wasn't the reason. It was because, when he was a boy, he had to work for a living."

Another night on the frozen ground; and during it, the Union commander pondered the situation. Marshall's forces were broken and demoralized. Though in full retreat, they might be overtaken and destroyed; but his own troops were half dead with fatigue and exposure, and had less than three day's rations. In these circumstances Garfield prudently decided to occupy Prestonburg, and await the arrival of additional supplies before dealing a final blow at the enemy.

On the day succeeding the battle, Garfield issued the following address to his army, which tells, in brief, the story of the campaign:

SOLDIERS OF THE EIGHTEENTH BRIGADE:—I am proud of you all! In four weeks you have marched, some eighty and some a hundred miles, over almost impassable roads. One night in four you have slept, often in the storm, with only a wintry sky above your heads. You have marched in the face of a foe of more than double your number—led on by chiefs who have won a national renown under the old flag—intrenched in hills of his own choosing, and strengthened by all the appliances of military art. With no experience but the consciousness of your own manhood, you have driven him from his strongholds, pursued his inglorious flight, and compelled him to meet you in battle. When forced to fight he sought the shelter of rocks and hills. You drove him from his position, leaving scores of his bloody dead unburied. His artillery thundered against you, but you compelled him to flee by the light of his burning stores, and to leave even the banner of his rebellion behind him. I greet you as brave men. Our common country will not forget you. She will not forget the sacred dead who fell beside you, nor those of your comrades who won scars of honor on the field. I have recalled you from the pursuit that you may regain vigor for still greater exertions. Let no one tarnish his well-earned honor by any act unworthy an American soldier. Remember your duties as American citizens, and sacredly respect the rights and property of those with whom you may come in contact. Let it not be said that good men dread the approach of an American army. Officers and soldiers, your duty has been nobly done. For this I thank you.

On the 11th of January, the troops took possession of Prestonburg; and the remainder of the campaign was but the working out in detail of the result already secured. In after years, speaking of this campaign, Garfield said: "It was a very rash and imprudent affair on my part. If I had been an officer of more experience I probably should not have made the attack. As it was, having gone into the army with the notion that fighting was our business, I didn't know any better." And Judge Clark, of the Forty-second Ohio, adds: "And during it all Garfield was the soldiers' friend. Such was his affection for the men, that he would divide his last rations with them, and nobody ever found anything better at head-quarters than the rest got." In illustration of this we will here introduce an incident. Garfield's treatment of soldiers was always thoughtful and tender. He would rise at four o'clock in the morning in cold weather and go out to see if the boys were comfortable, and frequently paused in his lonely rounds to tuck their blankets under them. "Thank you, sir," they would say, with tears in their eyes; "this reminds me of my boyhood days, and my good old mother." His desire was so great for their comfort that he had no scruples in robbing himself to serve them. On one occasion, when there had been no arrival of supplies for several inclement days, he was taking his regular morning walk, and discovered a man with only one boot on. "My poor fellow," he said, his eyes filling with tears, "the United States government is to be gravely rebuked for permitting this shocking outrage; here, take this." He relieved his left foot of the leather thereon, tossed the boot to the suffering soldier, and limped on, singing a psalm.

It is stated that had it not been for their brave commander, the Eighteenth Brigade, just after the engagement so successfully ended, would have been without anything to eat. Less than three days' rations were then on hand, and heavy rains had set in. The roads soon became impassable to wagon trains, and the outlook was anything but encouraging. Even before the first exultation of victory had passed they began to realize that they were hedged in more completely than if Marshall's forces surrounded them. The river was the only resource; but the Big Sandy was now swollen beyond its banks, and its rapid current, filled with floating logs and uptorn trees, rendered navigation a thing of seeming impossibility—at least the boatmen thought so. The oldest boatmen of the district shook their heads, and refused to attempt the perilous voyage. In these circumstances, Brown, the scout and ex-canal-boatman, who had returned from his circuit of Marshall's camp with a bullet through his hat, which had clipped off one of his black curls, said to Garfield, "It's which and t'other, Gineral Jim—starvin' or drownin'. I'd ruther drown nur starve. So, guv the word, and, dead or alive, I'll git down the river!" These two brave men—Garfield and Brown—boldly started down the treacherous stream in a small boat. Caring more for the comfort and good cheer of their companions than for any present danger, they were willing, at least, to make an effort to relieve the pressure which want must soon make. The river now was a raging torrent, sixty feet in depth, and, in many places above the tops of the tall trees which grew along its margin. In some deep and narrow gorges, where the steep banks shut closely down upon the stream, these trees had been undermined at the roots, and, falling inward, had locked their arms together, forming a net-work that well nigh prevented the passage of the small skiff and its two navigators. Where a small skiff could scarcely pass, could they run a large steamboat loaded with provisions? Other men might ask this question, but not the back-woods boy who had learned navigation on the waters of the Ohio and Pennsylvania Canal. Arriving at Catlettsburg, at the mouth of the river, in safety, he ordered a small steamer which belonged to the quartermaster's service, and known as the *Sandy Valley*, to take on a load of supplies and start on the return trip. The captain and crew were ordered to steam up at once, but refused, deeming the attempt as foolhardy and altogether beyond reason. Life and property must be at stake to contend against so many odds and the raging current; but Garfield knew no refusing, and would tolerate no hesitancy. The steamer was loaded, and having again ordered the captain and his crew on board, and stationing a competent army officer on deck to see that the captain did his duty, he himself went to the helm and set out, headed up stream. Still the captain protested, but he was silenced by Garfield's determination; and all he could do was to make the best of his situation. Brown he stationed at the bow, where, with a long fending pole in his hand, he was to keep one eye on the floating logs and uprooted trees, the other on the chicken-hearted captain. The river surged and boiled and whirled against the boat, tossing her about as if she were a cockle-shell. With every turn of her wheels she trembled from stem to stern, and with a full head of steam could only stagger along at the rate of three miles an hour. It was a wild torrent to run against; but the undaunted leader pressed on, himself standing at the wheel forty hours out of forty-eight. When night came the captain begged to tie up till morning, for breasting that flood in the dark was sheer madness; but Brown cried out, "Put her ahead, Gineral Jim;" and Garfield clutched the helm, and drove her on through the darkness.

It was during the second night that the most exciting incident occurred. At this time they came to a sudden bend in the stream, where the swift current formed a furious whirlpool, and this, catching the laboring boat, whirled her suddenly around, and drove her, head on, into the quicksands. Mattocks were plied, and excavations made around the imbedded bow, and the bowsman uttered oaths loud enough to have raised a small earthquake; but still the boat was immovable. She was stuck fast in the mud, and every effort to move her was fruitless. Garfield now conceived a new plan for moving the boat. Ordering a small boat to be lowered, and the men told to take a line to the other bank, by which to warp the steamer free; but the captain, and now the crew, protested it was certain death to tempt that foaming torrent at midnight. Indecision and hesitation never can accomplish anything, and Garfield knew this full well. Immediately our hero entered the small boat, the faithful Brown following. He took the helm, and laid her bow across the stream, but the swift current swept them downward. After incredible labor they made the opposite bank, but far below the steamboat. Closely hugging the shore, they now crept up the stream, opposite the *Sandy Valley*, and tying the line to a log fastened between two large trees, the boat was finally drawn off. Two impossibilities now conquered before the very eyes of the incredulous crew, there was no more doubting. They began to realize what manner of man he was with whom they were dealing, and further fears vanished. All that night and all the next day, and all the following night, they struggled with the furious river, Garfield never but once leaving the helm, and then for only a few hours' sleep, which he snatched in his clothes in the daytime. At last they rounded to at the Union camp, and then went up

THE PERILOUS TRIP UP THE BIG SANDY RIVER.

a cheer that might have been heard all over Kentucky. His waiting men, frantic with joy, seized their glorious commander, and were with difficulty prevented from bearing him on their shoulders to his quarters. Thus another noble deed of heroism was accomplished.

As we shall not have occasion again to make mention of Brown, the brave fellow who accompanied Garfield on this famous trip and performed other valuable services, some of which we have mentioned, it may be of interest to my readers to know what was his fate and fortune in later years. He came to a sad ending. In a letter Garfield once said of Brown: "I think he was never perfectly happy till he helped me to navigate the little steamer up the Big Sandy in the high water. Indeed, I could not have done that without his aid. He was about forty years old—a short, stocky, sailor-looking fellow, somewhat bloated with hard drinking; in short, he was a rare combination of good and bad qualities, with strong traits—a ruined man; and yet, underneath the ruins, a great deal of generous, self-sacrificing, noble-heartedness, which made one deplore his fall, and yet like him. He went North on some personal business just before I left the Sandy valley, and I received a dirty note from him, written from Buffalo, in which he said he should meet me somewhere in 'the tide of battle,' and fight by my side again, but I have not heard from him since."

This was in 1864. Twelve years afterward, General Garfield delivered an address at Ithaca, New York. After the meeting adjourned a heavy hand was laid upon his shoulder, and, turning about, he saw his ex-scout and old boat companion. Stepping up to the general he spoke one word—the old password which, known only to those two, had so often been used in the perilous times when Brown, unknown, and forced into a loss of his own identity, was nevertheless doing loyal service to his distressed country. At the familiar sound, the general started, as if thunderstruck, and then with the exclamation, "Brown! is this you?" he flung his arms about the poor fellow as if he had found a lost brother, and pressed him to that loving heart. Nor did the meeting end in a mere effusion of feeling. The noble general at once sought out prominent men in Ithaca, and commended Brown to their care, giving them an inkling of his valuable services. He was even a more perfect ruin than before—with bleared eyes, bloated face, and garments that were half tatters. He had come, he said, while the tears rolled down his cheeks, to that quiet place to die, and now he could die in peace, because he had seen his "gineral." Garfield gave him money, and got him quarters among some kind people, and left him, telling him to try to be a man; but, in any event, to let him know if he ever needed further help. A year or more passed, and no word came from Brown; but then the superintendent of the public hospital at Buffalo wrote the general that a man was there very sick, who in his delirium talked of him, of the Ohio Canal, and of the Sandy Valley expedition. Garfield knew at once that it was Brown, and immediately forwarded funds to the hospital, asking that he should have every possible care and comfort. The letter which acknowledged the remittance announced that the poor fellow had died—died muttering, in his delirium, the name, "Jim Garfield." Garfield gave him a decent burial, and wrote to certain gentlemen instructing them to see to the decoration of Brown's grave, and to render assistance in procuring a pension. And this was the last of the poor fellow.

Consternation filled the minds of the ignorant inhabitants, occupying the valley of the Big Sandy, after the Middle Creek battle. The terror-stricken rebels retreating, spread unwarranted stories of the inhuman treatment that all might expect at the hands of the "blue coats." Terrified and frightened they were rapidly desolating the country, flying to the mountains for protection and safety. To allay this alarm, and restore society to more of its normal condition, Garfield, during the week following the battle, issued the following proclamation:

HEAD-QUARTERS EIGHTEENTH BRIGADE,
PAINTVILLE, KY., Jan. 16, 1852.

CITIZENS OF THE SANDY VALLEY:—I have come among you to restore the honor of the Union, and to bring back the old banner which you all once loved, but which, by the machinations of evil men, and by mutual misunderstandings, has been dishonored among you. To those who are in arms against the Federal Government I offer only the alternative of battle or unconditional surrender; but to those who have taken no part in this war, who are in no way aiding or abetting the enemies of the Union, even to those who hold sentiments adverse to the Union, but yet give no aid and comfort to its enemies, I offer the full protection of the Government, both in their persons and property.

Let those who have been seduced away from the love of their country, to follow after and aid the destroyers of our peace, lay down their arms, return to their homes, bear true allegiance to the Federal Government, and they also shall enjoy like protection. The army of the Union wages no war of plunder, but comes to bring back the prosperity of peace. Let all peace-loving citizens who have fled from their homes, return, and resume again the pursuits of peace and industry. If citizens have suffered from any outrages by the soldiers under my command, I invite them to make known their complaints to me, and their wrongs shall be redressed, and the offenders punished. I expect the frends of the Union in this valley to banish from among them all private feuds, and to let a liberal-minded love of country direct their conduct toward those who have been so sadly estranged and misguided. I hope that these days of turbulence may soon end, and the better days of the Republic may soon return.

(Signed) J. A. GARFIELD,
Colonel commanding Brigade.

Encouraged by this promise of protection, the people soon issued from their hiding-places, and began to flock about the Union head-quarters. From them various reports were received of the whereabouts and intentions of Marshall. By some it was said that, re-enforced by three Virginia regiments and six field-pieces, he had made a stand, and was fortifying himself in a strong position about thirty miles above, on the waters of the Big Beaver; by others, that he was merely collecting provisions, and preparing to retreat into Tennessee as soon as the runs and rivers should become passable. The best information, however, indicated that Marshall had made a stand, and was still within the limits of Kentucky. It was very important that Garfield should learn his exact position, and to this end he dispatched a body of a hundred horsemen, under Captain Jenkins, of the Ohio cavalry, with orders to go up the Big Sandy as far as Piketon, and not to return until they had ascertained the position and intentions of the enemy. It was now established beyond a doubt that the rebel army had no more foot-hold in the State. Jenkins did his work well, and Garfield soon was in possession of the desired information. Marshall himself had evacuated Kentucky, but his forces were not entirely driven from the State, as sundry small parties still remained, endeavoring to secure recruits for the forces in Virginia, and destroying many things which would have been of use to the Union soldiers. They had fortified a strong position at Pound Gap, and radiating from there, swarms of guerillas were still overrunning all the lower counties, robbing and murdering defenceless men and women. More important still, was the information obtained by Jordan, the scout, after surmounting many difficulties and encountering great dangers, that Marshall had issued an order for a grand muster of the Confederate militia on the 15th of March. They were to meet at the "Pound," in the rear of their intrenchments, and it was expected they would muster in sufficient force to enter Kentucky, and drive the Union forces before them. To prevent this, Garfield dispatched the Eighteenth Brigade into Eastern Kentucky where it performed its last notable exploit.

Pound Gap is the best thoroughfare between Virginia and south-eastern Kentucky. It is a wild and irregular opening in the Cumberland Mountains, about forty-five miles south-west of Piketon. It is the only channel of wagon communication in that section, and takes its name from a fertile tract of meadow-land which skirts the southerly base of the mountains, and is enclosed by a narrow stream called Pound Fork. In the early history of the district this mountain locality was the home of a tribe of Indians, who made periodical expeditions into Virginia for plunder. Returning with the stolen cattle of the settlers, they pastured them in this meadow-enclosure, and hence it acquired the name of the "Pound," which in time it gave to both the Gap and streamlet.

In this "Pound," and on the summit of the gorge through which the road passes, the Confederates had built log-huts, capable of quartering twelve hundred men; and across the opening of the Gap they had erected a formidable breastwork that completely blocked the passage, where five hundred could hold against five thousand. For several weeks Pound Gap had been garrisoned by about six hundred Confederate militia, under Major Thompson; and though incapable of effective service in the field, they had held this gate-way into Virginia, and maintained a constant reign of terror among the Union citizens of all the lower counties. Issuing from their stronghold on the mountains, small parties of this gang would descend into the valleys, rob and murder peaceable inhabitants, and, before pursuit could be begun, would again return behind their breastworks, laden with booty and plunder. Many of these predatory bands had been captured, in consequence of the ceaseless activity of the loyal Kentucky cavalry; but as soon as one party was made prisoners another would appear in the valley, until it was evident that the only way to effectually stop their incursions was to break up their nest on the mountain. This Garfield had long determined to do. He had waited only for reliable information as to the strength and position of the guerillas, and for a definite description of the route to be taken to get in the rear of their intrenchments. Garfield at once determined to forestall the intended gathering of forces on the 15th of March, and to disperse the entire swarm of guerillas. With two hundred and twenty of the Fortieth

Ohio, under Colonel Cranor; two hundred of the Forty-second Ohio, under Major Pardee; one hundred and eighty of the Twenty-second Kentucky, under Major Cook; and a hundred cavalry, under Major M'Laughlin, he set out on the following morning, with three days' rations in the haversacks of the men, and a quantity of provisions packed on the backs of mules. The highways were deep in mud, and the countless rivulets which ramify through this mountain region were filled with ice, and swollen into rushing torrents; but pressing on over the rough roads, and in the midst of a drenching rain, the little army, late on the night of the second day, reached Elkhorn Creek, a small stream which flows along the northern base of the mountains, and empties into the Big Sandy, only two miles below the Confederate position. There they went into camp on the wet ground, and waited for the morning. Meanwhile Garfield endeavored to find out the enemy's exact position and numbers, as also the condition of the avenues of approach. Meager information was all that could be obtained, but it was sufficient to form a plan of attack. One main path led up to the gap. Garfield's plan was to send his small party of horsemen up the road to make a demonstration against the enemy's intrenchments, and to engage his attention, while, with the infantry, he should climb the steep side of the mountain, and filing along the narrow ledge of rocks on its summit, reach the Gap, and attack the flank of the Confederate position. To prove successful, the movement must be executed with the utmost secrecy, and a guide must be obtained to conduct the infantry over the mountain. Every male resident of the vicinity declared that there was no practicable route. The mountain was steep, and in some places precipitous. It was tangled with dense thickets, obstructed with fallen logs, and covered with huge bowlders, which, coated with ice and snow, formed an almost impassable barrier to the passage of any living thing save the panther or the catamount. But if, in the face of all these obstacles, the summit were at last gained by the adventurous band, they would be obliged to thread for a long distance a narrow ledge, which rose like a knife-edge, and was in places so narrow that two persons could not pass it abreast. This ledge was buried three feet deep in yielding snow; one false step would be death, and ten determined men could dispute the passage of an army. Though tempted with liberal offers of money, not one of the natives would undertake to guide the expedition. In these circumstances, Garfield lay down at midnight on the floor of a wretched log-shanty near the foot of the mountain. The prospect was in no way encouraging; in fact, the difficulties seemed well-nigh insurmountable. But turning back was out of the question. Guide or no guide, he would attempt to scale the mountain in the morning.

With these thoughts in his mind, he dropped off to sleep. Before morning he was aroused by a number of men entering his apartment—one of them said: "Colonel, this old fellow has just come into camp, and offers to guide us over he mountains. He says he knows every road of this region, and can lead us to he rebel nest in safety." Garfield raised himself on his blanket, and by the lim light of the logs that were smouldering on the hearth looked at the old native. He was apparently not far from seventy, with a tall, bent form, and long hair and beard which were almost snowy of whiteness. He wore the common homespun of the district, and over his shoulder carried, slung by a stout leather thong, a brightly burnished squirrel rifle. His enormous beard and huge slouch hat more than half hid his face, but enough of it was exposed to show a tawny, smoke-begrimed skin, and strongly marked, determined features. Hastily scanning him from head to foot, the Union officer said, smiling: "You! old man, do you think you can climb the mountain?" "I hev done it, gineral, many and many a time," said the native in a voice that sounded much like a cracked kettle. "I know, but in the winter the slope is a sheet of ice and three feet of snow on the summit." "I komed down it not ten days ago. Whar I kin come down ye kin go up." "I should think so—up or down. Is there a bridle-path we can follow?" "Yes, eight miles below. But ye'd better make yer own path. Ye must cum unto them unbeknown and sudden, and to do that ye must foller the path squirrels travil." "And do you think we can get over it safely?" "Yes, if ye's men of narve as means to do what they has come about." "Well," continued Garfield, after a pause, "what induces an old man like you to undertake a thing so hazardous?" "The hope to rid ther kentry of a set of murderin' thieves as is carrying terror and death inter every poor man's home in all the valley." "And what reward do you look for?" "Nary reward—only your word that I shall go as I come, with no one to let or hinder me." Garfield took a long, steady look at him, and replied, "Very well, I'll trust you. Be here early in the morning."

In the morning the snow was falling so thickly that objects only a few rods distant were totally invisible; but at nine o'clock the little body of cavalry was sent up the road to engage the attention of the enemy, and draw him from his intrenchments; and then the infantry was set in motion. In a long, bristling, serpent-like column, catching at every twig and shrub and fallen log that lay in their way, they clambered slowly up the icy mountain side, steadying their steps as well as they could by their bayonets and musket barrels. The ridge at this point rises two thousand feet above the valley, and half way up breaks into abrupt precipices, which defy the approach of any foot but that of the wild animal. The ascent was long and toilsome, but at last they reached the summit of the mountain; and here they paused to rest their tired limbs, and catch a glimpse of the magnificent view that stretched away far below them. They were above the storm, and the snow was falling thickly lower down the mountain, but here the eye could range for thirty miles, east and west, into three states, and over a most enchanting country. They now were two and a half miles from the point where the Confederate garrison was posted, and noiselessly they set out again, for discovery was only another name for destruction. It was a march of three hours. Garfield led the way through tangled thickets, over ice-coated logs, across abrupt chasms, to a point where a view was had of the fortifications in the Gap below them. "We are within half a mile of their position," he whispered to Lieutenant Lake, who had come up, and was standing beside him. "Yonder is their outside picket; but the way is clear—if we press on at the double-quick we have them." The picket had now descried the advancing column, and, firing his gun, he set out at the top of his speed for the intrenchments. A dozen muskets made shrill music about his ears, but he kept on, and the eager blue coats followed. When within sight of the camp, a line was thrown down along the eastern slope of the mountain, and, pressing rapidly forward, was formed along the deep gorge through which the high-road passes. Up to this time the Confederates had been skirmishing with the cavalry in front of their breastworks; but now they gathered on the hill directly opposite the advanced position of the Union infantry. To try the range, Garfield sent a volley across the gorge, and, as the smoke cleared away, he saw the unformed line melt like mist into the opposite forest. The enemy's position being now understood, the men of the Fortieth and Forty-second Ohio were ordered to the already formed left wing, and then along the line rang the words, "Press forward; scale the hill, and carry it with the bayonet." A ringing shout was the only answer, and then the long column swept down the ridge, across the ravine, through the Confederate camp, and up the opposite mountain. The enemy fell gradually back among the trees, but when the Union bayonets clambered the hill, they broke and ran in the wildest confusion. The Ohio boys followed, firing as they ran, and for a few moments the mountain echoed with the sharp, quick reports of half a thousand rifles; but pursuit in the dense forest was impossible, and soon the recall was sounded. In a fight of less than twenty minutes the Confederates were utterly routed, being chased by the Union cavalry far into Virginia; and their camp, consisting of sixty log houses, was in the hands of the attacking party.

After spending the night in these comfortable quarters, General Garfield burned the camp, and all the stores which he could not carry away, and returned to Piketon, in less than five days from the start, without the loss of a man, having marched over ninety miles in the worst of winter weather, and, with a handful of men, carried an almost impregnable position, defended by superior numbers. Only seven of his men were wounded; but this well nigh bloodless victory rid east Kentucky of Confederate rule forever. So ended the campaign in eastern Kentucky, of which Garfield was the principal actor. The gigantic scale on which the operations of our late war was conducted has dwarfed somewhat the achievements of individual actors. If in the history of either of the other wars in which our people have engaged, whether before or after the Declaration of Independence, such a chapter should be found as the narration of Garfield's Kentucky campaign, it would alone have made the name of its leader immortal. "The result of the campaign is a matter of history. The skill, the endurance, the extraordinary energy shown by Garfield, the courage he imparted to his men, raw and untried as himself, the measures he adopted to increase his force and to create in the enemy's mind exaggerated estimates of his numbers, bore perfect fruit in the routing of Marshall, the capture of his camp, the dispersion of his force, and emancipation of an important territory from the control of the Rebellion. Coming at the close of a long series of disasters to the Union arms, Garfield's victory had an unusual and extraneous importance, and in the popular judgment elevated the young commander to the rank of a military hero. With less than two thousand men in his entire command, with a mobilized force of only eleven hundred, without cannon, he had met an army of five thousand men and defeated them—driving Marshall's forces successively from two strongholds of their own selection, fortified with abundant artillery. Buell declared that his services had called into action the highest qualities of a soldier, and President Lincoln supplemented these words of praise by the more substantial reward of a brigadier-general's commission, to bear date from the day of his decisive victory over Marshall."* Fighting was over, and he was soon to be transferred to another sphere of action.

When the official news of Colonel Garfield's victory at Middle Creek reached the head-quarters of the department, the following general order was issued, indicating General Buell's appreciation of the results:

HEAD-QUARTERS DEPARTMENT OF THE OHIO,
LOUISVILLE, KY., January 20, 1862.

General Order, No. 40.

The General Commanding takes occasion to thank Colonel Garfield and his troops for their successful campaign against the rebel force under General Marshall on the Big Sandy, and their gallant conduct in battle. They have overcome formidable difficulties in the character of the country, the condition of the roads, and the inclemency of the season; and, without artillery, have in several engagements, terminating with the battle on Middle Creek on the 10th instant, driven the enemy from his intrenched positions, and forced him back into the mountains, with the loss of a large amount of baggage and stores, and many of his men killed or captured. These services have called into action the highest qualities of a soldier—fortitude, perseverance, courage.

By command of General Buell.

JAMES B. FRY,
A. A. G., Chief of Staff.

---

*Blaine's Eulogy.

CHAPTER X.

CHIEF OF STAFF TO ROSECRANS.

"Our best beloved of all the brave
That ever for freedom fought,
And, all the wonders of the wave
For fatherland were wrought!
He was the manner of man to show
How victories may be won;
So swift, you scarcely saw the blow;
You look'd—the deed was done."

'Tis a principle of war, that when you can use the lightning 'tis better than cannon.—NAPOLEON.

What success attended Garfield's commandership we have already seen. Upon the receipt of the congratulatory dispatch quoted in the preceding chapter, our young hero-commander's satisfaction was complete. What he had accomplished met the sanction of his superior officer, and this was sufficient of itself to demonstrate how well he had performed his duties. He had met the enemy and won the day. Humphrey Marshall was now far beyond the borders of Kentucky. The country shortly before terrorized and panic-stricken was once more composed; and the presence of the Union forces gave the inhabitants renewed confidence.

In every path of life how very essential is early success to young men. It is the animus they need to give them confidence in their powers. Just as the sunshine is necessary to the growth and development of vegetation, so is success and appreciation of success necessary to the man whose powers are expanding. True, success does not always attend the early efforts of many successful men, but this is no argument to disprove the fact already laid down. If the plant, whose growth depends upon this source of heat, is deprived of sunshine, it will be the more tardy of development, and oftentimes withers and dies before the highest development is reached. The success, therefore, attending Garfield's early undertakings gives us a key which will unlock some of the secrets of his later accomplishments. We have found Garfield strong in all directions, and when the time came for action he was always ready. Here is where young men fail too often.

Sufficient attention is seldom given to early efforts. That young man whose first undertakings are successful, other things being equal, will become the successful man in after years. There are some, again, who, failing with the first attempts, only strive the harder to be successful the second time; but the tendency is to discouragement and discomfiture. Were young men more careful and determined to be successful from the start, more would be accomplished by them. "It is a sad thing," says a certain writer, "to feel, even when we have done our best, that we have foundered in our earthly voyage, while those who set sail with us, pass by with streamers flying and swelling sail. There never was a truer sentiment uttered than that quoted some years years ago, at a scientific meeting in England, by Professor Owen, from the note-book of the late Dr. Hunter; namely, that no man was ever great who *wanted* to be. Great works do not make greatness; they only reveal it. They are the outlines of an inward being; they are the embodiments of the soul, which was *born great.* The world is always groping about for men of ability and integrity to fill its places of responsibility, and those who have these qualifications, if they do not hide them from shyness, are almost sure to find employment."

A reward greater than the thanks from head-quarters yet awaited Garfield. The news of the happy victory and close of the campaign hastened to Washington, and such was the satisfaction expressed by the authorities that Garfield was at once raised to the high position of Brigadier-General, with his commission dated back to January 10.

On the 19th of January, General Thomas defeated Zollicoffer's army, killed its general, and chased the remnants into Tennessee. Kentucky was now safe, and the extreme right wing of Johnston's Confederate army was broken. Grant followed immediately with his successful move on the left wing of that army. Other important actions soon followed, and the South was completely nonplussed. Enthusiasm ran high in the North, and triumphantly our armies began marching into the enemy's country.

Garfield's successes at this time were but the precursors of the greater ones that were to follow, and on that account they are the more valuable. This was the only independent command ever held by James A. Garfield; but by it he showed himself possessed of qualities which would, on a wider field, have ranked him among the great commanders of the Union. Thenceforward the military career of General Garfield was merged in that of the Army of the Cumberland. He held no separate command, and hence the traces of his great military abilities are lost in the general operations of the army, or only now and then seen in the complimentary allusions to his services which were so often made by his superior officers. It is no doubt true that to him, more than to any other man, was due the admirable organization of that army, which, despite its misfortunes, saved the South-west to the Union.

Previous to the Pound Gap expedition, General Garfield had corresponded with General Rosecrans, then commanding the Department of West Virginia, and they had united in proposing to the War Department a plan to destroy the East Tennessee, Virginia and Georgia Railroad, then the only direct line of communication between the Gulf States and Richmond. General Rosecrans was to send a force up New river, in West Virginia, to cut the railroad near Newbern, while General Garfield was to pass through Pound Gap, and cut it at Abingdon, Virginia, and destroy the salt-works at that place. The two great Confederate armies of the East and the West were at that time fully occupied, and the destruction could have been made very complete. Orders received by General Garfield, on the 23d of March, 1862, directed him to report, at once, with his command, to General Buell, at Louisville, and thus the plan was abandoned. From these instructions it was learned that the Army of the Ohio, under Buell, was to move southward into Tennessee, where they would join with the Army of the Tennessee, which, under General Grant, was on its way to the Tennessee River, after the victories of Forts Donelson and Henry, and with the united force, move forward to Corinth, Mississippi. A small force of Garfield's men were stationed in the valley of the Big Sandy, to hold it; with the rest he pushed on to Louisville, and there found an order to report to Buell in person, at Nashville. Arriving there, he learned that Buell was hurrying to the relief of Grant, at Pittsburg Landing; and, overtaking him on the 5th of April, about thirty miles south of Columbia, was at once assigned to the command of the Twentieth Brigade, Sixth Division of the Army of the Ohio, General Thomas J. Wood commanding. General Wood was making all possible effort to reach the Union forces under Grant, as the approaching battle with Sidney Johnson was anticipated as very probably a battle of the greatest importance. Being delayed at Duck River, General Nelson, upon learning that General Grant was already at Savannah, obtained permission of Buell to pass the river, as best they might, and hurry on to Grant's assistance. Word had been received from Grant, stating that he was in no present danger, and the request was granted Nelson very reluctantly. But this hurried march was what saved Grant's army at Shiloh. The remaining forces followed Nelson at intervals—Crittenden's division came second, McCook's third, and then Wood's (with whom was Garfield), and last, Thomas'. It had been decided to halt at Waynesboro for a day's rest, but the haste of Nelson impressed his commanders-in-arms with a like desire to be at the front, and they pushed on. In this manner Nelson reached Savannah on the 5th of April. Grant's army was at Pittsburg Landing, ten miles further up the river. Of the unexpected and disastrous battle which commenced on the morning of April 6, and lasted two days, all readers of history are familiar with. About ten that day, Grant, hearing that Wood, with the second division of Buell's army, had arrived at Savannah, sent him the following order: "You will move your command with the utmost dispatch, to the river at this point (landing), where steamers will be in readiness to convey you to Pittsburg." Still later in the day another message was sent to the commanding officer of Buell's forces, urging him to hurry up. It is not necessary to recount here how thoroughly the Union forces were whipped on the first day, and how extremely probable it seemed that the defeat would turn into a rout. But here, as on many other fields later in the bloody conflict, Ohio saved the day. When a halt was called on the evening of the 6th, it was determined by Grant that the Ohio troops were to form upon the left in the morning, and the attack was to be renewed. During the night of the 6th Buell busied himself in getting his troops up. Nelson's column, and nearly all of Crittenden's and McCook's divisions were ferried across the river and put in position. All night long the gun-boats dropped shells at intervals on the rebel lines, and the woods caught fire, lighting up the battle-field for miles away. But for a merciful shower of rain, thousands of helpless wounded would have been burned to death on that blazing battle-field. The orders were: "As soon as it is light enough to see, attack with a heavy skirmish line, and when you have found the enemy, throw upon him your whole force, leaving no reserve."

With the first gray of dawn this order was put in execution. The Ohio troops were given the left of the field. Grant's army, or what of it could be gathered together, undertook to form and maintain the right. As rapidly as the Ohioans could come up they went into action. As may be inferred, they fought with splendid energy. During the early part of the day, Grant met the First Ohio marching toward the northern part of the field, and immediately in front of a position which it was important should be taken. The regiment on the left was fighting hard, but about to yield; in fact, had given away, when Grant called upon the Ohio boys to change direction and charge. The soldiers, with a cheer, obeyed and the retreating troops, seing what was going on, took new courage, and rallying with loud shouts, drove the enemy from their strong position. Garfield had all this time been actively engaged in every possible exertion to bring up his brigade in time to assist before either defeat or victory silenced the cannonading that he so distinctly heard. About 1 P. M., he reached the front, and with a wild cheer his men dashed at the rebels, he leading through the storm of lead. The fresh onslaught, in which Garfield's brigade participated, changed the fortunes of the day, and the rebels were soon flying from where they had fought so long and well. The Union troops were too much exhausted for pursuit, and halting in the camps from which they had been driven the day before, were content to call it a victory. On the 9th, the War Department issued the following complimentary order to all concerned: "The thanks of the Department are hereby given to Generals Grant and Buell, and their forces, for the glorious repulse of Beauregard, at Pittsburg, in Tennessee."

On the morning of the 8th, Garfield's brigade formed a part of Sherman's advance, and participated in a sharp encounter with the enemy's rear guard, a few miles beyond the battle-field. Halleck, commander-in-chief, did not reach Pittsburg until April 11th, and the march then upon Corinth, the objective point of the campaign, and where Beauregard had retreated, was remarkably slow. Parallels of fortification to cover each day's advance were constructed; and six weeks were consumed in marching the thirty miles which lay between the army and Corinth. It was not until the 21st of May that the armies were fairly in line, three miles from Corinth, and everything was in readiness for the expected battle. But all the preparations for battle were of no use, and when Halleck was ready to engage Beauregard, the latter was no longer in Corinth. The wily enemy had evacuated the place without a struggle. The vast Union army, which had been massed for this campaign, having no foe to oppose it, was resolved into its original elements. Garfield's brigade had the empty honor of being among the earliest that entered the abandoned town. Then when General Buell, turning eastward, sought to prepare for a new aggressive campaign against Chattanooga, with his inadequate forces, General Garfield was assigned the task of rebuilding the bridges and reopening the Memphis and Chattanooga railroad, eastward from Corinth to Decatur. This road had to be almost entirely rebuilt, as the supplies for the army were to come along its line. If a culvert was to be built, Garfield planned a swift, but substantial way to build it; his mind was of the rare sort, which combines speculative with practical powers; his cheerfulness electrified the men, as it had the students at Hiram; and, in the drudgery of the work, from which the inspiration of battle was wholly wanting, it was he who encouraged their unwanton toil. Crossing the Tennessee here he advanced to Huntsville, where he remained during the rest of that campaign, carrying out every instruction received, with absolute fidelity, and at all times with perfect success.

One of the constant objects of General Buell during the time General Garfield was engaged in bridge-building, was the enforcement of discipline and the reduction of the somewhat loose habits of the men of his command to the army standard. Courts-martial were frequent, and it was not always easy to find officers thoroughly fitted for such duties. Garfield's legal mind, his dispassionate, full-reasoned judgment, singled him out from among his fellows for just such work. His first detail in this class of army experience was the case of Colonel Turchin, charged with committing gross excesses. These charges were neglect of duty, to the prejudice of good order and discipline, in permitting the wanton and disgraceful pillage of the town of Athens, Alabama; conduct unbecoming an officer and a gentleman in failing to pay a hotel bill in the town; insubordination in disobeying the orders against the molestation of peaceful citizens in persons and property. Some of the specifications particularized very shameful conduct. The court found him guilty (except as to the hotel bill story) and sentenced him to dismissal from the service. Six members recommended him to clemency, but by the determination of General Buell, the sentence was executed. The newspapers, and especially those of Chicago, took up the case and championed the colonel. Returning to Chicago, a public reception was tendered him, and the President, as if to endorse the deeds of the disgraced colonel, appointed him a brigadier.

While lying before Corinth, as well as throughout his military career, Garfield continued the study of the classics. His love of literature was still ardent, and the several volumes he carried with him were eagerly pursued as opportunity was granted While Garfield was in camp, after the battle of Shiloh, a trifling incident occurred, which showed the effects of his anti-slavery education. I give the narrative as it is related by a member of his staff.

"One day," says the officer, "I noticed a fugitive slave come rushing into camp with a bloody head, and greatly frightened. He had only passed my tent a moment when a regular bully of a fellow came riding up, and with a volley of oaths began to ask after his 'nigger.' General Garfield was not present, and he passed on to the division commander. This division commander was a sympathizer with the theory that fugitives should be returned to their masters, and that the Union soldiers should be made the instruments for returning them. He accordingly wrote a mandatory order to General Garfield, in whose command the negro was supposed to be hiding, telling him to hunt out and deliver over the property of the outraged citizen. I stated the case as fully as I could to General Garfield before handing him the order, but did not color my statement in any way. He took the order, and deliberately wrote on it the following endorsement: 'I respectfully, but positively, decline to allow my command to search for, or deliver up, any fugitive slaves. I conceive that they are here for quite another purpose.

The command is open, and no obstacles will be placed in the way of the search.' I read the endorsement, and was alarmed. I expected that, if it was returned, the result would be that the general would be court-martialed. I told him my fears. He simply replied: 'The matter may as well be tested first as last. Right is right, and I do not propose to mince matters at all. My soldiers are here for far other purposes than hunting and returning fugitive slaves. My people on the Western Reserve of Ohio, did not send my boys and myself down here to do that kind of business, and they will back me up in my action.' He would not alter the endorsement, and the order was returned. Nothing ever came of the matter further, although a court-martial, with a swift sentence of death, was the remedy for refusals to obey orders. But no court-martial was held. This was the first instance in which a Union officer refused to return a fugitive slave. The principle of Garfield's action was soon afterward embodied in a general order, and thus received the endorsement of the War Department. From that time the order obtained that no soldier in the army of the Republic should hound a human being back to fetters.

The work of reconstructing the railroad completed, Garfield established his head-quarters at Huntsville, Alabama, one of the most beautiful places in America. But the exposures of army life, the hardships encountered in rebuilding the railroad, the fierce rays of the sun, in an unaccustomed climate, weakened his constitution. The old tendency to fever and ague, contracted in the days of his tow-path experience on the Ohio Canal, was now aggravated in the malarious climate of the South, and Garfield returned home on sick-leave, on the 1st of August. Hardly had he started for Ohio, when the Secretary of War, who seems, at this early day, to have formed a high estimate of Garfield, which he continued to entertain through the war, issued orders to him to proceed to Cumberland Gap, and relieve General George W. Morgan of his command. But when they were received, Garfield was too ill to leave his bed. Garfield's reports of the various courts-martial, conducted to reduce the Army of the Ohio to a basis of strict military order, still further heightened the opinion of his abilities entertained there. A month later, the Secretary ordered him to report in person, at Washington, as soon as his health would permit. Shortly after this, he again bade farewell to his girlish wife, and started for the capital. On his arrival, soon after, it was found that the estimate placed upon his knowledge of law, his judgment and his loyalty, had led to his selection, by the Secretary of War, as one of the first members of the court-martial for the trial of the noted Fitz John Porter—the most important military trial of the war.

The charges preferred against Porter, by General Polk, are well known. He was accused of having disobeyed five distinct orders to bring his command to the front in time to take part in the second battle of Bull Run. The trial lasted forty-five days. Garfield was required to pass upon complicated questions, involving the rules of war, the situation and surroundings of Porter's command previous to the battle, the duties of subordinate commanders, and the military possibilities of the situation. In such a trial, the common-sense of a strong, but unprofessional mind, was more valuable than the technical training of a soldier. The question at issue was, whether Porter had kept his own opinions to himself and cheerfully obeyed his superior's orders, even if he did not approve them, or whether, through anger or jealousy, he had sulked in the rear, so as to insure the defeat which he prophesied. Garfield threw all his powers into the investigation, and at last was convinced of Porter's guilt, and gave his vote for the verdict by which General Porter was dismissed from the army and rendered incapable of holding any position of trust or profit under the United States Government. Such were the opinions of President Lincoln and other prominent men, and, no doubt, posterity will never change the verdict. The recent attempt made by Fitz John Porter and his friends, to have the verdict of the court overruled, and the free immunities of citizenship again restored to him, have resulted only in a partial accomplishment. The verdict that Garfield subscribed to, is, no doubt, that which the unfortunate Porter will ever be compelled to abide by, even though he may be restored to some of the high privileges of which the verdict deprived him.

The intimacy that sprung up during this trial between Garfield and Major-General Hunter, the president of the court-martial, and in command of our forces in South Carolina, led to an application for him to Secretary Stanton for Garfield's service in South Carolina, whither Hunter was about to start. The appointment was made. Garfield's strong anti-slavery views had been greatly strengthened by his experience thus far during the war, and the South Carolina appointment, under a commander so radical as Hunter, was on this account particularly gratifying. Garfield realized that while the war was being fought on the technical question of a state's right to secede, it was really a war to destroy the hideous and bloody institution of slavery, and his desire was to see it carried on for that purpose. As he afterward expressed it: "In the very crisis of our fate, God brought us face to face with the alarming truth that we must lose our freedom or grant it to the slave."

But an unexpected turn of affairs took place. Pending his departure with Hunter, Garfield's old army, now a part of the Army of the Cumberland, under the command of General Rosecrans, General Buell having been relieved, had, on the last day of 1862, plunged into the battle of Stone River. During the day's action a cannon-ball felled the beloved Colonel Garesche, chief of General Rosecrans' staff, and severed his head from his body. The need of a good officer in his place, and the prospect of satisfactorily filling it, not a little troubled the general. It required a man of high military ability to act as chief confidential adviser of the commanding general, both as to the general plan of a campaign and the imperious exigencies of battle. Rosecrans had relied implicitly in Garesche, and just at the time when so much was expected of the great Army of the Cumberland, by the War Department, the catastrophe had occurred. It was known by the high officials that Rosecrans easily became unmanageable, and though well-versed in the practice of warfare, might give way at an important crisis. It will thus be seen that an acceptable chief of staff must necessarily be a man of pleasant social qualities to fit him for the intimate relation. Much as the War Department at Washington thought of Rosecrans at this time, his violent temper and invincible obstinacy rendered it imperative that some one should be with him who would prevent an absolute rupture on trifling grounds. But in addition to these things, the chief of staff had to be a man of faultless generosity and unselfishness; he had to be a man who would exert his own genius for another's glory; he had to be willing to see the plans of brilliant campaigns, which were the product of his own mind, taken up and used by another; he had to be willing to see reports of victories, which were the results of his own military skill, sent to Washington over the name of the commanding general, in which his own name was never mentioned. He was to do the work and get no glory for it. All this he had to do cheerfully, and with a heart loyal to his superior. There must be no division of counsel, no lukewarm support, no heart-burnings at head-quarters. To the army and the world there was but one man—the general. In reality there were two—the general and his chief of staff. Looking carefully over the ground, and reviewing the subject thoroughly, Stanton at once fixed his eye on Garfield. The commission already given him for the South Carolina command was revoked. Garfield was thereupon commanded to report at once to Major-General Rosecrans, whose head-quarters were at Murfreesboro, Tennessee, as a result of the victory at Stone River. It is so stated that Rosecrans was somewhat displeased with the appointment of Garfield as his chief of staff. He had heard of him as a Campbellite preacher, and fond of theological debate, and a school-teacher. This catalogue of proclivities was sufficient to spoil any man for Rosecrans. Consequently the reception given his new chief, on the cold January morning, when Garfield presented himself, was much after the manner of the weather. It still remained optional with Rosecrans to accept or reject the appointment of the War Department for this position, and he had made up his mind to exercise his prerogative of rejection upon the slightest pretext. Garfield's appearance, to be sure, was greatly in his favor, and after a short conversation, Rosecrans decided to go slow before he rejected his services. Garfield was kept around head-quarters for several days, and questioned occasionally by the commanding general. The whole-souled Ohioan showed himself to be of the right kind of metal, and "Rosey," as the soldiers called him, irresistibly began admiring him. He found that he could not fathom the depth of Garfield's mind, and after each conversation his depths of reserve power seemed greater than before. Rosecrans now wanted him; but one thing was in the way. If Garfield preferred to go to the field, as he had himself prophesied from his name (Guard-of-the-field), just before leaving college, in 1856, Rosecrans was not the man to chain him up at head-quarters. The choice was open to Garfield; to take a division or accept the position of chief of staff. The latter had great responsibility and no opportunity whatever for fame. But without a moment's hesitation, Garfield quietly said: "If you want my services as chief of staff, you can have them." Most men would have taken the brigade, but Garfield chose to remain with the general. That Rosecrans never regretted the appointment as chief of staff, which he made immediately after the interview, is evidenced by what he has said: "We were together until the Chattanooga affair. I found him to be a competent and efficient officer, an earnest and devoted patriot, and a man of the highest honor. His views were large, and he was possessed of a thoroughly comprehensive mind." His appointment as chief of staff gave great satisfaction throughout the army, and it was everywhere expressed. The country was equally pleased, especially Ohio. Among other things, the following was said of the appointment: "We have known General James A. Garfield for several years, and entertain for him the highest personal regard. He is one of the most eloquent men in Ohio, as well as one of the ripest scholars. Socially and morally he has no superior. He is popular with all, as the attachment of his scholars, as well as his soldiers, for him demonstrates. In respect to abilities, nature has by no means been unfriendly to him; and he has neither despised nor slighted her gifts. A severe course of mental training, combined with the mental practice obtained by presiding over one of the colleges of Ohio, has fully developed his natural endowments. Above all these considerations, every one respects General Garfield for his stern, unyielding, uncompromising patriotism. The permanent good of his country, the restoration of its unity, and the perpetuation of the national power and glory through all coming time, are the objects which he keeps steadily in view." Once installed in his new position, he rapidly grew into a favorite. Possessed of sound, natural sense, an excellent judgment, a highly-cultivated intellect, and the deserved reputation of a successful military leader, he was soon to be the mentor of the staff, and his opinions sought and his counsels heeded by many who were older and not less distinguished than himself. Edmund Kirke, in his picturesque war story, "Down in Tennessee," written in 1863, draws the following pen-portrait of Garfield in his new capacity: "In a corner by the window, seated at a small pine desk—a sort of packing-box, perched on a long-legged stool, and divided into pigeon-holes, with a turn-down lid—was a tall, deep-chested, sinewy-built man, with regular, massive features, a full, clear, blue eye, slightly tinged with gray, and a high, broad forehead, rising into a ridge over the eyes, as if it had been thrown up by a plow. There was something singularly engaging in his open, expressive face, and his whole appearance indicated, as the phrase goes, 'great reserved power.' His uniform, though cleanly brushed, and sitting easily upon him, had a sort of democratic air, and everything about him seemed to denote that he was 'a man of the people.' A rusty, slouched hat, large enough to have fitted Daniel Webster, lay on the desk before him, but a glance at that was not needed to convince me that his head held more than the common share of brains. He glanced at me as I approached, and when I mentioned my name, rose, and extending his hand in a free, cordial way, said, 'I am glad to meet you. I have seen your handwriting—Edmund Kirke, his (X) mark.' 'And I have seen yours,' I replied. grasping his hand with equal cordiality. 'But *you* write with a *steel* pen—epics in the measure of 'Hail Columbia!' I sat down, and in ten minutes knew him as well as I might have known some other men in ten years."

CHAPTER XI.

THE FAMOUS TULLAHOMA CAMPAIGN.

All the gods' go with you! Upon your sword
Sit lauded victory, and smooth success
Be strew'd before your feet!

—SHAKESPEARE.

A mighty deed is like the heaven's thunder,
That wakes the nation's slumbers from their rest.

—RAUPACH.

The arms are fair
When the intent for bearing them is just.

—SHAKESPEARE.

Garfield had been Rosecrans' chief of staff but a short time until the utmost confidence was placed in his judgment. His ideas and plans were always found to be the best. This, together with his courteous manner, gives us the key to the confidence placed in him. The friendship and official relationship, therefore, of these two men became intimate and very pleasant. Garfield had proven himself equal to the various trying emergencies. He was looked upon as the most mature member of the staff, Rosecrans having a partiality for young and gallant spirits, like Captain Charles Thompson, Major Bond, Colonel Mickler, Captain Hunter Brooke, Major Horace Porter (subsequently on Grant's staff), and Major Morton McMichael. Not that Garfield was much older than these officers, but he always had a mature look, and his mood was ever serious, as if there was in the peril of the nation something more of personal concern and personal interest to him than to most of his associates.

About this time there appeared in Rosecrans' camp, with drooping feathers, but brazen face, the thing which patriotism denominated "a copperhead." The one to whom reference is made is Clement L. Vallandigham, a native of Ohio, and who had been ostracised from his own community—Montgomery county—for his treason. He, thereupon, came to the army at Murfreesboro, and was to have an escort to the enemy's camp, a few miles distant, at Tullahoma, by flag of truce

When brought into camp, Vallandigham was taken, in the usual course of business, to Rosecrans' head-quarters, and he and Garfield being acquaintances, it was natural they should fall into conversation, and equally natural that the conversation should turn upon the policy and conduct of the war, in a political sense. Vallandigham was to go off the next day, escorted as far as the rebel lines, in the vicinity of Tullahoma. He entered Rosecrans' tent at an early hour of the morning with an affectation of unconcern and light-heartedness which he could not have felt, threw himself into a tragic attitude, and in a mock heroic vein exclaimed, quoting from Romeo and Juliet:

> "Night's candles are burnt out, and jocund day
> Stands tiptoe on the misty mountain tops."

Here he hesitated, when Garfield quickly but quietly finished the speech, by adding, in a half aside, to the aid-de-camp in charge of the flag of truce escort, waiting to convey Vallandigham to the rebel lines,

> "I must begone and live, or stay and die."

Vallandigham, however, overheard and caught the hidden meaning of the citation, and blushed scarlet as he made its application.

A little later, President Hinsdale wrote to General Garfield concerning the treasonable views of some disloyal students at Hiram. More than anything else, Garfield detested a foe in the rear. For a man who declared his principles on the battle-field he had some degree of respect, but a traitor, a coward, a "copper-head," was to him despicable beyond all countenance. Here is the characteristic letter that he wrote in reply.

HEAD-QUARTERS DEPARTMENT OF THE CUMBERLAND,
MURFREESBORO, May 26, 1863.

Tell all those copperhead students for me that, were I there in charge of the school, I would not only dishonorably dismiss them from the school, but, if they remained in the place and persisted in their cowardly treason, I would apply to General Burnsides to enforce General Order No. 28 in their cases. If these young traitors are in earnest, they should go to the Southern Confederacy, where they can receive full sympathy. Tell them all that I will furnish them passes through our lines, where they can join Vallandigham and their other friends, till such time as they can destroy us, and come back home as conquerors of their own people, or can learn wisdom and obedience. I know this is apparently a small matter, but it is only apparently small. We do not know what the developments of a month may bring forth, and, if such things be permitted at Hiram, they may anywhere. The rebels catch up all such facts as sweet morsels of comfort, and every such influence lengthens the war and adds to the bloodshed.

Life in an encamped army is somewhat barren of incidents. One or two, however, are somewhat indicative of Garfield's character, and hence may be worthy of mention. Rosecrans was a late worker, and often kept the members of his staff up till very unseasonable hours. The result was, that if not actually engaged in some active duty, the young gentlemen would often drop off to sleep; and this more frequently happened with the poor orderlies, who were stationed in the hall outside, in readiness to go upon messages for the officers.

One night the officers' council lasted very late. The dozen orderlies being forbidden to talk together, and having nothing whatever to engage their attention, toward the small hours of the morning, deputed one of their number—Orderly Sergeant Daugherty—to remain on watch, to awake them in case any orders came from head-quarters, and went quietly to sleep at their posts. Tilting his chair against the wall by the general's door, the sergeant had stretched his legs out to their utmost length, and fallen fast asleep, when the door suddenly opened, and General Garfield emerged at a quick pace from the inner room. A single tallow candle lighted the hall only dimly, and not observing the sergeant's outstretched legs, the general stumbled over them, and fell on his hands and knees to the floor. Being a stout man, he came down heavily. The affrighted sergeant sprang to his feet, and, as the general rose, stood at "attention" and saluted, but expecting to be certainly cuffed, and perhaps kicked from one end of the hall to the other for his heedlessness. To his astonishment, the general quietly gathered himself up, and saying, kindly, "Excuse me, sergeant, I did not see you. I'm afraid you did not find me very light," passed on as if nothing had happened. This incident, though trifling in itself, shows that a man may be born in a log cabin and yet be a gentleman. It is easy to see also why the soldiers loved Garfield so devotedly.

Another incident, of more importance, is also illustiative of some traits in General Garfield's character. One day, an aid entered the room and handed Rosecrans a letter. He opened it, and became at once absorbed in its contents. Its date was May 18, 1863, and it began thus:

GENERAL:—A plan has been adopted for a simultaneous movement or rising to sever the rebel communications throughout the whole South, which is now disclosed to some general in each military department in the Secesh States, in order that they may act in concert, and thus insure us success. The plan is for the blacks to make a concerted and simultaneous rising, on the night of the 1st of August next, over the whole states in rebellion. To arm themselves with any and every kind of weapon that may come to hand, and commence operations by burning all railroad and county bridges, tearing up all railroad tracks, and cutting and destroying telegraph wires—and when this is done, take to the woods, the swamps, or the mountains, whence they may emerge, as occasions may offer, for provisions or for further depredations. No blood is to be shed except in self-defense. The corn will be in roasting ear about the 1st of August, and upon this, and by foraging on the farms at night, we can subsist. Concerted movement at the time named would be successful, and the Rebellion be brought suddenly to an end.

Our informant was re-reading the letter, when the general again said, "What do you think of it?" "It would end the Rebellion. Co-operated with by our forces, it would certainly succeed, but the South would run with blood," was the answer. "Innocent blood—women and children?" he asked. "Yes, women and children. If you let the blacks loose, they will rush into carnage like horses into a burning barn. St. Domingo will be multiplied by a million." "But he says no blood is to be shed except in self-defense." "He says so, and the leaders may mean it, but they cannot restrain the rabble. Every slave has some real or fancied wrong, and he would take such a time to avenge it." "Well, I must talk with Garfield. Come, go with me."

They crossed the street to Garfield's lodgings, and found him bolstered up in bed, quite sick with a fever. Rosecrans sat down on the foot of his bed, and handed him the letter. Garfield read it over carefully, and then laying it down, said, "It will never do, general. *We* don't want to whip by such means." "I knew you'd say so," said Rosecrans; "but he speaks of other department commanders—may they not come into it?" "Yes, they may, and that should be looked into. Mr. ——— has been speaking of going home every day for a fortnight. Now let him go, and send this letter by him to the President. Let Mr. Lincoln head off the movement."

In several days the letter was laid before President Lincoln. He read it over thoughtfully, and then said, "Is not this a hoax?" "It may be, sir, but it looks and sounds like a genuine document." "That is true; but what do Rosecrans and Garfield think of it?" The above interview was then stated. "And they want me to put my foot upon it?" "They do; and Garfield, particularly, urges that you give it immediate attention. He thinks the country will be seriously affected if the project is countenanced for a moment." "He is right; and I will give it immediate attention. I will thank you if you will write them to that effect."

This was in the latter part of May, and early in June following, Garfield wrote a letter, of which the following is an extract: "I am clearly of opinion that the negro project is every way bad, and should be repudiated, and, if possible, thwarted. If the slaves should, of their own accord, rise and assert their original right to themselves, and cut their way through rebeldom, that is their own affair; but the government could have no complicity with it without outraging the sense of justice of the civilized world. We should create great sympathy for the rebels abroad, and God knows they have too much already." The matter was again laid before Mr. Lincoln. He read the letters in his quiet, thoughtful way; then laying them down, and moving his one leg from where it dangled across the other, he said, emphatically, "That Garfield is a trump—there is no discount upon that."

The gentleman in question was in no frame of mind at that time to listen to a eulogy on Garfield, as the exigencies of the case in hand gave a different turn to his thoughts. He was about to ask Lincoln what he had done about the negro project, when he went on: "Do you know, that job of his on the Big Sandy was the cleanest thing that has been done in the war. It's something to have been born in a log-shanty."

"And to have split rails!" replied the visitor, smiling.

"Yes," he answered, "and I'll bet Garfield has done that."

"I don't know about him; but it is a fact that his mother has."

"Is that so?" he said laughing. "Well, that accounts for Garfield—he had a good mother."

Then subsiding into a serious tone he added, "But, as Garfield says, that negro business is bad every way, and we can't afford it. I think I have put my foot upon it."

"We all know that the insurrection did not take place, and it is doubtful if the intended uprising was so wide-spread and universal as the letters indicated; but when we reflect that a hundred, or even fifty, intelligent and resolute men, acting in concert in as many different localities, and aided by our troops, might at any time during the war have lighted a negro conflagration which, once started, would soon have involved the whole South, even the strongest statement of the possible danger will not seem improbable. The uprising was fixed for the first of August, and we know that serious outbreaks occurred among the blacks of Georgia and Alabama in September. May not those have been the work of subordinate leaders, who, maddened at the miscarriage of the main design, were determined to carry out their own part of the programme at all hazards? Mr. Lincoln was always very reticent about the part he took in the affair. To occasional indirect questions he always, but once, returned evasive answers, and then he said, 'When the right time comes, I will make known the whole of that story.' The assassin's bullet cut short the story."

One of the most prolific war writers—J. R. Gilmore—who spent a month with Rosecrans, gives us some interesting gem pictures of Garfield, as he was at this time, the spring and summer of 1863. "We rode one day out to Sheridan's head-quarters," says Gilmore, "and as we entered the forest encircling the town, Garfield broke out with Hosea Bigelow's poem:

"'I du believe in Freedom's cause,'

and if the 'down east poet' would have any appreciation of his own lines, he should hear them in such grand, old woods, the words echoed back from the great spreading trees and set to the music of an hundred horses' heels. He had scarcely ended, when Rosecrans began to tell how

"'Zekle crep' up, quite unbeknown,
An' peeped in thru the winder;
While there sot Huldy all alone
'Ith no one nigh to hinder.'

"'What would you give to have written that?' Rosecrans said, as he finished the recitation.

"'All the castles I ever built in the clouds,' was the reply.

"'So would I. You know what Wolfe said before his great battle?'

"'That he would rather have written Gray's Elegy than take Quebec. Would *you* have said that before Stone River?'

"He hesitated a moment, and then answered:

"'No, for now we need victories more than poems.'

While waiting at Murfreesboro, the tiresome routine of camp life was varied as much as possible by the invention of games and sports by both officers and men. An incident which occurred at the head-quarters of Phil. Sheridan, in the forest surrounding the town, where he had invented a novel game, which he called Dutch ten-pins, is worth relating. In front of his cabin, suspended from the limb of a high tree, was a rope with a small cannon ball attached to the end. Underneath the branch was placed the ten-pins, with space enough between to allow the ball freely to pass without hitting them. The first attempts of the little general were to throw the ball between the pins without hitting any. But with an increase of skill came new and more arduous attempts. His next trials were to throw the ball between the pins and have it strike them on the return. Sheridan became very fond of the exercise, and in the three throws allowed each player, he could bring down twenty pins of a possible thirty. The reputation of the game and Sheridan's skill at last reached head-quarters of the commanding general. One day Rosecrans, Garfield, and several other officers, went out to see "little Phil.," as he was called, and try their hand at the game. The guests were cordially received, and, after considerable jesting and many attempts, Sheridan began the game. At the first throw the ball in returning brought down six pins; at the second, seven; and the third the same number, making a score of twenty. Several other officers made a trial but all with poor success. Rosecrans at last made the attempt. The spectators laughed at his nervous way of handling the ball; and, after a lengthy aim, he threw, knocking down every pin. Other attempts were made, but he found it impossible to get the ball beyond the wooden line without knocking down the pins. Then General Garfield stepped forward, remarking: "It's nothing but mathematics. All you need is an eye and a hand." And with this he carelessly threw the ball. It passed safely through, and returning brought down seven pins. Everybody shouted, "Luck! Luck! Try that again." The chief of staff only laughed, and with still greater seeming indifference, brought down eight. The third throw resulted as the second, and a score of twenty-three was made, giving him the game, much to the discomfiture of "little Phil." It is no wonder that an officer said of him, "That man Garfield beats everything. No matter what he does, he is the superior of his competitors, without half trying."

On the 25th of April 1863, Garfield issued a circular to the entire Army of the Cumberland, containing an escaped prisoner's account of his treatment by the rebels in the Southern prison-pens. The barbarities and unspeakable outrages awaiting all those captured on the battle-field were pictured in most burning words. In concluding this address General Garfield said: "We cannot believe that the justice of God will allow such a people to prosper. Let every soldier know that death on the battle-field is preferable to a surrender, followed by such outrages as their comrades have undergone." And how true that circular was, those brave ones whose unhappy fortune it was to be imprisoned in these pens, remember with horror. The outrages committed on our soldiers at Libby and Andersonville, as well as numerous other places in the South, are unparalleled in history. In an enlightened age, when warfare occupies such a high plane, and when the hardships of civil and national contests-at-arms are expected to be conducted in a civilized, if not a Christian manner, there is no excuse or palliation, nor, in justice can there be, of the horrors which the South imposed upon Northern soldiers during our late war. And this is why Garfield importuned the soldiers to choose death rather than life with an imprisonment in the South. This will ever remain a stain against the chivalry, valor and good intentions of the South. It is the mark of Cain, which time cannot efface. For such a stain upon the escutcheon of any country, or part of a country, there can be no excuse. Even defeat in a cause which they deemed right and just, can be no excuse. Human life rises far above such considerations, and the South will ever have this to regret. The time may come, and now is more than at any time since the close of the war, when the South can be forgiven for fighting for principles which it then conceived to be right. The time has come when the North and South can shake hands across the old chasm—when the blue and gray alike unite in raising the stars and stripes, and that, too, with the same spirit of heroic devotion; when the sorrows of the North and South become alike the sorrows of each other, over the ruin once wrought by human folly; the right hand of fellowship has been extended—but the men who directly or indirectly caused or countenanced the starvation, the torture, the poisoned and rotten food, the abandonment to loathsome disease, the crowding of thousands of Union prisoners into stockades, and every other unparalleled and unjustifiable atrocity of the Southern prison—atrocities which violated every rule of known warfare; atrocities, to find the equals of which the history of barbarous and savage nations, without the light of religion, or the smile of civilization, will be ransacked in vain, shall be handed down to an eternity of infamy. *For all this the one man of all others, who is and was directly responsible, is Jeff. Davis—the renegade and traitor to his country.* All the North can do, is to try and forget; forgive it cannot. God only can mete out the just reward. It was unfortunate that the South had such leaders—men who did not scruple to institute such barbarities; for 'tis the South whom history will ever hold accountable.

While Garfield was chief of staff to Rosecrans, some Northern Republicans, prominent among whom was Horace Greeley, having become dissatisfied with Lincoln in 1862–3, and desiring a new candidate for the presidency in 1864, addressed Garfield upon the subject of nominating Rosecrans. These Northerners had been attracted by the signal successes made by General Rosecrans, and began to consider him as not only an available candidate, but a strong and popular one. The correspondence was opened up with Garfield, in whom they had the utmost confidence, and it was thought that with his assistance Lincoln could be irresistibly overcome in the nominating convention. Garfield, however, at once defeated the project by putting his foot on the ambitious scheme. He firmly believed, and history knows only too well how correct was that belief, that no man on earth could equal Lincoln in those trying hours. The fate of the nation rested with that noble man; and Garfield believed that by electing Rosecrans a wonderful President would be defeated, and an excellent soldier removed from a place where he was then most needed. Not a word of the scheme was whispered to his general, and so effectually was the plan smothered that history first informed Rosecrans of it. Cunning and contriving politicians have unwarrantedly endeavored to make capital out of this action on the part of Garfield. They would have us believe that his motives were selfish and sinister; but how far this is from being correct, all those who knew Garfield to love him, are ready to testify. No one, perhaps, would have been more persistent in advocating the claims of Rosecrans to this high place, than Garfield, had the spirit and exigencies of the times called for his advancement. But Lincoln was the only man then for the place, and the fate of the war depended, to a great extent, in keeping him at the head of the nation. History vindicates the action, and must free Garfield from any imputations other than those of patriotism and devotion.

Garfield impressed himself in various ways upon those with whom he came in contact. A certain chaplain who knew Garfield, gives the following testimony:

It was my privilege, and I esteem it as one of the sweetest privileges of my life, to know Mr. Garfield personally. I met him first in camp. We went together in the field. I was with him in his first battle. I watched his movements on that occasion. I had a position where I could see the battle and see our leader. I have seen him in the hospital after the battle was over. He was, with all his greatness, with all his learning and with his wonderful ability, as kind and gentle as a woman. There was not a man in the brigade who did not respect him. He had this peculiarity that all officers did not—he did not measure a man by the clothes he wore. Garfield respected the man in the blue blouse, and over and over again, as we were in camp in the same place about two months, I have seen General Garfield sitting in the room of the private soldiers and talking with them with as much interest and pleasure as though they had been a company of United States Senators. Garfield carried his religion into the army. It would be better for the country and better for a great many men if they did the same. He scrupulously observed God's law in regard to the Sabbath. I remember one morning in March when the snow was on the ground and the mercury below zero, and the weather was so bad I had been thinking we had better give up services for the day, that I received a note from Mr. Garfield saying: "My chaplain is absent, and if you please, we will join you in religious services to-day," and that grand man with his Websterian head stood uncovered as I tried to preach as best I could when it was freezing.

While our forces lay at Murfreesboro, General Garfield organized the admirable secret-service system of the Army of the Cumberland, which gave Rosecrans such perfect information of the movements of the enemy, and put an end to the extensive smuggling of cotton through the army lines which was being carried on by professed Union men high in civil and military positions. In this work he at first met with strenuous opposition, and then was offered enormous bribes to let things go on in their former routine; but this young officer, with a bare stipend of only three thousand dollars from his rank as brigadier, was proof against both bribes and blandishments, and, with the cordial help of Rosecrans, he soon cleaned out the Augean stables. The citizens were hostile, and had but two objects—one to serve the Confederacy, the other to make money for themselves. Smuggling was the great army vice. The profits of cotton, smuggled contraband through the Union lines to the North, and of medicines, arms, leather, whisky, and a thousand Northern manufactures, through to the South, were simply incalculable. Bribery was the most effective. The Southern women, famous the world over for their beauty and their captivating and passionate manners, would entangle the officers in their meshes in order to extort favors. To break up this smuggling, and get fresh information of any plot or pitfalls for the Union army, systems of army police had been organized at Nashville and Murfreesboro. After his appointment as chief of staff, Garfield undertook the task of making the work more available. A military bureau of information, with General D. G. Swaim for its head, was established. For efficiency it was never again equalled or approached during the war. Shortly after the establishment of this bureau of information, a determined attack was made on the whole institution. "It marshalled its friends and enemies in almost regimental numbers. Even in the army it has been violently assailed, not only by the vicious in the ranks, but by officers whose evil deeds were *not* past finding out." The accusations which were laid before Garfield were always investigated immediately, and always to the vindication of the police department. A special officer was at last detailed to investigate the entire department. His report of the wonderful achievements of the army police is monumental. Garfield was inexorable. Every officer guilty of smuggling had to come down, no matter how prominent he was. The chief of staff set his face like brass against the corruptions. The opportunities open to him for wealth were immense. Had he but done as others did—merely shut his eyes to this contraband traffic—he might have made, during the five months the army lay at Murfreesboro, at least a million of dollars. And yet we are told that at a subsequent period he sold himself to Oakes Ames for three hundred and twenty-nine dollars! General Garfield broke up stealing among the men. He established a system of regular reports from spies on the enemies. His police furnished him with the political status of every family in that section of the State. He knew just the temper of Bragg's troops, and had a fair idea of their number. He knew just what corn was selling at in the enemy's lines. Located in a hostile country, honey-combed with a system of rebel spies, he outspied the enemy, putting spies to watch its spies. In every public capacity, civil or military, virtue is more rare and more necessary than genius. General Garfield's incorruptible character alone saved the army police from destruction, and restored the Army of the Cumberland to order and honesty. He had, long before entering the army, shown wonderful ability for using assistants in accumulating facts for him. The police institution was an outcropping of the same thing. No commander during the war had more exact and detailed information of the enemy than Garfield had at this time.

The time of General Garfield's arrival at Rosecran's head-quarters, marks the beginning of that period of quarrels with the War Department in which General Rosecrans frittered away his influence and paved the way for his removal. That great strategist and gallant soldier was always unwise in caring for his own interests, and generally was very imprudent in his intercourse with his superiors. Yet he was nearly always right in his demands, especially when he made appeals to the War Department for more cavalry and revolving arms. The situation of affairs was about as follows: The Army of the Cumberland had no cavalry, the arms were inferior, and the terrible encounter at Stone River had greatly weakened it, and Rosecrans demanded re-enforcements before making another advance. The Department at Washington, and Halleck, commander-in-chief of the Union forces, thought that an advance should be made at once. Rosecrans, though possessing some high military skill, was sensitive, head-strong, absorbed in details, and violent of speech. His demands were reiterated. Sharper and sharper came the replies. In these requests Garfield was, at first, heart and soul with his superior. At the same time he did all in his power to soften the tone of asperity which his chief adopted in his dispatches to Washington. Sometimes he took the responsibility of totally suppressing an angry message. Often he ventured to soften the phraseology. But in all this there was a limit beyond which he could not go, and when Rosecrans had pronounced certain statements of the department, "a profound, grievous, cruel and ungenerous official and personal wrong," the good offices of the chief of staff were no longer efficacious—the breach was irreparable. Thenceforward he could only strive to make victories in the field atone for errors in council.

He regarded the organization of the army as vitally defective. Almost the first recommendation made by General Garfield was the displacement of A. M. McCook and T. L. Crittenden. This recommendation was made in course of a discussion on the battle of Stone River, in which Rosecrans explicitly said that these officers had shown themselves incompetent in that engagement. Garfield then, with his clear-headed judgment—utterly unmoved by popular prejudice, and thoroughly well able to perceive real ability beneath misfortune, recommended that McCook and Crittenden be replaced by Irvin McDowell and Don Carlos Buell. Garfield did not take the ground that Buell and McDowell had proved themselves equal to the high commands they had already held, but without discussing this, he argued at length their masterly qualifications for important subordinate positions, as well as the fact that this offer of an opportunity to come out from the cloud under which they rested would insure their gratitude and incite them to their very best efforts. With George H. Thomas already in command, with men like these as his associates, and with the energy and genius of Rosecrans to lead them, the Army of the Cumberland would have been the best officered army in the service of the nation. But "Rosecrans was unwilling to adopt the suggestion—for a reason creditable to his kindness of heart, but not to his military character—Crittenden and McCook ought to be removed, of that he had no doubt, but—'he hated to injure two such good fellows,' and the two good fellows remained with him until Chickamauga."

From January 4th to June 24th, Rosecrans lay at Murfreesboro. Through five months of this delay Garfield was with him. The War Department demanded an advance, and, when the spring opened, with unusual vehemence. General Rosecrans delayed, waiting for cavalry, for re-enforcements, for Grant's movements before Vickburg, for the movements of the enemy, for the opinions of the generals. The chief of staff at first approved the delays till the army should be strengthened and massed, but long before the delaying officers were ready he was urging movement with all his power. Finally, General Rosecrans formally asked his corps, division and cavalry generals as to the propriety of a movement. With singular unanimity, though for divers reasons, they opposed it. Out of seventeen generals not one was in favor of an immediate advance, and not one was even willing to put himself upon record as in favor of an early advance. It is to be remembered that among the seventeen generals were Thomas, Sheridan, Negley, Jeff. C. Davis, Hazen, and Granger. The opinions were in conformity with those of Rosecrans. But there was a man with genius at his side. Garfield, his confidential adviser, looked at the opinions of the generals in utter dismay. He saw that a crisis had arrived. The Department of War peremptorily demanded an advance; and to let the vast army, with its then excellent equipment, lie idle longer, meant, not only the speedy removal of Rosecrans from command, but the greatest danger to the

Union cause. General Garfield therefore collated the seventeen letters sent in from the generals in reply to the questions of their commander, and fairly refuted their substance. The paper began with a statement of the question to be discussed. Next it contained, in tabulated form, the opinions of the generals upon each question. Then followed a swift summary of the reasons presented in the seventeen opinions against the advance. Then began the answer. He presented an elaborate estimate of the strength of Bragg's army, probably far more accurate and complete than the rebel general had himself. It was made up from the official report of Bragg after the battle of Stone River, from facts obtained from prisoners, deserters, refugees, rebel newspapers, and, above all, from the reports of the army police. The argument showed a perfect knowledge of the rules of organization of the Confederate army. The mass of proofs accompanying the opinion, was overwhelming. Then followed a summary and analysis of the Army of the Cumberland. Summing up the relative strength of the two armies, he says, after leaving a strong garrison force at Murfreesboro, "there will be left sixty-five thousand one hundred and thirty-seven bayonets and sabers to throw against Bragg's forty-one thousand six hundred and eighty." He concludes with the following general observations:

Bragg's army is now weaker than it has been since the battle of Stone River, or is likely to be again for the present, while our army has reached its maximum of strength, and we have no right to expect re-enforcements for several months, if at all. * * * Whatever be the result at Vicksburg, the determination of its fate will give large re-enforcements to Bragg. * * * No man can predict with certainty the result of any battle, however great the disparity in numbers. Such results are in the hands of God. But, viewing the question in the light of human calculation, I refuse to entertain a doubt that this army, which, in January last, defeated Bragg's superior numbers, can overwhelm his present greatly inferior forces. * * * The most unfavorable course for us that Bragg could take, would be to fall back without giving us battle; but this would be very disastrous to him. Besides, the loss of *materiel* of war and the abandonment of the rich and abundant harvest now nearly ripe in Middle Tennessee, he would lose heavily by desertion. It is well known that a wide-spread dissatisfaction exists among his Kentucky and Tennessee troops. They are already deserting in large numbers. A retreat would greatly increase both the desire and the opportunity for desertion, and would very materially reduce his physical and moral strength. While it would lengthen our communications, it would give us possession of McMinnville, and enable us to threaten Chattanooga and East Tennessee; and it would not be unreasonable to expect an early occupation of the former place. * * * The defeat of Bragg would be in the highest degree disastrous to the rebellion. * * * The turbulent aspect of politics in the loyal States renders a decisive blow against the enemy at this time of the highest importance to the success of the Government at the polls, and in the enforcement of the conscription act. * * * You have, in my judgment, wisely delayed a general movement hitherto, till your army could be massed, and your cavalry could be mounted. Your mobile force can now be concentrated in twenty-four hours; and your cavalry, if not equal in numerical strength to that of the enemy, is greatly superior in efficiency. For these reasons I believe an immediate advance of all our available forces is advisable, and under the providence of God, will be successful.

Rosecrans read the opinion, examined the proofs, and was convinced. "Garfield," said he, "you have captured me, but how shall the advance be made?"

"The situation was about as follows: Imagine an isosceles triangle, with its apex to the north at Murfreesboro. Here the Army of the Cumberland was situated. The base of the triangle was about fifty miles long, and constituted the enemy's front, with its right terminating at McMinnville, the south-east corner of the triangle, and its left at Columbia, the south-west corner of the figure. At the middle of the base was the village of Wartrace, and almost due west of Wartrace, but a little below the base of the triangle, was Shelbyville, where the enemy's centre was situated, behind massive fortifications. Between Shelbyville and Wartrace was massed the enemy's infantry, the extreme wings being composed of cavalry. At a little distance north of the enemy's front, and forming the base of the triangle, was a 'range of hills, rough and rocky, through whose depressions, called gaps, the main roads to the south passed. These gaps were held by a strong detachment with heavy columns within supporting distance.' Any one can see the enormous strength of the enemy's position for defense. But it had still other sources of strength. Behind the enemy's left and centre was Duck river, a deep torrent, with tremendous banks. If they were pressed in front, the rebel army could fall back south of the river, burn the bridges, and gain ample time for retreat to the lofty range of the Cumberland Mountains, which were only a day's march to the rear. On a direct line with Murfreesboro and Wartrace, and at the same distance south of Wartrace, as Murfreesboro was north of it, was Tullahoma, the depot of the enemy's supplies, and hence the key to the situation. Posted in this almost impregnable situation, Bragg's army was the master of central Tennessee. It is evident that the campaign, which Garfield so powerfully urged, was a great undertaking. The narrow mountain gaps heavily fortified; behind the range of hills the great body of the rebel army intrenched in heavy fortifications; behind them the natural defense of Duck river, and still to the south, the Cumberland Mountains, formed an aggregation of obstacles almost insuperable. The plan of the campaign which followed must, in military history, be accredited to Rosecrans, because he was the general in command, but biography cares not for military customs, and names its author and originator, the chief of staff. The reason Garfield urged the advance, was that he had a plan, the merits of which we will examine hereafter, by which he was convinced it might be successfully made."

There were substantially three ways by which the Union army might advance, one lay along the west side of the triangle to Columbia, then attacking the enemy's left wing; another to march directly south to Shelbyville, and fall upon the enemy's centre; a third, to advance by two roads, cutting the base of the triangle about midway between the enemy's centre and extreme right. A fourth route was possible, along the eastern side of the triangle to McMinnville; but if the enemy's right was to be attacked, the Manchester roads were every way preferable, as being more direct. General Garfield's selection was the third route. His plan was to throw a heavy force forward on the road to Shelbyville, as if intending to attack the rebel centre. Then, under cover of this feint, swiftly throw the bulk of the army upon the enemy's right, turn the flank, cross Duck river, and march swiftly to the enemy's rear, threatening his supplies, thus compelling Bragg to fall back from his tremendous stronghold at Shelbyville, and either give battle in open country or abandon the entire region.

Rosecrans decided to act on Garfield's advice, and twelve days thereafter the army was set in motion. As it was about to break up camp, Major-General T. L. Crittenden, one of the three corps commanders, said to Garfield: "It is understood, sir, by the general officers of the army that this movement is your work. I wish you to understand that it is a rash and fatal move, for which you will be held responsible."

The rash and fatal move was the Tullahoma campaign—a campaign perfect in its conception, excellent in its general execution, and only hindered from resulting in the complete destruction of the opposing army by the delays which had too long postponed its commencement. It might even yet have destroyed Bragg but for the terrible season of rains which set in on the morning of the advance, and continued uninterruptedly for the greater part of the month. The artillery sunk hub-deep in the almost bottomless mire. Great teams of twelve or fourteen powerful horses stalled with small field-pieces Never a minute did the rain let up. The men's clothing was so drenched that it was not dry for two weeks. The army-wagons, hundreds in number, carrying the precious bacon and hard-tack, stuck fast on the roads; so fearful was the mire that on one day the army only advanced a mile and a half. With a week's earlier start it would have ended the career of Bragg's army in the war.

The first advance was made by General Granger's division toward Shelbyville, on June 23d. A demonstration was at the same time made toward the enemy's left, to create the belief that feints were being made to distract the enemy's attention from what would be supposed the main attack on Shelbyville. Meanwhile the bulk of the army was advanced along the two roads leading to the middle of the enemy's right—the east road leading through Liberty Gap, and the west through Hoover's Gap, a defile three miles long. The two gaps were soon taken; and the demonstrations on the enemy's left and centre were kept up with great vigor Bragg was wholly deceived by the numerous points of attack. On the 27th, the entire army was concentrated, and passed rapidly through Hoover's Gap, and on to Manchester. While the army was concentrating at Manchester, General Thomas on the 28th began the final move in the game—the advance upon Tullahoma. Both Shelbyville and Tullahoma were then evacuated by the enemy, and an attempt was made to intercept Bragg's retreat and force him to battle. But the terrible condition of the roads and rivers rendered the effort futile. Bragg crossed the Cumberland Mountains, and Central Tennessee was once more in the hands of the Union army. The rebel army of fifty thousand veterans had been driven from a natural stronghold of the most formidable character; and had lost all the fruits of a year's victories by a single campaign of nine days, conducted in one of the most extraordinary rains ever known in Tennessee.

There were seventeen hundred rebel prisoners taken, several packs of artillery, and an enormous amount of Confederate stores at Tullahoma. This campaign and its victory was not the result of battle, but of pure strategy, confessedly the highest art in war. And now let honor to whom honor belongs be given. There can be no question as to whom the credit of this campaign belongs. Certainly not to the fearful Crittenden and the seventeen generals of Rosecrans' staff. Certainly not to Rosecrans, although as we have seen, it is impossible to separate the double star of Garfield and Rosecrans by military etiquette. But aside from the fact that the campaign was begun as a result of Garfield's argument, in the face of unanimous opposition, even the lips of the enemy are now made to bear unwilling testimony to the glory and credit of the chief of staff.

In his report forwarded to the War Department, as he was setting out for this campaign, General Rosecrans hopes it will not be considered invidious if he specially mentions "Brigadier-General James A. Garfield, an able soldier, zealous, devoted to duty, prudent and sagacious. I feel," he says, "much indebted to him both for his counsel and assistance in the administration of this army. He possesses the instincts and energy of a great commander."

Historians are unanimous in their opinions that the Tullahoma campaign was one of the most masterly exhibitions of strategic genius possible to the commander of a great army. Mahan, author of the *Critical History of the Civil War*, who is ever ready to attack and expose the blunders of the Union generals, declares that this Tullahoma campaign shows *"as skillful combinations as the history of war presents."*

CHAPTER XII.

THE BATTLE OF CHICKAMAUGA—GARFIELD'S HEROISM.

O chief of staff, the nation's fate
  That red field crossed with thee;
The triumph of the camp and state,
  The hope of liberty!

O nation, from sea to sea,
  With Union blessed forever,
Not vainly heroes fought for thee
  By Chickamauga river!

—HEZEKIAH BUTTERWORTH.

But now the trumpet, terrible from far,
In shriller clangor animates the war;
Confed'rate drums in fuller concert beat,
And echoing hills the loud alarm repeat.

—ADDISON.

But the Tullahoma campaign was not the conclusion of the advance which General Garfield had so persistently urged, and the success of which had been so triumphantly demonstrated. An important line of defense had been broken up; an enormous piece of territory had been captured. Bragg still held Chattanooga, which was the objective point of the Army of the Cumberland. It will be remembered, that in Garfield's convincing argument already referred to, giving reasons why an immediate forward march should be made from Murfreesboro, that he used these words: "While it would lengthen our communications, it would give us possession of McMinnville, *and enable us to threaten Chattanooga and East Tennessee; and it would not be unreasonable to expect an early occupation of the former place.*" In the light of history, how true is the fulfillment of that prophecy. No sooner had the victories of the Tullahoma campaign been won, and Bragg had retreated behind the Tennessee river, than Rosecrans stopped. The delay was without reason, and again the War Department ordered an advance. Once more the commander refused to obey, and again Garfield urged that no delay take place. But Rosecrans was immovable. The Department waited; the army waited; the country waited. September was now nearly come, the summer almost gone, and the coming autumn was ripe in its promise of immediate results. The air was full of rumors of approaching conflicts, and the North waited the echo from the battle-field. On August 5th, General Halleck telegraphed Rosecrans peremptory orders to move. The thing required was stupendons, but the results show it was not impossible. Rosecrans quietly waited till the dispositions along his extended lines were completed, till stores were accumulated and the corn had ripened, so that his horses could be made to live off the country. On the 15th he was ready.

The problem now before him was to cross the Tennessee river and gain possession of Chattanooga, the key to the entire mountain ranges of East Tennessee and Northern Georgia, in the face of an enemy of equal strength, whose business it was to oppose him. Two courses were open. Forcing a passage over the river above Chattanooga, he might have essayed a direct attack upon the town. If not repulsed in the dangerous preliminary movements, he would still have had upon his hands a siege not less formidable than that of Vicksburg, with difficulties incomparably greater in maintaining his supplies. But, if this plan was not adopted, it then behooved him to convince the enemy that he had adopted it, while crossing below he hastened southward over the ruggedest roads, to seize the mountain gaps, whence he could debouch upon the enemy's line of supplies. More briefly, he could either attempt to fight the enemy out of Chattanooga or flank him out. He chose the latter alternative. Chattanooga is in the midst of mountains; and in 1863 had fifteen hundred inhabitants. Along the north-west front of the town runs the river, which would have to be crossed by the Union forces. On the southern side of the river, below Chattanooga, are three parallel ridges—Sand Mountain, Lookout Mountain, and Pigeon Ridge—the valleys between the ranges running up to the gap at Chattanooga. Chattanooga was south-east from where the Union army was situated. The town was the lock, and Bragg's army the key, to the door to Georgia, Virginia, and the Carolinas. To unlock this door was the task before the Army of the Cumberland. More than these natural obstacles in the way, Rosecrans had to depend upon Louisville, Kentucky, and the slender line of railway from that place, for his army supplies. Every advance made only weakened the army, by requiring that strong detachments be left behind to preserve the communications; while on the other hand, Bragg, already re-enforced, would grow stronger as he fell back. Garfield urged an advance upon Chattanooga, because he saw a way in which it could be made. The plan took shape when the order came to advance, and was adopted by Rosecrans. The theory of the advance was to pass the enemy's flank, march to the rear, threaten his line of supplies and compel him, by military strategy, to evacuate Chattanooga, as he had Shelbyville and Tullahoma. The army made the movement along three separate routes. Crittenden's corps, forming the left, was to advance by a circuitous route to a point about fifteen miles south-west of Chattanooga, and make its crossing of the Tennessee there. Thomas, as the centre, was to cross a little further down the stream, and McCook thirty miles further to the right. These real movements were to be made under cover of an apparent one. About seven thousand men marched directly to the river shore, opposite Chattanooga, as if a direct attack were to be made on the place. Bragg was again deceived. Absorbed in the operations in front of the place, he offered no resistance to the crossing of the Tennessee river by the main army.

By the 28th, the singular activity of the National forces along a front of one hundred and fifty miles, had blinded and bewildered Bragg as to his antagonist's actual intentions. Four brigades suddenly began demonstrating furiously against his lines above Chattanooga, and the plan was thought to be revealed. Rosecrans must be about attempting to force a passage there, and straightway a concentration to oppose him was ordered. Meantime, bridges, secretly prepared, were hastily thrown across thirty miles further down the river at different points, and, before Bragg had finished preparing to resist a crossing above, Rosecrans, handling with rare skill his various corps and divisions, had securely planted his army south of the Tennessee; and, cutting completely loose from his base of supplies, was already pushing southward—his flank next the enemy being admirably protected by impassable mountains. By September 3d, the Union forces were all on the southern side of the Tennessee. Immediately at the river, Sand Mountain rises abruptly. To repair and construct roads occupied some time; but Thomas and McCook pushed forward vigorously, and by the evening of the 6th were on the southern side of Sand Mountain, and occupied the valley in front of Lookout Mountain. Each of the corps had crossed the range opposite points where the river had been crossed, and though in the same valley, were thirty-five miles apart.

For Bragg, but one thing was feasible. As he had been forced out of Shelbyville, out of Wartrace, out of Tullahoma, precisely had the same stress been placed upon him by the same hand in a still stronger position; and in all haste he evacuated Chattanooga, leaving it to the nearest corps of Rosecrans' army to march quietly in and take possession. The very ease of this occupation proved its strongest element of danger. For men, seeing the objective point of the campaign in their hands, forgot the columns toiling through the mountains away to the southward, whose presence there alone compelled the rebel evacuation. But for them, the isolated troops at Chattanooga would have been overwhelmed. Thenceforward there was need of still greater generalship to re-unite the scattered corps. They could not return by the way they had gone, for the moment they began such a movement Bragg, holding the shorter line, and already re-enforced by Longstreet's veteran corps of the Army of Northern Virginia, could sweep back over the route of his late retreat. Rosecrans now made a fatal blunder. Instead of marching the corps of Thomas and McCook up the Lookout Valley to Chattanooga, and uniting them with Crittenden's, he ordered the crossing of the range as a flank movement to be continued in order to intercept Bragg's supposed retreat. Accordingly, on the 11th and 12th, Thomas re-commenced to push over Lookout Mountain through a pass, twenty-five miles south-east of Chattanooga; and thirty-five miles beyond Thomas, McCook was doing the same thing. And so it came about that a battle—the bloody one of Chickamauga—was fought to enable the Federal army to concentrate in the position one of its corps had already occupied for days without firing a shot. Unfortunately, the concentration was not speedy enough. Indeed, there are some plausible reasons for believing that Rosecrans was, perhaps for a few days, deceived by his easy success, into a belief that Bragg was still in full retreat. Certainly, the general-in-chief and the War Department did all they could to encourage such an idea, and even after Rosecrans, every nerve tense with the struggle to concentrate his corps, was striving to prepare for the onset of the re-enforced rebel army, General Halleck informed him of reports that Bragg's army was re-enforcing Lee, and pleasantly added, that after he had occupied Dalton it would be decided whether he should move still further southward! By this time, Bragg had gathered in every available re-enforcement.

Of the opening of this famous battle Garfield himself has said: "The Rossville road—the road to Chattanooga—was the great prize to be won or lost at Chickamauga. If the enemy failed to gain it, their campaign would be an unmitigated disaster; for the gate-way of the mountains would be irretrievably lost. If our army failed to hold it, not only would our campaign be a failure, but almost inevitable destruction awaited the army itself. The first day's battle (September 19th), which lasted far into the night, left us in possession of the road; but all knew that next day would bring the final decision. Late at night, surrounded by his commanders, assembled in the rude cabin known as the Widow Glenn House, Rosecrans gave his orders for the coming morning. The substance of his order to Thomas was this: Your line lies across the road to Chattanooga. That is the pivot of the battle. Hold it at all hazards; and I will re-enforce you, if necessary, with the whole army. During the whole night the re-enforcements of the enemy were coming in. Early next morning we were attacked along the whole line. Thomas commanded the left and centre of our army. From early morning he withstood the furious and repeated attacks of the enemy, who constantly re-enforced his assaults on our left. About noon our whole right wing was broken, and driven, in hopeless confusion, from the field. Rosecrans was himself swept away in the tide of retreat. The forces of Longstreet, which had broken our right, desisted from the pursuit, and, forming in heavy columns, assaulted the right flank of Thomas with unexampled fury. *Seeing the approaching danger*, he threw back his exposed flank toward the base of the mountain, and met the new peril."

The few words italicised reveal the turning and vital point of the battle. Thomas saw the approaching danger, and, seeing it, was able to check the enemy and save the army, and in telling how he came to see it, I shall relate one of the most brilliant exploits of the War of the Rebellion. The world knows of the awful conflict which followed. General Garfield was located at Widow Glenn's house, in the rear of the right wing. This was Rosecrans' head-quarters. General Thomas located himself at Kelley's farm-house in the rear of the left wing. For three nights General Garfield had not slept as many hours. Every anxious order, for the concentration of the army, had come from him; every courier and aid during those days and nights of suspense reported to him in person; before him lay his maps; each moment since the thirteenth he had known the exact position of the different corps and divisions of our vast army. Looking for the attack at any moment, it was necessary to constantly know the situation of the enemy among those gloomy mountains and sunless forests. "When the red tide of battle rolled through the valley, each part of the line was ignorant of all the rest of the line. The right wing could not even guess the direction of the left wing. The surrounding forests and hills shut in the centre so completely that it did not know where either of the wings were. Every division commander simply obeyed the orders from head-quarters, took his position, and fought. The line of battle was formed in the night. To misunderstand orders and take the

BATTLE OF CHICKAMAUGA.

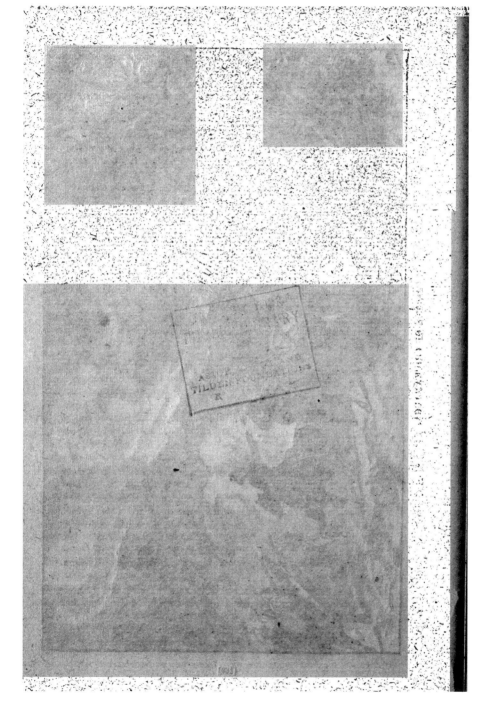

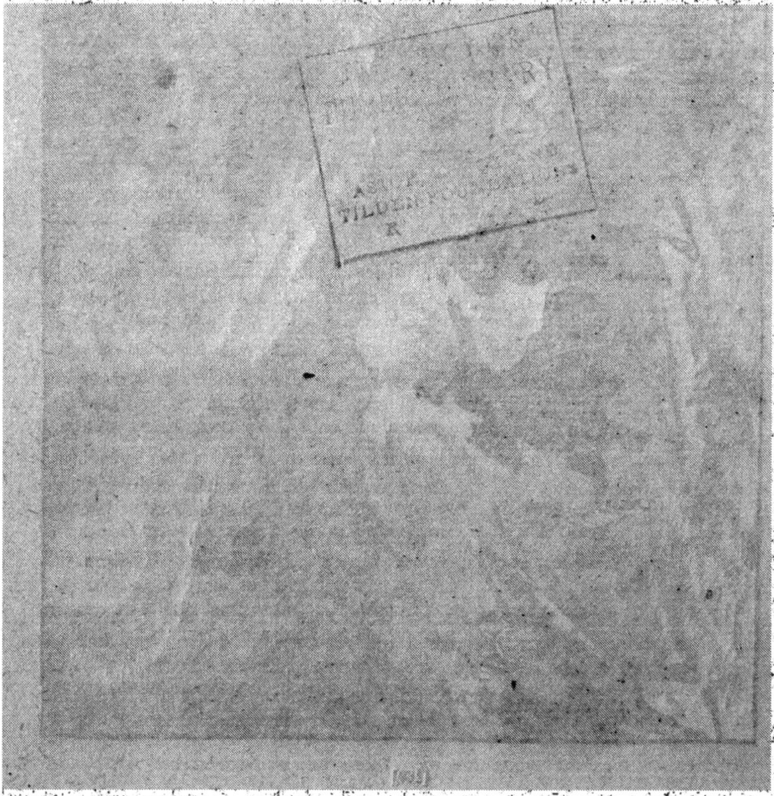

wrong position was easy. But so lucid were the commands, so particular were the explanations which came from the man at head-quarters, that the line of battle was perfect. Many battles of the war were fought with but few orders from head-quarters; some without any concerted plan at all. Pittsburg Landing, of the latter sort; Gettysburg, of the former sort. At Gettysburg the commander-in-chief, General Meade, had little to do with the battle. The country was open, the enemy's whereabouts were visible, and each division commander placed his troops just where they could do the most good. Not so at Chickamauga. No battle of the war required so many and such incessant orders from head-quarters. The only man in the Union army who knew the whole situation of our troops was General Garfield. Amid the forests, ravines and hills along the five miles of battle front, the only possible way to maintain a unity of plan and a concert of action was for the man at head-quarters to know it all. General Garfield knew the entire situation as if it had been a chess-board, and each division of the army a man. At a touch, by the player, the various brigades and divisions assumed their positions. Everything thus far said has been of the combatants. But there were others on the battle-field. There were the inhabitants of this valley, non-combatants, inviolate by the rules of civilized warfare. Of this sort were the rustic people at Widow Glenn's, where General Garfield passed the most memorable days of his life. The house was a Tennessee cabin. Around it lay a little farm with small clearings. Here the widow lived with her three children, one a young man, the others a boy and girl of tender age. As General Garfield took up his head-quarters there it is said to have reminded him powerfully of his own childhood home with his toiling mother. All the life of these children had been passed in this quiet valley. Of the outside world they knew little, and cared less. They did not know the meaning of the word war. They were ignorant and poverty-stricken, but peaceful. Shut in by the mountains of ignorance, as well as the lofty ranges along the valley, they had known no event more startling than the flight of birds through the air or the rustle of the wind through the forest. The soil was rocky and barren like their minds; yet, unvisited by calamity, they were happy.

"But suddenly this quiet life was broken into. The forests were filled with armed men. The cabin was taken possession of by the officers. A sentinel stood at the door. Outside stood dozens of horses, saddled and bridled. Every moment some one mounted and dashed away; every moment some other dismounted from his breathless and foam-flecked steed and rushed into the cabin. The widow, stunned and frightened, sat in the corner with an arm around each of her children. The little girl cried, but the boy's curiosity got somewhat the better of his fear. A time or two General Garfield took the little fellow on his knee, and quieted his alarm. The fences were torn down and used for camp fires. Great trees were hastily felled for barricades. In front of the house passed and repassed bodies of troops in uniform, and with deadly rifles. Now and then a body of cavalry dashed by in a whirlwind of dust. Great cannon, black and hideous, thundered down the rocky road, shaking the solid earth in their terrible race. The cabin-yard was filled with soldiers. The well was drained dry by them to fill their canteens. It was like a nightmare to the trembling inhabitants of the cabin. Their little crops were tramped into dust by the iron tread of war. On a hill in front of the cabin, where nothing more dangerous than a plow had ever been, a battery frowned. The valley, which had never been disturbed by any thing more startling than the screech of an owl, or the cackle of the barn-yard, was filled with a muffled roar from the falling trees and the shouts of men. When morning broke on this secluded spot, the clarion of the strutting cock was supplanted by the bugle-call. The moaning of the wind through the forest was drowned in the incessant roll of the drums. The movement of troops before the cabin from right to left became more rapid. The consultations within became more eager and hurried. Mysterious notes, on slips of white paper, were incessantly written by General Garfield and handed to orderlies, who galloped away into the forest. Spread out before him, on an improvised table, lay his maps, which he constantly consulted. At one time, after a long study of the map, he said to General Rosecrans: 'Thomas will have the brunt of the battle. The Rossville road must be held at all hazards.' Rosecrans replied: 'It is true. Thomas must hold it, if he has to be re-enforced by the entire army.' At another time a messenger dashed into the room, and handed the chief of staff an envelope. Quietly opening it, he calmly read aloud: 'Longstreet has re-enforced Bragg with seventeen thousand troops from Lee's Virginia army.'

"Toward nine o'clock in the morning, the movement of troops along the road ceased. The roar in the forest subsided. No more orders were sent by General Garfield. There was suspense. It was as if every one were waiting for something. The drums no longer throbbed; the bugle-call ceased from echoing among the mountains. A half hour passed. The silence was death-like. As the sun mounted upward it seemed to cast darker shadows than usual. The house-dog gave utterance to the most plaintive howls. The chickens were gathered anxiously together under a shed, as if it were about to rain. It was. But the rain was to be red. Passing over through the forest, one saw that the troops were drawn up in lines, all with their backs toward the road and the cabin, and facing the direction of the river. That was half a mile away, but its gurgle and plashing could be easily heard in the silence. It sent a shudder through one's frame, as if it were the gurgle and plashing of blood. The only other sound that broke the quiet was the whinnying of cavalry-horses far off to the right. The dumb brutes seemed anxious, and nervously answered each other's eager calls. Just as the hand of the clock reached ten there was a report from a gun. It came from the extreme left, miles away. General Garfield stepped quickly to the door and listened. There was another gun, and another, and fifty more, swelling to a roar. Turning to Rosecrans, Garfield said, 'It has begun.' To which the commander replied, 'Then, God help us.' Heavier and heavier became the roar. The engagement on the left was evidently becoming heavier. A quarter of an hour later messengers began to arrive. The enemy was endeavoring to turn the left flank, but was being repulsed with heavy loss. A few moments later came the word that the enemy had captured ten pieces of artillery. The order had been given for one division of the troops to fall back. It was obeyed. But the artillerymen had been unable to move the guns back in time. The heavy undergrowth in the forest, the fallen and rotting logs, had made it slow work to drag back the ponderous cannon. The red-shirted cannoneers were still bravely working to move their battery to the rear after the line had fallen back from them a long distance. Suddenly, with a fierce yell, the rebel column poured in upon them. Guns and gunners were captured.

"At 11:30 came a call from General Thomas for re-enforcements. General Garfield swiftly wrote an order for divisions in the centre to march to the left and re-enforce General Thomas. Another courier was dispatched to the right, ordering troops to take the place of those removed from the centre. At half past twelve these movements were completed. So far, the only attack had been on the left, though the tide of battle was rolling slowly down the line. General Rosecrans and General Garfield held an earnest consultation. It was decided to order an advance on the right centre, in order to prevent the enemy from concentrating his whole army against our left wing. Before long the din of conflict could be heard opposite the cabin. The advance was being fiercely contested. Messengers one after another came asking for re-enforcements. General Garfield received their messages, asked each one a question or two, turned for a few moments to his map, and then issued orders for support to the right centre. As the battle raged fiercer in front of the cabin, the sounds from the extreme left grew lighter. At two o'clock they ceased altogether. The battery had been recaptured, and the enemy silenced for the time being. Meanwhile the battle at the centre became more terrible. Ambulances hurried along; poor fellows, pale and bleeding, staggered back to the road. Occasionally a shell dropped near the cabin, exploding with frightful force. The roar was deafening. General Garfield had to shout to General Rosecrans in order to be understood. The domestic animals around the cabin were paralyzed with fright. No thunderstorm, rattling among the mountain peaks, had ever shaken the earth like the terrific roar of the shotted guns. A half mile in front of the cabin a dense smoke rose over the tops of the trees. All day long it poured upward in black volumes. The air became stifling with a sulphurous smell of gun-powder. The messengers, hurrying to and from the cabin, had changed in appearance. The bright, clean uniforms of the morning were torn and muddy. Their faces were black with smoke; their eyes blood-shot with fever. Some of them came up with bleeding wounds. When General Garfield called attention to the injury, they would say, 'It is only a scratch.' In the excitement of battle men receive death wounds without being conscious that they are struck. Some of the messengers sent out came back no more forever. Their horses would gallop up the road riderless. The riders had found the serenity of death. 'They were asleep in the windowless palace of rest.'"

It was impossible to predict the issue of the conflict in the centre. Once a dispatch was handed Garfield, saying that the line was broken, and the enemy pouring through. Before he had finished the reading, another message said that our troops had rallied, and were driving the enemy. This was repeated several times. The scene of this conflict was Vineyard's farm. It was a clearing, surrounded on all sides by the thickest woods. The troops of each army, in the alternations of advance and retreat, found friendly cover in the woods, or fatal exposure in the clearing. It was this configuration of the battle-field which caused the fluctuations of the issue. Time after time a column of blue charged across the clearing, and was driven back to rally in the sheltering forest. Time after time did the line of gray advance from the shade into the sunlight, only to retire, leaving half their number stretched lifeless on the field. It was a battle within a battle. The rest of the army could hear the terrific roar, but were ignorant of the whereabouts of the conflict. The farm and the surrounding woods was a distinct battle-field. Meanwhile, in hurrying re-enforcements to this portion of the line of battle, a chasm was opened between the centre and left. Troops were thrown forward to occupy it, but the enemy had discovered the weakness, and hurled forward heavy columns against the devoted Union lines. The struggle here was the counterpart of the one at the Vineyard farm. At the latter place the line was, at one time in the afternoon, driven back to the Lafayette road; but toward evening, the divisions which had repulsed the attack on General Thomas' extreme left were shifted down to the scene of these other conflicts, and the enemy was finally driven back with heavy loss.

When this was accomplished, the sun had already sunk behind the western range. Night swiftly drew her mantle over the angry field, and spread above the combatants her canopy of stars. The firing became weaker; only now and then a sullen shot was fired into the night. The first day of Chickamauga was done. In a little while ten thousand camp-fires blazed up in the forest, throwing sombre shadows back of every object. At every fire could be seen the frying bacon and the steaming coffee-pot, singing as merrily as if war and battle were a thousand miles away. The men had eaten nothing since five o'clock in the morning. They had the appetites of hungry giants. Many a messmate's place was empty. Many a corpse lay in the thicket, with a ball through the heart. But in the midst of horror the men were happy. The coffee and bacon and hard-tack tasted to the heroes like a banquet of the gods. With many a song and many a jest they finished the meal, rolled up in their blankets, and lying down on the ground, with knapsacks for pillows, were fast asleep in the darkness. The red embers of the camp-fires gradually went out. The darkness and the silence were unbroken, save by the gleam of a star through the over-arching branches, or the tramp of the watchful sentinels among the rustling leaves. But at Widow Glenn's cabin there was no sleep. General Garfield dispatched messengers to the different generals of the army to assemble for a council of war. It was eleven o'clock before all were present. Long and anxious was the session. The chief of staff marked out the situation of each division of the army upon his map. The losses were estimated, and the entire ground gone over. On the whole, the issue of the day had been favorable. The army having been on the defensive, might be considered so far victorious in that it had held its own. The line of battle was now continuous, and much shorter than in the morning. The general movement of troops during the day had been from right to left. The battle front was still parallel with the Chattanooga roads. General Thomas still held his own. The losses had been heavy, but not so severe as the enemy's. But it was evident that the battle would be renewed on the morrow. The troops, already exhausted by forced marches in the effort to concentrate before attack, had all been engaged during the day. It was tolerably certain, General Garfield thought, from the reports of his scouts, that the enemy would have fresh troops to oppose to the wearied men. This would necessitate all the army being brought into action again on the next day. In case the enemy should succeed in getting the roads to Chattanooga, there was no alternative but the entire destruction of the splendid Army of the Cumberland. Still further concentration of forces on the left, to re-enforce General Thomas, was decided on. Many of the tired troops had to be roused from their sleep for this movement. There was no rest at head-quarters. When morning dawned, the light still shone from the cabin window.

On the morning of September 20, 1863, a dense fog rose from the Chickamauga river, and mixing with the smoke from the battle of the day before, filled the valley. This fact delayed the enemy's attack. The sun rose, looking through the fog like a vast disk of blood. General Garfield noticed it, and pointing to the phenomenon, said, "It is ominous. It will, indeed, be a day of blood." By nine o'clock the fog lifted sufficiently for the attack. As on the day before, it began on the left, rolling down the line. From early morning General Thomas withstood the furious assaults of the constantly re-enforced enemy. The change of the line in the night had been such that it was the right wing instead of the centre which was now in front of the Widow Glenn's. The battle was fierce and more general than the day before. The demands for re-enforcements on the left came faster and faster. Division after division was moved to the left. In the midst of a battle these movements are dangerous. A single order, given from head-quarters without a perfect comprehension of the situation of the troops, a single ambiguous phrase, a single erroneous punctuation mark in the hastily-written dispatch, may cost thousands of lives in a few minutes. In a battle like Chickamauga, where the only unity possible is by perfect and swift obedience to the commands from head-quarters, a single misunderstood sentence may change the destiny of empires. The information received at Widow Glenn's up to ten o'clock of the 20th showed that the troops, though wearied, were holding their own. Up to this time, General Garfield, appreciating each emergency as it occurred, had directed every movement and written every order during the battle. Not a blunder had occurred. His clear, unmistakable English had not a doubtful phrase or a misplaced comma. Every officer had understood and executed just what was expected of him. The fury of the storm had so far spent itself in vain. At half past ten an aid galloped up to the cabin and informed General Rosecrans that there was a chasm in the centre, between the divisions of General Reynolds on the left and General Wood on the right. Unfortunate moment! Cruel fate! In a moment the blunder was committed which was almost to destroy our heroic army. In the excitement of the crisis, Rosecrans varied from his custom of consulting the chief of staff. General Garfield was deeply engaged at another matter. Rosecrans called another aid to write an order instantly directing Wood to close the gap by moving to his left.

Had General Garfield been consulted that order would never have been written. *Wood was not next to Reynolds. General Brannan's division was in the line between them.* Brannan's force stood back from the line somewhat. The aid, galloping rapidly over the field, did not know that a little farther back in the forest stood Brannan's division. It looked to him like a break in the line. General Rosecrans was either ignorant, or forgot that Brannan was there. General Garfield alone knew the situation of every division on the battle-field. *This fatal order was the only one of the entire battle which he did not write himself.* On receipt of the order, General Wood was confused. He could not close up on

Reynolds because Brannan was in the way. Supposing, however, from the words of the order, that Reynolds was heavily pressed, and that the intention was to re-enforce him, and knowing the extreme importance of obeying orders from head-quarters, in order to prevent the army from getting inextricably tangled in the forest, he promptly marched his division backward, passed to the rear of Brannan, and thus to the rear of and support of Reynolds. The fatal withdrawal of Wood from the line of battle was simultaneous with a Confederate advance. Failing in his desperate and bloody attacks upon the left, Bragg ordered an advance all along the line. Right opposite the chasm left by Wood was Longstreet, the most desperate fighter of the Confederacy, with seventeen thousand veteran troops from Lee's army. Formed in solid column, three quarters of a mile long, on they came right at the gap. Two brigades of Federal troops, under General Lytle, reached the space first, but were instantly ground to powder beneath this tremendous ram. Right through the gap came the wedge, splitting the Union army in two. In fifteen minutes the entire right wing was a rout. One half the army was in a dead run toward Rossville. Guns, knapsacks, blankets, whatever could impede them, were hastily thrown away. So sudden was the rout that the stream of fugitives, swarming back from the woods, was the first information received at Widow Glenn's that the line had been pierced. There was no time to be lost. Behind the fleeing troops came the iron columns of the enemy. In five minutes more the cabin would be in their hands. Hastily gathering his precious maps, Garfield followed Rosecrans on horseback, over to the Dry Valley road. Here General Garfield dismounted, and exerted all his powers to stem the tide of retreat. Snatching a flag from a flying color-bearer, he shouted at the deaf ears of the mob. Seizing men by their shoulders, he would turn them around, and then grasp others to try and form a nucleus to resist the flood. It was useless. The moment he took his hands off a man he would run.

Rosecrans had caught a distant sight of some scattering troops straggling over the hills, and he called out to Captain Gaw, as he approached, "What troops are those coming down the hill?" "They are a part of McCleve's reserves, general —the right centre is broken." In a moment more the hills were swarming with a disordered rabble, and turning to his chief of staff, this genuine soldier, who had never before lost a battle, cried out, his anxiety photographed in his face, "Garfield, what shall be done? Garfield, what shall be done?" Cool, clear-headed, and intrepid, this glorious man and wonderful soldier took in, on the instant, the whole extent of the disaster. As quietly as if on dress-parade, Garfield answers: "Send an order to General Mitchell (commanding the cavalry) to fall back on Chattanooga; send another to the officer in command at Rossville to withdraw his guards, and let the retreating troops pass; and send Captain Gaw to General Thomas, asking him to take command of all the forces, fall back on Rossville, and, with McCook and Crittenden, make a stand there, and hold the enemy in check until you can re-organize the broken divisions." Couriers are quickly dispatched with the several messages, and Captain Gaw has set out, when Rosecrans calls him back, and directs him to show them the shortest route to the Chattanooga Valley road. They set out, through a trackless forest of cedar-brake and bramble, in the direction of Nickajack Trace. Now and then the commanding general halts, turns his head to listen, and says, "Thomas is still intact;" then moves on in mournful silence. They come to the Dry Valley road, and find it crowded with a tangled mass of horses, wagons, and soldiers moving briskly, but without the energy of a stampede. As they pass this disorganized mass, the general's face reflects the humiliation he feels. Then they leave the highway, and go on again over a rugged, trackless waste. At last they reach the Chattanooga road, three miles by direct route from Thomas, and four from Chattanooga. Here they halt.

Thomas is only three miles away, but the noise of his fire is broken by the intervening hills and timber. They are in doubt, from the indistinct sounds, whether he is holding his ground, or is falling back, already broken. Rosecrans

GARFIELD'S RIDE AT CHICKAMAUGA.

and Garfield dismount from their horses, and, laying their ears to the ground, listen long and intently. Rosecrans is the first to speak. "It is a scattering fire," he says. "He is broken!"

"No," says Garfield. "He is holding his ground. They are regular discharges."

They listen again, and in a few moments Rosecrans exclaims, "You are mistaken, Garfield. He is giving way! We must hurry back, and hold Chattanooga." The chief of staff knows he is right, but argument is useless. He simply says, "Well, general, if you think you must go back, let me go on to Thomas." Rosecrans hesitates, then says, "As you will, general;" and then, reaching Garfield his hand, he adds, while his face shows his emotion, "We may not meet again; good-by—God bless you!" Though one of the bravest men and ablest soldiers that ever lived, Rosecrans has a heart as tender and gentle as a woman's. He thinks Garfield is going to a well nigh certain death, and he loves him as David loved Jonathan. Again he wrings his hand, and then they part—Rosecrans to the rear, to rally his broken troops, Garfield to a perilous ride in pursuit of Thomas.

" Undaunted 'mid the whirlwind storm of war,
The shock of surging foes, the wild dismay
Of shattered legions swept in blood away,
While the red conflict, thundering afar,
Raged on the left—yet all unseen, unknown—
Great chieftain! man of men! 'twas thine alone,
With faith and courage high, the guiding star
Of that disastrous field, to seek the fray
Where still the hosts of UNION hold their own,
With wasting lines that stand, and strive, and bleed,
Waiting the promise of a better day.
O steadfast soul! O heart of oak! No harm
Could reach thee then: thou hadst for shield His arm
Who kept thee for the nation's later need."

Then began the world-famous ride. No one knew the situation of the troops or the cause of the disaster, and the way to retrieve it, like the chief of staff. To convey that priceless information to Thomas, Garfield determined to do or die. It was a race between the rebel column and the noble steed on which Garfield rode. Up and down the stony valley road, sparks flying from the horses' heels, two of Garfield's comrades hatless, and all breathless, without delay or doubt, on dashed the heroes. Still the enemy was between them and Thomas. At last Garfield said, "We must try to cross now or never. In a half hour it will be too late for us to do any good." Turning sharply to their right, they found themselves in a dark, tangled forest. They were scratched and bleeding from the brier thickets and the overhanging branches. But not a rider checked his horse. General Garfield's horse seemed to catch the spirit of the race. Over ravines and fences, through an almost impenetrable undergrowth, sometimes through a marsh, and then over broken rocks, the smoking steed plunged without a quiver. Suddenly they came upon a cabin, a Confederate pest house. A crowd of unfortunates, in various stages of the small-pox, were sitting and lying about the lonely and avoided place. The other riders spurred on their way, but General Garfield reined in sharply, and, calling in a kind tone to the strongest of the wrecks, asked, "Can I do anything for you, my poor fellow?" In an instant the man gasped out, "Do not come near. It is small-pox! But for God's sake give us money to buy food." Quick as thought, the great-hearted chief of staff drew out his purse and tossed it to the man, and with a rapid but cheerful "good-by," spurred after his companions. Crashing, tearing, plunging, rearing, through the forest dashed the steed. Poet's song could not be long in celebrating that daring deed. All the while, General Garfield was in the most imminent danger. But of personal danger he never thought. The great fear in his mind was that he would fail to reach Thomas. At last they reached a cotton-field. If the enemy was near it was almost certain death. Suddenly a rifle ball whizzed past Garfield's face. Turning in his saddle he saw the fence on the right glittering with murderous rifles. A second later a shower of bullets rattled around the little party. Garfield shouted, "Scatter, gentlemen, scatter," and wheeled abruptly to the left. The two orderlies with him fell, and Garfield became the single target for the enemy. His own horse received two balls, but the noble animal kept straight on at a terrific speed. Garfield is mounted on a magnificent horse, that knows his rider's bridle-hand as well as he knows the route to his fodder. Putting spurs to his side, the horse leaps the fence into the cotton-field. The opposite fence is lined with gray blouses, and a single glance tells him that they are loading for another volley. He has been in tight places before, but this is the tightest. Putting his lips firmly together, he says to himself, "Now is your time; be a man, Jim Garfield!" He speaks to his horse, and lays his left hand gently on the rein of the animal. The trained beast yields kindly to his touch, and, putting the rowels into his side, Garfield takes a zigzag course across the cotton-field. It is his only chance; he must tack from side to side, for he is a dead man if they get a steady aim upon him.

He is riding up an inclined plane of about four hundred yards, and if he can pass the crest, he is in safety. But the gray fellows can load and fire twice before he reaches the summit, and his death is a thing certain, unless Providence has more work for him to do on this footstool. Up the hill he goes, tacking, when another volley bellows from out the timber. His horse is struck—a flesh wound—but the noble animal only leaps forward the faster. Scattering bullets whiz by his head, but he is within a few feet of the summit. Another volley echoes along the hill when he is half over the crest, but in a moment more he is in safety. As he tears down the slope, a small body of mounted blue-coats gallop forward to meet him. At their head is General Dan McCook, his face anxious and pallid. "My God, Garfield!" he cries, "I thought you were killed, certain. How you have escaped is a miracle." It was not long before this brave man was himself stretched upon such another shot-swept field at Knoxville. Captain Gaw had his horse shot under him at the first fire, and was considerably hurt by the fall; but somehow he managed to dodge the bullets, and crawl over the crest to the side of McCook and Garfield. McCook gives him another horse and they start again for the head-quarters of Thomas.

> "Through tongues of flame, through meadows brown,
> Dry valley roads concealed,
> Ohio's hero dashes down
> Upon the rebel field.
> And swiftly on reeling charger borne,
> He threads the wooden plain,
> By twice an hundred cannon mown,
> And reddened with the slain."

Garfield's horse has been struck twice; but he is good yet for a score of miles; and, at a break-neck pace they go forward, through plowed fields and tangled forests, and over broken and rocky hills, for four weary miles, till they climb a wooded crest, and are within sight of Thomas. In a slight depression of the ground, with a group of officers about him, he stands in the open field, while over him sweeps the storm of shotted fire that falls in thick rain on the high foot-hill which Garfield is crossing. Shot and shell and cannister plough up the ground all about Garfield; but in the midst of it he halts, and with uplifted right arm, and eyes full of tears, he shouts, as he catches sight of Thomas, "There he is! God bless the old hero! he has saved the army" For a moment only he halts, then he plunges down the hill through the fiery storm, and in five minutes is by the side of Thomas. He has come out unscathed from the hurricane of death, for God's good angels have warded off the bullets; but his noble horse staggers a step or two, and then falls dead at the feet of Thomas.*

The meeting of the two men I shall not attempt to describe, for it was too pathetic for description. In hurried, broken sentences Garfield tells Thomas that he is out-flanked, and that at least seventy thousand men are closing down upon his right wing, to crush his twenty-five thousand into fragments. He must withdraw his right wing and form line again upon the crested horse-shoe which is before them at the base of the mountain. Quick the orders are given, and quick the movement is executed, yet not a moment too soon; for yonder, from behind a clump of woods, emerges the head of Longstreet's bristling columns. But Thomas' men are few, and his line falls short by three hundred feet of the spur of the mountain. Longstreet sees this gap, heads his column for it, and in a moment more will have struck Thomas on flank and rear fatally. At this critical moment a heavy column is seen on the hill down which Garfield has just ridden, and in another moment a horseman, his steed covered with foam, is by the side of Thomas and Garfield. He is a slightly-formed man, a little slab-sided, with dark hair, projecting brows, and deep, black, cavernous eyes, from which now a black flame is flashing. It is Granger. He points with his sword to the men on the hill, and cries, "Where will you place us?" Thomas stretches his hand toward the three-hundred-feet gap, in the direction of which Longstreet is coming, and simply says "There!" Back, up the bullet-swept hill, Granger gallops, and in a moment his thirty-seven hundred men, led on by Steedman, are rushing down to the break in the lines, like a bristling avalanche. They are not a moment too soon, for Longstreet's heavy column is at the breach, and—now comes the collision. It is like two immense railway trains meeting in full career—the forward columns shivering to atoms, and going down as they come together. Steedman's horse is shot on the full gallop, and his rider is hurled fifteen feet forward by the momentum. He lights on his feet, and waves his sword for his men to come on as if nothing had happened. For forty minutes the onset lasted, and then a ghastly breastwork of three thousand mangled blue-coats and gray fills the narrow gap, but the Army of the Cumberland is saved from destruction. A thousand of our brave men killed and wounded paid for its possession; but we held the gap. And this is the result of Garfield's zigzag ride over that bullet-swept cotton-field. It gave Thomas the information which saved the army. Now, beaten and baffled, Longstreet withdraws his reeling columns, but along the rest of the line the conflict still rages. At its close, bleeding and dying and dead, twenty thousand men lie

*The details of this account are mostly from the statement of Captain William B. Gaw, then chief-engineer on the staff of General Thomas, who was Garfield's companion in this perilous ride.

about that smoking horse-shoe; but then the Confederates are in full retreat, and Garfield, shooting a battery of Napoleon guns, gives them a parting salutation. Begrimed with smoke and powder, Garfield had been everywhere during the battle, animating and encouraging the men; but toward the close of the fight, sheltered by a dead tree, he sat down on the ground, and indited a dispatch to Rosecrans, detailing the situation. As he sat there, during the heaviest of the firing, a white dove, after hovering above his head for a few moments, settled on the topmost branch of the tree which sheltered him. It remained there in all the leaden storm, nor flew away till he had finished his writing. "It is an omen of peace," said General Wood, who stood beside him. Garfield said nothing, but went on with his dispatch. Then the dove flew away to the North. Garfield went again into the battle, and the flash of his Napoleon guns was the last light that shone upon the bloody field of Chickamauga.

Toward the close of the fight Thomas' ammunition ran very low. His ammunition trains had become involved with the rout of the right, and were miles in the rear at Rossville. This want of ammunition created more fear than the assaults of the enemy. The last charge was repelled at portions of the line with the bayonet alone. But the hard-earned victory was won. The Rossville road was still held. The masterly skill and coolness of Thomas, when General Garfield reached him with information as to the rest of the army, which, it must be remembered, was never visible through the dense forests and jagged ridges of the valley, had saved the Army of the Cumberland from destruction. After night the exhausted men withdrew to Rossville and subsequently to Chattanooga. In the battle of Chickamauga General Rosecrans lost about seventeen thousand men, about five thousand having been taken prisoners; thirty-six pieces of cannon and over eight thousand small arms. The enemy's loss was eighteen thousand, and about two thousand were taken as prisoners. It was only the glorious stand made by the left wing of our army under General Thomas that saved the army from destruction or capture.

"A great battle is a memorable experience to one who takes part. There is nothing like it on earth. Henceforth the participant is different from other men. All his preceding life becomes small and forgotten after such days as those of Chickamauga. From that day he feels that he began to live. When the flames of frenzy with which he was possessed subside, they have left their mark on his being. Ordinarily the flames of battle have burnt out many sympathies. His nature stands like a forest of charred and blackened trunks, once green and beautiful, waving in their leafy splendor, but through which the destroying tempest of fire has passed in its mad career of vengeance. He can neither forget nor forgive the murderous foe. Before the battle he might have exchanged tobacco plugs with the man with whom he would have, with equal readiness, exchanged shots. But after the carnage of the battle, after the day of blood and fury, all this is passed. The last gun is fired on the field of battle. The last shattered line of heroes withdraws into the night. The earth has received its last baptism of blood for the time-being. Only burial parties, with white flags, may be seen picking their way among the fallen brave. The actual battle is over forever. Not so is it with the combatant. In his mind the battle goes on and on. He is perpetually training masked batteries on the foe. The roar of conflict never ceases to reverberate in his brain. Throughout his life, whenever recalled to the subject of the war, his mental attitude is that of the battle-field. In his thought the columns are still charging up the hill. The earth still shakes with an artillery that is never silenced. The air is still sulphurous with gunpowder smoke. The ranks of the brave and true still fall around him. Forever is he mentally loading and firing; forever charging bayonets across the bloody field; forever burying the fallen heroes under the protection of the flag of truce. This is the law of ordinary minds. The red panorama of Gettysburg and Chickamauga is forever moving before his eyes. The wrench or strain given to his mental being by those days is too terrific, too awful, for any re-action in the average mind. This fact has been abundantly proven in the history of the last twenty years. Chickamauga thus became a new birth to many a soldier. His life, henceforward, seemed to date from the 19th of September, 1863. His life was ever afterward marked off by anniversaries of that day. It is found that many soldiers die on the anniversaries of some great battle in which they were participants. Such is the influence mental states bear upon the physical organism. Chickamauga was all this to General Garfield. It was more than this to him. He was not merely a participant in the battle of bullets. He was also in the battle of brains. The field soldier certainly feels enough anxiety. His mental experience has enough of torture to gratify the monarch of hell himself. But the anxieties of the men at head-quarters are unspeakable. He sees not merely the actual horrors and the individual danger. He carries on his heart the responsibility for an army. He is responsible for the thousands of lives. A single mistake, a single blunder, a single defective plan, will forever desolate unnumbered firesides. More than this he feels. Not only the fate of the army, but the fate of the country rests in his hand. The burden is crushing. It may be said this is only upon the commander-in-chief. But General Garfield, as chief of staff, we have seen, was no figure-head, no amanuensis. He took the responsibilities of that campaign and battle to his own heart. At every step his genius grappled with the situation. Rosecrans was a good soldier; but in nothing was his ability so exhibited as in selecting Garfield for confidential adviser, and trusting so fully to his genius."

Thus the battle of Chickamauga entered into Garfield's mental experience in its greatest aspects. His profoundly sympathetic nature was subjected to an incalculable strain. The struggle of the first day, the beginning of the second, the fatal order, the apalling catastrophe, the fearful ride, the invincible courage of Thomas, the costly victory, all these things were incorporated into his life. He lived years in a single hour. He was only *thirty-one years old.* It was only seven years since he had graduated. But the education of Chickamauga gave him age. The maturity of the mind is not measured by time, but by experience. Previous to the Chattanooga campaign, General Garfield was a clever man. After the battle of Chickamauga he was a great man.

In their reports to head-quarters, Generals Rosecrans and Wood made special mention of Garfield's heroism and bravery at Chickamauga. A fortnight later the War Department commissioned Garfield a major-general, "for gallant conduct, and important services," in the battle of Chickamauga.

GARFIELD—THE STATESMAN.

GREATER THAN ALL.

Alexander conquered the world by the force of arms; Garfield by loftiness of character. Cæsar had great ambition; Garfield higher and nobler. Charlemagne founded an empire; Garfield a character that was greater than an empire. Frederick the Great made German nationality possible; Garfield made Christian statesmanship a reality. Napoleon overthrew feudalism; Garfield cemented American liberty. Each of these great characters was great in his sphere and age; but Garfield lived in a better and lived a better life, and has left the better example. Little wonder, then, is it that America mourns, and the sympathy of the world goes out to her, in this dark hour.

R. J. BURDETTE.

CHAPTER XIII.

RESIGNS HIS COMMISSION AND ENTERS THE WAR CONGRESS.

There is a mystery in the soul of State,
Which hath an operation more divine
Than breath or pen can give expressure to.
—SHAKESPEARE.

Turn him to any course of policy,
The Gordian knot of it he will unloose.
—SHAKESPEARE.

Again the course of our hero's life is turned into a new channel. The first visions of a glorious seaman's life had given away to the more pleasant pursuits of the student, and now as he is about to be rewarded by splendid promotions in the army, and his thoughts and longings are of military leadership, circumstances change all this. As in the former case, the change was to his advantage, so has time vindicated the wisdom of his leaving the army for Congress. It was this fortunate and providential change that made Garfield the twentieth President of his country.

The important fact to which we have now made reference as changing his career, was his nomination and election to Congress, which the people of the famous Western Reserve district had secured in the fall of 1862. Several months yet intervened before Congress would assemble, and for the time he put aside the tempting offer.

"Peace hath her victories no less renowned than war;" and we are now to follow Garfield in the walks of peace, but through many a well-contested struggle, crowned by many a hard-won victory. He had been elected to Congress from the Nineteenth District of Ohio, for so many years represented by Joshua R. Giddings. His term did not begin until December of 1863, and his constituents felt certain that the war would end before that time. The Tullahoma campaign came on, Garfield's military desires had only increased; and the congressional question still forced itself unpleasantly upon him. He thought and pondered over the matter; and the more he thought the greater became the difficulty of a decision. Peace was yet a thing wearing so much of futurity and uncertainty that few thoughts were given it. Had peace come in the year 1863, as was expected, the question in Garfield's mind would readily have been settled.

On an afternoon, while debating this subject in his mind—the army was then at Chattanooga—Garfield approached his commander, Rosecrans, and said to him: "General, I have been asked to accept the Republican nomination for Congress from the Ashtabula district. What ought I to do? What is your advice? Ought I to accept? Can I do so honorably?"

"I am glad, for your sake," returned Rosecrans, "that you have a new distinction, and I certainly think you can accept with honor, and, what is more, I deem it your duty to do so. The war is not over yet, nor will it be for some time to come. There will be of necessity, many questions arising in Congress which will require not alone statesmanlike treatment, but the advice of men having an acquaintance with military affairs. For this, and other reasons, I believe you will be able to do equally good service to your country in Congress as in the field. Now, let me give you a piece of advice. When you go to Congress, be careful what you say. Don't talk too much, but when you do talk speak to the point. Be true to yourself, and you will make your mark before the country."

But even the encouragement given by Rosecrans did not decide his mind. He still waited. It was while in this strait of uncertainty that the Chattanooga campaign came on. Of course Garfield was engaged in this so incessantly that he thought little of the congressional offer. The idea of chaining himself down to the monotonous sessions of Congress, was not at all pleasing for him to contemplate. The enthusiasm of his military ancestry aroused him. He saw his fitness to grapple with the great problem of the rebellion on the field, and was loath to relinquish such pursuits. But his brother officers urged him to accept. Military men were needed in the Nation's Congress no less than on the field of battle. Such men were the only ones who could understand rightly the wants of the army. To future success it was absolutely necessary that Congress should assist the army with money and equipments.

The battle of Chickamauga over he started to Washington, where the Department of War, relying in Garfield's spotless integrity, demanded a full explanation of the disastrous campaign, why so many thousand lives were sacrificed, and the exact situation of affairs, with the present needs of the army.

An incident which occurred while he was *en route*, as told by Mr. George Q. Gardner, will be appropriate at this place:

Generals Garfield, Steedman and myself happened to go down from the hotel in Louisville to the ferry-boat in the same 'bus, on the top of which were Garfield's and Steedman's negro servants. It appears that, owing to the fact that the emancipation proclamation was not general, and did not at that time apply to Kentucky, that State's Legislature had taken advantage of it and passed laws regarding the kidnapping and confiscating of every stray negro the gangs of civil officers and citizens could lay their hands upon. Officers with posses were stationed at the levees, instructed and authorized to seize all negroes attempting to cross the river on the boats, no matter where they were from. When we went on the boat we were all in ignorance of this State law, and of the fact that a strong force of men were on the boat for the purpose of seizing any unlucky darkey who might be going North with the Union officers. My attention was first called to the fact by hearing General Garfield ask a pompous-looking man, "What do you want with that boy?"

I looked out of the 'bus window and noticed that the man, in company with others, was ordering the two boys to get down from the 'bus and go ashore with them. The man, who claimed to be the sheriff, said the boys could not go across the river; that he should take possession of them, etc., and proceeded to force them off the boat. At this, Garfield and Steedman jumped out of the 'bus. Garfield was mad; he told these insolent men that he had been fighting rebels in the field for two years, that he would now do some fighting on the water, and if they did not leave the boat at once they would get hurt. He stood between the negroes and the officers, and shook his fist in their faces, and dared them to touch the black boys who had so faithfully stood by him in the camp and on the battle-grounds of Stone river and Chickamauga. General Steedman was mad; he pulled off his coat and marched into the crowd.

It was an exciting time for them. Those in the 'bus came to the assistance of the Union generals. The captain having been ordered by the sheriff not to move his boat, came to Garfield, and told him that he, the captain, could not take the boys across the river without incurring a heavy fine, and therefore would not move the boat. General Garfield said he would relieve him of responsibility, so he announced he would pilot the boat across if some one would volunteer to run the engine. Upon several of the soldiers agreeing to do it, the captain caved and ordered the boat untied, saying he would take the crowd across, and stop the 'tarnal fuss. The boat started and the row ended.

Garfield embraced the opportunity of visiting his modest home at Hiram while on his way to the Capital. The Hiram cottage where Mrs. Garfield still lived seemed dearer to him than ever before. But grief was also a visitor there. While at home, his first-born, "Little Trot," only three years of age, was seized with a fatal illness. The little one died, and sadness filled their hearts. The parents had no picture of the child, to whom they were both tenderly attached, and an artist was called in to take its photograph after death. Garfield was in his uniform, his civilian suit not being yet ready; and when he took the little creature on his lap, and glanced down upon its pallid features, his eye fell on the buttons of his new rank of major-general. Sitting thus, with death in his arms, how little, he thought, is there in all the honors and glory of the world! The funeral over, and the first pangs of grief subdued, he was compelled to hurry onward to Washington. Reader, imagine if you can James Garfield's feelings as he journeyed toward the Capital!

Almost heart-broken, and with great responsibility entrusted to him, he at last arrived at New York, where he remained over night with his old college classmate and bosom friend, Henry E. Knox. To him he put the same question he had put to Rosecrans, and received, in substance, the same answer; but still he was undecided. At last he said to his friend, "I will state the case to Mr. Lincoln when I arrive at Washington, and leave it to his decision." Never was a man so unwilling to accept a seat in Congress. He felt he had a great prospect before him in the army, and he desired to realize it.

Arriving at Washington, he sought out the President, and made him acquainted with the state of his mind, and Mr. Lincoln said, "The Republican majority in Congress is very small, and it is often doubtful whether we can carry the necessary war measures; and, besides, we are greatly lacking in men of military experience in the House to regulate legislation about the army. It is your duty, therefore, to enter Congress."

Garfield often expressed regret that he did not fight the war through. Had he done so he would no doubt have ranked at its close among the foremost of the victorious generals of the Republic, for he displayed in his Sandy Valley campaign and at the battle of Chickamauga the highest qualities of generalship. A brilliant opening awaited him in the Army of the Cumberland.

It was evident to Garfield that his mission to Washington would result either in the vindication or removal of Rosecrans. The troubles already mentioned, existing between the War Department and this general, had reached such a point that the government had decided upon an investigation. Garfield determined to save Rosecrans if it was in his power. Secretary Stanton was visited, a detailed account of the actions of the Army of the Cumberland given, and with maps at command, Garfield made an elaborate presentation of facts, from the long delay at Murfreesboro down through the Tullahoma and Chattanooga campaigns. He did all he could for his general, and gave a masterly review of the situation. Montgomery Blair, one of the ablest men at the Capital, after listening to General Garfield's masterly presentation of the facts, said to a friend, "Garfield is a great man." President Lincoln said, "I never understood so fully and clearly the necessities, situation and movements of any army in the field."

But the die was cast. No amount of importuning in Rosecrans' favor would avail. Stanton and the commander-in-chief were firm, and Rosecrans had to go. His obstinate refusals at Murfreesboro, his insulting letters, his violent temper and uncontrollable stubbornness, had ruined him long before Chickamauga. Enemies were now ready to destroy him. Chickamauga gave the opportunity. The fatal order, the rout of the right wing, the loss of presence of mind, and the ride to the rear—which was in telling contrast with General Garfield's heroic and intrepid ride to the front—bore down upon him like an avalanche. The strategy of the campaigns was regarded as splendid, even Napoleonic. No fault of the Department could excuse Rosecrans, and he was relieved. The chief of staff, rightly regarded by Stanton as the back-bone and originator of the successful movements, was advanced.

This mission ended, he now finally decided the matter of entering Congress. With the implicit understanding that his rank would be restored to him if he desired to return to the army, General Garfield reluctantly resigned his new major-generalship. He left the Army of the Cumberland, followed by the regrets and good wishes of every man in it—for each was his friend—and he laid down his sword, to enter an arena where he has won a prouder fame, a soldier of few but shining laurels. A distinguished military critic thus sums up his soldierly achievements: "He proved himself a good, independent commander in the small but important operations in the Sandy valley. His campaign there opened our series of successes in the West, and, though fought against superior forces, began with us the habit of victory. After that he was only a subordinate. But he always enjoyed the confidence of his immediate superiors and of the Department. As chief of staff, he was unrivaled. There, as elsewhere, he was ready to accept the gravest responsibilities in following his convictions. The bent of his mind was aggressive; his judgment in military matters was always good; his papers on the Tullahoma campaign will stand a monument of his courage and his far-reaching soldierly sagacity; and his conduct at Chickamauga will never be forgotten by a nation of brave men."

A prominent writer of the day has said:

The greatest men seem often to have been those who were suddenly lifted out of the career of life which they had chosen, and to which they seemed to be pre-eminently adapted, and forced, as it were, by the exigencies of the times into a new channel. Julius Cæsar, whose lofty character, unapproachable genius, and sorrowful death, are hardly equalled in the annals of any age or country, had chosen for himself the career of a civil and religious officer of state. His chosen field was in the stately sessions of the Roman Senate, or before the turbulent multitudes of the forum. It was said of him by his enemies, that in speaking he excelled those who practiced no other art. It was said that, had he continued in his chosen career, he would have outshone, in his eloquence, every orator whose name and fame has been transmitted by Rome to later generations. But from this career he was unexpectedly taken. The dangers to the state from Gallic tribes, and the restless Roman appetite for conquest, required a military leader. Almost by accident Cæsar was drawn away from the senate and the forum to take up the profession of arms.

Unlike the great Roman, Garfield, under the stress of public necessity, was almost by accident withdrawn from the career of arms, in which it may be truly said of him that he, too, excelled those who practiced no other art, to enter upon the career of a legislator. Cæsar exchanged the assembly for the camp, while the great American left the camp for the assembly. Each did so at the call of the state, and each was to become, in his new field, the master spirit of his generation.

On the 5th day of December, 1863, General Garfield entered the House of Representatives of that United States, bearing the credentials entitling him to a seat and voice in the body. The Thirty-Eighth Congress is pre-eminently entitled in history to the designation of the War Congress. It was elected while the war was flagrant, and every member was chosen upon the issues involved in the continuance of the struggle. The Thirty-Seventh Congress had, indeed, legislated to a large extent on war measures, but it was chosen before any one believed that secession of the States would be actually attempted. The magnitude of the work which fell upon its successor was unprecedented, both in respect to the vast sums of money raised for the support of the Army and Navy, and of the new and extraordinary powers of legislation which it was forced to exercise. Only twenty-four States were represented, and one hundred and eighty-two members were upon its roll. Among these were many distinguished party leaders on both sides, veterans in the public service, with established reputations for ability, and with that skill which comes only from parliamentary experience. Into this assemblage of men Garfield entered without special preparation, and it might almost be said, unexpectedly. The question of taking command of a division of troops under General Thomas or taking his seat in Congress was kept open till the last moment, so late, indeed, that the resignation of his military commission and his appearance in the House were almost contemporaneous. He wore the uniform of a major-general of the United States Army on Saturday, and on Monday, in civilian's dress, he answered to the roll-call as a Representative in Congress from the State of Ohio. He was the youngest member of that body, as he had been of the Ohio Legislature, and the youngest brigadier in the army.

Before proceeding further it may be well to pause and inquire who sent him there, and learn what we may of his constituency. We premise beforehand that it must have been an intelligent and progressive community, for such a man they chose to represent them, and it will generally be found that congressional representatives are good indices of their constituency. But stronger proof is forthcoming. We are acquainted with the fact that nine times the length of a Congressional term, and an equal number of times that measures the political life of a majority of Congressmen, James A. Garfield was returned to the House as the Representative of this same district. All this time he was an active participant in the events that have transpired in congress, and he has left the imprint of his ability and patriotism as thoroughly upon the legislation of the country as any man recently in public service. Garfield, we know, was great, and hence we cannot but form favorable conclusions concerning his constituency.

The congressional district in which he lived is generally called the Ashtabula district, and has been more faithful to its representatives than any of those of the North. It now consists of the counties of Ashtabula, Portage, Geauga and Trumbull, and contains a voting population of about twenty-five thousand. The county of Lake, which was a part of it when Garfield was first elected, has been detached. The district is the nineteenth, and is situated in the Western Reserve—the New England of the North-west—in North-east Ohio. It was originally settled by New Englanders, and its population has the thrift, the keen intelligence, the habits of local self-government, the political instincts, and the morals of New England. Well educated, thrifty, thoroughly intelligent in affairs, acutely discerning of character, not quick to bestow confidence, and slow to withdraw it, they were at once the most helpful and most exacting of supporters. Their tenacious trust in men in whom they have once confided is illustrated by the unparalleled fact that Elisha Whittlesey, Joshua R. Giddings and James A Garfield represented the district for fifty-four years. There is no population of equal numbers on the long line reaching from New York to Chicago, that writes so many letters and receives through the mails so much reading matter. There is less illiteracy in proportion to the population, than in any other district in the United States. Free schools are at every cross-road, and in some sections one may ride a whole day without coming upon a dram-shop. They are manly, energetic, freedom-loving, and God-fearing; but with these qualities, it may be, there exist among them some faint traces of the bigotry, narrowness, and cast-iron theology of rural New England as it was fifty years ago. The district is essentially a rural one, with the exception of some iron-working portions in the southern end. It early became deeply interested in the anti-slavery movement, and this greatly quickened the interest of its people in public affairs. It was this intelligent interest in national welfare that made the district accessible to General Garfield's earnest, straight-forward exposition of solid political doctrines, to his high bearing, to the impact of his mental and moral power upon intelligent and honest minds, rather than by any managing or demagogic measures. Giddings, the anti-slavery champion, had served them faithfully for nearly a quarter of a century, when one day they learned that, in reckoning his mileage, he went to Washington by the way of New York, while Ben Wade, who lived on the other side of the street from him, made the same journey by the shorter route *via* Harrisburg, and thus saved the district two hundred dollars a year. Two hundred dollars divided among twenty-five thousand tax-payers is less than one cent to each; but every one of these tax-payers felt that the whole amount came out of his individual pocket, and they arose in the spirit of Seventy-six and threw Mr. Giddings, as their fathers had thrown the boxes of tea, overboard. Grown careless of the arts of politics toward the end of his career, he came to look upon a nomination and re-election as a matter of course. His over-confidence was taken advantage of by an ambitious lawyer named Hutchins, to carry the convention of 1858 against him. Giddings was defeated, and lost his influence. But the country was kinder than his constituency; it gave the good old man the consulate at Montreal, and thus he was not left in his age altogether "naked to his enemies." The friends of Giddings never forgave Hutchins, and cast about for a means of defeating him. In a short time the majority of the district became dissatisfied with their new representative, and, repenting of their unkindness, the leading men laid their suffrages again at the feet of their old Congressman. The old man was comfortably quartered in his consulate at Montreal, and did not care to make fight to get back to Congress. So, his supporters made use of the popularity of General Garfield, and nominated him while he was with his brigade. He had no knowledge of any such movement in his behalf. He had recently made his brilliant campaign in Eastern Kentucky, and they vividly remembered his important services in the State Senate, so without asking his leave, or even notifying him, they put him in nomination for Congress.

Now, into what kind of an arena was it that these people sent their champion to stand for them? The House of Representatives at this time confronted innumerable difficulties in the way of legislation. The war left only northern men as the component parts of Congress.

And it was to help complete the gigantic tasks of Congress during this momentous time that Garfield was sent there. The House of Representatives contained many able men, but most of these belonged to a closing period. They had grown up in opposition, not in administration. A new group of men was now about to take the lead, and re-construct the Union on a foundation whose corner-stone should be Union and Liberty, instead of Slavery and State Rights. The old generation of leaders were still there with their wisdom and valuable experience; but the spirit of a new era now came in, which should outlive Thaddeus Stevens and his compeers. About this time there came into Congress, Blaine and Boutwell and Conkling and—Garfield, destined to do more than any of them in restoring prosperity, peace, public justice, and, above all, a harmonious Union, which this age shall not again see broken. The usefulness of a legislator has in all times been popularly ascribed to his work in the open assembly. But this was never wholly true, and in no existing legislature in the world is it even half true at this day. Public business of this sort is so vast and so complicated that no assembly can give it all a fair consideration. To remedy this trouble we have the committee system, by which the special study of a few informs the many who rely upon their reports, and merely pass upon their recommendations. Several months passed before Garfield manifested much interest in the public proceedings of Congress. What work he did was mainly done in the committee rooms, as the Congressional records make mention of no speech delivered by him until early in the year 1864. But that he was active and diligent in his committee work is certain.

We are sometimes too prone to misjudge a Congressman or Representative on this account. In the majority of cases a member of Congress cannot be judged by the figure he presents on the floor of the house. In this arena he may be silent and yet the author and originator of some of the most summary and important measures before Congress. His worth may pass current for another person, who expresses on the floor what he has advanced in the committee rooms. But Garfield did more than either of these. He came to be master and leader in debate not only on the floor, but also in the private consultations of the committees of which he was an important member. On the floor he showed himself to be a clear and logical debater, and was little sought as an opponent. He was valuable to the committees, because his researches were wide, and his wonderful industry made him a valuable member.

We have seen that the Thirty-Eighth Congress began its session while the war was still in existence. Naturally the most important committee then was the Military Committee, as it ever was during the war. This committee was composed as follows: Robert C. Schenck, of Ohio; John F. Farnsworth, of Illinois; George H. Yeaman, of Kentucky; James A. Garfield, of Ohio; Benjamin Loan, of Missouri; Moses F. Odell, of New York; Henry C. Deming, of Connecticut; F. W. Kellogg, of Michigan; Archibald McAllister, of Pennsylvania—all prominent and leading men. The position which the chairman intended should be given Garfield on this committee was that of second instead of fourth. His experience and presence in the army had been in his favor, and, hence, it was the more desirable that he should occupy a leading position. In this capacity his activity, industry, military knowledge, and familiarity with the wants of the army brought him into immediate requisition, and, with his ability in debate, gave him at once a prominence in the House which he might not have acquired in a much longer time in other circumstances.

General Garfield's time was now devoted to public business. Every subject likely to come before his committee was investigated through all the avenues of information. He set himself a wide course of reading on finance, on constitutional law, and a great group of kindred subjects. These were studied in the Garfield way, which was to read all the literature he could find on a topic, or that could in any way affect the discussion thereof. It was this prodigious labor, matching his capacity for keeping the run of what would have overwhelmed most men with confusion, that made him at the same time a remarkably ready and a wonderfully reliable man, either in committee or as a speaker on the floor of the House. General Garfield had not been in Congress long before his occasional brief statements began to attract attention. Of course it was not till after a considerable period that he became a recognized leader; but his force began to be felt very soon, and grew every day until, by steady development of his abilities and his influence, he finally reached the summit of power, as leader of his party in the Lower House of Congress.

We have seen that he was not a politician in the popular sense of the word. He had been sent to Congress rather against than with his inclinations, and was above posturing and plotting for re-election. Even after he had reluctantly given up his commission as major-general in the army, he was ready to return on call. In fact, he did once almost determine on going back. General Thomas, having succeeded Rosecrans in his command, wrote a private letter asking Garfield to accept the command of a corps in his army. Thomas urged this upon him in a private letter, and it brought up again to Garfield the question whether his duty did not lie in that direction. Another consideration which may properly have weighed with him, was the fact that he had a young and growing family, and that his salary as a Congressman—then only three thousand dollars—was barely sufficient for their support, and less than half what his pay would be as a major-general. He was a poor man, and this last, therefore, was a weighty consideration. The offer was tempting, and duty seemed to point the way. Mr. Lincoln, however, was having trouble to get his measures through Congress, and needed support.

Almost immediately after the opening of the Thirty-Eighth Congress occurred the great war-legislation of this momentous period. On the 26th of January, 1864, was introduced a bill for the confiscation of rebel property, and Garfield made his first regular speech in Congress. House Resolution No. 18 was offered, so amending a resolution of the preceding Congress that no punishment or proceedings under it should be so construed as to make a forfeiture of the estate of the offender, except during life. Out of this little motion there grew a great crop of controversy, and, among others, General Garfield took part. His first speech of any length, on January 28th, gave ample promise in the bud of the flowers of powerful oratory so soon to bloom. For it shows the swing of his mind and the character of his oratory, as well as his mental stature at this early date in his Congressional career. It was a reply to his Democratic colleague, Mr. Finck, who had just taken his seat at the close of a long set speech, and was in favor of the confiscation of rebel property. We quote from its brilliant passages:

The war was announced by proclamation, and it must end by proclamation. We can hold the insurgent States in military subjection half a century, if need be, until they are purged of their poison and stand up clean before the country. They must come back with clean hands, if they come at all. I hope to see in all those States the men who fought and suffered for the truth, tilling the fields on which they pitched their tents. I hope to see them, like old Kasper of Blenheim, on the summer evenings, with their children upon their knees, and pointing out the spot where brave men fell and marble commemorates it.

* * * * * * *

I deprecate these apparently partisan remarks; it hurts me to make them, but it hurts me more to know they are true. I conclude by returning once more to the resolution before me. Let no weak sentiments of misplaced sympathy deter us from inaugurating a measure which will cleanse our Nation and make it the fit home of freedom and glorious manhood. Let us not despise the severe wisdom of our Revolutionary fathers, when they served their generation in a similar way. Let the republic drive from its soil the traitors that have conspired against its life, as God and his angels drove Satan and his host from heaven. He was not too merciful to be just, and to hurl down in chains and everlasting darkness the "traitor angel" who "first broke peace in heaven," and rebelled against him.

This was not the kind of man to stultify himself for the sake of public favor; and therefore it is not surprising to find his speech on the "Bounty Question" opposed to the whole House. At this time in the war, volunteering had become so rare a thing that new measures had to be devised to keep up the ever-dwindling ranks of the army. Two methods were advocated. One was to draft men forcibly, and put them into the service; the other was to induce men to volunteer by payment of a bonus for enlistment. Out of these two principles a hybrid policy had been formed, resulting in the Conscription Act, of March 3, 1863. This act provided for a draft, but allowed a commutation in money, which was fixed at three hundred dollars. In addition, thirteen exceptions were allowed by which the draft could be escaped. To compensate for these losses, three hundred dollars bounty money was given to every raw recruit, and four hundred dollars to every re-enlisted veteran. The result of all this was a rapidly decreasing army. The Government urged stronger measures; and it was before these measures had been perfected that an incident occurred in which General Garfield first indicated his opinions on the subject.

According to a law passed, the bounties above mentioned could be paid only up to January 5, 1864. On January 6th, the Military Committee reported a joint resolution to continue this limit over till March 1st. Mr. Garfield did not approve of the resolution, although every man in the House seemed against him. His reasons are given in the *Congressional Globe*, wherein the following is reported:

MR. GARFIELD.—Mr. Speaker, I regret that I was not able to meet with the Military Committee when this resolution was under consideration. I did not reach the city until a few hours before the House met this morning; but if I understand the matter correctly from the public journals, the request of the President and the War Department was to continue the payment of bounties until the 1st of February next; but the resolution before the House proposes to extend the payment until the 1st of March. And while the President asks us to continue the payment of bounties to veteran volunteers only, the resolution extends it to all volunteers, whether veterans or raw recruits. If the resolution prevails, it seems to me we shall swamp the finances of the Government before the 1st of March arrives. I can not consent to a measure which authorizes the expenditure of so vast a sum as will be expended under this resolution, unless it be shown absolutely indispensable to the work of filling up the army. I am anxious that veterans should volunteer, and that liberal bounties should be paid to them. But if we extend the payment to all classes of volunteers for two months to come, I fear we shall swamp the Government. Before I vote for this resolution, I desire to know whether the Government is determined to abandon the draft. If it be its policy to raise an army solely by volunteering and paying bounties, we have one line of policy to pursue. If the conscription law is to be anything but a dead letter on the statute book, our line of policy is a very different one. I ask the gentleman from Illinois to inform me what course is to be adopted. I am sorry to see in this resolution the indication of a timid and vacillating course. It is unworthy the dignity of our Government and our army to use the conscription act as a scarecrow, and the bounty system as a bait, to alternately scare and coax men into the army. Let us give liberal bounties to veteran soldiers who may re-enlist, and for raw recruits use the draft.

The discussion among the members having closed, the vote was taken, resulting in yeas 112, noes 2. Mr. Grinnell, of Iowa, made the second negative, changing his vote after Garfield had voted. The system had been tried before, and it had gathered in a host of bounty-jumpers and wretched fellows who would have shamed the raw recruits of Falstaff. The bill was popular with the soldiers, for it offered recruits—whether they jumped the service or served out their time honestly—a large premium for enlistment. Congress was unanimously in favor of the measure, for the members wanted to be friendly with the soldiers who were their constituents. This vote at once brought a letter of censure, signed by twenty of the most influential of Garfield's constituents. His resignation was demanded, but conscious of the integrity of his views he only answered by saying that within a year they would all agree with his action and vindicate him. This was a fearless action. But right was right, and he did not propose to give any vantage ground to that which he regarded as wrong. He had acted according to his views of the needs of the country. Within a year, his action was praised by the very men who first had censured him. Salmon P. Chase, then Secretary of the Treasury, congratulated him, admiring his firmness and adherence to principle, but cautioned him to be very careful against such antagonism to his party, and advised him to indulge in it sparingly. As we know the man now, this advice was scarcely necessary, for Garfield ever showed himself to be a shrewd man, and not at all factious. He simply had the courage of conviction.

It was not long before the bounty system broke down, and Congress came to Garfield's opinion. The system of bounties had proved a failure. We had attempted coercion on the States, and the only way to succeed was by further coercion of our own citizens. Legislation on the enrollment of soldiers must now come. The people objected; and Congressmen were afraid of the coming fall election of 1864. Garfield could not understand how men could value their political lives in such a crisis.

The army at this time numbered about seven hundred and fifty thousand; but one day Mr. Lincoln came to the room of the Committee on Military Affairs, and told them—what he did not dare say in public, and they did not dare to disclose to the House—that at a certain time not far ahead, say, one hundred days, the term of three hundred and eighty thousand men would expire, and the army be reduced below four hundred thousand. "Unless I can replace those three hundred and eighty thousand," he said, "we not only cannot push the rebellion, but we cannot stand where we are. Sherman will have to come back from Atlanta, Grant from the peninsula. I ask you to give me the power to draft men to fill the ranks." Some of his Republican friends on the committee remonstrated with him; they represented that it was just on the eve of his re-election, and that the country would not tolerate a draft-law; that men who had already paid large sums for substitutes to meet the quotas would not now submit to be drafted, and would raise a tempest which would carry the country for the Democracy. Mr. Lincoln raised his awkward but manly figure up to its full height, as he said: "Gentlemen, it is not necessary that I should be re-elected; but it *is* necessary that I should put down this Rebellion. If you will give me this law, I will put it down before my successor takes his seat." Thereupon the committee drew a draft-bill, and reported it to the House. It was voted down by a two-thirds majority.

This would never do. The friends of the bill re-constructed it, and determined to put it through. On the 21st of June the effort was made. General Garfield was, perhaps, more intensely wrought up on the subject than any man except Lincoln, and his speech was full of fire, and bristling like a regiment of bayonets. It was replete with learning, logic, and eloquence. This bill was the result of conditions in national affairs which Garfield had long forseen; he had prophesied at the time of his vote against extending bounties, that the end of such extension would be ruin to the Union cause. That ruin was now impending, and the closing appeal in his great speech suggests his earnestness:

I ask gentlemen who oppose this repeal, why they desire to make it easy for citizens to escape from military duty? Is it a great hardship to serve one's country? Is it a disgraceful service? Will you, by your action here, say to the soldiers in the field, "This is a disreputable business; you have been deceived; you have been caught in a trap, and we will make no law to put anybody else in it?" Do you thus treat your soldiers in the field? They are proud of their voluntary service, and if there be one wish of the army paramount to all others, one message more earnest than all the others which they send back to you, it is that you will aid in filling up their battle-thinned ranks by a draft which will compel lukewarm citizens who prate against the war to go into the field. They ask that you will not expend large bounties in paying men for third-rate patriotism, while they went with no other bounty than their love of country, to which they gave their young lives a free offering, but that you will compel these eleventh-hour men to take their chances in the field beside them. Let us grant their request, and, by a steady and persistent effort, we shall, in the end, be it near or remote, be it in one year or ten, crown the nation with victory and enduring peace.

It carried the house by storm; the bill was passed after a lengthy discussion, and Mr. Lincoln made the draft for five hundred thousand men, and the immortal work was enabled to be finished.

This readiness at trenchant debating proved, in some respects, injurious to his rising fame. Garfield spoke so readily that members were constantly asking his services in behalf of favorite measures, and in the impulsive eagerness of a young man and a young member, he often consented. He thus came to be too frequent a speaker, and the House wearied a little of his polished periods, and began to think him too fond of talking. His superior knowledge, too, used to offend some of his less learned colleagues at first. They thought him bookish and pedantic, until they found how solid and useful was his store of knowledge, and how pertinent to the business in hand were the drafts he made upon it. But this in time wore off. His genial personal ways soon made him many warm friends, and re-action set in. The men of brains in both Houses, and in the departments, were not long in discovering that here was a fresh, strong intellectual force that was destined to make its mark upon the politics of the country. They sought his acquaintance, and before he had been long in Washington, he had the advantage of the best society in the capital.

It was during this session, February 17th, that a resolution was introduced in the House, tendering the thanks of Congress to General George H. Thomas for his important services at the battle of Chickamauga, but omitting all mention of Rosecrans. Mr. Garfield, upon the resolution being read twice, moved to amend it by inserting the name of Major-General W. S. Rosecrans before that of General Thomas, so that it would read, "to Major-General W. S. Rosecrans and Major-General George H. Thomas, and to the officers and men under them." Several members objected, thinking separate resolutions would be better. In support of his motion General Garfield said:

I regret that this resolution has come before the House of Representatives, as it is now presented. Since this session began we have not only thanked officers who were chiefs in armies, but also those who held subordinate positions in the various armies of the Republic. In many of the instances referred to, I have had no knowledge of the merits of the case. But when it comes so close to my own experience and knowledge of the history of the war, I cannot permit a resolution of this kind to pass without my protest against this hasty and thoughtless style of legislation. I now appeal to your sense of justice whether it be right to single out a subordinate officer, give him the thanks of Congress, and pass his chief in silence. On what grounds are you now ready to ignore the man who has won so many of the proudest victories? This resolution proposes to thank Major-General Thomas and the officers and men under his command for gallant services in the battle of Chickamauga. It meets my hearty approval for what it contains, but my protest for what it does not contain. I should be recreant to my sense of justice did I allow this omission to pass without notice. No man here is ready to say—and if there be such a man I am ready to meet him—that the thanks of this Congress are not due to Major-General W. S. Rosecrans, for the campaign which culminated in the battle of Chickamauga. It is not uncommon throughout the press of the country, and among many people, to speak of that battle as a disaster to the army of the United States, and to treat of it as a defeat. If that battle was a defeat, we may welcome a hundred such defeats. I should be glad if each of our armies would repeat Chickamauga. Twenty such would destroy the rebel army and the Confederacy utterly and forever.

What was that battle, terminating as it did a great campaign whose object was to drive the rebel army beyond the Tennessee, and to obtain a foothold on the south bank of that river, which should form the basis of future operations in the Gulf States? We had never yet crossed that river, except far below, in the neighborhood of Corinth. Chattanooga was the gateway of the Cumberland Mountains, and until we crossed the river and held the gateway, we could not commence operations in Georgia. The army was ordered to cross the river, to grasp and hold the key of the Cumberland Mountains. It did cross in the face of superior numbers; and after two days of fighting, more terrible, I believe, than any since this war began, the army of the Cumberland, hurled back, discomfited and repulsed the combined power of three rebel armies, gained the key to the Cumberland Mountains, gained Chattanooga, and held it against every assault. If there has been a more substantial success against overwhelming odds since the war began, I have not heard of it. We have had victories—God be thanked—along the line, but in the history of this war, I know of no such battle against such numbers; forty thousand against an army of not less by a man than seventy-five thousand. Who commanded the army of the Cumberland? Who organized, disciplined and led it? Who planned its campaign? The general whose name is omitted in this resolution, Major-General W. S. Rosecrans. And who is this General Rosecrans? The history of the country tells you, and your children know it by heart. It is he who fought battles and won victories in Western Virginia under the shadow of another's name. When the poetic pretender claimed the honor and received the reward as the author of Virgil's stanza in praise of Cæsar, the great Mautceau wrote on the walls of the imperial palace: "*Hos ego versiculos feci, tulit alter honores.*" So might the hero of Rich Mountain say, "I won this battle, but another has won the laurels." From Western Virginia he went to Mississippi, and there won the battles of Iuka and Corinth, which have added materially to exalt the fame of that general upon whom this House has been in such haste to confer the proud rank of Lieutenant-General of the Army of the United States, but who was not upon either of these battle-fields. Who took command of the Army of the Cumberland, fought that army at Bowling Green in November, 1862, as it lay disorganized, disheartened, driven back from Alabama and Tennessee, and led it across the Cumberland, planted it in Nashville, and thence, on the first day of the new year, planted his banners at Murfreesboro in torrents of blood, and in the moment of our extremest peril throwing himself into the breach, saved by his personal valor the Army of the Cumberland and the hopes of the Republic? It was General Rosecrans. From the day he assumed the command at Bowling Green the history of that army may be written in one sentence—it advanced and maintained its advanced position, and its last campaign under the general it loved was the bloodiest and most brilliant. The fruits of Chickamauga were gathered in November, on the heights of Mission Ridge and among the clouds of Lookout Mountain. The battle at Chattanooga was a glorious one, and every loyal heart is proud of it. But, sir, it was won when we had nearly three times the number of the enemy. It ought to have been won. Thank God that it was won! I would take no laurels from the brow of the man who won it; but I would remind gentlemen here that while the battle of Chattanooga was fought with vastly superior numbers on our part, the battle of Chickamauga was fought with still vaster superiority against us. If there is any man upon earth whom I honor it is the man who is named in this resolution—General George H. Thomas. But I say to gentlemen here, that if there is any man whose heart would be hurt by the passage of this resolution as it now stands, that man is General George H. Thomas. I know, and all know, that he deserves well of his country, and his name ought to be recorded in letters of gold; but I know, equally well, that General Rosecrans deserves well of his country. I ask you, then, not to pain the heart of a noble man who will be burdened with the weight of these thanks that wrong his brother officer and his superior in command.

The nation now knows that Garfield was right; that Rosecrans was one of the ablest soldiers and purest patriots that helped to crush the Rebellion.

In March, 1864, the Committee on Military Affairs reported a bill "to declare certain roads military roads, and post roads, and to regulate commerce." Its principal object, as far as the government was concerned, was to enlarge its facilities of communication between Washington, Philadelphia and New York. The only existing postal route between the commercial capital and the political capital, was by the Camden and Amboy Railroad. This bill was presented on petition of the Raritan and Delaware Bay Railroad Company, asking that it be given similar rights to those held by the Camden and Amboy; which latter road of course used all its influence to defeat the measure. Both the power and the duty of Congress to pass the bill were violently assailed and denied. Mr Garfield favored its passage, and made a speech on the subject which ran through parts of two days—March 24, and 31. This address was very powerful, and was called by some members "the speech of the session."

On the 8th of April, 1864, the House of Representatives resolved itself into the committee of the whole upon the state of the Union, whereupon Mr. Alexander Long, of Cincinnati, Ohio, took the floor, and, in a speech of much bitterness, arraigned the administration, not for its conduct of the war, but for carrying on the war at all. "*An unconstitutional war can only be carried on in an unconstitutional manner,*" said Mr. Long. His demand now was for peace. This was the first sound of Democratic preparation for the presidential election, the key-note of their campaign. Mr. Long said:

MR. CHAIRMAN:—I speak to-day for the preservation of the government. In the independence of a representative of the people I intend to proclaim the deliberate convictions of my judgment in this fearful hour of the country's peril. The brief period of three short years has produced a fearful change in this free, happy and prosperous government—so pure in its restrainments upon personal liberty, and so gentle in its demands upon the resources of the people, that the celebrated Humboldt, after traveling through the country, on his return to Europe said, "The American people have a government which you neither see nor feel." So different is it now, and so great the change, that the inquiry might well be made to-day, "Are we not in Constantinople, in St. Petersburg, in Vienna, in Rome, or in Paris?" Military governors and their provost marshals override the laws, and the echo of the armed heel rings forth as clearly now in

America as in France or Austria; and the President sits to-day guarded by armed soldiers at every approach leading to the executive mansion. So far from crushing the Rebellion, three years have passed away, and from the day on which the conflict began, up to the present hour, the Confederate army has not been forced beyond the sound of their guns from the dome of the capitol in which we are assembled.

The remainder of the speech continued in the same spirit. The war could not be put down. Moreover, it was wrong, and ought not to be put down.

These were the sentiments of a Democratic politician in Congress; they would be scattered broadcast over the whole land. Some of the arguments were specious; they would be echoed from a thousand platforms during the summer. It was incumbent upon the opposition to furnish a speedy and strong reply. When Mr. Long took his seat, as if by common consent, all eyes were turned toward the young member from Ohio. They expected a reply, and they were not disappointed. Garfield at once rose, and his first words struck on the House like the notes of a bugle. Members from the remoter seats crowded about him, and in the midst of intense excitement, broken by frequent applause, he poured forth a torrent of invective, which has rarely been surpassed for power and eloquence. Mr. Garfield said:

MR. CHAIRMAN:—I should be obliged to you if you would direct the sergeant-at-arms to bring a white flag and plant it in the aisle between myself and my colleague who has just addressed you. I recollect on one occasion when two great armies stood face to face, that under a white flag just planted, I approached a company of men dressed in the uniform of the rebel Confederacy, and reached out my hand to one of the number, and told him I respected him as a brave man. Though he wore the emblems of disloyalty and treason, still, underneath his vestments I beheld a brave and honest soul. I would produce that scene here this afternoon. I say, *were* there such a flag of truce—but God forbid me if I should do it under any other circumstances—I would reach out this right hand and ask that gentleman to take it, because I honor his bravery and his honesty. I believe what has just fallen from his lips are the honest sentiments of his heart, and in uttering it he has made a new epoch in the history of this war; he has done a new thing under the sun; he has done a brave thing. It is braver than to face cannon and musketry, and I honor him for his candor and frankness. But now, I ask you to take away the flag of truce; and I will go back inside the Union lines and speak of what he has done. I am reminded by this of a distinguished character in *Paradise Lost*. When he had rebelled against the glory of God, and "led away a third part of heaven's sons, conjured against the Highest;" when, after terrible battles in which hills and mountains were hurled down "nine times the space that measures day and night," and after the terrible fall lay stretched prone on the burning lake—Satan lifted up his shattered bulk, crossed the abyss, looked down into Paradise, and, soliloquizing, said:

"Which way I fly is hell, myself am hell;"

it seems to me in that utterance he expressed the very sentiments to which you have just listened uttered by one not less brave, malign and fallen. This man gathers up the meaning of this great contest, the philosophy of the moment, the prophecies of the hour, and, in sight of the paradise of victory and peace, utters them all in this wail of terrible despair, "Which way I fly is hell." He ought to add, "Myself am hell." I am reminded by the occurrences of this afternoon of two characters in the war of the Revolution, as compared with two others in the war of to-day. The first was Lord Fairfax, who dwelt near the Potomac, a few miles from us. When the great contest was opened between the mother country and the colonies, Lord Fairfax, after a protracted struggle with his own heart, decided he must go with the mother country. He gathered his mantle about him and went over grandly and solemnly. There was another man who cast in his lot with the struggling colonists, and continued with them till the war was well nigh ended. In an hour of darkness that just preceded the glory of the morning, he hatched the treason to surrender forever all that had been gained to the enemies of his country. Benedict Arnold was that man! Fairfax and Arnold find their parallel of to-day. When this war began, many good men stood hesitating and doubting what they ought to do. Robert E. Lee sat in his house across the river here, doubting and delaying, and going off at last almost tearfully to join the army of his state. He reminds one, in some respects, of Lord Fairfax—the stately royalist of the Revolution. But now, when tens of thousands of brave souls have gone up to God under the shadow of the flag; when thousands more, maimed and shattered in the contest, are sadly awaiting the deliverance of death; now, when three years of terrific warfare have raged over us; when our armies have pushed the Rebellion back over mountains and rivers, and crowded it into narrow limits, until a wall of fire girds it; now, when the uplifted hand of a majestic people is about to hurl the bolts of its conquering power upon the Rebellion; now, in the quiet of this hall, hatched in the lowest depths of a similar dark treason, there rises a Benedict Arnold and proposes to surrender all up, body and spirit, the Nation and the flag, its genius and its honor, now and forever, to the accursed traitors to our country! And that proposition comes—God forgive and pity my beloved state—it comes from a citizen of the time-honored and loyal commonwealth of Ohio! I implore you, brethren in this house, to believe that not many births ever gave pangs to my mother state such as she suffered when that traitor was born! I beg you not to believe that on the soil of that state another such a growth has ever deformed the face of nature, and darkened the light of God's day. For the first time in the history of this contest it is proposed in this hall to give up the struggle, to abandon the war, and let treason run riot through the land! I will, if I can, dismiss feeling from my heart and try to consider only what bears upon the logic of the speech to which we have just listened. First of all, the gentleman tells us that the right of secession is a constitutional right. I do not propose to enter into the argument. I have hitherto expressed myself on state sovereignty and state rights, of which this proposition of his is the legitimate child. But the gentleman takes higher ground—and in that I agree with him; namely, that five million or eight million people possess the right of revolution. Grant it; we agree there. If fifty-nine men can make a revolution successful, they have the right of revolution? If one state wishes to break its connection with the Federal Government, and does it by force, maintaining itself, it is an independent state. If the eleven Southern states are resolved and determined to leave the Union, to secede, to revolutionize, and can maintain that revolution by force, they have the revolutionary right to do so. I stand on that platform with the gentleman. And now the question comes, is it our constitutional duty to let them do it? That is the question. And in order to reach it, I beg to call your attention, not to argument, but to the condition of affairs that would result from such action—the mere statement of which becomes the strongest possible argument. What does this gentleman propose? Where will he draw the line of division? If the rebels carry into secession what they desire to carry; if their revolution envelops as many states as they intend it shall envelop; if they draw the line where Isham G. Harris, the rebel governor of Tennessee, in the rebel camp near our lines, told Mr. Vallandigham they would draw it—along the line of the Ohio and Potomac—if they make good their statement to him, that they will never consent to any other line, then I ask, what is the thing the gentleman proposes to do? He proposes to leave to the United States a territory reaching from the Atlantic to the Pacific, and one hundred miles wide in the centre!! From Wellsville on the Ohio to Cleveland on the lakes, is one hundred miles. I ask you, Mr. Chairman, if there be a man here so insane as to suppose that the American people will allow their magnificent national proportions to be shorn to so deformed a shape as this? Suppose the policy of the gentleman was adopted to-day. Let the order go forth; sound the "recall" on your bugles, and let it ring from Texas to the far Atlantic, and tell the armies to come back. Call the victorious legions back over the battle-field of blood forever now disgraced. Call them back over the territory which they have conquered. Call them back, and let the minions of secession chase them with derision and jeers as they come. And then tell them that the man across the aisle, from the free state of Ohio, gave birth to the monstrous proposition.

Mr. Chairman, if such a word should be sent forth through the armies of the Union, the wave of terrible vengeance that would sweep back over this land could never find a parallel in the records of history. Almost in the moment of final victory, the "recall" is sounded by a craven people not desiring freedom. We ought, every man, to be made a slave should we sanction such a sentiment. The gentleman has told us that there is no such thing as coercion justifiable under the Constitution. I ask him for one moment to reflect, that no statute ever was enforced without coercion. It is the basis of every law in the universe,—God's law as well as man's. A law is no law without coercion behind it. When a man has murdered his brother, coercion takes the murderer, tries him and hangs him. When you levy your taxes, coercion secures their collection; it follows the shadow of the thief and brings him to justice; it accompanies your diplomacy to foreign courts, and backs a declaration of the nation's right by a pledge of the nation's power. Again, he tells us that oaths taken under the amnesty proclamation are good for nothing. The oath of Galileo was not binding upon him. I am reminded of another oath that was taken; but perhaps it was an oath on the lips alone to which the heart made no response. I remember to have stood in a line of nineteen men on that carpet yonder on the first day of the session, and I remember that another oath was passed round and each member signed it as provided by law, utterly repudiating the Rebellion and its pretenses. Does that gentleman not blush to speak of Galileo's oath? Was not his own its counterpart? He says that the Union can never be restored because of the terrible hatred engendered by the war. To prove it, he quotes what some Southern man said a few years ago, that he knew no hatred between people in the world like that between the North and the South. And yet that North and South have been one nation for eighty-eight years! Have you seen in this contest any thing more bitter than the wars of the Scottish border? Have we seen anything more bitter than those terrible feuds in the days of Edward, when England and Scotland were the deadliest foes on earth? And yet for centuries those countries have been cemented in an indissoluble union that has made the British nation one of the proudest of the earth! I said a little while ago that I accepted the proposition of the gentleman that rebels had a right of revolution; and the decisive issue between us and the Rebellion is, whether they shall revolutionize and destroy, or we shall subdue and preserve. We take the latter ground. We take the common weapons of war to meet them; and if these be not sufficient, I would take any element which will overwhelm and destroy; I would sacrifice the dearest and best beloved; I would take all the old sanctions of law and the Constitution and fling them to the winds, if necessary, rather than let the Nation be broken in pieces and its people destroyed with endless ruin. What is the Constitution that these gentlemen are perpetually flinging in our faces whenever we desire to strike hard blows against the Rebellion? It is the production of the American people. They made it; and the creator is mightier than the creature. The power which made the Constitution can also make other instruments to do its great work in the day of dire necessity.

The debate waxed warm and was participated in by a number of representatives. General Garfield appeared often in debate during this session of Congress; and some of his speeches at this time—notably that on the Constitutional Amendment to abolish slavery—are among the best he ever delivered. We will now leave the halls of Congress and look at the state of the country, and review briefly the fall election of 1864.

CHAPTER XIV.

GARFIELD IN THE ASCENDANT.

"While the races of mankind endure,
Let his great example stand,
Colossal, seen of every land,
And keep the soldier firm, the statesman pure."

"In the New World man climbs the rugged steep
And takes the forefront by the force of will
And daring purpose in him."

The famous speech made by Mr. Long attracted the attention of the whole country. The day following its delivery Speaker Colfax introduced a resolution in the House, for the expulsion of Representative Long. He did this, he said, in the performance of a high public duty—a duty to his constituents and to the soldiers in the field. He believed in the freedom of speech, and had during this Congress heard nothing, save this single speech, which could have prompted him to offer such a resolution. The flag of the Confederacy had been boldly unfurled by a gentleman who had taken an oath at the opening of the session, that up to that time, he had not given aid, countenance, or encouragement to the enemies of the United States. If such an oath was necessary to membership, then he who could thus publicly give the encouragement which he had sworn not to have given in the past, was an unworthy member, and ought not to remain. When the vote was called there were eighty-one ayes and fifty-eight nays, thus lacking the necessary two thirds majority. But a vote of censure was passed, and thus the House put itself in the proper light before the country.

The national and congressional elections of 1864 soon come on. A presidential election was now to be decided in the midst of war, as the one four years previous had been under its projected shadows. Undoubtedly the people of the South longed for peace. The whole people desired peace, except a few to whom war was money. But peace was impossible until either the Government or the rebels were defeated, except by the abandonment on one side or the other of the very object for which it was fighting. No proposition indicating the willingness of the Confederate government to surrender its independence upon any conditions had ever been made. Davis' declaration was that the "war must go on till the last of this generation falls in his tracks, and his children seize his musket and fight our battles, unless you acknowledge our right to self-government. We are not fighting for slavery; we are fighting for independence, and that or extermination we will have." Certainly this declaration did not improve the prospects of the opposition party in the North in the approaching elections.

Upon the issues of the pending campaign rested the fate of a Republic. All the forces which had ever antagonized the war for the Union were arrayed on the one side; those which demanded that the war should be vigorously pursued until rebellion was forever put down, withstood them on the other side. It was a hand-to-hand struggle. Garfield took the stump and ably advocated the Republican cause. He traveled nearly eight thousand miles, and made sixty-five speeches. Late in the season his constituents met to nominate a congressman. Garfield was very popular in the district, which had been pleased with his ability and the patriotic spirit of his conduct. But, after the adjournment of Congress, an incident occurred which caused trouble in the Republican ranks, and seemed likely to drive him out of the field. The subject of the re-admission of conquered Southern States to the full enjoyment of their political rights, had occupied the attention of the Thirty-Eighth Congress; and that body, on the day of its adjournment, had passed and sent for the President's approval, a bill providing for the government of such States. Mr. Lincoln had let the bill go over unsigned till after adjournment; and soon issued a proclamation referring to the subject, which offended many of the friends of the bill. Among these were Ben. Wade and Winter Davis, who issued to the public a reply to Mr. Lincoln, censuring him in very severe language. The President was therein charged with favoring a policy subversive of human liberty, unjust to the friends of the administration, and dangerous to the Republic. This Wade–Davis manifesto caused a great furore of excitement. Wade and Davis were denounced; the people would hear nothing against Mr. Lincoln. When the congressional convention of the Nineteenth District met at Warren, Mr. Garfield was sent for. He had been charged by some with the authorship of the Wade–Davis paper, and by many with holding to its views. When he appeared before them, the chairman stated to him the charge, with a strong intimation that if he cared for a re-nomination he must declare war against all disagreement with the President's policy. The convention was eager to nominate him, but it was objected, and the objection seemed to have some force with the delegates, that he had not condemned the manifesto.

Then the young general and statesman having entered the hall arose, and stepped forward to face the assembly. They listened to hear their former hero explain away the terrible opinion attributed to him, and, like the fawning politician he was not, trim his sails according to the popular pleasure. Mr. Garfield spoke for only half an hour, and said that he was not the author of the manifesto which the chairman had mentioned. Only of late had he read that great protest. But, having read, he approved; and only regretted that there had been any necessity for such a thing. The facts alleged were truly asserted. This was his belief. If they preferred a representative not of the same mind as himself, not a free agent, they should by all means hasten to nominate their man. As he warmed up to his subject, he captivated the convention with his plain, hard reasoning and his glowing eloquence. Having somewhat haughtily spoken these brave words, Garfield took his hat and strode out, with the intention of returning to his hotel. As he reached the street, a great shout was heard. "That sound, no doubt, means my defeat and another's nomination," he muttered. But, with nothing to regret, he went his way. Meanwhile, what did the convention actually do? They were dumb with astonishment for a moment; a heroic deed had been done before them, and admiration for the chief actor was the uppermost sentiment in every heart. Then a young man from Ashtabula called out: "Mr. Chairman, I say that the man who has courage enough to oppose a convention like that ought not to be discarded. I move that James A. Garfield be nominated by acclamation." Without a dissenting voice it was done.

Governor Todd closed the meeting with the remark: "A district that will allow a young fellow like Garfield to tweak its nose and cuff its ears in that manner, deserves to have him saddled on it for life." General Garfield, speaking of this incident, said he knew it was a bold action for a youngster, but he believed both Mr. Wade and Mr. Davis to be right, and he determined to stand by them. "This showed me completely the truth of the old maxim, that 'Honesty is the best policy,' and I have ever since been entirely independent in my relations with the people of my district." The news of his action spread far and wide. A day or two afterward he met Ben. Wade, who seized him by the hand, and roared out: "Look here, do you know you did a brave thing at that convention the other day?" "It was my duty, Mr. Wade, to say what I did, as I believed you and Mr. Davis to be in the right," replied Garfield. "Bosh," cried old Ben., "I say it was very brave. Why, not one fellow in a dozen but would have given Davis and I the go-by. All you had to do was to go in and teter a little before the convention, and they would have promised in advance to re-nominate you. But you didn't do it; devil the bit did you do it. You took the bull by the horns like a man, and told the convention it was wrong, and I say it was brave in you to do so. Now, mind you, Garfield, you have got that district, and they won't fool with you any more. The people of Ohio like a bold and honest man, and they have found one in you, and they ain't going to give you up soon. Just you go ahead, they know you are worth a dozen limber-jacks, and they will stick by you. It's a clear case you won't turn for anybody—you had the best chance to turn the other day before that convention you will ever have, and you didn't do it. The people hate a trimmer, and I tell you your action before that convention has given the men and women of your district a new idea of you. As for me," added old Ben, the tears starting to his eyes, "I won't say how much I am obliged to to you for the way you stood by me, but I shall never forget it, never, sir, while I live on this earth." Then the old war-horse went abruptly away, and the young statesman knew he had made a friend for life of the oldest and best statesman Ohio ever had. The election came off in the fall of 1864, and Garfield was returned by a majority of nearly twelve thousand votes.

The session of Congress which met in December of 1864 was marked by the great debates on the Thirteenth Amendment to the Constitution, which was presented to the States for ratification on the first of February, 1865. Perhaps the strongest opposition to that amendment was from George H. Pendleton, of Ohio.

He spoke against it on the 13th of January. The chief argument was that purely State institutions could not properly be interfered with by the Nation, without the consent of the State or States concerned. To this speech Mr. Garfield made a reply. On taking the floor, he began:

MR. SPEAKER: We shall never know why slavery dies so hard in this Republic and in this hall till we know why sin is long-lived, and Satan is immortal. It has been declared here and elsewhere to be in the several stages of mortality—wounded, moribund, dead. I know of no better illustration of its condition than is found in Sallust's admirable history of the great conspirator, Catiline, who, when his final battle was fought and lost, his army broken and scattered, was found, far in advance of his own troops, lying among the dead enemies of Rome, yet breathing a little, but exhibiting in his countenance all the ferocity of spirit which had characterized his life. So, sir, this body of slavery lies before us among the dead enemies of the Republic, mortally wounded, impotent in its fiendish wickedness, but with its old ferocity of look, bearing the unmistakable marks of its infernal origin. All along the coast of our political sea lie the victims of slavery, like stranded wrecks, broken on the headlands of freedom. In its mad arrogance it lifted its hand to strike down the fabric of the Union, and since that fatal day it has been a "fugitive and a vagabond upon the earth." Like the spirit that Jesus cast out, it has, since then, "been seeking rest and finding none." It has sought in all the corners of the Republic to find some hiding-place in which to shelter itself from the death it so richly deserves. It sought an asylum in the untrodden territories of the west, but, with a whip of scorpions, indignant freemen drove it thence. My gallant colleague (Mr. Pendleton), for I recognize him as a gallant and able man, has followed slavery in its flight, until at last it has reached the great temple where liberty is enshrined—the Constitution of the United States—and there, in that last retreat, declares that no hand shall strike it. It reminds me of that celebrated passage in the great Latin poet, in which the serpents of the Ionian sea, when they had destroyed Laocoon and his sons, fled to the heights of the Trojan citadel and coiled their slimy lengths around the feet of the tutelar goddess, and were covered by the orb of her shield. So, under the guidance of my colleague (Mr. Pendleton), slavery, gorged with the blood of ten thousand freemen, has climbed to the high citadel of American nationality, and coiled itself securely, as he believes, around the feet of the statue of Justice and under the shield of the Constitution of the United States. We desire to follow it even there, and kill it beside the very altar of liberty. Its blood can never make atonement for the least of its crimes. On the justice of the amendment itself no arguments are necessary. The reasons crowd in on every side. To enumerate them would be a work of superfluity. To me it is a matter of great surprise that gentlemen of the other side should wish to delay the death of slavery. I can only account for it on the ground of long-continued familiarity and friendship.

Five days after this address, Mr. Garfield, together with Henry Winter Davis, made a lively attack on the War Department. At this time the writ of *habeas corpus* was suspended, and the art of imprisoning men without warrant or accusation was reaching a high state of perfection. The Carroll and Old Capital prisons were full of victims who could not find out why they were thus arbitrarily confined. This tyrannical practice having been brought before the Committee on Military Affairs, some of them investigated the subject. As a result, a resolution was offered calling for a public inquiry, which resolution passed. The next day Thaddeus Stevens attempted to get it rescinded, whereupon he was met by a fiery speech from Mr. Garfield, which saved the resolution; and in a few days there was a general freeing of all prisoners against whom no sufficient charges could be made. In his speech, Mr. Garfield graphically told of the great injustice which was being done, especially to men who had served the country in the field. One of these was a colonel in the Union army, who had been wounded and discharged from the service, but now, for some unknown reason, perhaps maliciously, had been deprived of his liberty. Mr. Garfield had been an admirer of Stanton, and recognized the great Secretary's ability and patriotism; but this could not save either him or his subordinates from just censures. This action was the occasion of much admiring notice from the public, and even from Stanton himself. For such was the reputed roughness of Stanton's temper that few men ever had enough boldness to criticise him. He had already attained a very high rank among his colleagues, and men of brains in both houses had discovered that here was a fresh, strong intellectual force, which was destined to make its mark upon the politics of the country. Of his power over a popular audience a single incident, which occurred about this time, will afford illustration.

On the night of April 14, 1865, the war-heated blood of this nation was frozen with sudden horror at a deed which then had no parallel in American history— the murder of Abraham Lincoln. That night General Garfield was in New York City. In the early morning hours a colored servant came to the door of his room at the hotel, and in a heart-broken voice announced that Mr. Lincoln, the emancipator of his race from bondage, had been shot down by a traitor to the country. While in the midst of the universal rejoicing over the return of peace, the President was shot down. Instantly the telegraph flashed the news from one end of the land to the other, and the country became excited to its utmost tension. Every one of my readers must know what a spell such a calamity produces on the public mind. Those who number their years sufficiently to remember the occurrence of which we are now speaking, will know full well what the assassination of the chief executive meant then; those of less years and experience will recall, as if an occurrence of but yesterday, the pall cast over the whole world when Garfield himself fell a martyr to the cause of liberty.

The dark night of despair and uncertainty passed away, and morning dawned. But what a morning! The return of day did not bring with it a return of peace and hope. The messengers of the morning, bearing across the heavens the sprites of light to cheer the world and build up the animate of nature, only deepened the darkness of soul, and chilled the pulse of the North. New York City, on the morning after the assassination, seemed ready for the scene of the French Revolution. The newspaper head-lines were in the largest type. Crowds were about the bulletin boards, and the high crime was on every one's tongue. Fear took possession of men's minds as to the fate of the government, for in a few hours the news came that Seward, too, had been murdered, and that attempts had been made upon the lives of other of the government officers. Placards were put up everywhere, in great, black letters, calling upon the loyal citizens of New York, Brooklyn, Jersey City, and neighboring cities to meet around Wall Street Exchange, and give expression to their sentiments. It was a dark and terrible hour. What might come next no one could tell, and men spoke with bated breath. The wrath of the workingmen was simply uncontrollable, and revolvers and knives were in the hands of thousands, ready at the first provocation to avenge the death of the martyred President upon any and all who dared to utter a word against him. Everybody left business, left home, left all other considerations and filled the streets. The tragedy was the topic of the hour. Every lip gave utterance to the sentiments of horror. No business, no mirth, no laughter, but all was silence, painful and unknown before. It was impossible for a man so large-hearted, so patriotic as was Garfield, not to have felt keenly the death of Abraham Lincoln. He saw that it was not the hand of one man, but the spirit of secession aiming a last despairing blow at the great principles that had conquered it. Naturally, then, his was the tongue to give some expression to the Nation's grief. And in the exciting hours that followed Booth's cowardly pistol shot, when the whole North was roused with a whirlwind of mad passion, Garfield's hand was apparent in staying the impending storm, in counseling that course that led to the wiser way, the better plan. In the incident we are about to relate, the extraordinary moral power always exerted over men by Garfield, was perhaps never shown to a better advantage. The incident is contributed to this volume by a distinguished public man, who was an eye-witness of the exciting scene:

Fifty thousand people crowded around the Exchange building, cramming and jamming the streets, and wedged in tight as men could stand together. With a few to whom a special favor was extended, I went over from Brooklyn at nine A. M., and, even then, with the utmost difficulty, found my way to the reception room for the speakers in the front of the Exchange building, and looking out on the high and massive balcony, whose front was protected by a heavy iron railing. We sat in solemnity and silence, waiting for General Butler, who, it was announced, had started from Washington, and was either already in the city or expected every moment. Nearly a hundred generals, judges, statesmen, lawyers, editors, clergymen and others were in that room waiting Butler's arrival. We stepped out to the balcony to watch the fearfully solemn and swaying mass of people. Not a hurrah was heard, but for the most part a dead silence, or a deep, ominous muttering ran, like a rising wave, up the street toward Broadway, and again down toward the river on the right. At length the batons of the police were seen swinging in the air, far up on the left, parting the crowd and pressing it back to make way for a carriage that moved slowly, and with difficult jogs, through the compact multitude. Suddenly the silence was broken, and the cry of 'Butler!' 'Butler!' 'Butler!' rang out with tremendous and thrilling effect, and was taken up by the people. But not a hurrah! Not once! It was the cry of a great people, asking to know how their President died. The blood bounced in our veins, and the tears ran like streams down our faces. How it was done I forget, but Butler was pulled through and pulled up, and entered the room, where we had just walked back to meet him. A broad crape a yard long hung from his left arm—terrible contrast with the countless flags that were waving the Nation's victory in the breeze. We first realized, then, the truth of the sad news that Lincoln was dead. When Butler entered the room we shook hands. Some spoke, some could not; all were in tears. The only word Butler had for us all, at the first break of the silence, was, '*Gentlemen, he died in the fullness of his fame!*' and as he spoke it his lips quivered and the tears ran fast down his cheeks. Then, after a few moments, came the speaking. And you can imagine the effect, as the crape fluttered in the wind, while his arm was uplifted. Two men lay bleeding on one of the side streets, the one dead, the other next to dying: one on the pavement, the other in the gutter. They had said a moment before that 'Lincoln ought to have been shot long ago!' They were not allowed to say it again. Soon two long pieces of scantling stood out above the heads of the crowd, crossed at the top like the letter X, and a looped halter pendent from the junction, a dozen men following its slow motion through the masses, while 'Vengeance' was the cry. On the right, suddenly, the shout rose, 'The World!' 'the World!' 'the office of the World!' 'World!' 'World!' and a movement of perhaps eight thousand or ten thousand turning their faces in the direction of that building began to be executed. It was a critical moment. What might come no one could tell, did that crowd get in front of that office. Police and military would have availed little or been too late. A telegram had just been read from Washington, 'Seward is dying.' Just then, at that juncture, a man stepped forward with a small flag in his hand, and beckoned to the crowd. 'Another telegram from Washington!' And then, in the awful stillness of the crisis, taking advantage of the hesitation of the crowd, whose steps had been arrested a moment, a right arm was lifted skyward, and a voice, clear and steady, loud and distinct, spoke out, 'Fellow-citizens! Clouds and darkness are around about Him! His pavilion is dark waters and thick clouds of the skies! Justice and judgment are the establishment of His throne! Mercy and truth shall go before His face! Fellow-citizens! God reigns, and the Government at Washington still lives!' The effect was tremendous. The crowd stood rivited to the ground with awe, gazing at the motionless orator, and thinking of God and of his providence over the Government and the Nation. As the boiling wave subsides and settles to the sea when some strong wind beats it down, so the tumult of the people sunk and became still. As the rod draws the electricity from the air, and conducts it safely to the ground, so this man had drawn the fury from that frantic crowd, and guided it to more tranquil thoughts than vengeance. It was as if some divinity had spoken through him. It was a triumph of eloquence, a flash of inspiration such as seldom comes to any man, and to not more than one man in a century. Webster nor Choate, nor Everett, nor Seward ever reached it. Demosthenes never equalled it. The man for the crisis had come, and his words were more potent than Napoleon's guns at Paris. A murmur went through the crowd, "Who is he?" The answer came in low whispers, "General Garfield, of Ohio."

Providence thus furnished the man for the occasion, and soon it lent him the inspiration. By this wonderful utterance the popular fury was stayed. What a few moments before would have been considered impossible, had now been accomplished. The "World" had been saved, but this was but little; the safety of the city had been secured and this was everything. Other meetings were held in New York City on that memorable day, and the magnetic speaker of the morning was called out again. In the course of an address that afternoon he uttered these words:

By this last act of madness, it seems as though the Rebellion had determined that the President of the soldiers should go with the soldiers who have laid down their lives on the battle-field. They slew the noblest and gentlest heart that ever put down a rebellion upon this earth. In taking that life they have left the iron hand of the people to fall upon them. Love is on the front of the throne of God, but justice and judgment, with inexorable dread, follow behind; and when law is slighted and mercy despised, when they have rejected those who would be their best friends, then comes justice with her hoodwinked eyes, and with the sword and scales. From every gaping wound of your dead chief, let the voice go up from the people to see to it that our house is swept and garnished. I hasten to say one thing more, fellow-citizens. For mere vengeance I would do nothing. This nation is too great to look for mere revenge. But *for security of the future* I would do every thing.

It is a remarkable fact that when the nation gave expression to its sorrow over Lincoln's death, Garfield should have been so notably *the voice* which spoke that sorrow. A year passed on. In April of 1866, Congress, busy with the important legislation of that period, neglected to remember the approaching anniversary. On the morning of April 14th, the newspapers announced that, according to President Johnson's order, the Government offices would be closed that day out of respect to the murdered Lincoln. Congressmen at the breakfast-table read this announcement, and hurried to the Capitol, inquiring what corresponding action should be taken by the two Houses of Congress. General Garfield was in the committee-room, hard at work on the preparation of a bill, when, shortly before time for the House to come to order, Speaker Colfax came hurriedly in, saying that Mr. Garfield must be in the House directly and move an adjournment. At the same time Garfield should make an address appropriate to such an anniversary. That gentleman protested that the time was too short, but Colfax insisted, and left the room. Remaining there alone for a quarter of an hour, the general thought of the tragic event, and what he should say.

Just as the clerk had finished reading the previous day's journal of the house, Mr. Garfield arose and said:

MR. SPEAKER:—I desire to move that this House do now adjourn; and before the vote upon that motion is taken, I desire to say a few words.

This day, Mr. Speaker, will be sadly memorable so long as this nation shall endure, which, God grant, may be "till the last syllable of recorded time," when the volume of human history shall be sealed up and delivered to the Omnipotent

Judge. In all future time, on the recurrence of this day, I doubt not that the citizens of this Republic will meet in solemn assembly to reflect on the life and character of Abraham Lincoln, and the awful tragic event of April 14, 1865,—an event unparalleled in the history of nations, certainly unparalleled in our own. It is eminently proper that this House should this day place upon its records a memorial of that event. The last five years have been marked by wonderful developments of human character. Thousands of our people before unknown to fame, have taken their places in history, crowned with immortal honors. In thousands of humble homes are dwelling heroes and patriots whose names shall never die. But greatest among all these developments was the character and fame of Abraham Lincoln, whose loss the nation still deplores. His character is aptly described in the words of England's great laureate—written thirty years ago—in which he traces the upward steps of some

"Divinely gifted man,
Whose life in low estate began,
And on a simple village green:

Who breaks his birth's invidious bar,
And rasps the skirts of happy chance,
And breasts the blows of circumstance,
And grapples with his evil star:

Who makes by force his merit known,
And lives to clutch the golden keys
To mold a mighty State's decrees,
And shape the whisper of the throne:

And moving up from high to higher,
Becomes on Fortune's crowning slope,
The pillar of a people's hope,
The centre of a world's desire."

Such a life and character will be treasured forever as the sacred possession of the American people and of mankind. In the great drama of the Rebellion, there were two acts. The first was the war, with its battles and sieges, victories and defeats, its sufferings and tears. That act was closing one year ago to-night, and just as the curtain was lifting on the second and final act, the restoration of peace and liberty,—just as the curtain was rising upon new events and new characters,—the evil spirt of the Rebellion, in the fury of despair, nerved and directed the hand of the assassin to strike down the chief character in both. It was no one man who killed Abraham Lincoln; it was the embodied spirit of treason and slavery, inspired with fearful and despairing hate, that struck him down in the moment of the nation's supremest joy.

Ah, sirs, there are times in the history of men and nations when they stand so near the veil that separates mortals from immortals, time from eternity, and men from their God, that they can almost hear the beatings and feel the pulsations of the heart of the Infinite! Through such a time has this nation passed. When two hundred and fifty thousand brave spirits passed from the field of honor through that thin veil to the presence of God, and when at last its parting folds admitted the martyr President to the company of the dead heroes of the Republic, the nation stood so near the veil that the whispers of God were heard by the children of men. Awe-stricken by his voice, the American people knelt in tearful reverence and made a solemn covenant with him and with each other that this nation should be saved from its enemies, that all its glories should be restored, and, on the ruins of treason and slavery the temples of freedom and justice should be built, and should survive forever.

General Garfield was a thorough-going temperance man. On returning to his home in Painesville, Ohio, in the summer of 1865, he found the good people of that place in trouble on account of a brewery which had been established in their midst. All efforts to have it removed had been unavailing. Public meetings were held. Garfield attended one of these, and while there announced that he would that day remove the brewery. He just went over to the brewer and bought him out for $10,000. The liquor on hand, and such brewing machinery as could not be used for any thing else, he destroyed. When autumn came he used his new establishment as a cider-mill. The cider was kept till it became good vinegar, and then sold. The general thus did a good thing for the public, and it is said, made money out of the investment, until, after several years, he sold the building.

The House was thereupon declared adjourned. It is now necessary to hasten on to the Thirty-Ninth Congress, wherein General Garfield, no longer under the disadvantages of being a new member, continued to develop rapidly as an able worker.

When Congress met in December, 1865, it had to face a great task. The Rebellion had been put down, but at great cost; and they had an enormous debt to provide for. Four years of war had disorganized every thing, and great questions of finance, involving tariffs, and taxation, and a thousand vexed themes of public policy, hung with leaden weight over the heads of our national legislators. Garfield was one of the few men who were both able and willing to face the music and bury themselves in the bewildering world of figures which loomed in the dusky foreground of coming events. The interest alone on our liabilities amounted to $150,000,000. When Speaker Colfax made up his committees, he asked Garfield what he would like. Garfield replied that he would like to have a place which called for the study of finance. Justin S. Morrill, Chairman of the Committee on Ways and Means, also asked for him. He was, accordingly, put upon that committee, and immediately began to study the subjects which were connected with its prospective work. Conceiving that our financial condition was in some respects parallel to that of England at the close of the Napoleonic wars, he carefully investigated the conditions, policy and progress of that government from the time of Waterloo until the resumption of specie payments. The most remarkable periods of our own financial history were also studied, especially that wherein the great Alexander Hamilton appears the master mind. These pursuits, and a wide-reaching knowledge of the existing conditions in our own country, were the foundations on which Garfield built the structure of a set of opinions which were then received as good, and which still withstand the test of time.

About this time General Garfield won his first case as a lawyer, and it was in the Supreme Court of the United States—in other words, he began where most lawyers are content to end. It is the general impression that he was not a regular member of the legal profession, and hence some people suppose that the fee of five thousand dollars, which was paid him in the De Golyer case, was more to secure his influence as a Congressman than his services as a lawyer. For the benefit of such persons, I will say that General Garfield was regarded by the members of the Supreme Court as one of the ablest constitutional lawyers in this country, and that some of his fees for arguments before the United States bench have been as large as any ever paid to Daniel Webster. He was not admitted to the bar by the usual routine, but he was no less a very able lawyer. The usual tread-mill route to legal preferment is, to enter when a small boy a lawyer's office, sweep the floor for two or three years, engross long legal documents for two or three more, pettifog in a justice's court for even a longer time, and then slowly and gradually, as the older heads die off, appear in the higher courts; and when he has done this fifteen or twenty years, become admitted to the Supreme Court, when he is perhaps a man of sixty, have his first case, and glory over it as the red-letter day in his history. Garfield did not reach the bar of the Supreme Court by this slow and tedious process. He studied law as thoroughly, perhaps, as any man ever did study it; but he studied it in his own room at Hiram, while he was teaching his class in the college, lecturing on geology, supplying the pulpit for good "Father" Ryder, and doing a thousand other things, that would have broken down any man not of his iron constitution.

Judge Black knew what Garfield had said two years before in Congress, concerning *habeas corpus*, and asked if he was willing to say the same thing in an argument before the Supreme Court. Garfield's answer was, "That depends altogether upon the nature of your case." Judge Black then gave him briefly the facts of the case, and the record of the trial. Garfield read it, and on meeting Judge Black again, said, "I believe in that doctrine." The astute old lawyer then said to the young Congressman, "Young man, it is a perilous thing for a young Republican in Congress to endorse such doctrines, and I don't want you to injure yourself." "That consideration," answered Garfield, "does not weigh with me. I believe in English liberty and English law; but, Judge Black, I am not a practitioner in the Supreme Court, and I never tried a case in any court in my life." The Judge answered, "How long ago were you admitted to the bar?" "About six years," said Garfield. "That will do," said Judge Black; "you must now be admitted to the Supreme Court, and try this case with me." Garfield was admitted, and at once entered upon this important case.

In 1864, L. P. Milligan, W. A. Bowles, and Stephen Horsey, three citizens of Indiana, were arrested in that State on charges of treason, in conspiring against the Government in preventing enlistments, and encouraging desertions from the army. There was no doubt they were guilty of the crime. But, unfortunately, they were not tried according to law. No government can long hold such absolute powers as was given to our Government during the Rebellion, without developing in some degree a carelessness of the forms of law which is fatal to liberty. Indiana was not the scene of war. Her courts, and the United States courts there, were open for the prosecution of criminals. Yet these men were arrested by the military department, tried by a military commission, and condemned to be hanged. The sentence was approved by President Johnson, and the day of execution fixed for Friday, May 19th, 1865. At this juncture a petition was presented to Judge Davis, then holding United States Circuit Court at Indianapolis, for a writ of *habeas corpus*, to test the legality of these arbitrary proceedings. The judges of that court not agreeing, the points on which they disagreed were certified up to the Supreme court.

The sentences were finally commuted to imprisonment for life, and they were placed in the State prison at Columbus, Ohio. This was the case. The eminent counsel engaged therein were: Hons. Joseph E. McDonald, of Indiana; Jeremiah S. Black, of Pennsylvania; James A. Garfield, and David D. Field, of New York, for petitioners; Hons. Benjamin F. Butler, James Speed, and Henry Stanbery, for the Government.

After two days and nights of preparation, Mr. Garfield had decided upon the points of his argument. Needless to say, it was a complete and unanswerable presentation of those great English and American constitutional principles which secure the free people of those countries from star chambers and military despotisms. It showed forth clearly the limits of military power, and demonstrated the utter want of jurisdiction of a military court over civilian citizens.

On the day before the trial, the counsel for the prisoners met in Washington to determine upon the conduct of the case. As soon as they had come together Judge Black said, "We will hear first from our youngest member. Garfield, what do you intend to say?" The scene was very much like that which I have described when—a young colonel—Garfield stood before Buell at Louisville. These men were the foremost lawyers in the land, and the young lawyer, not ten days admitted, was to show his hand before them. It required more pluck than to face the fire of Chickamauga. But he took his points coolly, and stated succinctly the line of his argument. When he was through, they said to him with one accord, "Don't change one word or one point." On the following day the case was tried in the Supreme Court. McDonald opened for the prisoners; Garfield followed him; Black followed him; and David Dudley Field closed the argument. And the case was decided in their favor. Garfield spoke for two hours; and his argument, which was reported in short-hand, was printed in pamphlet form, and given a wide circulation. When General Garfield had finished his speech, he had established every essential point of the case beyond a peradventure. By eminent legal authority it was pronounced conclusive and masterly. It gave him at once a high standing in the Supreme Court, and soon brought him many important cases. The men he had defended were poor and in prison. Garfield had never seen them, never had any relation with them, and was never paid for his services in any other way than by the valuable practice which came to him in consequence of defending them. His speech closed with these eloquent words in appeal to the court:

> Your decision will mark an era in American history. The just and final settlement of this great question will take a high place among the great achievements which have immortalized this decade. It will establish forever this truth, of inestimable valuable to us and to mankind, that a republic can wield the vast enginery of war without breaking down the safeguards of liberty; can sup-

press insurrection and put down rebellion, however formidable, without destroying the bulwarks of law; can, by the might of its armed millions, preserve and defend both nationality and liberty. Victories on the field were of priceless value, for they plucked the life of the Republic out of the hands of its enemies; but,

"Peace hath her victories
No less renowned than war;"

and if the protection of law shall, by your decision, be extended over every acre of our peaceful territory, you shall have rendered the great decision of the century. When Pericles had made Greece immortal in arts and arms, in liberty and law, he invoked the genius of Phidias to devise a monument which should symbolize the beauty and glory of Athens. That artist selected for his theme the tutelar divinity of Athens—the Jove-born goddess, protectress of arts and arms, of industry and law, who typified the Greek conception of composed, majestic, unrelenting force. He erected on the heights of the Acropolis a colossal statue of Minerva, armed with spear and helmet, which towered in awful majesty above the surrounding temples of the gods. Sailors on far-off ships beheld the crest and spear of the goddess, and bowed with reverent awe. To every Greek she was the symbol of power and glory. But the Acropolis, with its temples and statues, is now a heap of ruins. The visible gods have vanished in the clearer light of modern civilization. We cannot restore the decayed emblems of ancient Greece, but it is in your power, O Judge, to erect in this citadel of our liberties a monument more lasting than brass; invisible, indeed, to the eye of flesh, but visible to the eye of the spirit as the awful form and figure of Justice crowning and adorning the Republic; rising above the storms of political strife, above the din of battle, above the earthquake shock of rebellion; seen from afar and hailed as protector by the oppressed of all nations; dispensing equal blessings, and covering with the protecting shield of law the weakest, the humblest, the meanest, and, until declared by solemn law unworthy of protection, the guiltiest of its citizens."

Other and very able arguments were made on both sides of the case; but the law was sustained and the prisoners set free. For this act Garfield was denounced by many newspapers and many individuals in his own state and elsewhere. But, as usual, he weathered it all, and was re-elected to Congress in the fall; for the Reserve people had come to the point of believing in Garfield, though he did not follow their opinions. In from one to three years afterward they generally discovered that he had been right from the start.

Garfield was a splendid lawyer. It is only because his course was pushed aside into the great lines of war and of politics that his history is not largely the story of great triumphs at the bar. When he was examined for admission to the bar of Ohio, the lawyers who examined him pronounced his legal knowledge phenomenal for a man to have acquired in the short time he had been reading. But he never practiced in any court until 1866. Afterwards he had about thirty cases in the Supreme Court, and often appeared in State courts. At one time Judge Jeremiah S. Black, a lawyer of national reputation, offered him a partnership. Financially it would have been a good thing for Garfield, but fortunately for his constituents and for the country, he refused. Yet, in the language of Stanley Matthews, now of the United States Supreme Court, Mr. Garfield actually ranked "as one of the very best lawyers at the bar of the whole country."

The Committee on Ways and Means is one of the most important in the House of Representatives. Consequently, its members are chosen by the Speaker with the greatest care and are selected from the ablest members. Garfield at once set to work to master thoroughly these immense subjects. He studied carefully the history of English finance during the Napoleonic war; went over the debates and speeches in the English parliament, and the writings of the English financiers of that time; and then traced the subject down through our own revolutionary period, and through Hamilton's and Jackson's time, making copious notes as he went along. His speech on the public debt and specie payments, delivered March 16, 1865, was the first in which he displayed the extensive knowledge he had acquired on these subjects, but it is also shown in many of his speeches at a later period. Mr. Chase spoke of him at this time as one of the best informed men on such topics then in public life. He was industrious in his work in the committee room, assiduous in his private study of pending questions, an able debater on the floor of Congress, and, because he kept in the line of the current thought of the time, always prepared to speak understandingly and eloquently upon any subject that came up, however sudden or unexpected the occasion.

On February 1, 1866, Garfield made that masterly address on the Freedman's Bureau, in which he so clearly set forth his views on the nature of the Union, and the states of which it is composed. On March 16, 1866, he made a remarkable speech on "The Currency and Specie Payments." Other noted speeches were the "Restoration of the Rebel States," and "The National Bureau of Education." A man of Garfield's intellect and scholarly acquirements could not fail to be interested in the cause of education, always and everywhere. He was himself a splendid result of the free-school system of Ohio, and had been an enthusiastic teacher. It was natural, therefore, that he should endeavor to interest Congress in the condition of the American schools. At the request of the American Association of School Superintendents, General Garfield, in February, 1866, prepared a bill for the establishment of a National Bureau of Education. The principal object of the bureau was to collect statistics and other facts, and so to arrange and publish them as to enlighten the people as to our progress in the means of education. The bill was opposed on account of the expense, as it called for an appropriation of fifteen thousand dollars! Speaking on this bill, June 8, 1866, Mr. Garfield called attention to the subject of national expenditures for extra governmental purposes. We had expended millions on a coast survey bureau, on an astronomical observatory, on a light-house board, on exploring expeditions, on the Pacific Railroad survey, on agriculture, on the patent office—why not a few dollars on education? "As man is greater than the soil, as the immortal spirit is nobler than the clod it animates, so is the object of this bill of more importance than any mere pecuniary interest." The National Bureau of Education was established, and the results of its work have fully vindicated the opinions of its founders. Garfield's idea of what should be taught in our schools and colleges was as broad and deep as the domain of knowledge; but, withal, very practical. That he loved the classics, his own study of them demonstrates; but he saw that something better adapted to the scientific and practical character of our country was needed. In an address at Hiram, on June 14, 1867, he gave emphatic expression to this idea:

A finished education is supposed to consist mainly of literary culture. The story of the forges of the Cyclops, where the thunderbolts of Jove were fashioned, is supposed to adorn elegant scholarship more gracefully than those sturdy truths which are preaching to this generation in the wonders of the mine, in the fire of the furnace, in the clang of the iron mills, and the other innumerable industries, which, more than all other human agencies, have made our civilization what it is, and are destined to achieve wonders yet undreamed of. This generation is beginning to understand that education should not be forever divorced from industry; that the highest results can be reached only when science guides the hand of labor. With what eagerness and alacrity is industry seizing every truth of science and putting it in harness!

Moreover, Mr. Garfield believed strongly in a liberal political education for the youth of the land. On this point, in the address above mentioned, he said:

It is well to know the history of these magnificent nations, whose origin is lost in fable, and whose epitaphs were written a thousand years ago; but, if we cannot know both, it is far better to study the history of our own Nation, whose origin we can trace to the freest and noblest aspirations of the human heart—a Nation that was formed from the hardiest, purest, and most enduring element of European civilization; a nation that by its faith and courage has dared and accomplished more for the human race in a single century than Europe accomplished in the first thousand years of the Christian era. The New England township was the type after which our Federal Government was modeled; yet it would be rare to find a college student who can make a comprehensive and intelligible statement of the municipal organization of the township in which he was born, and tell you by what officers its legislative, judicial, and executive functions are administered. One half of the time which is now almost wholly wasted in district schools on English grammar, attempted at too early an age, would be sufficient to teach our children to love the Republic, and to become its loyal and life-long supporters. After the bloody baptism from which the Nation has risen to a higher and nobler life, if this shameful defect in our system of education be not speedily remedied, we shall deserve the infinite contempt of future generations. I insist that it shall be made an indispensable condition of graduation in every American college, that the student must understand the history of this continent since its discovery by Europeans, the origin and history of the United States, its constitution of government, the struggles through which it has passed, and the rights and duties of citizens who are to determine its destiny and share its glory. Having thus gained the knowledge which is necessary to life, health, industry, and citizenship, the student is prepared to enter a wider and grander field of thought. If he desires that large and liberal culture which will call into activity all his powers, and make the most of the material God has given him, he must study deeply and earnestly, the intellectual, the moral, the religious, and the æsthetic nature of man; his relations to nature, to civilization, past and present; and, above all, his relations to God. These should occupy nearly, if not fully, half the time of his college course. In connection with the philosophy of the mind, he should study logic, the pure mathematics, and the general laws of thought. In connection with moral philosophy, he should study political and social ethics—a science so little known either in colleges or congresses. Prominent among all the rest, should be his study of the wonderful history of the human race, in its slow and toilsome march across the centuries—now buried in ignorance, superstition, and crime; now rising to the sublimity of heroism and catching a glimpse of a better destiny; now turning remorselessly away from, and leaving to perish, empires and civilizations in which it had invested its faith and courage and boundless energy for a thousand years, and, plunging into the forests of Germany, Gaul, and Britain, to build for itself new empires better fitted for its new aspirations; and, at last, crossing three thousand miles of unknown sea, and building in the wilderness of a new hemisphere its latest and proudest monuments.

In August, 1866, the gentleman who had been set aside by his district on the occasion of Garfield's first election to Congress, made an effort to secure the nomination. He thoroughly canvassed the district, and was aided in his opposition by the iron-producers of the Mahoning valley, who opposed Garfield's re-nomination on the ground that he did not favor so high a tariff on iron as they considered their interest demanded. Garfield was, however, re-nominated by an overwhelming vote, and elected by his usual majority. He afterward convinced these opponents that a moderate duty, affording a reasonable margin for protection, was better for them than a high prohibitory tariff.

This subject of the tariff was always one of General Garfield's favorites, and while in Congress he made several of his ablest and most recondite speeches upon it. Garfield's assistance in the direction of an equitable system of protection has been very valuable to the cause of home industry, when it was in serious peril from free-trade attacks. In the first speech which he made in Congress upon the tariff question in 1866, he goes fully into the history of protection; states the policy of England toward the Colonies, which led to the Revolution, and shows how she made of our fathers mere "hewers of wood and drawers of water"—simply farm-laborers to supply the raw material for her manufactories; and in subsequent ones he discusses more fully the philosophy of the subject. His studies led him to believe that, as a mere abstract theory, free-trade is the true doctrine; but that in a country situated like ours it can be made to work practically only as we come up to it through a long series of protections, until, one by one, the various articles of manufacture are placed so well on their feet as to stand alone. He was opposed to prohibitory protection, but in favor of a tariff high enough to enable our people to compete fairly with foreign industries, and keep our own alive; yet not so high as to enable our manufacturers to combine and monopolize prices, and altogether shut out foreign competition.

He early took his stand on this middle doctrine. It was not satisfactory to the free-traders, because they wanted absolutely no restriction; nor was it to the extreme protectionists, because they desired the highest possible tariff, to give them a monopoly of their business. He was denounced by the protectionists as a free-trader, and by the free-traders as a protectionist. In fact, it is the only position where he ever stood in the middle between two extremes. On every other question he has been at one pole or the other. Here he has stood on the equator, and insisted that the true position is the point of stable equilibrium where a tariff could be held that would not be let down whenever the free-traders held sway, or forced up whenever the protectionists got into power. What the country needs is a permanent and settled policy, the tendency of which will be constantly toward amelioration and lesser duties. He has held this equitable ground throughout his congressional career, against the assaults of first one side and then of the other; and to have held that steady equipoise is, perhaps, the greatest of his achievements in statesmanship.

Early in 1867 his constant application began to wear upon him; his health broke down, and by the advice of his physician, in the summer of that year, accompanied by his wife, General Garfield went to Europe, sailing from New York in the steamer "City of London," which carried them across the Atlantic in thirteen days. Remembering the ambitions of his boyhood to become a sailor, Garfield enjoyed his voyage as few men do who cross the sea. As they steamed up the Mersey, General Garfield significantly remarked, looking into its muddy waters, "The quality of Mersey is not strained." He was absent from New York seventeen weeks, and in that time made the tour most familiar to travelers. He landed at Liverpool, and went down to London, stopping at Chester—which is near the home of his ancestors. He remained in London about a week, and while there listened to the great reform debate which resulted in giving the ballot to seven hundred thousand Englishmen. He saw Gladstone, Disraeli, Bright, and other great Englishmen, and after a week of sight seeing and studying here, visited other parts of England. He then visited Scotland, making the tour of the lakes, and then crossing the North Sea, landed at Rotterdam. Mr. Blaine and Mr. Morrill were with them in Scotland. There the general visited the home of Burns and re-read "Tam O'Shanter." Thence he went to Brussels, and up the Rhine to Switzerland, and then across the Alps into Italy, visiting Florence and Rome. Hear a year of life was crowded into a week, while Garfield lived amid the wrecks of antiquity and the decayed remnants of that dead empire whose splendid history can not be forgotten till "the last syllable of recorded time." At Milan and Venice he made short stops; but at Rome he remained a week, studying its ruins and monuments, and being carried back to the classic times, which, since his college days have been the delight of his imagination. On his return, he spent another week in Paris where they met several American friends, among them the artist, Miss Ransom, and then, after a few days in London and Liverpool, crossed to Kingston, and after a trip through Ireland, set sail for home. This journey widened his knowledge of men and things, and gave him what he sought—restored health.

The Fortieth Congress met in December, 1867, and Mr. Garfield, contrary to his wishes, was dropped from the Committee of Ways and Means, and made

Chairman of the Committe on Military Affairs. In this committee he had plenty of work to do looking after the demands of the discharged soldiers for pay and bounty, of which many had been deprived by red-tape decisions of the Government accounting officers. Among his most important speeches, in this connection, were that on the "Military Control of the Rebel States," made in February, 1867, and that delivered January 17, 1868, on the then all-absorbing theme, "Reconstruction."

In the conflict between President Johnson and the majority in Congress, about the government of the late rebel states, General Garfield was, of course, sternly opposed to that outrageous policy of the President, whose main object seemed to be the undoing of all the beneficial results of the war. When the articles of impeachment against Johnson were passed, Garfield was not in Washington, but on his return he took occasion to say that if he had been present he should have voted for them. He had formerly opposed such action because he thought it would be unsuccessful. Johnson's later actions, however, especially his arbitrary dismissal of Secretary Stanton, were such clear violations of the Constitution that he supposed the President's guilt could be judicially established, and therefore he favored the attempt.

During the month of May in this year another address on the currency was delivered by General Garfield. His financial views were still in advance of his party, and the unsound views advanced by various politicians gave opportunity for many a well-directed shot from his well-stored armory of facts, figures, and principles. In 1868 occcured one of the many attempts made by politicians to reduce the public debt by extorting money from the Nation's creditors. In July General Garfield considered, at great length, and with all his usual clearness and ability, one of these measures, which, in this case, was a bill for the taxation of bonds. He was too honest a man and at the same time too sound a financier, to be blind to the wrong as well as the impolitic character of such a law.

On May 30, 1868, occurred the first general observance of that beautiful national custom, the annual decoration of the soldier's graves. On that day, the President and his Cabinet, with a large number of Congressmen and other distinguished persons and about fifteen thousand people, met on Arlington Heights to pay their repects to the Nation's dead, and listen to an address. The orator of the day was Garfield. No more touching and sincere expression of patriotic sentiments was ever uttered than he spoke there that day. Indeed, his reverence for the time and place was deeper than his words could tell. To this he referred in the beginning, saying:

If silence is ever golden, it must be here, beside the graves of fifteen thousand men, whose lives were more significant than speech, and whose death was a poem the music of which can never be sung. With words we make promises, plight faith, praise virtue. Promises may not be kept; plighted faith may be broken; and vaunted virtue may be only the cunning mask of vice. We do not know one promise these men have made, one pledge they gave, one word they spoke; but we do know they summed up and perfected, by one supreme act, the highest virtues of men and citizens. For love of country they accepted death; and thus resolved all doubts, and made immortal their patriotism and their virtue. For the noblest man that lives there still remains a conflict. He must still withstand the assaults of time and fortune; he must still be assailed with temptations before which lofty natures have fallen. But with *these*, the conflict ended, the victory was won, when death stamped on them the great seal of heroic character, and closed a record which years can never blot.

This memorable address closed thus:

"And now, consider this silent assembly of the dead. What does it represent? Nay, rather, what does it not represent? It is an epitome of the war. Here are sheaves reaped, in the harvest of death, from every battle-field of Virginia. If each grave had a voice to tell us what its silent tenant last saw and heard on earth, we might stand, with uncovered heads, and hear the whole story of the war. We should hear that one perished when the first great drops of the crimson shower began to fall, when the darkness of that first disaster at Manassas fell like an eclipse on the Nation; that another died of disease while wearily waiting for winter to end; that this one fell on the field in sight of the spires of Richmond, little dreaming that the flag must be carried through three more years of blood before it should be planted in that citadel of treason; and that one fell when the tide of war had swept us back, till the roar of rebel guns shook the dome of yonder capitol, and re-echoed in the chambers of the executive mansion. We should hear mingled voices from the Rappahannock, the Rapidan, the Chickahominy, and the James; solemn voices from the Wilderness, and triumphant shouts from the Shenandoah, from Petersburgh, and the Five Forks, mingled with the wild acclaim of victory and the sweet chorus of returning peace. The voices of these dead will forever fill the land, like holy benedictions. What other spot so fitting for their last resting place as this, under the shadow of the capitol saved by their valor? Here, where the grim edge of battle joined; here, where all the hope and fear and agony of their country centred; here let them rest, asleep on the Nation's heart, entombed in the Nation's love! The view from this spot bears some resemblance to that which greets the eye at Rome. In sight of the Capitoline Hill, up and across the Tiber, and overlooking the city, is a hill, not rugged or lofty, but known as the Vatican Mount. At the beginning of the Christian era, an imperial circus stood on its summit. There, gladiator slaves died for the sport of Rome, and wild beasts fought with wilder men. In that arena, a Galilean fisherman gave up his life, a sacrifice for his faith. No human life was ever so nobly avenged. On that spot was reared the proudest Christian temple ever built by human hands. For its adornment, the rich offerings of every clime and kingdom had been contributed. And now, after eighteen centuries, the hearts of two hundred million people turn toward it with reverence when they worship God! Seen from the western slope of our capitol, in direction, distance and appearance, this spot is not unlike the Vatican Mount, though the river that flows at our feet is larger than a hundred Tibers. Seven years ago this was the home of one who lifted his sword against the life of his country, and who became the great imperator of the Rebellion. The soil beneath our feet was watered by the tears of slaves, in whose hearts the sight of yonder proud capitol awakened no pride, and inspired no hope. The face of the goddess that crowns it was turned toward the sea, and not toward them. But, thanks be to God, this arena of rebellion and slavery is a scene of violence and crime no longer! This will be forever the sacred mountain of our capital. Here is our temple; its pavement is the sepulcher of heroic hearts; its dome, the bending heaven; its altar candles, the watching stars.

As the thread of our story continues, how grandly before us rises the hero of this volume! Spotless and irreproachable, his career presents a type than which there is no higher. From it there comes an appeal for excellence, which youth cannot study but to respect; if to respect, then to imitate; and if to imitate, to be like him—NOBLE AND TRUE.

CHAPTER XV.

AN ORNAMENT OF CONGRESS.

He spake, and into every heart his words
Carried new strength and courage.

BRYANT.

"Yet remember all
He spoke among you, and the man who spoke;
Who never sold the truth to serve the hour,
Nor paltered with eternal God for power."

General Garfield had been in Congress about four years, when the famous inflation cry was raised in the country. Everything soon seemed drifting toward greenbacks and repudiation. General Garfield was from the outset a consistent advocate, both in Congress and on the stump, of "honest money." He has opposed every form of inflation and greenbackism, and had at this time succeeded in making his opinions on this subject the thought of the majority of his district; but on his return from Europe, he found that the Republicans of Ohio had adopted a wretched platform, which looked to the payment of the bonds of the Government in greenbacks, and that they had already fought the fall campaign on that issue. His friends proposed to give him a public reception at Jefferson before his departure for Washington, and, knowing his opinions, they said to him: "The state is swept into the greenback current, and there is no stemming the torrent; so, say nothing on this subject, for the feeling is too strong to be resisted. An indiscreet word may cost you the nomination." He was not to be in Ohio again before the holding of the nominating convention; but he attended the reception, and when called upon to address the assemblage, rose and made a speech in favor of the honest payment of the public debt, right in the teeth of the platform. And he said to them: "Much as I value your opinions, I here denounce this theory that has worked its way into this state, as dishonest, unwise, and unpatriotic; and if I were offered a nomination and election for my natural life, from this district, on this platform, I should spurn it. If you should ever raise the question of re-nominating me, let it be understood you can have my services only on the ground of the honest payment of this debt, and these bonds, in coin, according to the letter and spirit of the contract."

Garfield was too much of a leader and statesman, too far ahead of the party of which he was a conspicuous member, too far in advance of the thinking of the politicians—not to see the evil results sure to follow in the path of the inflation idea. The country hailed the new money era with delight. The government presses were idle; all over the country were poor men. Why not set the presses to work, and make sufficient greenbacks to make every man rich, and able to live in easy circumstances? Why should there be this seeming inconsistency of a few rich and many poor? It was a capital idea! It was the very panacea needed, and soon every one was to be rich and happy! All over the West, and particularly in Garfield's own state, the satisfaction of the people at the happy prospects was great. The fountain of wealth which was present to the people all the time, without once being suspected, was hailed as the harbinger of a happy and prosperous future. To further equalize the matter, it was decided to compel the Nation's bondholders to accept greenbacks instead of gold for their bonds. One was just as good as the other in their eyes, and why not force the public credit, and make our creditors take them! An objection on their part was not to be considered. And this was the sentiment General Garfield found pervading the Republican party on his return. His own constituents were for inflation without reserve. His declarations had always been for hard money, and for the payment of the bonds in gold. Garfield had been re-elected at each of the congressional elections of his district since he first took his seat. Ordinarily, to secure a re-nomination, a congressman would gradually swing around to the popular sentiment and feelings of his constituents about the time for holding the convention, and if he did not incorporate them as his own ideas and opinions, would at least do so from policy sake. But in every different occasion we have found General Garfield never once carping and fawning in this matter. Every time he had maintained his own sentiments, and upon them he was chosen. He preferred to remain a free moral agent, rather than subscribe to that which he did not believe. He took a bold stand; as his views were opposed to those of many leading men of his party, and to the declarations of the Republican State Committee of Ohio, he indeed seemed to hazard his re-nomination, but he did not hesitate firmly and fully to avow his convictions. The following extract from a letter written to his confidential friend, Hinsdale, dated March 8, 1868, declares:

"The state convention at Columbus has committed itself to some financial doctrines that, if I understand them, I cannot and will not endorse. If my constituents approve them they cannot approve me. Before many weeks my immediate political future will be decided. I care less about the result than I have ever cared before."

And there Garfield stood unmoved and immovable. Office, position, influence and immediate success could not move this brave man. What a lesson to the legislators of the day! How incalculably better, and freer from censure, would be our public men and measures if such was their candor and honesty. What is more distasteful than an Uriah Heep official. It has begun to be an idea of ridicule, that "the office should seek the man." In these times of dishonesty, avarice and selfishness, the man who talks the most of his selfish ends, and winds himself, spiral-like, around the popular cant of the day, is the one who occupies the positions where the best of men should be. And even this tendency is becoming so strong and grounded that honest, pure men, are fearful of the results when they enter the arena of politics. Perhaps our statement is too sweeping;

perhaps not. That there are good men and noble men to-day in our halls of legisture is true, beyond any question of a doubt. But even these are placed at a great disadvantage, from the fact that the public mind has begun to look upon the occupation of the politician and legislator as selfish and low. We say, Success to the man who stands or falls upon his own integrity of purpose and principle. Garfield's public life and the way he obtained position will bear the scrutinizing gaze of all eyes. It is well worthy of imitation. He thus took "the bull by the horns," and then went to Washington. The result was, that, when the convention met, he was renominated by acclamation.

In the nominating convention of 1868, Garfield was opposed by Darius Cadwell, of Ashtabula county, who secured forty votes, chiefly from his own county, and had the pleasure of seeing his opponent elected by one of his overwhelming majorities. When he reached Congress he was appointed Chairman of the Committee on Banking and Currency. It would be useless to attempt to give more than a very brief sketch of the immense activities of General Garfield in Congress from this time on. The voluminous reports of which he was the author, the comprehensive debates in which he was a chief figure-head, embracing every topic and question of the science of government, finance, tariff and the many other questions of political science, his immense and varied committee work, would fill volumes were it attempted. His speeches are incomparable for their profound learning and logic. Glancing over the records of these sessions, one is forcibly struck with his great superiority. No compeer excels him, and very few equal. In fact, it may be said that he is above and alone. There were others whose powers were great, and whose efforts outside the light of Garfield's sun, would have been as stars of the first magnitude.

On December 14, 1868, he introduced a bill "To strengthen the public credit." Ultimately this was a part of the great bill making our bonds payable in gold. Garfield fought all attempts to repeal it with singular success; and in 1879, when resumption was accomplished, the law still remained on the statute books. February 26, 1869, General Garfield, as Chairman of the Military Committee, made the monster report upon the re-organization of the army. It contained one hundred and thirty-seven printed pages. This question, the re-adjusting of the armies of the Republic, on a peace footing, had occupied Garfield's attention for years. All the leading army officers had been examined by him, and the report was the result. It contained the history of each department of the army. It illuminated all the dark corners, the secret channels, the hidden chambers of corruption which had been constructed in the military policy of the country, and was the product of immense labor. Early in 1869, General Garfield introduced a resolution for the appointment of a committee upon the subject of the Ninth census. Of this committee he was made chairman. Upon the great subject of statistics his speeches are most characteristic. They show Garfield in the light of a political scientist. The enormous reach of his mind is remarkable. He proved himself to be abreast of the leading scientific thought of the day. Nowhere in or out of Congress can be found so succinct and admirable a statement of the importance of statistics. He showed that a legislator without statistics to guide him, was like a mariner at sea without a compass. The thing that should be settled is whether the rich men are becoming richer and the poor man poorer. We need a new chart to guide us, he argued, like the seaman who starts out on a voyage after a thousand volcanoes have belched forth in mid-ocean.

Again on December 16, 1869, General Garfield spoke on this same subject. In this effort, the principle upon which statistical science rests, and the objects it proposes to reach, were discussed. He showed that the cultivation of statistics developed the truth that society is an organism whose elements and forms conform to laws as constant and pervasive as those which govern the material universe; that their development is causing history to be re-written; that statistical science is indispensable to modern statesmanship, which consists rather in removing causes than in punishing or evading results. He suggested that a record of the vital statistics be taken, measuring as accurately as possible the effective physical strength of the people. Then a record in regard to the dwellings should be made, as indicating more fully the condition of the people. The next paragraph is devoted to the question of determining the number of voters. The Fourteenth Amendment to the Constitution reduced a state's representation in Congress to the measure of its votes. This was thought at the time to refer merely to the states where negroes were not allowed to vote, but Garfield found that in all the states there were eighty restrictions in the right to vote, besides color and crime, ranging all the way from residence to education and character. Upon the subject of agricultural products, he thought that the amended schedule would enable us to ascertain the elements which have made our country the granary of the world. He was persuaded that a very important question to be confronted would be that of corporations, and their relation to the interests of the people and to the national life. The learning and advanced views, together with the phenomenal grouping of the social statistics in this speech, is something unique in the wilderness of congressional oratory. After all this work, re-search and labor, the bill failed to pass the Senate, and the Ninth census was taken under the old law. The body of the bill, however, eventually became the law under which the unequaled census of 1880 was taken.

The next most significant action and famous speech of General Garfield was concerning the celebrated "Black Friday." There are few but will remember the gold panic of September 24, 1869. It originated in the greatest financial conspiracy known in history. In the House of Representatives an investigation was demanded, and this was given into the hands of the Committee on Banking and Currency, of which General Garfield was Chairman, having received the appointment at the opening of the Forty-first Congress. General Garfield proceeded at once to New York, entered the Gold Room, without making his person known, heard the secret examination by the Gold Board, made copious notes and obtained his clue. When he returned to Washington, a faithful substitute was left, and each witness was attached and taken immediately to Washington for examination there. Gould and Fisk, the chief schemers, each were forced to disclose the terrible secrets. General Garfield's report, made March 1, 1870, goes to the very bottom of this darkest conspiracy ever planned. It reads like a novel, and contains the material for a whole library of fiction. In brief, some idea of the foul plot may be obtained from the following summary;

Gould and Fisk raised and lowered the price of gold to suit their purposes for some time. They finally, through the assistance of A. R. Corbin, a brother-in-law of President Grant, and also a conspirator, secured the appointment of General Butterfield as assistant treasurer, at New York, who they desired to assist them in their nefarious schemes. In the investigation it was proven, however, that the latter gentleman was in no way acquainted with the corrupt schemes. While the President was *en route* in one of the Messrs. Fisk and Gould Fall River steamers to Boston, the schemers endeavored to obtain from President Grant his views in regard to finance. The President said "there was a certain amount of fictitiousness about the prosperity of the country, and that the bubble might as well be tapped in one way as another." This remark had the effect of a wet blanket. It was evident now that some other means would have to be adopted, to prevent a further decline of gold, which would certainly interfere with their purposes of speculation. This was to be effected by facts and arguments presented in the name of the country and its business interests. The theory was that the business interests of the country required an advance in the price of gold; that, in order to move the fall crops and secure the foreign market for our grains, it was necessary that gold should be put up to 145. This plan was pushed persistently. Newspapers, previously bought by the conspirators, filled their columns with editorials and arguments in favor of the new scheme. Upon the President there was brought to bear all manner of argument and memorial. Pamphlets came by every mail. On every hand came the plea for the poor country. If the Government would sell no gold, the conspirators would have the market in their own hands. By this arrangement, persons having obligations to fulfill in gold, would be compelled to purchase of the conspirators at any price. The President remained silent, but his silence gave the conspirators more hope and they made additional heavy purchases of gold. Gould now secured a partner. Fisk joined the movement upon learning that persons in authority from the President down to General Butterfield were corruptly connected with the project, and that the Secretary of the Treasury had been ordered not to sell any gold. The price of gold was now pushed from 135½, where it stood on the morning of the 13th of September, until on the evening of the 22d, they held it firm at 140½. They now held sixty millions of gold. Everything depended on Grant's preventing the sale of gold. Brother-in-law Corbin was to manage that. Every cent advanced in gold added $15,000 to Corbin's profit. He now wrote a letter to the President, importuning him not to interfere. A faithful servant carried the letter in person to Washington, Pennsylvania, where the President was staying. The letter being delivered and no answer given in return, the letter-carrier went to the nearest telegraph-office and sent to Fisk this dispatch: "Letters delivered all right." This he interpreted as meaning the President was all right for them, and would not interfere, and consequently, large additional purchases were made. The receipt of the letter by the President, under the circumstances, urging a certain policy upon the administration, evidently for personal ends, excited the President's suspicion. He believed Mr. Corbin guilty of speculations at the cost of the government. He thereupon urged Mrs. Grant to write to Mrs. Corbin, stating that the President had received rumors of Corbin's speculations, and urged her to persuade him to disengage himself at once. Corbin received the letter on the 22d, and disclosed its contents to Gould. No little alarm was now created in their minds. Corbin tried to get Gould to buy him out, so that he could tell the President he was not interested in the market. Gould plotted to save himself by ruining his co-conspirators. A meeting was held, and Gould secretly sold his interest to Fisk. It was then decided to push the price of gold up to 160 the next day ("Black Friday"), publish a list of all firms who had contracts to furnish gold, offer to settle with them at the price named before three o'clock, but threatening higher prices to all who delayed. Business now began to be paralyzed all over the country. The telegraph could not keep up with the fluctuations in gold. The President returned to Washington on the 23d, and at once held a consultation with the Secretary of the Treasury concerning the condition of the gold market. They decided to protect the business interests of the country should gold be pushed higher. The next morning the price advanced rapidly, and telegrams poured into Washington from every quarter, urging the government to interfere and prevent a financial crisis. Shortly before noon the crack of doom came. Butterfield, Assistant Treasurer at New York, was ordered to sell on the following day four millions of gold, and buy four millions bonds. In fifteen minutes the price fell to 133, and in the language of one of the witnesses, half of Wall street was involved in ruin.

General Garfield was by this time recognized as the highest authority on the intricate subjects of finance, revenue, and expenditure, in the House. It will be seen that these topics fall within the general head of political economy, "the dismal science." Of these he was the acknowledged master. Accordingly, at the beginning of the Forty-second Congress, in 1871, Garfield was made chairman of the Committee of Appropriations, as successor to Henry L. Dawes. This position he held until the Democrats got control of the House in 1875, and during that time he largely reduced the expenses of the Government, "reformed the system of estimates and appropriations, providing for closer accountability on the part of those who spend the public money, and a clear knowledge of those who vote it, of what it is used for." It is probable that in this capacity he never had an equal. He had been returned at this time for his fifth two years without opposition, either in the convention or the field. Something must be said of his work. In order to master the great subject of public expenditures, he studied the history of those of European nations. He read the "budget speeches" of the English chancellors of the exchequer for a long period. He refreshed his German, and studied French, in order to read the best works in the world on the subjects, the highest authorities being in those languages. He examined the British and French appropriations for a long period. After an exhaustive study of the history of foreign nations, he commenced with our own country at the time of the Revolution. Charles Sumner was the greatest reader, and had the longest book list at the Congressional Library of any man in Washington. The library records show that General Garfield's list was next to Sumner's, being but slightly below it. After Sumner's death, the man who was second became first. This gathering of facts was followed by wide inductions. National expenditures were found by him to be subject to a law as fixed as that of gravitation. There was a proportion between population, area of country, and the necessary outlay for public expenses, which was fixed. Anything beyond this was waste. No covering could hide official robbery from the reach of such a detective as the establishment of this law. Every miscreant left a tell-tale track.

The results of his studies were embodied in an elaborate speech on January 22, 1872, in the introduction of his appropriation bill. The speech is the result of an immense induction, by which he arrives at the conclusion that the expenditures of a war cannot be brought down to a peace level until a subsequent period twice as long as the war itself. He shows that it had been so in the wars of England, and in our own wars ever since the formation of the Government; that expenditures rise to their height at the close of a war; that then they begin to fall—to gradually and uniformly decline until they strike the new level of peace; when they again began to rise gradually, keeping pace with the growth and prosperity of the country. The late war, he said, was substantially five years long, ending, financially, in 1866. Apply his rule to this, and the peace level will have been reached in 1876. On April 4, 1871, he delivered a speech in opposition to a Republican bill for the enforcement of the Fourteenth Amendment. At the time it brought down upon him the censure of his party. But he was firm. There could be no doubt of his loyalty to the Nation, and his distrust of the malignant South. But he was too conservative for the war leaders and politicians. A compromise was effected, with which, however, his opponents were much dissatisfied. Another notable speech was made on the bill to establish an educational fund from the proceeds of the sale of public lands. The speech abounded in citations from English, French, and German authorities on the subject of education. One doctrine enunciated was that matters of education belonged to the State governments, not to the nation; that Congress made no claim to interfere in the method, but only to assist in the work.

In the summer of 1872, General Garfield undertook a delicate mission to the Flat-Head Indians. Their removal was required by the Government. But the noble red man refused to stir an inch from his ancestral hunting-grounds. Garfield's mission was to be the last pacific resort. He was successful when the department had given up hope in any resource but war. On his return from the West, General Garfield found the Credit Mobilier scandal looming up like a cyclone in the congressional sky. Living a life of study, research, and thought, of spotless character and purest intention, he was inexpressibly pained. His correspondence at this time with President Hinsdale, in which he uncovers his secret heart, is full of expressions of disgust with politics, "where ten years of honest toil goes for naught in the face of one vote," as he says. Once he declares: "Were it not for the Credit Mobilier, I believe I would resign." How plainly Garfield's motives appear in the following little extract:

> You know that I have always said that my whole public life was an experiment to determine whether an intelligent people would sustain a man in acting sensibly on each proposition that arose, and in doing nothing for mere show or for demagogical effect. I do not now remember that I ever cast a vote of that latter sort. Perhaps it is true that the demagogue will succeed when honorable statesmanship will fail. If so, public life is the hollowest of all shams.

In another letter to Colonel Rockwell, he speaks from his heart: "I think of you as away, and in an eylsium of quiet and peace, where I should love to be, out of the storm and in the sunshine of love and books. Do not think from the above that I am despondent. There is life and hope and fight in your old friend yet."

On one occasion, when delivering one of his famous "budget speeches," as they came to be called, he said:

The necessary expenditures of the Government form the base line from which we measure the amount of our taxation required, and on which we base our system of finance. We have frequently heard it remarked since the session began, that we should make our expenditures come within our revenues—that we should "cut our garment according to our cloth." This theory may be correct when applied to private affairs, but it is not applicable to the wants of nations. Our national expenditures should be measured by the real necessities and the proper needs of the Government. We should cut our garment so as to fit the person to be clothed. If he be a giant, we must provide cloth sufficient for a fitting garment. The Committee on Appropriations are seeking earnestly to reduce the expenditures of the Government, but they reject the doctrine that they should at all hazards reduce the expenditures to the level of the revenues, however small those revenues may be. They have attempted rather to ascertain what are the real and vital necessities of the Government; to find what amount of money will suffice to meet all its honorable obligations, to carry on all its necessary and essential functions, and to keep alive those public enterprises which the country desires its Government to undertake and accomplish. When the amount of expenses necessary to meet these objects is ascertained, that amount should be appropriated, and ways and means for procuring that amount should be provided. On some accounts, it is unfortunate that our work of appropriations is not connected directly with the work of taxation. If this were so, the necessity of taxation would be a constant check upon extravagance, and the practice of economy would promise, as its immediate result, the pleasure of reducing taxation.

Referring to Garfield's tariff record, it is both just and proper that we should state that the protectionists of the country who have kept watch over tariff legislation during the past twenty years, and who have assisted in shaping and maintaining the present tariff, are perfectly satisfied with his tariff votes and speeches. They and all other protectionists have, indeed, abundant reason to be thankful to him for valuable assistance rendered to the cause of home industry when it was in serious peril from free-trade attacks. His votes and speeches have been uniformly and constantly in favor of the protective policy.

About the same time he delivered his celebrated speech on the Railway Problem. The pending question was upon making certain appropriations for river, harbor, and canal surveys, as a preliminary to cheaper transportation. General Garfield favored the appointment of a similar commission on the railway question. The speech is one of his great efforts and shows the grasp and handling of a master mind.

CHAPTER XVI.

"INTER FOLIA FRUCTUS."

Wise in the council, stalwart in the field!
Such rank supreme a workman's hut may yield.
His onward steps like measured marbles show,
Climbing the height where God's great flame doth glow.

—JULIA WARD HOWE.

Step by step, to higher stair
Forward he leaps,
Broader his vision sweeps,
Till he the loftiest summit gains.

—ALCOTT.

So full of labor have appeared the years of Garfield's life that we have just been scanning, that one would think all the efforts of the man had been mentioned. But how far from the truth such a conjecture would be, this chapter shall show. Garfield seems to be absolutely beyond the possibility of sounding. We cast the plummet-line out at the close of every day's sailing, and yet it cannot be perceived that the bottom is reached. In a previous chapter it was shown that Garfield was great in every direction we might choose to view him. His powers seemed to know no fatigue. His labors were stupendous. At Hiram, Garfield had crowded many years of work in a course of but a few years. At Williams he had accomplished much the same thing, while at the same time he was preacher and leader. In the army he rose without occupying many of the intermediate stages; he reached the Supreme Court without first going to the lower courts, and did so while his principal work lay in other channels. Knowing these facts then, we naturally look around us for other labors that Garfield probably performed while his main work was on the floor of the House of Representatives and in the various committee rooms. And we will not search in vain. His mind must have action to maintain its vigor—and that action must go out in various directions.

During the years that we have just been reviewing, Garfield's marvelous achievements in the National House had been such as to give any man the reputation which all congressmen esteem. But Garfield was much more than his great efforts. At the distance of a decade we admire Garfield's achievements, but above them all he stands pre-eminently superior. As the inventor is in every way greater than his invention, so is the man of genius still above his greatest works. Even when the excitement of debate was highest in the House, he still found time to keep up his literary studies. This was his recreation, and to him it was far more enjoyable than absolute cessation from all labor. It is related of him that during one of the busy sessions he was found behind a big barricade of books, which proved upon examination to be different editions of Horace, and works relating to that poet. "I find I'm overworked, and need recreation," he said. "Now, my theory is that the best way to rest the mind is not to let it lie idle, but to put it at something quite outside the ordinary line of employment. So, I am resting by learning all the Congressional Library can teach about Horace, and the various editions and translations of his poems." And an application of this theory to his every-day life made him a student, and ripened a scholarship rare among public men. The first oration which we will mention under this caption as coincident with his numerous public duties was that delivered June 29, 1869, before the Commercial College in Washington City, on the "Elements of Success." In this speech are to be found some of the choicest and best thoughts. Let us select a few thought-flowers:

I feel a profounder reverence for a boy than a man. I never meet a ragged boy on the street without feeling that I owe him a salute, for I know not what possibilities may be buttoned up under his shabby coat. When I meet you in the full flush of mature life, I see nearly all there is of you; but among these boys are the great men of the future—the heroes of the next generation, the philosophers, the statesmen, the philanthropists, the great reformers and molders of the next age. Therefore, I say, there is a peculiar charm to me in the exhibitions of young people engaged in the business of education. * *

Speaking of the modern college curriculum, he said:

The prevailing system was established at a time when the learning of the world was in Latin and Greek; when, if a man would learn arithmetic, he must first learn Latin; and if he would learn the history and geography of his own country, he could acquire that knowledge only through the Latin language. Of course, in those days it was necessary to lay the foundation of learning in a knowledge of the learned languages. The universities of Europe, from which our colleges were copied, were founded before the modern languages were born. The leading languages of Europe are scarcely six hundred years old. The reasons for a course of study then are not good now. The old necessities have passed away. We now have strong and noble living languages, rich in literature, replete with high and earnest thought—the language of science, religion and liberty—and yet we bid our children feed their spirits on the life of dead ages, instead of the inspiring life and vigor of our own times. The present chancellor of the British exchequer, the Right Honorable Robert Lowe, one of the brightest minds in that kingdom, said, in a recent address before the venerable University of Edinburgh: "I was a few months ago in Paris, and two graduates of Oxford went with me to get our dinner at a restaurant, and if the white-aproned waiter had not been better educated than all three of us, we might have starved to death. We could not ask for our dinner in his language, but fortunately he could ask us in our own language what we wanted." There was one test of the insufficiency of modern education. * * * * * * * * * * * *

Let me beg you, in the outset of your career, to dismiss from your minds all idea of succeeding by luck. There is no more common thought among young people than that foolish one that by and by something will turn up by which they will suddenly achieve fame or fortune. No, young gentlemen; things don't turn up in this world unless somebody turns them up. Inertia is one of the indispensable laws of matter, and things lie flat where they are until by some intelligent spirit (for nothing but spirit makes motion in this world) they are endowed with activity and life. Luck is an *ignis fatuus*. You may follow it to ruin, but not to success. The great Napoleon, who believed in his destiny, followed it until he saw his star go down in blackest night, when the Old Guard perished around him, and Waterloo was lost. A pound of pluck is worth a ton of luck. * * * Poverty is uncomfortable, as I can testify; but nine times out of ten the best thing that can happen to a young man is to be tossed overboard, and compelled to sink or swim for himself. In all my acquaintance I have never known one to be drowned who was worth saving. This would not be wholly true in any country but one of political equality like ours. The editor of one of the leading magazines of England told me, not many months ago, a fact startling enough in itself, but of great significance to a poor man. He told me that he had never yet known, in all his experience, a single boy of the class of farm laborers (not those who own farms, but mere farm laborers) who had ever risen above his class. Boys from the manufacturing and commercial classes had risen frequently, but from the farm-labor class he had never known one. The reason is this: In the aristocracies of the Old World, wealth and society are built up like the strata of rock which compose the crust of the earth. If a boy be born in the lowest stratum of life, it is almost impossible for him to rise through this hard crust into the higher ranks; but in this country it is not so. The strata of our society resembles rather the ocean, where every drop, even the lowest, is free to mingle with all others, and may shine at last on the crest of the highest wave.

His correspondence is full of glimpses of literary life. At one time he breaks into glee over a new book. At another he solemnly urges the necessity of his friend Hinsdale and himself mastering French and German. Again he sighs for more time to read, and then gives an elaborate criticism of some book he had just finished. Once he says:

I can't see that John Stuart Mill ever came to comprehend human life as a reality from the actual course of human affairs beginning with Greek life down to our own. Men and women were always, with him, more or less of the nature of abstractions; while, with his enormous mass of books, he learned a wonderful power of analysis, for which he was by nature surprisingly fitted. But his education was narrow just where his own mind was originally deficient. He was educated solely through books; for his father was never a companion. His brothers and sisters bored him. He had no playfellows; *and of his mother not a word is said in his autobiography.*

Every peep of his private life has an exquisite charm. It perpetually surprises one with its frankness, its simplicity, and artless affection. "In Homer's *Iliad*, the great Hector, clad in dazzling armor and helmet, stoops to kiss his child before going forth to mortal combat. But the child drew back, afraid of his strange and terrible aspect. Swiftly the father removed the panoply of war, and then stooped to the child to be received with outstretched arms. In the fierce arena of debate we see Garfield clad with the stern helmet and buckler of battle. But in his private life he laid aside the armor, and stood forth in all the beauty of a grand, simple and affectionate nature." During the period covered by this chapter his home remained at Hiram, Ohio, where he spent his vacations from Congress. Here he lived in a very modest manner, keeping neither carriage nor horse, and borrowing or hiring when he desired to be conveyed to the railroad station, four miles off.

Mr. Frederick E. Warren, an attorney of Cincinnati, Ohio, was a student at Hiram College from 1869 to 1875. During this time he became acquainted with General Garfield. Of his impressions and acquaintance, he furnishes a vivacious narrative. He says:

General Garfield's return home was always an event with the college boys, by whom he was greatly admired and beloved. My earliest impressions of him, as he came one morning striding up the old plank walk that stretched across the college campus, realized all that I had heard spoken of him as to his appearance and bearing. Even God had seemed to set his seal upon him, "to give the world assurance of a *man*." Subsequent acquaintance merely ripened this impression. None of us required a formal introduction to him. The boys and he instinctively knew each other. He took the stranger cordially by the hand, gave him a kindly and encouraging word, and made him feel at once that he was his *friend*, and you may rest assured that the boy was forever *his*.

We learned much from the general's "talks," as he styled them. Whenever at home, he regularly attended the chapel exercises each morning. As soon as the religious services were concluded, he invariably was called upon to say something; to give us a "talk." He never failed to respond. His remarks were usually brief, but delightfully instructive, and there was a freshness and novelty which characterized them that I have never met with in any other public speaker or teacher.

On one occasion, when going to chapel, he saw a horse-shoe lying at the side of the path, which he picked up and carried along with him. After prayer, when asked as usual to say something to us (I must sorrowfully confess that a majority of the boys were impatient of prayers when the general was about), he produced the horse-shoe, and proceeded to explain its history and use from the remotest period, in so entertaining a manner that I am sure that no one who was present has ever forgotten it. At another time he delivered a similar off-hand lecture upon the hammer, suggested by one he had found somewhere about the college premises. In all he said to the students he was eminently practical, and it seemed to us that he could convey more information in fifteen minutes' talk than the combined faculty could have done in an hour. The general effect of these frequent brief discourses can readily be imagined. The more thoughtful vacated the playground, and gathered in groups about the boarding places, to discuss some question of interest suggested by the general, or retired to their rooms for reading and reflection upon the subject, inspired with a new love of knowledge, and desire for improvement. His application to business and study was extraordinary. It appeared to make no difference at what hour of the day or night one called upon him, he would be found in his library at work. If there was a "night owl" *par excellence* in Hiram College from the winter of 1869 to the winter of 1875, it was myself, yet however late the hour I retired might be, I had but to look three doors westward to see the light still burning in General Garfield's window; and he was nearly always up with the sun. It was often asked if he ever slept.

Apropos of this, I am able to recall a very agreeable incident, and one highly characteristic of the man. I was reading late one night Momssen's "History of Rome," and several times came across the word "symmachy," which I failed to find in the English dictionary. Somewhat puzzled with its recurrence, and seeing that the general was still up, I decided, although it was two o'clock in the morning, to call upon him for the meaning of the word. I found him hard at work, and after excusing myself for the interruption, explained the object of my unseasonable visit. He immediately replied: "It is coined from the Greek, a frequent practice with Momssen;" and taking from a book-case a Greek lexicon, he quickly furnished me with the information I was in quest of. He then insisted upon my sitting down, and for a couple of hours entertained me with an account of a recent trip to Europe. I noticed upon his shelves a copy of Bryant's translation of Homer. He complained that the book-seller had sent him an imperfect copy, there being one hundred and ninety lines at the beginning of the first volume omitted through the carelessness of the binder. He repeated some of the omitted lines, and spoke of them in terms of high critical eulogy. It was quite daylight before he allowed me to depart. The general was very peculiar in the discipline of his children. One evening an agent for a Babcock fire extinguisher was exhibiting the machine on a pile of lighted tarred boxes, on the public square, in the presence of a large crowd, among them General Garfield and his little son Jim, who is a chip off the old block, as the saying is. A gentleman accidentally stepped on the boy's foot. He did not yell, as most boys might have done under such a pressure, but savagely sprang at the gentleman and dealt him a blow with his fist somewhere in the region of the abdomen, about as high as he could reach. The father observed it, and immediately had the crowd open and ordered the fireman to turn the hose upon Jim, which was done, and the boy was extinguished in less than a minute. When he was in Washington, and we wanted—as frequently happened—any public documents or any facts to aid us in our society debates, which were not accessible from any other source, all we had to do was to write to the general for them, and it was flattering to us how promptly he complied with these requests.

What better proof can we have of the greatness of any man than such a testimony as this? Two Southern ladies engaged in charitable work connected with their church society, once became interested in the case of a family consisting of a blind man, his invalid wife and a lame daughter. The latter was at work in the fourth story of a government building in Washington at a salary of $400 per annum, and to get this small amount, she was obliged to walk (using a crutch) nearly three miles each way between her house and the printing room, and to climb four flights of stairs to her labors. This so exhausted the poor child that she was fast losing her health. These two Southern ladies looked about them to see who among the influential men in Washington had the broadest human sympathy, and they decided that James A. Garfield, then a member of Congress, was the man most likely to help them in benefiting this afflicted family. They accordingly visited General Garfield's house, and found a carriage before the door. Though complete strangers to him, they sent their cards to the general, who immediately came down stairs. He had his overcoat thrown over his arm, but very courteously greeted the ladies and asked what he could do for them. They said, "We notice that you appear to be leaving, and perhaps we detain you." He replied, "I am about to take the cars, but I will delay till next train if I can in any way be of service to you," and he showed them into the parlor and introduced them to his wife. When he was told of the case he replied that he should be away from Washington for two or three days, but if they would remind him on his return he would do all he could to assist them. Mrs. Garfield engaged to remind the general on his return, which she did, and through his kindness and effort this lame girl was transferred from the fourth floor to the first, and her salary made $1,200 instead of $400. This simple instance serves to illustrate the man's kindness of heart.

Previous to 1869, General Garfield had boarded a part of the time in Washington, and lived in a rented house for the remainder. It was during this year that his beautiful residence at the corner of Thirteenth and I streets, opposite Franklin Square, was built, in which he continued to reside until he was elected President. This is a modest, unpretentious brick mansion, plain and square built. It was small; comfortably, but by no means lavishly, furnished. Just over the grand piano hung a picture of General Garfield's mother. Opposite hung a portrait of the general's first daughter, a face of surpassing sweetness. Over the mantel there hung a relic of an idea, a half portrayed inspiration. The general one evening, in the company of some literary and artistic men, in the course of a discussion on Shakespeare, remarked that none of the illustrations of Falstaff satisfied his conception. An artist present begged him to describe his ideal, and from the description then given attempted the picture over the mantel. The artist dying before it was completed, the half finished sketch was framed by the general. The finished portion embraces the figure of the rollicking knight leaning his right arm on the inn table, and balancing in his left hand an empty glass. In the background the "drawer" is bringing in a fresh cup of sack. The conception is quite effective, even in its present state. The particular shrine in the Garfield home to which one always willingly hastened his steps was the library, situated just over the dining-room. This was the man of energy's workshop. It was here the student and the scholar lived. It was here the politician rested. Occupying the centre was a double walnut office desk, with the addition of pigeon-holes, and boxes, and drawers on one end, while just above hung a heavy chandelier. It was very evident from the orderly disorder of the room that the owner cared far more for immediate convenience than general symmetry. Half a dozen bookcases occupied the available space around the walls, and three thousand volumes filled their shelves. No two of these cases were of the same height, width or make. It suggested to the visitor, that from time to time, as the books overflowed their limits, another case was hastily procured in which to accommodate the surplus, and then when that was full another was added, and so on. And, undoubtedly, the overflow has been regular, as you could go nowhere in the general's home without coming face to face with books. They confronted you in the hall when you entered, in the parlor and the sitting-room, in the dining-room and even in the bath-room, where documents and speeches were corded up like fire-wood. And what was a wonderful point in their owner's favor, there was not one trashy volume among them. They were law, history, biography, poetry, politics, philosophy, government and standard works of all sorts, the accumulation of years of study and the patient research of the scholar. This house was in every sense a scholar's retreat. Books were everywhere. All of Garfield's reading was done under a system. Special fields were investigated at special times. In this way he was able to digest and retain more of what he read.

He was a great lover of scrap-books, and he had in his library a shelf full of them, containing articles and paragraphs relating to the subjects lettered on their backs. In this work Mrs. Garfield rendered him valuable aid, cutting and sorting the scraps which he would mark in newspapers. He was a maker of commonplace or reference books. Said he to an English visitor: "You see, political life fossilizes a man unless he has the strength to introduce a vivifying element, and for many years I have been busy in the House of Representatives during the session, and during the recesses at Washington, aiding the Republican cause by stump speaking or by any other means that offered by which to advance the party which is, as I think, most fitted to maintain the country's integrity. Yet there never was a time when I was too busy to study the works of great thinkers, and to make notes and comments on their wisdom. During my military life I looked into the subject of the histories of armies since the days of Sesostris; here you see my notes on that course of reading." So saying, he took up a large book, full of memoranda, of queries, of quotations and of original dessertations in his own handwriting, in Greek and Latin, in French, German and English. "At another time," he continued, "I became deeply interested in the Gothean literature. Here are my cullings from that mine of gold, with original comments. Again, I wanted to know what all the great thinkers of the world had had to say about women; so here you see excerpts gleaned from innumerable sources, in various languages. Another of my literary occupations has been that of making collections of the charming things we read in current journalism. We see something that strikes us as beautiful in a daily or weekly newspaper—something we should like to read again—to let our children read. The paper gets lost, torn up, and the little literary gem has vanished forever. My wife and I have had a habit of cutting such pretty things out and pasting them in scrap-books." This habit was begun on his first entrance into public life.

"It is perfectly astounding," said the general, "how much we are indebted to other people for our opinions. Comparatively few men or women take the trouble to think for themselves. Most persons frame their opinions from what they read or hear others say. I noticed this early in life, but never saw the evil of it until I went to Congress. Committees appointed to investigate particular subjects would meet together, and no one would say much at first. After a while some one would get up and state his opinion positively, give his reasons for thinking so, and in nine cases out of ten that man's opinion would be adopted as the opinion of the committee. The other members either had not or did not care to investigate the matter, and rather than take the trouble to look up the facts, would accept this member's opinion as their own."

It was this that made him such a close student, and caused him to read so much on matters that affected congressional legislation. He warned every one against the pernicious practice of taking other people's opinions as correct, and holding that ever man and woman should try and find out the fact and think for themselves. In addition to this he had daily records covering his whole line of actions and thoughts, so that almost his entire intellectual life is preserved. But more than either of these he had numerous labeled drawers, in which were filed away newspaper cuttings, items, pamphlets and documents. These were carefully classified. We now have the reason of Garfield's great knowledge and information on all subjects which presented themselves. A question would come up, some statement be made which he could not rebut. At evening the scrap-books would be examined, the subject thoroughly studied, and when his turn for reply came, he presented his point with great freshness. His collection was of incalculably more value to him than any encyclopedia. But we need not dwell here, however refreshing it may be to peep occasionally into the private life of our hero.

Among other great productions delivered during this period, was one on November 25, 1870, before the Army of the Cumberland, on the "Life and Character of George H. Thomas." As an argument defending Thomas from Robert E. Lee's charge of disloyalty, it is overwhelming. Garfield loved Thomas as a brother; and with the dead hero for a theme, the orator rose to the loftiest heights. Among his opening remarks were the following:

There are now living not less than two hundred thousand men who served under the eye of General Thomas; who saw him in sunshine and storm—on the march, in the fight, and on the field when the victory had been won. Enshrined in the hearts of all these, are enduring images and most precious memories of their commander and friend. Who shall collect and unite into one worthy picture, the bold outlines, the innumerable lights and shadows which make up the life and character of our great leader? Who shall condense into a single hour the record of a life which forms so large a chapter of the Nation's history, and whose fame fills and overfills a hemisphere? No line can be omitted, no false stroke made, no imperfect sketching done, which you, his soldiers, will not instantly detect and deplore. I know that each of you here present sees him in memory at this moment, as we often saw him in life; erect and strong, like a tower of solid masonry; his broad, square shoulders and massive head; his abundant hair and full beard of light brown, sprinkled with silver; his broad forehead, full face, and features that would appear colossal, but for their perfect harmony of proportion; his clear complexion, with just enough color to assure you of robust health and a well-regulated life; his face lighted up by an eye which was cold grey to his enemies, but warm, deep blue to his friends; not a man of iron, but of live oak. His attitude, form, and features, all assured you of inflexible firmness, of inexpugnable strength; while his welcoming smile set every feature aglow with a kindness that won your manliest affection. If thus in memory you see his form and features, even more vividly do you remember the qualities of his mind and heart. His body was the fitting type of his intellect and character; and you saw both his intellect and character tried, again and again, in the fiery furnace of war, and by other tests not less searching. Thus, comrades, you see him; and your memories supply a thousand details which complete and adorn the picture.

In closing what might be called more particularly the biographical portion of the address he said:

Thomas' life is a notable illustration of the virtue and power of hard work; and in the last analysis, the power to do hard work is only another name for talent. Professor Church, one of his instructors at West Point, says of his student life, that "he never allowed anything to escape a thorough examination, and left nothing behind that he did not fully comprehend." And so it was in the army. To him a battle was neither an earthquake nor a volcano, nor a chaos of brave men and frantic horses, involved in vast explosions of gunpowder. It was rather a calm, rational concentration of force against force. It was a question of lines and positions; of weight of metal and strength of batallions. He knew that the elements and forces which bring victory are not created on the battle-field, but must be patiently elaborated in the quiet of the camp, by the perfect organization and outfit of his army. His remark to a captain of artillery, while inspecting a battery, is worth remembering, for it exhibits his theory of success: "Keep every thing in order, for the fate of a battle may turn on a buckle or a linch-pin." He understood so thoroughly the condition of his army, and its equipment, that when the hour of trial came, he knew how great a pressure it could stand, and how hard a blow it could strike.

His character was as grand and as simple as a colossal pillar of chiseled granite. Every step of his career as a soldier was marked by the most loyal and unhesitating obedience to law—to the laws of his government and to the commands of his superiors. The obedience which he rendered to those above him he rigidly required of those under his command. His influence over his troops grew steadily and constantly. He won his ascendancy over them neither by artifice nor by any one act of special daring, but he gradually filled them with his own spirit, until their confidence in him knew no bounds. His power as a commander was developed slowly and silently; not like volcanic land lifted from the sea by sudden and violent upheaval, but rather like a coral island, where each increment is a growth—an act of life and work.

Power exhibits itself under two distinct forms—strength and force—each possessing peculiar qualities, and each perfect in its own sphere. Strength is typified by the oak, the rock, the mountain. Force embodies itself in the cataract, the tempest, the thunderbolt. The great tragic poet of Greece, in describing the punishment of Prometheus for rebellion against Jupiter, represented Vulcan descending from heaven, attended by two mighty spirits, Strength and Force, by whose aid he held and bound Prometheus to the rock.

In subduing our great rebellion, the Republic called to its aid men who represented many forms of great excellence and power. A very few of our commanders possessed more force than Thomas—more genius for planning and executing bold and daring enterprises; but, in my judgment, no other was so complete in embodiment and incarnation of strength—the strength that resists, maintains, and endures. His power was not that of the cataract which leaps in fury down the chasm, but rather that of the river, broad and deep, whose current is steady, silent, and irresistible.

From the peroration the following is taken:

The language applied to the Iron Duke, by the historian of the Peninsula War, might also be mistaken for a description of Thomas. Napier says, "He held his army in hand, keeping it with unmitigated labor, always in a fit state to march or to fight. * * * * * * * Sometimes he was indebted to fortune, sometimes to his natural genius, always to his untiring industry; for he was emphatically a painstaking man."

The language of Lord Brougham, addressed to Wellington, is a fitting description of Thomas: "Mighty captain! who never advanced except to cover his arms with glory; mightier captain! who never retreated except to eclipse the glory of his advance." If I remember correctly, no enemy was ever able to fight Thomas out of any position he undertook to hold. On the whole, I can not doubt that the most fitting parallel to General Thomas is found in our greatest American, the man who was "first in war, first in peace, and first in the hearts of his countrymen." The personal resemblance of General Thomas to Washington was often the subject of remark. Even at West Point, Rosecrans was accustomed to call him General Washington. He resembled Washington in the gravity and dignity of his character; in the solidity of his judgment; in the careful accuracy of all his transactions; in his incorruptible integrity, and in his extreme but unaffected modesty. * * * * But his career is ended. Struck dead at his post of duty, a bereaved nation bore his honored dust across the continent and laid it to rest on the banks of the Hudson, amidst the tears and grief of millions. The nation stood at his grave as a mourner. No one knew until he was dead how strong was his hold on the hearts of the American people. Every citizen felt that a pillar of state had fallen; that a great and true and pure man had passed from earth. There are no fitting words in which I may speak of the loss which every member of this society has sustained in his death. The general of the army has beautifully said, in his order announcing the death of Thomas: "Though he leaves no child to bear his name, the *Old Army of the Cumberland*, numbered by tens of thousands, called him father, and will weep for him in tears of manly grief."

To us, his comrades, he has left the rich legacy of his friendship. To his country and to mankind, he has left his character and his fame as a priceless and everlasting possession.

"O iron nerve to true occasion true!
O fallen at length that tower of strength
Which stood four-square to all the winds that blew!"
* * * * "His work is done;
But while the races of mankind endure,
Let his great example stand
Colossal seen of every land,
And keep the soldier firm, the statesman pure,
Till in all lands and through all human story,
The path of Duty be the way to Glory."

In an address delivered at Hudson College, on the "Future of our Country," that country which he loved so well, he said:

Our great dangers are not from without. We do not live by the consent of any other nation. We must look within to find elements of danger. The first and most obvious of these is territorial expansion, overgrowth, and the danger that we shall break to pieces by our own weight. This has been the commonplace of historians and publicists for many centuries, and its truth has found many striking illustrations in the experience of mankind. But we have fair ground for believing that new conditions and new forces have nearly if not wholly removed the ground of this danger. Distance, estrangement, isolation have been overcome by the recent amazing growth in the means of intercommunication. For political and industrial purposes California and Massachusetts are nearer neighbors to-day, than were Philadelphia and Boston in the days of the Revolution. It was distance, isolation, ignorance of separate parts, that broke the cohesive force of the great empires of antiquity. Fortunately, our greatest line of extension is from east to west, and our pathway along the parallels of latitude are not too broad for safety—for it lies within the zone of national development. The Gulf of Mexico is our special providence on the south. Perhaps it would be more fortunate for us if the northern shore of that gulf stretched westward to the Pacific. If our territory embraced the tropics, the sun would be our enemy. "The stars in their courses" would fight against us. Now these celestial forces are our friends, and help to make us one. Let us hope the Republic will be content to maintain this friendly alliance. Our northern boundary is not yet wholly surveyed. Perhaps our neighbors across the lakes will some day take a hint from nature, and save themselves and us the discomfort of an artificial boundary. Restrained within our present southern limits, with a population more homogeneous than that of any other great nation, and with a wonderful power to absorb and assimilate to our own type the European races that come among us, we have but little reason to fear that we shall be broken up by divided interests and internal feuds, because of our great territorial extent. Finally, our great hope for the future—our great safeguard against danger, is to be found in the general and thorough education of our people, and in the virtue which accompanies such education. And all these elements depend in a large measure, upon the intellectual and moral culture of the young men who go out from our higher institutions of learning. From the standpoint of this general culture we may trustfully encounter the perils that assail us. Secure against dangers from abroad, united at home by the stronger ties of common interest and patriotic pride, holding and unifying our vast territory by the most potent forces of civilization, relying upon the intelligent strength and responsibility of each citizen, and, most of all, upon the power of truth, without undue arrogance, we may hope that in the centuries to come our Republic will continue to live and hold its high place among the nations as

"The heir of all the ages in the foremost files of time."

From our Republic and its future, we turn aside to gather in a literary scrap, an address on Burns, in which we find this, from a fine comparison of three of the world's song-writers:

To appreciate the genius and achievements of Robert Burns, it is fitting to compare him with others who have been eminent in the same field. In the highest class of lyric poetry their names stand eminent. Their field covers eighteen centuries of time, and the three names are Horace, Beranger and Burns. It is an interesting and suggestive fact, that each of these sprang from the humble walks of life. Each may be described as one

"Who begs a brother of the earth,
To give him leave to toil,"

and each proved by his life and achievements that, however hard the lot of poverty, "a man's a man for a' that."

A great writer has said that it took the age forty years to catch Burns, so far was he in advance of the thoughts of his times. But we ought not to be surprised at the power he exhibited. We are apt to be misled when we seek to find the cause of greatness in the schools and universities alone. There is no necessary conflict between nature and art. In the highest and best sense art is as natural as nature. We do not wonder at the perfect beauty of the rose, although we may not understand the mysteries by which its delicate petals are fashioned and fed out of the grosser elements of earth. We do not wonder at the perfection of the rose because God is the artist. When he fashioned the germ of the rose-tree he made possible the beauties of its flower. The earth and air and sunshine conspired to unfold and adorn it—to tint and crown it with peerless beauty. When the Divine Artist would produce a poem, he plants a germ of it in a human soul, and out of that soul the poem springs and grows as from the rose-tree the rose. Burns was a child of nature. He lived close to her beating heart, and all the rich and deep sympathies of life glowed and lived in his heart. The beauties of earth, air and sky filled and transfigured him.

With an extract from one more of Garfield's miscellaneous speeches, we will close this chapter. All through life he seemed to have the happy and useful faculty of inspiring young men. His speeches frequently related to them, and how to win success, was a theme in which both tongue and pen delighted. This address was upon "The Key to Success:"

In order to have any success in life, or any worthy success, you must resolve to carry into your work a fullness of knowledge—not merely a sufficiency, but more than sufficiency. In this respect follow the rule of the machinists. If they want a machine to do the work of six horses, they give it nine horse power, so that they may have a reserve of three. To carry on the business of life you must have a surplus power. Be fit for more than the thing you are now doing. Let every one know that you have a reserve in yourself; that you have more power than you are now using. If you are not too large for the place you occupy, you are too small for it. How full our country is of bright examples, not only of those who occupy some proud eminence in public life, but in every place you may find men going on with steady nerve, attracting the attention of their fellow citizens, and carving out for themselves names and fortunes from small and humble beginnings, and in the face of formidable obstacles. Let me cite an example of a man I recently saw in the little village of Norwich, New York. If you wish to know his name, go into any hardware store and ask for the best hammer in the word; and if the salesman be an intelligent man, he will bring you a hammer bearing the name of D. Maydole. Young gentlemen, take that hammer in your hand, drive nails with it, and draw inspiration from it. Thirty years ago a boy was struggling through the snows at Chenango valley, trying to hire himself to a blacksmith. He succeeded and learned his trade; but he did more. He took it into his head that he could make a better hammer than any other man had made. He devoted himself to the task for more than a quarter of a century. He studied the chemistry of metals, the strength of materials, the philosophy of form. He studied failures. Each broken hammer taught him a lesson. There was no part of the process that he did not master. He taxed his wit to invent machines to perfect and cheapen his processes. No improvement in working steel or iron escaped his notice. What may not twenty-five years of effort accomplish when concentrated on a single object? He earned success; and now, when his name is stamped on a steel hammer, it is his note, his bond, his integrity embodied in steel. The spirit of the man is in such hammers, and the work, like the workman, is unrivaled. Mr. Maydole is now acknowledged to have made the best hammer in the world.

Garfield was an active and honored member of the Washington Literary Society, an organization embracing the most prominent men and women in music, art and literature of the National capital. He was almost always present at the meetings, and took an earnest, yet modest, part in the discussions. He was usually accompanied by his wife, who was his companion, counsellor and friend. So much for his literary work.

CHAPTER XVII.

THE VICTIM OF CALUMNY.

"An honest man
Is open as the light,
So search as keenly as you can,
You'll only find—all right."

"Aye! blot him black with slander's ink,
He stands as white as snow.
You serve him better than you think,
And kinder than you know.
Yes! be the scandal what you will,
Or whisper what you please;
You do but fan his glory still
By whistling up a breeze."

Five times had General Garfield been chosen to represent the old Giddings district without serious opposition in his own party, and without a breath of suspicion being cast upon his personal integrity. With one exception, all his nominations had been made by acclamation. In his sixth canvass, however, a storm of calumny broke upon him. A concerted attack was made upon him for the purpose, if possible, of defeating him in the convention, and failing in that, to beat him at the polls. He was charged with bribery and corruption in connection with the Credit Mobilier and the DeGolyer pavement contract, and with responsibility for the Salary Grab. In 1873 General Garfield wrote from Washington to his old friend Hinsdale: "The district is lost, and as soon as I can close up my affairs here I am coming home to capture it." What was this tidal wave, this chilling north wind, that all but lost for him his constituency?

Was James Abram Garfield honest? Where is the voice that would now declare him dishonest? No one could have known him and thought him otherwise than possessed of honesty and spotless integrity. Examine the life now passing in review before us and point to anything but honesty. "His character was as clear as crystal; truth illumined his soul alway, and there the shadows of insincerity never fell." But even such a man could not escape the foul reproach of calumny. No public man ever has. Even Washington, the father of his country, had his enemies and his accusers. The grandeur and nobility of the man was a burning reproach to dishonesty. It is an easy matter to accuse of crime, but to prove the truth of such assertions is a more difficult task. To-day a defense of Garfield's character would seem useless and unnecessary, for the whole world believes Garfield was pure and free of the stain that designing ones would have placed upon him. When assailed he manfully met the charge and entirely vindicated himself. The best proof of this lies in the fact that his own district—one of the most conservative and Puritan to be found, as we have already seen—ratified his action by their votes. And now time and history free him from any stint, and point to him as an honest man. We have referred to the formidable array of charges made against him. These charges came upon him almost simultaneously. One array of facts and charges were hardly put down, until another confronted him.

The year 1874 was the year of the Democratic tidal wave, the Credit Mobilier and the Salary Grab having alienated many of the Republican thousands. Nowhere did these two affairs make a deeper impression than in the sensitive and jealous constituency represented by Mr. Garfield. Mr. Whittlesey and Mr. Giddings, who had preceded Mr. Garfield, were men of unsullied reputation. The faintest semblance of any thing like a wrong or improper course of conduct was enough to draw forth the honest, plain-spoken indignation of men who were not ready to justify the slightest departure from the line of right. The district felt very proud of Garfield. No representative held his constituency with a firmer hand. His tenure promised to be as long as that of Whittlesey or Giddings. But now all was changed. A Republican convention that met in Warren for some local purpose, demanded his resignation. Most men denounced, all regretted, few defended, what had been done. All that the staunchest friends of General Garfield presumed to do was to say: "Wait until you hear the case; hear what Garfield has to say before you determine that he is a dishonest man."

Before returning to Hiram Garfield had prepared two exhaustive pamphlets—one entitled, "Review of the Transactions of the Credit Mobilier Company," and the other "The Increase of Salaries." These papers, and the general discussions which were going on at the same time, threw much light upon the subjects. But the opportunity was too good for politicians to lose, and it was only after a desperate struggle that Mr. Garfield was re-nominated and re-elected in 1874. The opposition to him did not bring forward a candidate, but merely cast blank votes. His enemies then nominated a second Republican candidate. General Garfield met the charges against him before the jury of his constituents. He visited all parts of the district, speaking day and night at township meetings. The verdict of the election was a complete vindication of his character and actions, and in 1876 and 1878 his constituents nominated him by acclamation and elected him by increased majorities.

It has not been deemed necessary at this time to go into detail concerning the charges of calumny which were made against Garfield. The storm is past, and from under the reproaches and accusations General Garfield came vindicated and irreproachable. Few are the public men who have not been misjudged.

One of the great public works of the Union, of which the whole country is justly proud, is the Pacific Railroad, extending from the Missouri river to the Pacific ocean. The early history of the great road is a story of constant struggles and disappointments. It seemed to the soundest capitalist a mere piece of fool-hardiness to undertake to build a railroad across the continent and over the Rocky Mountains, and, although Government aid was liberally pledged to the undertaking, it did not, for a long time, attract to it the capital it needed. At length, after many struggles, the doubt which had attended the enterprise was ended. Capital was found, and with it men ready to carry on the work. In September, 1864, a contract was entered into between the Union Pacific Company and H. W. Hoxie, for the building by said Hoxie of one hundred miles of the road from Omaha west. Mr. Hoxie at once assigned this contract to a company, as had been the understanding from the first. This company, then comparatively unknown, but since very famous, was known as the Credit Mobilier of America. The company had bought up an old charter that had been granted by the Legislature of Pennsylvania to another company in that State, but which had not been used by them. The stockholders of the Credit Mobilier were also the stockholders of the Union Pacific Company. Oakes Ames, the principle manager, and also a member of Congress, succeeded in interesting sixteen prominent congressmen in the project.

Reduced to plain English, the story of the Credit Mobilier is simply this: The men entrusted with the management of the Pacific Road made a bargain with themselves to build the road for a sum equal to about twice its actual cost, and pocketed the profits, which have been estimated at about THIRTY MILLIONS OF DOLLARS—this immense sum coming out of the pockets of taxpayers of the United States. This contract was made in October, 1867. Subsequently the vast property interests of the Pacific Road were appropriated by the Credit Mobilier. In the summer of 1872, some trouble having arisen between several of the principal managers, the inside history of the Mobilier were made public; and the names of the congressmen to whom shares of stock were said to have been sold were published. Of course such an announcement created a storm of excitement all over the country. Oakes Ames allotted one thousand dollars of Credit Mobilier stock to Garfield. In point of fact Garfield never subscribed for it; never paid for it; never received it; but there was a dividend of three hundred and twenty-nine dollars, upon the stock, which it has been claimed Garfield accepted from Ames. But even this Garfield always denied. The only money received by the late President from Ames was a loan of three hundred dollars, just after returning from his trip to Europe; and this he subsequently repaid. So that he never accepted a dollar on the Credit Mobilier account. This is all there is in the Credit Mobilier affair, and Garfield was as innocent of any guilt connected with it as any reader of these pages. Upon the assembling of Congress an investigation was called for. Blaine and Garfield, having been charged as accessories in the scheme, promptly urged the matter of an investigation upon the House, and thereupon the famous Poland Committee was appointed. Suffice it to say that the integrity of Garfield's motives was shown beyond a peradventure. That he was not guilty of any charges made, the investigating committee first, the country, his friends and partisans last, unite in declaring. General Garfield realized the truth of the lines,

> "Be thou as chaste as ice, as pure as snow,
> Thou shalt not escape calumny."

The testimony is overwhelmingly in favor of Garfield. Further than what has already been given it may be of interest to read the following remarks of President Hinsdale of Hiram College, who has known General Garfield intimately for twenty-five years, and during all of that period has been a resident of his district. In an address he used the following language:

"It was in the winter of 1872-73 that the Credit Mobilier developments aroused and alarmed the country. They seemed to point to a corruption in public life that had not been generally suspected. Mr. Garfield's name, from no real fault of his own appeared in the history. No sooner had the House of Representatives disposed of the Mobilier than the salary legislation was enacted. The Forty-second Congress had been unpopular; the Mobilier transactions had scandalized the country; the public had always been jealous of congressmen voting up their own pay; so that everything conspired to stir the public indignation to its depths. A wave of abjuration, bearing upon its breast "steal," "robber," "grab," starting on the Atlantic shore, rolled to the Pacific and back again. Mr. Garfield had vigorously opposed the increase of salaries. But when it was forced upon one of the great appropriation bills by a decided vote, when the Conference Committee insisted that it should remain, when further resistance was either nugatory or would involve an extra session of Congress, he concluded that it was his duty to acquiesce and vote for the bill with the obnoxious measure. In so doing, he may have been wrong; that queston I do not argue; my proposition is that he was honest and patriotic. Perhaps I may be indulged in saying that I was in Washington at the time, that I was thoroughly familiar with all the history, and then, as now, I was as confident of his uprightness as I can be of any man's uprightness. But my great point is yet before me. Returning home from Washington after the adjournment, I found myself in the midst of the tempest. Cleveland editors hesitated to publish any statement of the salary matter that varied from the current version. One of them said to me, "This vote has taken us in the pit of the stomach." Perhaps the best illustration that I can give of the intensity of feeling is this: Knowing as I did the grounds of General Garfield's action, and the spirit in which he had acted, I felt it my duty to say in private conversation, in the newspapers, and even in the Hiram pulpit: "General Garfield is not a thief. He has not robbed the Treasury. Whether he is right or wrong, I do not argue; but whether right or wrong, he has acted honestly and with an eye single to the public good." And some of my neighbors said: "Mr. Hinsdale has a private right to think General Garfield honest if he can; but let him keep his opinion to himself; he has no right to injure the college of which he is president, as he will do by bearing public testimony." Only those who had been very violent in opposition now stood out. These had to be won back, one by one. Nor should I fail to mark how the victory was won, how the district was re-captured. It was not accomplished by management; James A. Garfield was no "manager." It was not by flattering the people and appealing to popular passions. General Gerfield was no demagogue. It was by the earnest, straightforward exposition of solid political doctrine; it was by the high bearing of the man; in a word, it was by the impact of his mental and moral power upon intelligent and honest minds.

Garfield, examined in the best light possible, was guiltless of all three of the charges. Acting always with honesty of purpose and integrity of principle, his countrymen, long before death met him, realized that the charges of corruption and bribery which were hurled against him, were without foundation in truth. I shall not relate the circumstances of these slanders. Garfield is to be remembered not by these charges, but by his goodness and greatness. He was the victim of injustice, not of conscious wrong. His actions bear the scrutiny of the most searching investigation. Such a record should be the prized patrimony of every legislator. Young men should follow it, and then politics would be purged of much that is polluting and selfish.

As we have already seen, the Congress which met in December, 1875, was Democratic. Hitherto the legislative work of General Garfield had been constructive. Now he was called upon to defend this work against the assaults of the party which step by step had opposed its accomplishment, and which by the aid of the solid support of the late rebel element had gained power in Congress.

Of the Forty-fourth Congress, Michael C. Kerr, of Indiana, was made Speaker, Blaine having been ousted by the opposition party. As a consequence the various committees were re-organized, and Democratic leaders placed at their heads. Garfield had served for four years as Chairman of the Appropriation Committee, and now he found himself almost last on the Committee of Ways and Means. After his re-election in 1876, he served as a member of the House Committee on Rules, his knowledge of parliamentary rules giving him special adaptability for the work.

It was not long until Garfield became thoroughly dissatisfied with Democratic statesmanship. To tear down what had been built up soon became the order of the day, and organized opposition was formed. This Confederate Congress began introducing measures favorable to themselves and the rebel generals. The first direct collision occurred in January, 1876. It will be remembered that after the close of the war, when the Southern States had been restored to their place in the Union, many of her citizens were debarred from the rights of citizenship on account of treason. By subsequent acts of Congress the majority of these had been restored to the "inalienable rights," and the restrictions were removed. The Amnesty bill was now introduced, extending pardon unconditionally to all ex-Confederates. To this Mr. Blaine offered an amendment excepting Jefferson Davis and seven hundred and fifty others, until they should renounce their treason by taking the oath of allegiance to the United States, and made the charge that the bill was altogether too sweeping. The exception was not accepted by the friends of the measure, and a drawn battle ensued. Samuel J. Randall, of Pennsylvania, had charge of the bill, between whom and Blaine there was considerable light firing and skirmishing. Exasperated at length, the "plumed knight," as he is known, rushed forward and in one of the most brilliant charges on record, arraigned the Confederate President in the most bitter manner. He held him directly responsible for the unwarrantable and merciless cruelties imposed on the soldiers of the Union, while confined in southern prison-pens. The horrors of Andersonville and Libby stood out in their awful terror. Davis' celebrated "Order Thirteen" was read, which authorized the rebel guns to be turned on the suffering and dying thousands at Andersonville, while Sherman was approaching. Before God and the American people he held this man responsible, and Davis should not, ought not, in the name of humanity and justice, ever again be permitted to hold any honorable public position within the domain of the United States. Cox and Hill followed Blaine. Hill succeeded in meeting Blaine's charges, and in great part, succeeded in overcoming the impressions made by the "member from Maine." The whole Democracy were now rejoicing. An easy victory seemed near. They thought Hill's speech absolutely unanswerable. Garfield having given notice previously that he would speak on the bill, followed on the 12th of January. All eyes turned to him, and it was not long until he was the hero of the hour. Garfield, by a brilliant stroke of parliamentary strategy, forced a Democrat to testify to the falsity of Hill's charge. He said that the Elmira, New York, district where was located during the war the principal prison for captured rebels, was represented in the House by a Democrat. He did not know him, but he was willing to rest his case wholly on his testimony. He called upon the member from Elmira to inform the House whether the good people of his city had permitted the captured Confederate soldiers in their midst to suffer for want of food. The gentleman thus appealed to rose promptly and said that to his knowledge the prisoners had received exactly the same rations as the Union soldiers guarding them. While this statement was being made a telegraphic dispatch was handed to General Garfield. Holding it up, he said, "The lightnings of heaven are aiding me in this controversy." The dispatch was from General Elwell, of Cleveland, who had been the quartermaster at the Elmira prison, and who telegraphed that the rations issued to the rebel prisoners were in exact quantity and quality as those issued to the Union soldiers. Garfield said:

I do not object to Jefferson Davis because he was a conspicuous leader. Whatever we may believe theologically, I do not believe in the doctrine of vicarious atonement in politics. Jefferson Davis was no more guilty for taking up arms than any other man who went into the rebellion with equal intelligence. But this is the question: In the high court of war did he practice according to his well-known laws—the laws of nations? Did he, in appealing to war, obey the laws of war; or did he so violate those laws, that justice to those who suffered at his hands, demands that he be not permitted to come back to his old privileges in the Union? That is the whole question; and it is as plain and fair a question for deliberation as was ever debated in this House.

From this point Mr. Garfield proceeded by a long argument, well supported by authorities, to show forth the real history of the atrocities mentioned, and to demonstrate the responsibility of Jefferson Davis for them. He ended this portion of the discussion in these words:

It seems to me incontrovertible that the records I have adduced lay at his door the charge of being himself the author, the conscious author, through his own appointed instrument, of the terrible work at Andersonville, for which the American people still hold him unfit to be admitted among the legislators of this nation.

And now, Mr. Speaker, I close as I began. Toward those men who gallantly fought us on the field I cherish the kindest feeling. I feel a sincere reverence for the soldierly qualities they displayed on many a well-fought battle-field. I hope the day will come when their swords and ours will be crossed over many a doorway of our children, who will remember the glory of their ancestors with pride. The high qualities displayed in that conflict now belong to the whole nation. Let them be consecrated to the Union, and its future peace and glory. I shall hail that consecration as a pledge and symbol of our perpetuity.

I join you in all, in every aspiration that you may express to stay in this Union, to heal its wounds, to increase its glory, and to forget the evils and bitterness of the past; but do not, for the sake of the three hundred thousand heroic men who, maimed and bruised, drag out their weary lives, many of them carrying in their hearts horrible memories of what they suffered in the prison-pen—do not ask us to vote to put back into power that man who was the cause of their suffering—that man still unaneled, unshriven, unforgiven, undefended. . . .

As the autumn of 1876 approached, it became evident that the Democratic party, already dominant in the House, would make a desperate struggle at the November elections to get complete control of the Government. Before the long session of that hot summer ended, Mr. Lamar, of Mississippi, took occasion to deliver in the House a powerful speech, stating reasons why the Democratic party should be put into power at the next election. The speech was delayed until within two or three days of the close of the session; but it came to be whispered about that it would be a strong campaign document, and be delivered so late that no reply could be made to it by the Republicans. The moment Mr. Lamar sat down General Garfield rose, and got the floor. It was late in the afternoon, and the House at once adjourned, but he had secured the right to reply on the following morning. Lamar's speech was withheld from publication in the *Congressional Record*, and Garfield was forced to rely upon the brief notes of it which he had taken, and the short summary that had appeared in the morning journals. He had but little time for preparation, and had to work nearly all night in preparing his "points," but the speech is one of the best he ever made, and should be read by millions. It is as applicable to-day as to the time when it was delivered.

Here are several paragraphs from this masterly speech:

The antagonisms which gave rise to the war and grew out of it were not born in a day, nor can they vanish in a night.

Mr. Chairman, great ideas travel slowly, and for a time noiselessly, as the gods, whose feet were shod with wool. Our war of independence was a war of ideas, of ideas evolved out of two hundred years of slow and silent growth. When, one hundred years ago, our fathers announced as self-evident truths the declaration that all men are created equal, and the only just power of governments is derived from the consent of the governed, they uttered a doctrine that no nation had ever adopted, that not one kingdom on the earth then believed. Yet to our fathers it was so plain that they would not debate it. They announced it as a truth "self evident." Whence came the immortal truths of the Declaration?

To me this was for years the riddle of our history. I have searched long and patiently through the books of the *doctrinaires* to find the germs from which the Declaration of Independence sprang. I found hints in Locke, in Hobbs, in Rousseau, and Fenelon; but they were only the hints of dreamers and philosophers. The great doctrines of the Declaration germinated in the hearts of our fathers, and were developed under the new influences of this wilderness world, by the same subtle mystery which brings forth the rose from the germ of the rose-tree. Unconsciously to themselves, the great truths were growing under the new conditions until, like the century-plant, they blossomed into the matchless beauty of the Declaration of Independence, whose fruitage, increased and increasing, we enjoy to-day.

"But that is not all of the situation. On the other hand, we see the North, after leaving its 350,000 dead upon the field of battle and bringing home its 500,000 maimed and wounded to be cared for, crippled in its industries, staggering under the tremendous burden of public and private debt, and both North and South weighted with unparalleled burdens and losses—the whole nation suffering from that loosening of the bonds of social order which always follows a great war, and from the resulting corruption both in the public and the private life of the people. These, Mr. Chairman, constitute the vast field which we must survey in order to find the path which will soonest lead our beloved country to the highway of peace, of liberty and prosperity. Peace from the shock of battle; the higher peace of our streets, of our homes, of our equal rights, we must make secure by making the conquering ideas of the war everywhere dominant and permanent.

Thus the defense and aggrandizement of slavery, and the hatred of Abolitionism, became not only the central idea of the Democratic party, but its master-passion—a passion intensified and inflamed by twenty-five years of fierce political contest, which had not only driven from its ranks all those who preferred freedom to slavery, but had absorbed all the extreme pro-slavery elements of the fallen Whig party. Over against this was arrayed the Republican party, asserting the broad doctrines of nationality and loyalty, insisting that no state had a right to secede, that secession was treason, and demanding that the institution of slavery should be restricted to the limits of the states where it already existed. But here and there, many bolder and more radical thinkers declared, with Wendell Phillips, that there never could be union and peace, freedom and prosperity, until we were willing to see John Hancock under a black skin.

Mr. Chairman, after the facts I have cited, am I not warranted in raising a grave doubt whether the transformation occurred at all except in a few patriotic and philosophic minds? The light gleams first on the mountain peaks; but shadows and darkness linger in the valley. It is in the valley masses of those lately in rebellion that the light of this beautiful philosophy, which I honor, has not penetrated. It is safer to withhold from them the custody and supreme control of the precious treasures of the Republic until the midday sun of liberty, justice, and equal laws shall shine upon them with unclouded ray.

I walk across that Democratic camping-ground as in a graveyard. Under my feet resound the hollow echoes of the dead. There lies slavery, a black marble column at the head of its grave, on which I read: Died in the flames of the civil war; loved in its life; lamented in its death; followed to its bier by its only mourner, the Democratic party, but dead! And here is a double grave: Sacred to the memory of Squatter Sovereignty. Died in the campaign of 1860. On the reverse side: Sacred to the memory of the Dred-Scott-Breckinridge doctrine. Both died at the hands of Abraham Lincoln! And here a monument of brimstone: Sacred to the memory of the Rebellion; the war against it is a failure; *Tilden et Vallandigham fecerunt*, A. D. 1864. Dead on the field of battle; shot to death by the million guns of the Republic. The doctrine of Secession; of State Sovereignty. Dead. Expired in the flames of civil war, amidst the blazing rafters of the Confederacy, except that the modern Æneas, fleeing out of the flames of that ruin, bears on his back another Anchises of State Sovereignty, and brings it here in the person of the honorable gentleman from the Appomatox district of Virginia [Mr. Tucker]. [Laughter.] All else is dead.

Now, gentlemen, come with me for a moment into the camp of the Republican party and review its career. Our central doctrine in 1860 was that slavery should never extend itself over another foot of American soil. Is that doctrine dead? It is folded away like a victorious banner; its truth is alive for evermore on this continent. In 1864 we declared that we would put down the Rebellion and secession. And that doctrine lives, and will live when the second Centennial has arrived! Freedom, national, universal, and perpetual—our great constitutional amendments, are they alive or dead? Alive, thank the God that shields both liberty and Union. And our national credit, saved from the assaults of Pendleton; saved from the assaults of those who struck it later, rising higher and higher at home and abroad; and only now in doubt lest its enemy, its only enemy, the Democracy, should triumph in November.

Never had a speaker secured a more complete victory. The Democracy were discomfited, the Republicans triumphant. Garfield again showed himself to be complete master of the situation. He won new friends, new laurels, and saved his party from defeat and chagrin. The speech throughout is absolutely unanswerable. Every paragraph produced telling effect. The imprint of a master is seen in every sentence.

CHAPTER XVIII.

LEADER AND STATESMAN.

"Tell proudly how, with penury's chill hand,
This son of freedom fought his way to place;
Passing his compeers in the upward race,
Until he stood the foremost in the land."

"To seek honor is no honor." Garfield never did anything for the empty praise and approbation which an action might give him. His nobility was of a stronger, better kind. In all his public career he was actuated by the highest motives. He sought the good of his country, and in this way received the applaudits which even his enemies could not withhold. So continuously and well has Garfield coursed his way that little is left for the historio-biographer but to gather up his eloquent words and present them in their natural order and sequence.

On the 19th day of December, 1876, the state of Massachusetts presented to the United States—according to an arrangement made years ago, that each state of the Union should be allowed to place in the halls of Congress two statues of distinguished citizens—statues of John Winthrop and Samuel Adams. In speaking on the resolution accepting these gifts, General Garfield made one of the finest and most polished orations of which congressional lore can boast. We must omit all but one paragraph:

As, from time to time, our venerable and beautiful hall has been peopled with statues of the elect of the states, it has seemed to me that a Third House was being organized within the walls of the Capitol—a house whose members have received their high credentials at the hands of history, and whose term of office will outlast the ages. Year by year we see the circle of its immortal membership enlarging; year by year we see the elect of their country in eloquent silence, taking their places in this American Pantheon, bringing within its sacred circle the wealth of those immortal memories which made their lives illustrious; and year by year that august assembly is teaching a deeper and grander lesson to all who serve their brief hour in these more ephemeral Houses of Congress. And now two places of great honor have just been most noblv filled.

Of a truth, General Garfield understood and appreciated the greatness of the Republic, and the grandeur of the character which belonged to its founders!

The American people will not soon forget the presidential election of 1876. The uncertainty of the result, the long delay occasioned, the Electoral Commission, are still vivid before the mind of all of this generation. Nor will the lessons of those hours be soon forgotten. The "visiting statesmen" watching the count in the three doubtful states before the famous Returning Board, and the final result, which, by an eight to seven vote, gave the chief executiveship to Rutherford B. Hayes—these will long linger in their memory.

During the early part of November, General Garfield went to Washington, and upon the personal request of President Grant, accompanied a small party of Republican and Democratic politicians to New Orleans. Arriving there on the 14th, he, as well as the other Republicans, refused to take part in any movement to intimidate the Returning Board. He was a witness and not a participant. Members of both political parties were present all the time, being furnished with a copy of all the testimony taken. That the work might be the more readily accomplished, the members of the delegation were given different testimony to examine. General Garfield examined carefully the testimony in relation to the election in one parish—East Feliciana. He wrote out a brief and judicial statement of the official testimony as to the conduct of the election in that district, analyzing the movements of the Ku-Klux Rifle Club which broke up the election, and adding his own conclusions. When the Potter Committee came to make its investigations afterward, "it found no fault in him" whatever, and it must be remembered that the undertaking was a trying one. A public man certainly run great risks of doing himself harm. But Garfield kept himself clear of suspicion. The canvass of votes over, Garfield, together with most of the other visiting congressmen, returned to Washington.

As is well known, the deciding of the cases at New Orleans did not end the matter. As late as January it was feared that trouble would still come. Many thought any attempt to decide the question by the existing laws without the help of further legislation might lead to serious difficulties. Accordingly, on January 29, 1877, there was passed in the House a law providing for the Electoral Commission, a body to be composed of five Associate Justices of the Supreme Court, five Senators, and five Representatives, to whom should be committed the duty of deciding, by their recommendation, the votes of any disputed states. Who originated the plan is a matter of uncertainty.

General Garfield opposed it in a speech in which he took the ground that, under the Constitution it was the duty of the Vice-President to count the vote, and that in attempting to do it, Congress was usurping a power it did not legally possess. The two Houses could be present only as witnesses, but not as actors in the great solemn ceremony. Mr. Garfield voted against the bill, but it was carried by a large majority, the Democrats joining heartily in its support. After it was decided that the Republicans in the House should appoint upon the Commission two members, he and Mr. Hoar, of Massachusetts, were unanimously chosen. "Since you have appointed me," he said, "I will serve; I can act on a committee when I do not believe in its validity."

It is impossible even to hint at more than a small portion of the vast field of work which occupied General Garfield during this and the succeeding Congress. June 22, 1876, was to him the "sad occasion dear" of a revival of precious memories. In the preceding December his old friend and fellow-student of Hiram, Miss Booth, had died, and this day in June was appointed there for a memorial address by General Garfield. As at all such times when he spoke, we are struck with a sense of the wonderful delicacy of this man's nature, which responded so perfectly to every delicate and holy sentiment known to the human heart. His very first words were:

MR. PRESIDENT: You have called me to a duty at once most sad and most sacred. At every step of my preparation for its performance, I have encountered troops of thronging memories that swept across the field of the last twenty-five years of my life, and so filled my heart with the lights and shadows of their joy and sorrow that I have hardly been able to marshal them into order or give them coherent voice. I have lived over again the life of this place. I have seen again the groups of young and joyous students, ascending these green slopes, dwelling for a time on this peaceful height in happy and workful companionship, and then, with firmer step, and with more serious and thoughtful faces, marching away to their posts in the battle of life. And still nearer and clearer have come back the memories of that smaller band of friends, the leaders and guides of those who encamped on this training-ground. On my journey to this assembly, it has seemed that they, too, were coming, and that I should once more meet and greet them. And I have not yet been able to realize that Almeda Booth will not be with us. After our great loss, how shall we gather up the fragments of the life we lived in this place? We are mariners, treading the lonely shore in search of our surviving comrades and the fragments of our good ship, wrecked by the tempest. To her, indeed, it is no wreck. She has landed in safety, and ascended the immortal heights beyond our vision.

The death of Michael C. Kerr having made necessary the selection of a new Speaker, the Democratic majority in the House elected Samuel J. Randall, and the complimentary vote of the Republicans went to General Garfield. He was also their candidate in the two succeeding Congresses. He had divided the honor of leadership pretty evenly with Mr. Blaine, until, in 1877, the latter gentleman went to the Senate, and left Garfield without a rival. Fourteen years of able and faithful service had done their work grandly for his power and his fame.

On February 12, 1878, Mrs. Elizabeth Thompson, of New York City, presented to Congress that great painting of Carpenter, "Lincoln and Emancipation." At her request the presentation address was made by General Garfield. His important speeches during this Congress were even more numerous than usual; especially in the special session held in the spring and summer of 1879. One of the best was that of February 19, 1878, on the "Policy of Pacification, and the Prosecutions in Louisiana." At this time there were two serious political storms brewing in the air. First, there were divisions in the Republican party, and an alienation of some of its leaders from President Hayes; second, the Democratic party, with its cries of "fraud," concerning the last election, and its Potter Committee, and its prosecutions against the members of the Louisiana Returning Board, was trying to destroy the people's confidence in the Government as then constituted. The latter quarrel, no doubt, was the salvation of the party concerned in the former. Its members rallied and united. Garfield was leader and chief promoter of Republican harmony, as well as the strongest bulwark against the enemy. This speech, of February 19, contains the following pithy paragraph, descriptive of the way in which the nation had passed through the transformations of war:

There was, first, the military stage—the period of force, of open and bloody war—in which gentlemen of high character and honor met on the field, and decided by the power of the strongest the questions involved in the high court of war. That period passed, but did not leave us on the calm level of peace. It brought us to the period of transition, in which the elements of war and peace were mingled together in strange and anarchic confusion. It was a period of civil and military elements combined. All through that semi-military period the administration of General Grant had, of necessity, to conduct the country. His administration was not all civil, it was not all military; it was necessarily a combination of both; and out of that combination came many of the strange and anomalous situations which always follow such a war.

During the years 1878 and 1879, the public speeches made by Garfield, on the floor of the House and on the stump, were numerous. Almost every subject of national importance was touched upon. The recital of even the subjects of Garfield's speeches may be tedious, but where is the American statesmen who can show a better list of titles? We are reminded of the table of contents of Webster's speeches.

On the 21st of June, 1879, he spoke concerning a proposed survey of the Mississippi river, when he said:

But for myself, I believe that one of the grandest of our material national interests—one that is national in the largest material sense of that word—is the Mississippi river and its navigable tributaries. It is the most gigantic single natural feature of our continent, far transcending the glory of the ancient Nile or of any other river on the earth The statesmanship of America must grapple with the problem of this mighty stream. It is too vast for any State to handle; too much for any authority less than that of the Nation itself to manage. And I believe the time will come when the liberal-minded statesmanship of this country will devise a wise and comprehensive system, that will harness the powers of this great river to the material interests of America, so that not only all the people who live on its banks and the banks of its confluents, but all the citizens of the Republic, whether dwellers in the central valley or on the slope of either ocean, will recognize the importance of preserving and perfecting this great natural and material bond of national union between the North and the South—a bond to be so strengthened by commerce and intercourse that it can never be severed.

Immediately after President Hayes' inauguaration the Republicans in the Ohio Legislature desired to elect General Garfield to the United States Senate in place of John Sherman, who had resigned his seat to enter the Cabinet. Mr. Hayes made a personal appeal to him to decline to be a candidate and remain in the House to lead the Republicans in support of the Administration. General Garfield acceded, in the belief that his services would be of more value to the party in the House than in the Senate, and withdrew his name from the canvass, greatly to the disappointment of his friends in Ohio, who had already obtained pledges of the support of a large majority of the Republican members of the Legislature.

According to his custom, General Garfield spoke often during the Ohio campaign of 1879. During the regular sessions of the Forty-sixth Congress his activity was undiminished. In his speech of March 17, during the discussion of a bill to pay the United States marshals for the year ending June 30, 1880, we find such sterling utterances as these:

Here is the volume of our laws. More sacred than the twelve tables of Rome, this rock of the law rises in monumental grandeur alike above the people and the President, above the courts, above Congress, commanding everywhere reverence and obedience to its supreme authority. Yet the dominant party in this House virtually declares that "any part of this volume that we do not like and cannot repeal we will disobey. We have tried to repeal these election laws; we have failed because we had not the constitutional power to destroy them; the Constitution says they shall stand in their authority and power; but we, the Democratic party, in defiance of the Constitution, declare that if we cannot destroy them outright by the repeal, they shall be left to crumble into ruin by wanton and lawless neglect."

Mr. Chairman, by far the most formidable danger that threatens the Republic to-day is the spirit of law-breaking which shows itself in many turbulent and alarming manifestations. The people of the Pacific coast, after two years of wrestling with the spirit of communism in the city of San Francisco, have finally grappled with this lawless spirit, and the leader of it was yesterday sentenced to penal servitude as a violator of the law. But what can we say to Denis Kearney and his associates, if to-day we announce ourselves the foremost law-breakers of the country and set an example to all the turbulent and vicious elements of disorder to follow us?

I ask, gentlemen, whether this is a time when it is safe to disregard and weaken the authority of law. In all quarters the civil society of this country is becoming honeycombed through and through by disintegrating forces—in some states by the violation of contracts and the repudiation of debts; in others by open resistance and defiance; in still others by the reckless overturning of constitutions and letting the "red fool fury of the Seine" run riot among our people and build its blazing altars to the strange gods of ruin and misrule. All these things are shaking the good order of society and threatening the foundations of our government and our peace. In a time like this, more than ever before, this country needs a body of lawgivers clothed and in their right minds, and who have laid their hands upon the altar of the law as its defenders, not its destroyers.

April 5, 1880, General Garfield made a trenchant argument against the pet measure of the greenback apostle, Mr. Weaver. Five days afterward occurred a debate between Garfield and McMahon, also of Ohio, on the pending appropriation bill.

On May 1st he made a personal explanation, defending his committee action in regard to the so-called wood-pulp monopoly. This pulp is obtained from soft wood and used in the manufacture of paper. The newspapers everywhere were calling for a removal of the duty on this their great necessity. Garfield stood out for a ten per cent. tariff, as a protection to our manufacturers from the Canadian manufacturers, who had no royalties to pay, and therefore could have undersold us. In this speech Garfield met the charge of being a monopoly supporter, and vindicated his policy on the disputed question.

Turning aside from this well fought field where Garfield had so long stood, as a great representative of all that is good in the recent legislative history of our country, it is time to view the new honors which were now preparing for him.

"As it was in the district, so it was in the state. In a sense, in 1873, he had come to be the representative of Ohio. He passed through a state as well as a district ordeal, and came out approved. What then was more natural than that when the election of 1879 gave the Ohio Legislature to the Republicans, and the party looked around for a successor to Allen G. Thurman on the 4th of March 1880, Mr. Garfield should be the man. He had received the complimentary vote of the Republican members in the caucus two years before—1878—and after a protracted and bitter contest in that caucus, his name was withdrawn, and it was resolved to cast only blank votes in the two houses. This time ex-Senator Stanley Matthews, ex-Attorney-General Alphonso Taft and ex-Governor William Dennison had also entered into a canvass for the place, but by the time the caucus met the general sentiment of the state was so earnest and enthusiastic in favor of Garfield, that his three competitors withdrew without waiting for a ballot, and he was nominated on the 14th of January, 1880, unanimously by a rising vote, an honor never accorded to any other man of any party in the State of Ohio. So thoroughly had Garfield recovered from the wave of scandal which a few years earlier had swept over but could not overwhelm him, that he was the unanimous choice of his party; and the Democratic minority itself cordially united to make his election unanimous. All this came entirely without solicitation from him for such an honor." It will be *apropos* to go back a bit here to relate a little incident. Soon after A. G. Thurman's election and Ben Wade's retirement from the Senate, it was proposed by the latter's friends in Ohio that the "Old War Horse" should be sent to the House. Wade lived in Garfield's district, and as soon as the general heard of the proposition to send Wade to the House, he cordially indorsed it, saying: "The nation can better afford to spare me from its councils than it can to spare Ben. Wade—let him be sent to the House in my place." When Wade heard of what was on foot, he said: "Now, put a stop to it, and at once. What a devil of an idea! Sending me to the House, as if I were an essential to its existence! Why, I wouldn't go if I was unanimously nominated and elected. You have a good representative in Garfield, and I advise you to stick to him. I am old, and had better be getting ready to die than thinking of office. I have had enough of public office, and only wish to be let alone now. Garfield is young, faithful and able; send him back, and keep him there—stick to him. I tell you, there is no telling how high that fellow may go." At an informal reception held in the Capitol at Columbus, the evening after his election as United States Senator, General Garfield was called upon for a speech. In response, he made a brief and appropriate address. The following is an extract therefrom:

FELLOW CITIZENS:—I should be a great deal more than a man, or a great deal less than a man, if I were not extremely gratified by this mark of your kindness you have shown me in recent days. I did not expect any such meeting as this. I knew there was a greeting awaiting me, but I did not expect so cordial, generous, and general a greeting, without distinction of party, without distinction of interests, as I have received here to-night. And you will allow me in a moment or two to speak of the memories this chamber awakens.

I recognize the importance of the place to which you have elected me, and I should be base if I did not also recognize the great man whom you have elected me to succeed. I say for him, Ohio has had few larger-minded, broader-minded men in the records of our history than that of Allen G. Thurman. Differing widely from him as I have done in politics, and do, I recognize in him a man high in character and great in intellect; and I take this occasion to refer to what I have never before referred to in public—that many years ago, in the storm of party fighting, when the air was filled with all sorts of missiles aimed at the character and reputation of public men, when it was even for his party interest to join the general clamor against me and my associates, Senator Thurman said in public, in the campaign, on the stump—where men are as likely to say unkind things as at any place in the world—a most generous and earnest word of defense and kindness for me, which I shall never forget as long as I live. I say, moreover, that the flowers that bloom over the garden wall of party politics are the sweetest and most fragrant that bloom in the gardens of this world; and where we can early pluck them and enjoy their fragrance, it is manly and delightful to do so.

And now, gentlemen of the General Assembly, without distinction of party, I recognize this tribute and compliment made to me to-night. Whatever my own course may be in the future, a large share of the inspiration of my future public life will be drawn from this occasion and these surroundings, and I shall feel anew the sense of obligation that I owe to the State of Ohio. Let me venture to point a single sentence in regard to that work. During the twenty years that I have been in public life, almost eighteen of it in the Congress of the United States, I have tried to do one thing. Whether I was mistaken or otherwise, it has been the plan of my life to follow my convictions at whatever personal cost to myself. I have represented for many years a district in Congress whose approbation I greatly desired; but though it may seem, perhaps, a little egotistical to say it, I yet desired still more the approbation of one person, and his name is Garfield. He is the only man that I am compelled to sleep with, and eat with, and live with, and die with; and if I could not have his approbation, I should have bad companionship. And in this larger constituency which has called me to represent them now, I can only do what is true to my best self, applying the same rules. And if I should be so unfortunate as to lose the confidence of this larger constituency, I must do what every other fair-minded man has to do—carry his political life in his hand and take the consequences. But I must follow what seems to me to be the only safe rule of my life; and with that view of the case, and with that much personal reference, I leave the subject. Thanking you again, fellow-citizens, members of the General Assembly, Republicans and Democrats —all, party man as I am—thanking you both for what you have done and for this cordial and manly greeting, I bid you good-night.

We have now passed in review the splendid achievements of this great man, while he so ably—so well—represented his constituency on the floor of the House. We have found him as splendid and successful a general in dealing with men and things on the forensic battle-field as on the field of carnage. Garfield always took a genuine pride in the historical achievements of the Republican party, with which he was identified from its birth. He had a traditional leaning toward all measures for the advantage of the freedmen, or of curtailing the influence of the party which he held to have been responsible for the rebellion. Nevertheless, he was by no means deficient in generous impulses toward the South, and more than once exerted his influence to prevent the passage of rash partisan legislation against the interests of that section. The "Confederate brigadiers" in Congress found him a determined and loyal adversary, but he never stooped to take unfair advantage of the numerical preponderance of his party. As a leader of the Republican minority in the House of Representatives he knew how to reconcile the party fealty with a conciliatory disposition toward the party in power, and was not unduly obstructive of any legislation which did not, in his opinion, transcend the fair limits of party predominance. He was in all things a calm, courteous, determined leader of men.

With the single exception of 1867, when he spent several weeks in Europe, partly in company with Senator Blaine and Senator Morrill, he did hard work on the stump for the Republican party in every campaign since he entered Congress. On the stump, he was one of the best orators in his party. He had a good voice, an air of evident sincerity, great clearness and vigor of statement, and a way of knitting his arguments together, so as to make a speech deepen its impression on the mind of the hearer, until the climax clinched the argument forever. He went directly to the reason of his hearers. There was never any sophistry in his speeches, or any appeal to prejudice, or any trick of suppression or half-statement. He approached his audiences neither in a way of mock deference nor of superiority, but as if he were one of them, come to talk with them on terms of intellectual equality, and desirous only of convincing their minds by a perfectly fair presentation of facts and arguments. He had a strong, far-reaching voice, pitched in the middle key, a dignified, manly presence, and an abundance of the quality which, for want of a better term, we call personal magnetism. His manner in his speeches was first engaging by reason of its frankness and moderation, and afterward impressive by its earnestness and vigor. At the climax of a speech he gathered up all the forces of statement and logic he had been marshaling, and hurled them upon his listeners with tremendous force. His eyes dilated, his form seemed to expand, his voice took on a sort of explosive quality, his language gained the height of simple and massive eloquence, and his gestures became so energetic and forcible that he seemed, at times, to be beating down opposition with sledge-hammer blows, throwing his arguments forward like solid shot from a cannon. He usually reserved half his time for the Ohio canvass, and gave the other half to other States. The November election generally found him worn and haggard with travel and speaking in the open air, but his robust constitution always carried him through, and after a few weeks' rest on his farm, he appeared in Washington refreshed and ready for the duties of the session.

It will, no doubt, be of considerable interest to a large number of readers to know the opinions of General Garfield upon the "Chinese Question," as it is called. His position is not stated in any speech, and was only lightly touched upon in his letter of acceptance. In 1877, a prominent paper in one of the Eastern States, succeeded in drawing from Garfield his views upon this subject. Alluding to the idea, quite strongly held by many writers, that the Chinese intend a conquest of Europe, Garfield said:

The Mongolian race is capable of great personal prowess. Being fatalists, they dare everything for the end they have in view. Their food is simple, easily supplied and easily transported. Their endurance of fatigue is proverbial. Once organized and in motion they could swarm into Russia as irresistibly as the locusts of Egypt, and upon the Pacific coast of this continent as numerous and destructive as the grasshoppers. Once started, where would they stop? Civilization would retire before them as from a plague. Look at the plague spots in San Francisco to-day. Nobody lives in them but Chinese. Nobody else can live in them. I have seen in a space no greater than the length and height in a sleeping-car berth, in a Chinese tenement quarter in San Francisco, the home of twelve Chinamen. In that space they actually lived—yes, actually lived most of their time. There they crouched (all doubled up), and there they cooked, ate, slept, and, in a word, lived. They cooked with a little lamp a mess of stuff that they import from China, which, like their rice food, is very cheap, and a mere pittance in the way of earnings on the street will supply them food and clothes for an indefinite time. A few cents per day is more to them than a dollar to the commonest American laborer. Hence the lowest grade of poor paid labor retires before them as it would before a pestilence.

This is not all. They have no assimilation whatever with Caucasian civilization. The negro assimilates with the Caucasian. He wants all that we want. He adopts our civilization—professes our religion—works for our wages, and is a customer for everything that civilization produces. Hence (using a figure of physiology) we can take him up in the circulation of the body politic and assimilate him—make a man and a brother of him, as the phrase goes; but not so in the least degree with the Chinaman. And this brings me to say that one of the great questions that now press upon Congress and the country for immediate attention and solution, is what shall we do with reference to Chinese immigration? We have always refused to citizenize them. Shall we continue the treaty under which they are immigrating to our shores?

Our next inquiry will be concerning Garfield's statesmanship. Hall says: "A statesman, we are told, should follow public opinion. Doubtless—as a coachman follows his horses, having a firm hold on the reins, and guiding them." True, statesmanship occupies a far higher plane than mere politics. The statesman is not an intriguer—rather a thinker and doer. He must mold and form public opinion. His generalship must be of a higher order, if possible, than martial. Was Garfield, then, a statesman? Who can have any doubts in this direction? For

> "With grave
> Aspect he rose, and in his rising seemed
> A pillar of State; deep on his form engraved,
> Deliberation sat and public care;
> And princely counsel in his face showed majestic."

In considering the question that we have now proposed, it is first necessary to consider what are the leading vital themes upon which American statesmanship must rest or fall. Questions there are which present themselves hourly to the man in public stations of no intrinsic importance, and are merely partisan. Hence it is that in the history of the life of public men, many sections will be found which merely tell of victories won, and battles fought. But on the other hand, there appears a very marked class of questions which rise to the level of perpetual interest, affecting not only the destinies of the hour, but pregnant with the fate of the future. "Not questions of the day are these, passing like a shadow over the landscape of current events; but shining rather like those orbs from whose disks the effulgence is shed which makes shadows possible." These are the questions for the statesman, for they vitally effect the very existence of the nation; and that one only, who in the heated arena of public life, shows himself able to grapple with such problems, is worthy the name of statesman. A prominent writer of the day has divided this class of discussions into the following leading heads:

I. Questions affecting THE NATIONALITY OF THE UNITED STATES. II. Questions affecting the FINANCIAL AND MONETARY SYSTEMS OF THE UNITED STATES. III. Questions affecting the REVENUE AND EXPENDITURES OF THE UNITED STATES. IV. Questions concerning the GENERAL CHARACTER AND TENDENCY OF AMERICAN INSTITUTIONS.

If it has appeared that James Abram Garfield was able to grasp and discuss any or all of the great questions under the above heads, in such a manner as that new light was thrown upon them, and public opinion fixed concerning them, and to that extent fixed more securely than hitherto the substructure of American greatness, then indeed is he worthy of the name of statesman.

In the abstracts of many of Garfield's speeches, which we have already made, it will be seen that his considerations and discussions fell under the four chief divisions. And this being true, his name is the peer and fit companion of the greatest in American history, for he must rank with Hamilton, and Adams, and Webster and Sumner.

Garfield's speeches must be the foundation for his fame. To these history will turn as a basis for its estimate. The first thing which is to be said of them, is that they dealt *with the real problems of the epoch.* That he was a great orator is true; that he was much more than this is equally true. He was so radical in opinion that on almost every question he was ahead of his party and the country. This was the case in his arguments on the status of the rebel states, and what ought to be done with them; in his arguments in favor of a reduction of the tariff as prices declined after the war, and in his discussion of the currency and banking problems. Yet so nearly right was he in every one of these instances that Congress and the army gradually moved up to and occupied the position which he had taken in advance of them.

"Those unfamiliar with Garfield's industry, and ignorant of the details of his work, may, in some degree, measure them by the annals of Congress. No one of the generation of public men to which he belonged has contributed so much that will be valuable for future reference. His speeches are numerous, many of them brilliant, all of them well studied, carefully phrased, and exhaustive of the subject under consideration. Collected from the scattered pages of ninety royal octavo volumes of the *Congressional Record*, they would present an invaluable compendium of the political history of the most important era through which the National Government has ever passed. When the history of this period shall be impartially written, when war legislation, measures of reconstruction, protection of human rights, amendments to the Constitution, maintenance of public credit, steps toward specie resumption, true theories of revenue, may be reviewed, unsurrounded by prejudice and disconnected from partisanism, the speeches of Garfield will be estimated at their true value, and will be found to comprise a vast magazine of fact and argument, of clear analysis and sound conclusion. Indeed, if no other authority were accessible, his speeches in the House of Representatives from December, 1863, to June, 1880, would give a well connected history and complete defense of the important legislation of the seventeen eventful years that constitute his parliamentary life. Far beyond that, his speeches would be found to forecast many great measures, yet to be completed —measures which he knew were beyond the public opinion of the hour, but which he confidently believed would secure popular approval within the period of his own lifetime, and by the aid of his own efforts."*

In other respects he also differed from the men around him. He was a scholar in the broadest sense. His speeches are absolutely unequaled anywhere for their scientific method. In their philosophical discussions they were the product of the ripest scholarship; in their practical suggestions and arguments, they were, they are, the product of the highest statesmanship. Finally, a man of more spotless honor and loftier integrity never trod the earth than James A. Garfield. He lived in an atmosphere of purity and unselfishness, which, to the average man, is an unknown realm. After all, there are men enough with intellect in politics, but too few with character. An estimate of Garfield would be incomplete which failed to include the inflexible honesty of the great orator and legislator, whether in affairs public or private. History shows that while no institutions ever decayed because of the intellectual weakness of the people among which they flourished, empire after empire has perished from the face of the earth through the decay of morals in its people and its public men. History repeats itself. What has been, will be. Name after name of the great men of the new Republic is stained with private immorality and public crime. The noblest part of Garfield, with all his genius, was his spotless character. There was, there is, no greater, purer, manlier man.

*Blaine's Eulogy.

GARFIELD—THE NATION'S CHIEF EXECUTIVE.

IN MEMORIAM.

In grief we humbly bow,
As tear-dimmed eyes behold our stricken chief
Laid low by death. In vain we try to grasp
The lesson Thou wouldst teach a sorrowing world.
The arm that oft has stayed the approaching tide
Of party feud and strife, no longer holds
The helm; the mind, replete with golden thoughts,
Forever striving after clearer truth
And light, is now at rest; the tender heart,
Aglow with love, and aspirations grand,
Is cold and still.
* * * Death's call brooks no delay.
It comes to all; and as the parent's hearts
Are joined more firmly o'er a loved one's grave,
So o'er our chief to-day, now cold in death,
A nation's union is more strongly knit.
From East and West, from North and South, the hearts
Of millions beat as one with poignant grief,
And faction's angry voice is hushed once more.

* * * * *

We leave in faith and hope our doubts, our fears,
Our country's future destiny, our all,
With Thee, our Father and our country's God.

—F. W. Reeder.

CHAPTER XIX.

NOMINATED FOR THE PRESIDENCY.

Even to the dullest peasant standing by
Who fastened still on him a wondering eye,
He seemed the master spirit of the land.

—JOANNA BAILLIE.

Things of the noblest kind his genius drew,
And looked through nature at a single view;
A loose he gave to his unbounded soul,
And taught new lands to rise, new seas to roll;
Called into being scenes unknown before,
And, passing nature's bounds, was something more.

—CHURCHILL.

In no other country has there grown up such an institution as the political party of America. In every government there are factions and divisions based on political differences; but in this country alone do we see the full fruition of the political party, nurtured in freedom and liberty. That it is a powerful agency in molding and shaping the character and destiny of government, no one for a moment can doubt. While its action is regular and measured, yet spontaneous outbursts which change the onward progress of affairs, are often the result of party manipulating. Its work, for the most part, is like the gradual upheaval which goes on imperceptibly in the earth, but often like the volcano it bursts forth, leaves its bounds, and if it does not bury cities and desolate fields, at least brings us face to face with radical changes. Such forces were at work at the birth of the Republican party. In this manner the old Whig and Tory parties were changed to those of to-day. By such a revolution and sudden upheaval Abraham Lincoln became the President of his country; by such did the war begin and end; and in a certain sense it made James Abram Garfield the twentieth President of the United States. In this I do not wish to be misunderstood. Even the volcano does not always burst forth in anger—it does not always threaten sudden destruction. Frequently it belches forth its lava in the flow of a majestic stream, until by age it increases, and rushing on carries all before it. In such a manner was the subject of this volume caught up, and became by common consent, the greatest of his contemporaries.

The year 1880 was one of great political excitement. The country did not have a war on its hands; it was not called upon to choose its chief executive either in the shadow or broad day of internal or national strifes. But like all years in which a president is chosen, business waited on the result. From the first assembling of the Republicans at Chicago, the citizens of the entire country, of all parties and creeds, waited in breathless suspense the announcement of the result. In another way this year was a peculiarly exciting and interesting one. In it was decided one of the most troublesome questions, and likely at some time to become very formidable. That question was whether any man could, under the precedents of our country, receive a third term to the office of President. General Grant was the exponent and advocate of the doctrine. Having filled the office of President two successive terms, by an absence of a few years in visiting other countries and studying the various systems of governments, returned to ask of his countrymen another term of office. This was the prominent issue to be decided. Grant had warm and ardent friends throughout the entire country, and the result promised to be one of the most interesting in modern politics. With this question to be solved, to decide also the arbitrary vote under a unit-rule, and these questions decided upon, to nominate the candidates accordingly, the delegates assembled in Chicago early in the month of June. A brief history of this convention is, therefore, valuable for present reading, and most happily illustrates the peculiar fortunes of General Garfield, who, while ever in patient waiting, had his long succession of honors seek him openly. It is a curious story of cause and effect.

On the second day of June the convention first assembled. To accomodate the seven hundred and fifty-five delegates and the immense concourse of spectators naturally attracted by such a momentous gathering, the great Exposition building was called into requisition. This is the Crystal Palace of Chicago. In the south half of the structure there is a hall four hundred feet long by one hundred and fifty feet wide, with galleries all round, and so arranged that ten thousand people can be easily accommodated. The building is simply a huge show of wood and iron and glass, built upon a long series of semi-circular arches. It has a dome, but no other characteristic except that of vast emptiness. Within this structure a huge wood box had been built, and this was the convention hall. It was altogether typical of Chicago. A great strip of bunting ran along the roof of the hall from end to end. A luxuriant drapery of flags, picturesquely arranged, covered all the walls with their bright hues. Busts of Franklin, Washington, Lincoln, Clay and Jackson, which stood on brackets upon the low walls rising from the floor to the edge of the galleries, were the centres of vivid rosettes of the red, white and blue. Over the stage was a beautiful decoration. The building is composed in great part of glass. It is located on the lake shore, and before it towards the east, lies the blue water. We remember that years before on the shores of another lake, while still a boy, an inspiration to greatness had possessed Garfield, and now does not the same feeling come over him? Then he was chopping wood and giving encouragement to the longings within him, now he is the hero of the hour, the applauded of the multitude, and he is to be made the candidate for the greatest office of which any government can boast.

Long before the convention was to assemble, the many hotels of Chicago were crowded to overflowing. The convention was the theme of conversation on every street corner, not only of Chicago, but of the entire country. Every incoming train brought delegations and spectators from every section of the land. It was a great gathering of rival clans, which did not wait the order of their generals to advance, but charged upon each other the moment they came upon the field. There were two battles in progress—the one of the masses, the other of the leaders.

Public meetings were held in various places in the city, in favor of the "Grant" and "anti-Grant" issue. Active in the interest of third-term rule, or for Grant, were such men and speakers as Senators Conkling, Logan, Carpenter, Woodford, of New York, Emory Storrs, Lincoln and Stephen A. Douglas. Little interest was shown in the way of a demonstration for Grant. A growing sentiment was possessing the multitude that Grant could not and should not be nominated. But never had a candidate such ardent and successful workers.

The anti-element was not nearly so well organized. The only thing the various leaders opposed to Grant had in common, was a deep-seated aversion to third-term rule. More than this, such leaders as Garfield, Frye, Chandler, and others, from the nature of the case, could not be in entire harmony. Each had his own candidate whose interests he made it his duty to advance. At all the public gatherings for the purpose of expressing opposition to Grant, the speeches were most radical. The tone of the meetings were unmistakable. The people declared that "they would not submit to boss rule; that they would not have a third term; but that they would defeat the villainous attempt to deprive them of their liberties." People came there determined to be pleased with every thing or any thing but Grant. But they hissed the third term. They shouted themselves hoarse for Blaine, Washburne, and Edmunds.

About the meetings of the National Committee, which was holding secret sessions at the Palmer House, great interest centred. It was known that a majority of this committee were anti-Grant men, and that its chairman was a most decided Grant advocate. Nearly every State was represented. Soon after Senator Cameron had called the meeting to order, Mr. William E. Chandler introduced a resolution, the import of which was that "the call for the National Republican Convention, as issued by its officers, inviting two delegates from each Congressional District, four delegates-at-large from each State, two from each Territory, and two from the District of Columbia," be approved and ratified. This was carried unanimously. Great excitement was caused among the third-term members of the committee, by the introduction of a resolution which had been agreed upon previously by the anti-Grant members, by ex-Senator Chaffee, that "the committee recognize the right of each delegate in the convention to freely cast and to have counted his individual vote, according to his own sentiment, and have it so decided as against any unit-rule or other instructions passed by the State Convention, which right was conceded without dissent, and was exercised in the conventions of 1860–'68, and was also fully debated and confirmed by the convention of 1876, and has thus become a part of the law of Republican conventions, and until reversed by the convention itself, must remain the governing principle." The chairman refused to put the resolution before the committee. The unit-rule was not to die so easily. More than this, Chairman Cameron positively and unconditionally refused to entertain any appeal from his decision. Mr. Chandler thereupon, in a vigorous speech, demurred to such ruling, and wound up by also appealing from the decision of the chair. To further aggravate matters, Cameron again refused to entertain the appeal. This brought Frye, of Maine, to his feet, and in a caustic speech he told the chairman that the committee had rights which he (the chairman) was bound to respect. Mr. Chandler significantly remarked that if the chairman would not pay any respect to the committee, the same power that made him chairman would remove him. It was thereupon decided that a committee should be appointed to select a candidate to preside at the temporary organization. After a recess, the committee reported in favor of Senator George F. Hoar, of Massachusetts. Acting under the same resolution, the chairman of the special committee, Mr. William E. Chandler, was empowered to call the convention to order in case the chairman of the National Committee was absent or unable to perform that duty. Mr. McCormick followed with a second resolution of the caucus, directing that in all questions pertaining to the temporary organization, the chairman shall rule that every delegate was at liberty to vote as he chooses, regardless of instructions. Messrs. Gorham, Filley, and others, made great opposition, and Mr. Cameron ruled that this resolution would not be entertained, since it was not in the power of the committee to instruct the chairman as to his rulings.

Several protests, prominent among which were those from the states of New York and Pennsylvania, were circulated against the unit-rule, to effect that many of the delegates from these states deemed that the nomination of General Grant would be to insure national defeat to the party in November. Early on the morning of June 1st, a caucus of "anti-Grant" delegates decided to defeat the unit-rule at all hazards, even if it was necessary to depose Mr. Cameron from the chairmanship. At this juncture the Grant leaders offered a flag of truce, desiring to harmonize all differences. The result of the compromise was that Senator Hoar was accepted as temporary chairman of the convention, and it was agreed that no attempt should be made to enforce the unit-rule. This was accepted, and on Wednesday, June 2d, after days and even weeks of intriguing, caucusing and speech making, the first session of the National Republican Convention for the year of 1880 was held. The day was a beautiful one. "The rageful features of the past day or two went into their tents at such sunshine and calm godliness of sky." Shortly after one o'clock, Senator Cameron called the convention to order, and after a short prayer by Rev. Dr. Kittredge, and a brief plea for Grant by the chairman, he then nominated Mr. Hoar for temporary chairman. Having been conducted to the chair, Mr. Hoar made a speech reviewing some of the prominent issues of the day. An organization was thus effected, and the chagrined Grant men, with the best grace possible, resigned the control of the preliminary organization to their opponents.

On motion of Eugene Hale, of Maine, the roll of States and Territories was called, and the committees made up. After a slight stir over Utah, and a sharp encounter between Conkling and Frye, the opening business was completed, and the convention adjourned for that day. A newspaper dispatch sent out of the room during this session said:

There is a good deal of talk about Garfield. Some significance is attached to the fact that when the name was mentioned in the convention to-day as a member of the Committee on Rules it was loudly applauded.

That night the popular battle in the streets and lobbies continued, attended with ever growing excitement. Grant men and Blaine men loudly proclaimed their confidence in a victory for their respective favorites, on the first or second ballot. Each of these two leaders claimed about three hundred reliable votes; but, in fact, they had not six hundred between them. Sherman, Edmunds, Washburne and Windom men felt sure that neither Blaine nor Grant could be nominated on account of the violent opposition to their factions. This gave hope to each of these smaller sections, and made "dark-horse" talk plausible.

At eleven o'clock of June 3d, the second day's fight of the convention began. As the delegations took their places, the great crowd of spectators occupied themselves in getting acquainted with the men who were to give and receive the hard blows to be dealt by both sides when the contest opened. All these men—Conkling, Garfield, Frye, Hale and Logan—were cordially received, though there were degrees in the favor. The most spontaneous of the greetings given any one of the leaders was to Garfield. One of the ovations to him gave rise to a ludicrous affair for Conkling. The latter had made his usual late and pompous entrance, had been received with much noise, and walked slowly up to his seat near the front. Just as he rose to show himself further and address the chair, General Garfield came in at the rear. A tremendous and rapidly spreading cheer broke out, which the New York "Duke" mistook for his own property. The second day was now passing, and the preliminaries were not yet complete. It was the policy of the Grant men to make delay, and wear out the strength of all opponents. They had come, as Cameron said, "to stick until we win." The Blaine leaders, on the other hand, had no such reliable, lasting force. They must dash in boldly and carry off their prize at once, or be forever defeated. To-day the Blaine men came in jubilant, for they had beaten the Grant faction in the committees. Conkling opened the proceedings from the floor at the earliest moment. He moved to adjourn until evening to await the report of the Committee on Credentials. Hale opposed this. Conkling, in his haste, forgetting his parliamentary knowledge, claimed that his motion to take a recess was not debatable. The chairman overruled this, much to the annoyance of Conkling. He soon poured out a little vial of wrath on Hale, and sneered at him as his "amiable friend." To this Hale retorted that he had not spent his time in cultivating sarcastic and sneering methods in argument; and if the Senator from New York was less amiable than others this morning the convention understood the reason well. At this reference to the general defeat of the Grant forces in the committees during the last evening, the people laughed loudly at Conkling, and that gentleman deigned to laugh also. Later on, a report was asked for from the Committee on Rules. Of this committee General Garfield was chairman. It had been decided by the committee to defer the reading of their report until the report of the Committee on Credentials had been presented. As General Garfield mounted a chair to have a better opportunity to explain the action of his committee, he was greeted with tremendous and hearty applause. It was a magnificent, spontaneous tribute to his worth and universally recognized public services. General Garfield's explanation was satisfactory, and Frey offered a motion proposing a recess until five P. M. It was half past that hour, however, before the convention came to order again. The galleries were packed as before with interested spectators. As soon as the convention was ready for business, Mr. Henderson, of Iowa, announced that the Committee on Credentials would not be ready to report at that session, and moved that the Committee on Rules be requested to report, so that the convention could proceed to business. This the Grant men resisted, and for this reason: The rules which had been agreed to by the committee only allowed five minutes debate on the matter of each individual contested seat. The Grant men did not want the report adopted before the Committee on Credentials reported, because they wanted to ascertain just what the latter report would be. Logan led the fight for Grant, supported by Boutwell and others. Henderson held his own very well. Finally, after an hour of this running fire of debate, Mr. Sharpe moved to amend the pending motion by substituting an order that the Committee on Credentials report at once. On this amendment a vote was soon reached, which proved to be the most significant event of the day; for it was the first vote taken by states; it was a test vote between the Grant men on the one side and the allied anti-Grant factions on the other, and it settled the fate of the "unit-rule." Upon Alabama being called the chairman of the delegation, Mr. Dunn, announced twenty ayes.

Mr. Allen Alexander, of Alabama, a colored delegate—I desire to vote, "No."

The Chairman—Does the gentleman from Alabama desire that his vote should be received in the negative?

Mr. Alexander—Yes, sir.

The Chairman—It will be so recorded.

Several other States offered divided votes.

The result was against Sharpe's substitute, by a vote of 318 to 406. About forty delegates were absent or did not vote. There was great rejoicing among the anti-Grant factions when it became certain that Hoar would allow no "unit rule" until forced to do so by an order of the convention. On motion of Mr. Brandagee, of Connecticut, Henderson's motion was laid on the table, and adjournment till the next day followed immediately.

The night intervening was an exciting one. Two days now the convention had been in session. Its work in one way had been momentous, and yet every one realized that the result, so far as nominations were concerned, could not be known for many days. Friday dawned rather unpropitious. It was one of those dark, damp and chilly days which all cities in close proximity to large bodies of water are familiar with. Storm clouds of passion had swept over the convention frequently since the opening of its sessions. The character of the weather now made every thing look gloomy, and augured more decided antagonism for the day. As General Garfield and Senator Conkling entered the assembly, at intervals of a few minutes, they were again applauded, but the ovation given the former was in striking contrast to that of the leader from New York.

The discussion of the morning opened upon a resolution presented by Senator Conkling. It was the meaning of this resolution that "every member of the convention is bound in honor to support its nominee, whoever that may be; and that no man should hold a seat who is not ready to so agree."

This furnished the key-note for a debate that illustrated fairly the direction in which the leaders were driving. The Associated Press report of the debate was as follows: Mr. Hale, mounting his chair, said he supposed that a Republican convention did not need to be instructed that its first duty after naming its candidate was to proceed to elect him over the Democratic candidate. [Applause.] They all had their preferences, but when the deliverance was had from all the labor of the convention he had no doubt that they should all be found hand in hand, shoulder to shoulder, marching on to the election of their candidate. When the vote was taken it was found that there were three negative votes among the delegates of West Virginia. Mr. Conkling then offered the following:

Resolved, That the delegates who have voted that they will not abide the action of the convention do not deserve to have seats, and have forfeited their votes in the convention. [Subdued applause and some hisses.]

Mr. Campbell, of West Virginia, who had cast the vote of that State, defended his position. He had suffered contumely and violence for his Republican principles, and if he was now to be denied the free expression of his opinion in a Republican convention, he was willing to withdraw from that convention. He had imbibed his Republican principles from the great New York statesman, William H. Seward. He had been a newspaper editor since the John Brown raid at Harper's Ferry, and had always consistently supported the national Republican nominee. But he felt that there was a principle in this question. He would never go to any convention and agree beforehand that whatever might be done by it should have his endorsement. He always intended to guard his own sovereignty. [Applause.] He never intended that any body of men should take that sovereignty from him. As he had not been afraid to stand up for Republican principles in West Virginia, he was not afraid to go home and face his constituents. The two remaining dissenters expressed themselves in as positive and emphatic a manner. In the course of this debate General Garfield arose and declared himself as follows against Conkling's pending resolution:

There never can be a convention, of which I am one delegate, equal in rights to every other delegate, that shall bind my vote against my will on any question whatever on which my vote is to be given. I regret that these gentlemen thought it best to break the harmony of this convention by their dissent; but, when they tell the convention that their dissent was not, and did not mean, that they would not vote for the nominee of this convention, but only that they did not think the resolution at this time wise, they acted in their right, and not by my vote. I do not know the gentlemen, nor their affiliations, nor their relations to candidates, except one of them. One of them I knew in the dark days of slavery, and for twenty long years, in the midst of slave-pens and slave-drivers, he stood up for liberty with a clear-sighted courage and a brave heart equal to the best Republicans that live on this globe. And if this convention expel him, then we must purge ourselves at the end of every vote by requiring that so many as shall vote against us shall go out.

The sequel of the matter was the withdrawal of the resolution by Conkling. The business of the convention was hastened as much as possible. The contested seats of the delegates from several states were passed upon, and decisions made. The contest over the Illinois delegates was the most exciting. After the discussion had gone on for some time, Mr. Raum replied for the sitting delegates. Eliott Anthony spoke for the opposition, and was succeeded by Mr. Storrs, of Illinois, who made a speech, the principal effect of which was to cause wild bursts of applause for Blaine and Grant. The sentence, "Nominate James G. Blaine, if you will," was the signal for another grand outburst of applause, which was renewed and intensified when he finished the sentence thus: "And then those who now shout in the galleries shall by and by be reposing under the influence of the summer sun; but the followers of the grand old silent soldier will still be found wide awake and watching by their camp-fires and carrying the banners of the sluggards."

The scene which followed and continued for several minutes was most exciting, the uproar dying away, then breaking out again many times, a perfect epidemic of cheers. What came next was thus described by a correspondent:

Mr. Conkling was conspicuous in leading the chorus, first by waving his handkerchief and later by standing on his chair and waving the illuminated little banner placed to designate the seats of the New York delegation. Finally some one started the campaign songs: "We'll Rally 'Round the Flag, Boys, Shouting the Battle-cry of Freedom," and "Marching through Georgia." At this time nearly every person within the hall was on his feet, each cheering for his own favorite. Flags, shawls, parasols, hats and all other movable things within reach were swung furiously to and fro. Bob Ingersoll, seizing a lady's shawl, waved it frantically from the platform. In the centre of the stage, just back of the chair, a fine-looking lady, with a flag in one hand and parasol in the other, swung them to and fro and repeated time and again, "Hurrah for Blaine!" She appeared to be in company with Governor Jewell, of Connecticut. Finally, she obtained two flags, and with one in each hand continued her enthusiastic efforts as long as the uproar lasted. It may safely be said that no public assemblage ever before witnessed such a scene. People seemed actually to have lost their senses in the giddy whirl. For half an hour this continued before the chair made any effort to control the members. The Illinois cases were then disposed of in favor of the majority, and, worn out with excitement, the convention shortly after adjourned to Saturday morning.

Saturday, June 5th, was like Friday, dark and gloomy. The vast crowd, after the preceding night of excitement, was, of course, dull and sleepy. It was noted, however, that when Garfield came into the hall the audience waked up and gave a hearty cheer. The roll was called at about twelve o'clock. After finishing the matters connected with the credentials, the convention, on the motion of General Garfield, adopted the report of the Committee on Rules.

The Committee on Resolutions next reported, and the platform was adopted; after which the convention adjourned till evening. Skirmishing ended, now would come serious work. The triumvirate and its legions had exhausted every parliamentary resource for delay, and at last had to face "the inevitable hour" which must lead, for them, to glory, or the common grave of all their plans. It was a magnificent audience which poured into the great hall that evening to witness the beginning of the end of this tremendous political conflict. After some preliminaries, Mr. Hale, of Maine, moved that the roll of States be called alphabetically and that nominations for candidates for President be made. General Logan inquired whether the rules permitted the seconding of nominations for candidates for President. The chairman said no, that the rules did not provide for it. Garfield thought there would be no objection to the seconding of nominations. Unanimous consent was accorded for five-minute speeches in seconding nominations. Hale's motion was then adopted without opposition.

The alphabetical roll call of States now begun to place in nomination candidates for President. When Michigan was reached James F. Joy arose and nominated James G. Blaine. The speech made by Mr. Joy was of rather a modest nature; and when he closed, although great enthusiasm was manifested over the nomination of such a popular candidate, yet the audience, believing that more masterly efforts were to follow, were not electrified. It did not arouse the enthusiasm of the audience to its highest pitch. Mr. Pixley, of California, seconded the nomination in a speech of considerable length. All in all, the Blaine men were disappointed, and to remedy matters, Mr. William P. Frye followed, having obtained the floor by consent, in an electric speech of ten minutes, which set the galleries wild again.

Minnesota was next called; whereupon E. F. Drake placed in nomination William Windom, of Winona, a very able and distinguished Senator from that State.

Now was heard the call for New York; a call which meant Roscoe Conkling and the nomination of the great General and ex-President, Ulysses S. Grant. As Mr. Conkling advanced to the front, he was greeted with tremendous cheers. Taking a commanding position on one of the reporters tables, he stood a few moments and regarded the audience while they grew silent at an imperious wave of his hand He briefly reviewed the third-term objections to Grant, and urged that it was no objection to any man that he had been weighed in the balance and not found wanting, or that he had obtained experience which rendered him better fitted for the duties confided to his care. When he had occupied thirty minutes there were loud calls from the galleries of "Time! Time!" but he paid no attention to them and was soon permitted to proceed. A little later he referred to General Grant as being without telegraph wires running from his house to this convention, which was evidently construed as an insinuation against Mr. Blaine. This was greeted with laughter and a storm of hisses and loud cries of "Time! Time!". which continued until a delegate appealed to the American people to listen to the gentleman, and asked them to hear him finish. He was then permitted to proceed until he referred to "electioneering contrivances,", which excited another outburst of objection.

Toward the conclusion, Mr. Conkling said the convention was master of a supreme opportunity. It could make the next President, and also make sure of his peaceful inauguration. It could break that power which mildews the South. Democratic success was a menace to order and progress, which the convention could overthrow and emancipate a solid South. It could make the Republican army march to certain victory with its greatest marshal at its head. The speech was throughout a magnificent display of studied oratory. The appeal for third-term and for Grant was unsurpassable. There were fears among many anti-Grant men that the speech could not be equalled. It was fully twenty minutes before order could be restored. The Grant men in the convention and galleries took a regular jubilee, and President Hoar had to sit down and let disorder tire itself out. The Grant delegation "pooled" the flags which marked their seats, marched round the aisles and cheered and yelled as if they were dwellers in Bedlam, just home after a long absence. Finally Mr. Bradley, of Kentucky, was allowed to speak, seconding Grant's name.

When Ohio was called Mr. Garfield rose, and amid tremendous cheering, advanced to the place Mr. Conkling had just vacated. Order being restored, he spoke in the following magnificent strain:

MR. PRESIDENT: I have witnessed the extraordinary scenes of this convention with deep solicitude. No emotion touches my heart more quickly than a sentiment in honor of a great and noble character. But as I sat on these seats and witnessed these demonstrations, it seemed to me you were a human ocean in a tempest. I have seen the sea lashed into fury and tossed into spray, and its grandeur moves the soul of the dullest man. But I remember that it is not the billows, but the calm level of the sea from which all heights and depths are measured. When the storm has passed and the hour of calm settles on the ocean, when sunshine bathes its smooth surface, then the astronomer and surveyor takes the level by which he measures all terrestrial heights and depths. Gentlemen of the convention, your present temper may not mark the healthful pulse of the people. When our enthusiasm has passed, when the emotions of this hour have subsided, we shall find the calm level of public opinion, below the storm, from which the thoughts of a mighty people are to be measured, and by which their final action will be determined. Not here, in this brilliant circle, where 15,000 men and women are assembled, is the destiny of the Republic to be decreed; not here, where I see the enthusiastic faces of 755 delegates waiting to cast their votes into the urn and determine the choice of their party; but by 5,000,000 Republican firesides, where the thoughtful fathers, with wives and children about them, with calm thoughts inspired by love of home and love of country, with the history of the past, the hopes of the future, and the knowledge of the great men who have adorned and blessed our nation in days gone by—there God prepares the verdict that shall determine the wisdom of our work to-night. Not in Chicago, in the heat of June, but in the sober quiet that comes between now and November, in the silence of deliberate judgment, will this great question be settled. Let us aid them to-night. [Great applause.]

But now, gentlemen of the Convention, what do we want? [A voice, Garfield.] Bear with me a moment. Hear me for this cause, and for a moment, be silent that you may hear. Twenty-five years ago this Republic was wearing a triple chain of bondage. Long familiarity with the traffic in the body and souls of men had paralyzed the consciences of a majority of our people. The baleful doctrine of State sovereignty had shocked and weakened the noblest and most beneficent powers of the National Government, and the grasping power of slavery was seizing the virgin Territories of the West and dragging them into the den of eternal bondage. At that crisis the Republican party was born. It drew its first inspiration from the fire of liberty which God has lighted in every man's heart, and which all the powers of ignorance and tyranny can never wholly extinguish. The Republican party came to deliver and save the Republic. It entered the arena when beleaguered and assailed territories were struggling for freedom, and drew around them the sacred circle of liberty, which the demon of slavery has never dared to cross. It made them free forever. Strengthened by its victory on the frontier, the young party, under the leadership of that great man, who on this spot, twenty years ago, was made its leader, entered the national capital and assumed the high duties of the Government. The light which shone from its banner dispelled the darkness in which slavery had enshrouded the Capitol and melted the shackles of every slave, and consumed, in the fire of liberty, every slave-pen within the shadow of the Capitol. Our national industries, by an impoverishing policy, were themselves prostrated, and the streams of revenue flowed in such feeble currents that the treasury itself was well nigh empty. The money of the people was the wretched notes of two thousand uncontrolled and irresponsible state bank corporations, which were filling the country with a circulation that poisoned rather than sustained the life of business. The Republican party changed all this. It abolished the Babel of confusion and gave the country a currency as national as its flag, based upon the sacred faith of the people. It threw its protecting arm around our great industries, and they stood erect as with new life. It filled with the spirit of true nationality all the great functions of the Government. It confronted a rebellion of unexampled magnitude, with a slavery behind it, and, under God, fought the final battle of liberty until victory was won. Then, after the storms of battle, were heard the sweet, calm words of peace uttered by the conquering nation, and saying to the conquered foe that lay prostrate at its feet, "This is our only revenge, that you join us in lifting to the serene firmament of the Constitution, to shine like stars forever and forever, the immortal principles of truth and justice, that all men, white or black, shall be free and stand equal before the law." Then came the questions of reconstruction, the public debt, and the public faith.

In the settlement of these questions the Republican party has completed its twenty-five years of glorious existence, and it has sent us here to prepare it for another lustrum of duty and of victory. How shall we do this great work? We can not do it, my friends, by assailing our Republican brethren. God forbid that I should say one word to cast a shadow upon any name on the roll of our heroes. This coming fight is our Thermopylæ. We are standing upon a narrow isthmus. If our Spartan hosts are united, we can withstand all the Persians that the Xerxes of Democracy can bring against us.

Let us hold our ground this one year, for the stars in their courses fight for us in the future. The census to be taken this year will bring re-enforcements and continued power. But, in order to win this victory now, we want the vote of every Republican, of every Grant Republican in America, of every Blaine man and of every anti-Blaine man. The vote of every follower of every candidate is needed to make our success certain; therefore I say, gentlemen and brethren, we are here to calmly counsel together, and inquire what we shall do. [A voice: "Nominate Garfield."—Great applause.]

We want a man whose life and opinions embody all the achievements of which I have spoken. We want a man who, standing on a mountain height, sees all the achievements of our past history, and carries in his heart the memory of all its glorious deeds, and who, looking forward, prepares to meet the labor and the dangers to come. We want one who will act in no spirit of unkindness toward those we lately met in battle. The Republican party offers to our brethren of the South the olive branch of peace, and wishes them to return to brotherhood, on this supreme condition, that it shall be admitted, forever and forever more, that, in the war for the Union, we were right and they were wrong. On that supreme condition we meet them as brethren, and no other. We ask them to share with us the blessings and honors of this great Republic.

Now, gentlemen, not to weary you, I am about to present a name for your consideration—the name of a man who was the comrade, and associate, and friend of nearly all those noble dead whose faces look down upon us from these walls to-night; a man who began his career of public service twenty-five years ago, whose first duty was courageously done in the days of peril on the plains of Kansas, when the first red drops of that bloody shower began to fall which finally swelled into the deluge of war. He bravely stood by young Kansas then, and, returning to his duty in the national legislature, through all subsequent time his pathway has been marked by labors performed in every department of legislation.

You ask for his monuments. I point you to twenty-five years of the national statutes. Not one great beneficent statute has been placed on our statute books without his intelligent and powerful aid. He aided these men to formulate the laws that raised our great armies and carried us through the war. His hand was seen in the workmanship of those statutes that restored and brought back the unity and married calm of the States. His hand was in all that great legislation that created the war currency, and in a greater work that redeemed the promises of the Government, and made the currency equal to gold. And when, at last, called from the halls of legislation into a high executive office, he displayed that experience, intelligence, firmness, and poise of character which has carried us through a stormy period of three years. With one half the public press crying, "Crucify him!" and a hostile Congress seeking to prevent success—in all this he remained unmoved until victory crowned him. The great fiscal affairs of the nation and the great business interests of the country he has guarded and preserved, while executing the law of resumption and effecting its object without a jar, and against the false prophecies of one half of the press and all the Democracy of this continent. He has shown himself able to meet with calmness the great emergencies of the Government for twenty-five years. He has trodden the perilous heights of public duty, and against all the shafts of malice has borne his breast unharmed. He has stood in the blaze of "that fierce light that beats against the throne," but its fiercest ray has found no flaw in his armor, no stain on his shield.

I do not present him as a better Republican, or as a better man than thousands of others we honor, but I present him for your deliberate consideration. I nominate John Sherman, of Ohio.

Of this masterly effort, the Chicago *Inter-Ocean*, a strong Grant paper, said the following morning:

When Ohio is called, a form—which probably comes nearer the people's ideal type of a statesman than any other in the convention—arises near the centre of the middle aisle and moves toward the stage amid the sharp clapping of thousands of hands, which increases, as General Garfield mounts the same table upon which Senator Conkling stood, to the roar of voices mingled with the noise of stamping feet. It is noticeable that in this ovation a large number of delegates and alternates have joined. To the attention which Garfield always attracts is now added the romance of a possibility that is in every one's mind, and whenever he has moved into sight of the galleries during this convention, he has been warmly greeted. As he stands now on the table where Conkling but a few moments ago stood, many thousands are doubtless comparing the two men who, among many great men, have almost monopolized and about equally shared the attention of the people. There is much of similarity, and, at the same time, great dissimilarity between the two men. Both are large in stature, and both would be noted, if strangers, among thousands, as remarkable types of physical development. The verdict of the great majority would be probably that Garfield looks more like the statesman than the New York senator. There is a grace and eloquence in the person and manners of Conkling that approaches too near airiness to be always strong in its effect, but the figure we now see before us is rough-hewn in form and rugged of feature. The verdict of the ladies in the gallery, many times during the convention, is that Conkling is "so handsome," and Garfield "so plain." But the Ohio school-teacher, minister, legislator, and statesman, is not plain-looking. To the beauty of great strength is added the grace with which an illustrious and radiant renown will clothe any man. Large of form, with a huge head, the figure fixed like a rock on that table, while the building trembles with the applause, is imposing, peerless and grand. To all of this, Garfield's nature adds a charm possessed by few men—the beauty of a generous and affectionate nature. A big heart, a sympathetic nature, and a mind keenly sensitive to everything that is beautiful in sentiment, are the artists that shade down the gnarled outlines and touch with soft coloring the plain features of a massive face. The conception of a grand thought always paints a glow upon Garfield's face, which no one forgets who has seen him while speaking. His eyes are a cold gray, but they are often—yes, all the time in this speech—lit brilliantly by the warm light of worthy sentiments, and the strong flame of a great man's conviction. In speaking, he is not so restless as Conkling; his speech is an appeal for thought and calm deliberation, and he stands still like the rock of judgment while he delivers it. There is no invective or bitterness in his effort, but there is throughout an earnestness of conviction and an unquestionable air of sincerity, to which every gesture and intonation of voice is especially adapted.

Other prominent journals spoke in the highest terms of General Garfield. Garfield's speech made a profound impression, not only on the convention, but on the country, and strengthened the already powerful sentiment in favor of making himself the nominee.

Edmunds and Washburne were the only other nominations proposed. They, with Sherman, were minor candidates, whose only hope lay in the enmity of the Grant and Blaine factions, whose evenly-balanced powers might prevent the success of either.

At twelve o'clock that night the Convention adjourned over till Monday. Many of the delegates wanted to continue the balloting after midnight, and some urged the chairman to ignore the Sabbath and let the convention go on. "Never," he replied; "this is a Sabbath-keeping nation, and I cannot preside over this convention one minute after twelve." The Sunday intervening was passed in feverish excitement. Never had Chicago seen such a Lord's-day. Notwithstanding the fact that the regular session of the convention was not held, scheming, plotting, and combinations were being made. The beginning of the end was at hand. The regular candidates were before the convention. The hotel lobbies were filled with an excited crowd. There were few of the political leaders but that were engaged in hard work for their candidate. Garfield had sought out a little Disciple congregation in a secluded part of the city. Here, forgetting the turmoil and excitement of the days before, he entered into the services of worship. To him it was a day of rest and worship. He dined with Marshall Field. At the table, addressing a friend who sat beside him, Garfield said: "Yes, this is a day of suspense, but it is also a day of prayer; and I have more faith in the prayers that will go up from Christian hearts to-day, than I have in all the political tactics which will prevail in the convention."

But the day passed only to open with renewed excitement. Sunday had been as a calm before a storm. Monday opened bright, and as the sun began his march upward in the cloudless sky, the contest commenced. Soon the first ballot was called. The incidents of the ballot were few and not very remarkable. Grant had received 304; Blaine 284; Sherman 93; Washburn 30; Edmunds 34 and Windom 10. The moment the vote was announced the President ordered another, holding that nothing was in order but voting; and before the leaders could look to their lines they were in action again by the prompt roll-call. The second ballot was uneventful, the third and fourth the same. The changes in these, and the succeeding ballots in the afternoon, were very slight—except the nomination of Garfield by a vote from Grier, a Pennsylvania delegate, and made without any particular idea of permanency. Eighteen ballots were taken during the morning session; and then a recess was taken until evening. The last ballot stood as follows; Grant 305; Blaine 283; Sherman 91; Edmunds 31; Washburn 35; Windom 10. The evening session opened noisily. The announcement of the first ballot at the evening session was greeted by the Sherman men with cheers, who saw their candidate was making a hole in the Blaine column. There was nothing of importance to disturb the situation of the Grant people. They held their own through the recess, and came back showing their determination to stick by their candidate to the last. It was very clear there had been no wholesale repairing of fences since the adjournment, and it began to look like an all-night siege. After the twenty-seventh ballot, Morse, of Massachusetts proposed an adjournment till the next morning. It was nearly half past nine, and the hall was excessively hot. Not less than twelve thousand people were overlooking the progress of the ballot, and at the conclusion of each call, while the secretaries were footing up the totals, this immense audience would rise with one accord to rest, by change of position, and the movement was suggestive of the distant roar of a coming storm. It was undeniably a brilliant scene at this time, but nobody could shut his ear to the fact that the multitude of spectators was a hindrance to business. After the twenty-eighth ballot, in which Garfield had received two votes, an adjournment was secured until the next morning.

The convention had now been in session for five days, and no nominations had been made; the country was impatient, the people were anxious for the termination of the battle. All Chicago rose on June 8th, with a settled wish that "today might settle it." The wish was father to the thought. The politicians believed it would as they strolled out of their hotels, boarding houses and resting places, and streamed in the direction of the Exposition building. General Garfield came forth from the Grand Pacific, arm-in-arm with his friend, Governor Foster, of Ohio. The suspicion that he would before nightfall be the nominee of the strongest party in the country for its President, never entered his head.

"I think, Charlie," said Garfield, "we shall get through with this business of president-making, to-day."

"Yes," returned Foster, "the delegates are all getting tired and want to go home." "I am quite sure they will select a candidate before another adjournment," continued Garfield.

"I hope it will be our man," answered Foster. "Honest John Sherman will be nominated, and again will Ohio be made proud by the work of the convention." "Amen," said Foster; "let us all take heart and work." "Yes, that is the word," cried Garfield. "Work! work! work!" And the two friends continued on down the street. As Garfield turned a corner, one of the hundreds of people who were thrusting advertisements, circulars and political squibs into the hands of passers-by, pressed a little piece of paper upon him, which he accepted mechanically, and as mechanically glanced at it. His eye caught "Acts 4.11 and 12." Thinking he would not throw a Bible leaf into the mud, he rolled it up and put it into his pocket, where he afterward found it, and continued his walk. Had he read it, the spirit of its prophecy would, no doubt, have struck him, as the words of those verses are: "This is the stone which was set at naught of you builders, which is become the head of the corner. Neither is there salvation in any other: for there is none other name under heaven given among men, whereby we must be saved." These, however, are but curious coincidences that, no doubt, would have exceedingly worked upon people of a superstitious turn of mind. But it was only the action of the convention which met an hour late that morning, that gave them their value. When it was opened, the reverend gentleman who asked the blessing of the Almighty, voicing the popular heart, prayed that the delegates might soon be restored to their friends.

It was at this point that Wisconsin pointed out the way to victory. Garfield's manly course in the convention had created a favorable impression on all sides, the result of which in the Wisconsin delegation was that he was freely talked of for second choice. They held no caucus, and during the night of Monday were anxiously waiting to see some other state make the break for Garfield. After the adjournment on Monday night the matter was talked up in the delegation, and it was agreed that, if no other solution offered itself within three or four ballots, the delegation would throw its solid strength to Garfield. No consultation was had on the subject with the other leaders, as it was intended to operate as a feeler, Wisconsin being among the last states called on the roll. The result of this feeler is now a matter of history. The thirty-fifth ballot developed a Garfield strength of fifty votes.

Amid the most intense excitement another call was ordered. It was GRANT or GARFIELD—which?

Here General Garfield rose to a question of order. He challenged the vote on the ground that the votes had been given for him without his consent, which consent he absolutely refused to give. The point was overruled. The roll call proceeded. When Connecticut was reached, eleven of the twelve votes were given for Garfield. This was the beginning of the excitement. Then Illinois gave seven votes for Garfield, followed by Indiana with twenty-nine votes. Next came Iowa, which had voted for Blaine on every ballot, with its full twenty-two votes for Garfield. When Maine was reached it voted for Garfield. This settled the question. Blaine was out of the field, and Garfield was speedily nominated. Vermont, Edmunds' state, gave a solid vote for Garfield.

At this point the people could no longer be controlled. The breeze had grown into a storm of enthusiasm. Delegates crowded around Garfield; the people in the galleries, ignoring the lines that had divided them, cheered and waved their hats and handkerchiefs. In this 10,000 people were engaged. It was taken up by almost as many people on the outside, where cannon were also discharged. The scene was one that will not soon be forgotten by those who were present. Republicans, without regard to previous differences, felt and acted as if a great and crushing weight had been removed, and as if they had safely emerged from an impending danger—a danger that threatened the very existence of the party. The result was read out as follows: Whole number of votes, 755; necessary to a choice, 378; Grant, 306; Blaine, 42; Sherman, 3; Washburne, 5; Garfield, 399. There was immense cheering, and the chairman found it difficult to restore order. But order being secured, he said: "*James A. Garfield is nominated for President of the United States.*" In the midst of all this, Garfield sat deeply moved. He was overwhelmed. Loud calls of "Platform" and "Speech" were unheard by him, and he sat silently in the heart of the hurricane which had caught him up. As soon as a hearing could be obtained, Mr Conkling arose, and after a few remarks on the subject of unity and harmony, and in praise of the nominee, moved that the nomination be made unanimous. This motion was seconded, with warm pledges of support, by several distinguished gentlemen, previous leaders of factions, now leaders of a united and satisfied political party. At half past two o'clock the convention adjourned to meet again at seven in the evening. In view of the fact that the man nominated for the second place on the national ticket was, in fact, to become a future President, it may be well to give this closing session a passing notice.

As we have already seen, indications were not wanting that Garfield's name might possibly be brought before the convention as a candidate; but he did not share the confidence of his friends. Whenever the matter was suggested as a possibility, Garfield always expressed a desire to round out his legislative career in the United States Senate. Colonel Rockwell contributes the following little incident: "Whenever I referred to the probability or possibility of his nomination, while he looked forward with an honest ambition to the highest honor to be conferred by his fellow citizens, he would say, 'Not yet; I must make my record in the senate.' I shall not soon forget my last interview with him in his library, before his departure for Chicago. While he was fully alive to the important result of the great convention, and his first thoughts were in the direction of the welfare of his party and the country, with the spirit of the gladiator he longed for the conflict of debate. Rising from his chair, he said, slowly and musingly, 'Well, I will go to Chicago!' Then, drawing himself up, he added, 'And if any one attempts to bulldoze that convention, I propose measuring lances with him!'"

When the time of re-assembling came, business was begun at once. The principal names presented for Vice-President were, Elihu B. Washburne, of Illinois; Marshall Jewell, of Connecticut; and Chester A. Arthur, of New York. On the first and only ballot the New York gentleman received 468 votes to 288 for all others. A vote to make the nomination unanimous carried with a good will, and Garfield and Arthur were at last before the country on their records and their characters, both to be approved and both to be elected.

"On the day of the general's nomination for President, at about the very moment of absolute time (as the Signal Service Bureau would say) that the nomination was made, allowing for the difference in longitude between Washington and Chicago, a magnificent bald eagle, after circling round the park, swooped down and rested on the general's house. Before the eagle rose from its strange perch a dozen people noticed and commented upon it. An old Roman would have seen in this an augury of the most inspiring character. But we Americans are free from superstitions, and so it was a mere 'coincidence.'" Yet, as a coincidence, a most inspiriting one.

CHAPTER XX.

ELECTED AND INAUGURATED AS PRESIDENT.

Nor fame I slight, nor for her favors call;
She comes unlook'd for, if she comes at all.

—POPE.

Though he in all the people's eyes seem'd great,
Yet greater he appeared in his retreat.

—SIR J. DENHAM.

In an incredibly short time after Garfield had been declared the choice of the great convention, the news had spread like wild-fire. The telegraph bore it to every state. In every city, from the Atlantic to the Pacific, the news was being read, and as the entire people realized that the Chicago nominee was one in which the nation trusted, satisfaction was expressed. Garfield had not left the Exposition building ere congratulatory dispatches began pouring in from every quarter, and from politicians and prominent men of all creeds and beliefs. In leaving the hall, an immense crowd surrounded him. He was finally permitted to be seated in a carriage, but the people attempted to unhitch the horses and haul him to his hotel themselves. The driver, not understanding the nature of the demonstration, endeavored to urge his horses forward. This, with great difficulty, he was permitted to do.

At the Grand Pacific hotel an ovation was tendered him, but being deeply moved, he declined saying anything more than expressing his thanks. During the evening more than six hundred telegrams expressing congratulations were received. Among these were expressions from President Hayes, John Sherman, and James G. Blaine. When General Grant received the news, he said, "It is all right; I am satisfied."

It had been announced that he would leave Chicago for home at five o'clock P. M., and General Butterworth was assigned the duty of providing a procession to accompany him to the station. Wisconsin, the first state to break for him, volunteered cheerfully, and the thousands of Ohioans in town were no less ready. A band was provided, and everything was prepared, when the general decided to stay until morning. In order to avoid the press of congratulations, he engaged parlors on another corridor, the knowledge of which was confined to a few. The Wisconsin delegates, however, became apprised of it, and soon a throng, hundreds strong, was marching through the rooms for the purpose of shaking hands with the distinguished man who was the centre of all interest. One of the Ohio men came up wearing the red badge, which had already been struck off, bearing the words, "For President, James A. Garfield." The wearer called the attention of the owner of the name. "That reminds me of a saying of Holmes," the general said. "He wrote that three things require age—wine, meerschaum pipes and poetry. That badge might be added to the list. It's too new yet. I can't realize it." When asked if he would respond to the demands that were already coming in for a speech, he said, "There is not power enough in Chicago to draw a speech out of me to-day."

In the evening, after the second place on the ticket had been filled, in deference to the wishes of many delegates, the general held a reception. A magnificent stand of flowers was upon the table, and beside this the nominee stood for an hour. The stream of congratulations was incessant, many ladies in elaborate evening toilette adding brilliancy to the event, and vieing with the men in the fervor of their declarations of satisfaction. In accepting the congratulations, the general bore himself with quiet dignity, seldom extending his replies beyond the hope that the nomination might prove acceptable to the Republican party and the country. Later a serenade was tendered him, for which he merely bowed his thanks. Near midnight, Senator Hoar, at the head of the committee appointed to notify General Garfield, appeared at the Grand Pacific, and notifying the general of his nomination, received the following reply:

"MR. CHAIRMAN AND GENTLEMEN: I assure you that the information you have officially given to me brings the sense of very grave responsibility, and especially so in view of the fact that I was a member of your body—a fact that could not have existed with propriety had I had the slightest expectation that my name would be connected with the nomination for the office. I have felt, with you, great solicitude concerning the situation of our party during the struggle; but believing that you are correct in assuring me that substantial unity has been reached in the conclusion, it gives me a gratification far greater than any personal pleasure your announcement can bring. I accept the trust committed to my hands. As to the work of our party, and as to the character of the campaign to be entered upon, I will take an early occasion to reply more fully than I can properly do to-night. I thank you for the assurances of confidence and esteem you have presented to me, and hope we shall see our future as promising as are indications to-night."

The next morning General Garfield left Chicago for his home at Mentor. Along the entire route popular demonstrations were made. Seldom are men permitted to return home under similar circumstances. The eyes of the nation were upon him. A great concourse of people followed him to the depot. A special car carried him, and with him were a multitude of distinguished friends. At Cleveland there was an immense demonstration. The spacious depot was crowded with an enthusiastic throng that burst out with far-resounding cheers as the general's train came in. The city was all in a flutter, and it became evident that *the people* were up and stirring. The great Ohioan was driven to a hotel, and in response to a speech of welcome, said:

FELLOW CITIZENS OF MY NATIVE COUNTY AND OF MY STATE: I thank you for this remarkable demonstration of your good-will and enthusiasm on this occasion. I can not at this time proceed upon any speech. All that I have to say is, that I know that all this demonstration means your gladness at the unity and harmony and good-feeling of a great political party, and in part your good feeling toward a neighbor and old friend. For all of these reasons I thank you, and bid you good night.

The following day, the 10th of June, was passed at Cleveland, and on the morrow General Garfield visited his old school at Hiram. The commencement exercises were set for that day, and the distinguished nominee was under promise to speak. Here were gathered his old friends and neighbors. Here he first met his wife since the nomination. She, with the boys, was now a part of her husband's audience. What fond recollections crowded around him now! Here the very inspiration to greatness and power had come to him. As he approached the college grounds the students came out in a body to greet him. His address to the vast audience was full of tenderness. One passage is particularly striking:

If the Superior Being of the universe would look down upon the world to find the most interesting object, it would be the unfinished, unformed character of the young man or young woman. Those behind me have probably in the main settled this question. Those who have passed into middle manhood and middle womanhood are about what they shall always be, and there is but little left of interest, as their characters are all developed.

After a few days of rest at his winter home, General Garfield journeyed on to Washington, and everywhere along the route he was received with enthusiasm. General Garfield continued acting in the capacity of congressman until Congress adjourned. The night after he arrived he was serenaded at his hotel, and the response to the cheers which his presence evoked from the crowd, was one of his most happy speeches:

FELLOW CITIZENS: While I have looked upon this great array, I believe I have gotten a new idea of the majesty of the American people. When I reflect that wherever you find sovereign power, every reverent heart on this earth bows before it, and when I remember that here for a hundred years we have denied the sovereignty of any man, and in place of it we have asserted the sovereignty of all in place of one, I see before me so vast a concourse that it is easy for me to imagine that the rest of the American people are gathered here to-night, and if they were all here, every man would stand uncovered, all in unsandled feet in presence of the majesty of the only sovereign power in this government under Almighty God. [Cheers.] And, therefore, to this great audience I pay the respectful homage that in part belongs to the sovereignty of the people. I thank you for this great and glorious demonstration. I am not, for one moment, misled into believing that it refers to so poor a thing as any one of our number. I know it means your reverence for your government, your reverence for its laws, your reverence for its institutions, and your compliment to one who is placed for a moment in relations to you of peculiar importance. For all these reasons I thank you.

The following night a grand banquet was tendered him. Then, after a brief stay at Washington, he returned to Mentor, hoping to enjoy a respite from the excitements of the hour. But there was little hope of rest for one who by the will of millions had thus been whirled into the blazing focus of expectation. On July 3d, he delivered an address at Painesville, Ohio, at the dedication of the soldiers' monument. His address created great enthusiasm, especially among the veteran soldiers. General Garfield said:

FELLOW CITIZENS: I cannot fail to respond on such an occasion, in sight of such a monument to such a cause, sustained by such men. [Applause and cheers.] While I have listened to what my friend has said, two questions have been sweeping through my heart. One was, "What does the monument mean?" and the other, "What will the monument teach?" Let me try and ask you for a moment to help me answer, "What does the monument mean?" Oh! the monument means a world of memories, a world of deeds, a world of tears, and a world of glories. You know, thousands know, what it is to offer up your life to the country, and that is no small thing, as every soldier knows. Let me put the question to you: For a moment suppose your country in the awfully embodied form of majestic law, should stand above you and say: "I want your life. Come up here on the platform and offer it." How many would walk up before that majestic presence and say, "Here I am; take this life and use it for your great needs." [Applause.] And yet almost two millions of men made that answer [applause], and a monument stands yonder to commemorate their answer. That is one of its meanings. But, my friends, let me try you a little further. To give up life is much, for it is to give up wife, and home, and child, and ambition. But let me test you this way further. Suppose this awfully majestic form should call out to you and say, "I ask you to give up health and drag yourself, not dead, but half alive, through a miserable existence for long years, until you perish and die in your crippled and hopeless condition. I ask you to volunteer to do that," and it calls for a higher reach of patriotism and self-sacrifice; but hundreds of thousands of you soldiers did that. That is what the monument means also. But let me ask you to go one step further. Suppose your country should say, "Come here, on this platform, and in my name, and for my sake, consent to be idiots. [Voice—Hear, hear.] Consent that your very brain and intellect shall be broken down into hopeless idiocy for my sake." How many could be found to make that venture? And yet there are thousands, and that with their eyes wide open to the horrible consequences, obeyed that call.

* * * * * * * *

Now, what does it teach? What will it teach? Why, I remember the story of one of the old conquerors of Greece, who, when he had traveled in his boyhood over the battle-fields where Miltiades had won victories and set up trophies, returning he said, "These trophies of Miltiades will never let me sleep." Why, something had taught him from the chiseled stone a lesson that he could never forget, and, fellow-citizens, that silent sentinel, that crowned granite column will look down upon the boys that will walk these streets for generations to come, and will not let them sleep when their country calls them. [Applause.] More than the bugler on the field from his dead lips will go out a call that the children of Lake county will hear after the grave has covered us all and our immediate children. That is the teaching of your monument.

To go back somewhat in point of time, we will enter the National House of Representatives, and see what was the expression and sentiment upon the announcement of Garfield's nomination. The House was in session, and as soon as the news was announced, business was suspended for a time, and Democrats and Republicans alike, could not but congratulate the party and the country upon the happy result. Business having been resumed, and the roll-call being under way while a vote was being taken on some public measure, as soon as the name of Garfield was reached it was the signal of great cheering.

At Williams college, as soon as the announcement was made, a Garfield club was formed. The excited students knew no bounds to their applause. But a little over a quarter of a century before, Garfield had first entered Williams. Then he was unknown to fame; now the world hailed his nomination to the Presidency with warm admiration.

It was during this period that an incident occurred, which, in the light of history, is of considerable interest. A prominent gentleman of Cleveland had been so greatly impressed with the circumstantial details of an organized plan for the assassination of General Garfield, that he had driven out to Mentor, by night, to acquaint him with the facts. As the result of the interview, it was arranged that the man who had made known the existence of the alleged plot should visit the general the next day, that he might examine and cross-question him. Pending his arival, General Swaim and Colonel Rockwell were made acquainted with the case, and were advised to watch the manner and bearing of the man, with a view to the detection of indications of insanity. In the course of the conversation the probability of the story and the necessity of action were discussed. Finally, after musing awhile, Garfield said, somewhat sadly and impressively, "Well, if assassination is to play its part in the campaign, and I must be the sacrifice, perhaps it is best. I think I am ready." The examination of the following day disclosed enough of mental wryness in the informer to prove that the plot was an hallucination, and the subject was dropped.

The next most important public utterance of General Garfield, is his letter of acceptance. This he sent on July 12th, having been so incessantly busy since the 8th of June, when he was nominated, that he had been unable to finish it sooner. This was one of the most sterling pronunciamentos of Republican doctrines and beliefs that modern politics have produced. This document expressed a cordial endorsement of the platform that had been adopted by the convention. Throughout, it was a masterly presentation of the Republican principles. As soon as the Cincinnati convention was over, and the standard-bearer of the Democracy was announced in Major-General Winfield S. Hancock, the contest was fairly on. The Democratic candidate was a strong man. He had been a distinguished officer in the war, and the result of the election became a matter of great concern. The platforms of the two parties had both been made with a view to political advantage rather than to uphold any distinctive principles.

In a modified form the old questions of the war were revived and paraded. During the time these great movements in political circles were taking place, General Garfield remained during the greater part of the time at his home in Mentor. Several public addresses were made, but in the main, his activities were less in the line of public speaking during this period than ever before. He had declared as false, the idea that a candidate for high office should remain silent. He believed that he could talk and still maintain the serious dignity which the majority of his predecessors in nomination had seen fit to exercise. And he was right. Fully ten thousand persons were in attendance upon the dedication exercises of a soldiers' monument, at Geneva, Ohio, on the 3d of August, when General Garfield spoke. Soon after this he went to New York, to confer with the principal Republicans there, concerning the campaign.

It will be remembered that as soon as the result was announced declaring General Garfield the Republican nominee, Senators Conkling, Logan and others had pledged their hearty support during the progress of the campaign. But these men held back, sulking in their tents. Mr. Blaine went earnestly to work, Mr. Sherman set just as good an example, and, with a will, the rank and file took up the march. Mr. Conkling was not, however, seen or heard. With an impertinence born of disgust and defeat, he held aloof, while his friends urged upon General Garfield the necessity and propriety of calling on him, and so enlisting his services. This advice General Garfield wisely disregarded. While he saw the want of dignity and the loss of prestige, in his making the first advances to Senator Conkling, he by no means underestimated the value in the election of the State of New York, which was thought by a heedless few to be in the power of Mr. Conkling to give or withhold. Mr. Garfield, seizing the situation, boldly determined to capture the State by going among its voters and talking to them. The wisdom of this was almost immediately apparent.

The Conference which he attended was one of the most notable political gatherings ever held in the country. Men of high repute in politics from all parts attended. Never before had so many gentlemen distinguished in the annals of the country been brought together on a notice so informal.

Garfield participated in these counsels of his friends. At the conclusion of the conference a great public demonstration was held in the city. Its character and enthusiasm was unmistakable. Garfield and his friends now started on their return. Everywhere they were received with the greatest ovations. Cheering, speech-making, fire-works and cannon were heard at every stop of the train. Generals Garfield and Hancock the rival candidates had been invited to spend the Sabbath at Lake Chautauqua, the guests of the Assembly. General Garfield accepted the invitation, and the following Sunday after leaving New York, was spent at this place. The Chautauqua salute was extended him, and although no popular demonstration, such as is ordinarily seen on political occasions, was permitted, it was not difficult to see that deep down in the hearts of the vast multitudes assembled to see the great man, there was the deepest love and reverence for him. And when Monday came, the people arose bright and early, and as the first rays of the sun were reaching up in the heavens, Garfield was introduced to the Chautauquans and delivered a spirited address on "Leisure."

Several addresses delivered at the re-unions of his comrades-in-arms, during the month of August, only served to increase the enthusiasm in his behalf among the soldiers. Here in the midst of a great campaign, when our hero's name was known to every tongue in the land, when his election was the earnest of one of the greatest parties of history, we pause. We have watched the unfolding of a career, than which there is none grander and purer. The race to pre-eminence has been a steady one. No man is born great, but only wins greatness by his own individual endeavors. It is strikingly true that success is a growth and expansion. Planted in Garfield's nature at birth were the germs which under proper culture would make the man of power and greatness. These could only be brought to their full fruition by culture and guidance. The most beautiful plant of which any herbarium can boast, owes its beauty of form, leaf and blossom to its proper culture, next only to its individuality of seed, and yet we admire the plant for what it really is, and do not estimate it by the fact that sunshine, rain and all favorable conditions were present during its growth. So with man. Each individual after all, is what he makes of himself; and if the man is great we admire him because he chose to be great.

But we shall leave Garfield so far as his further career during the campaign is concerned. His life thus far is a grand one; and furnishes us with a noble and powerful example to the young men of the country.

The campaign was hotly contested thereafter. As the time to autumn elections grew shorter, the boasts of victory that always fill the air in days of political excitement, grew more and more extravagant. For in several of the State elections the Republicans were defeated overwhelmingly. The famous Morey letter, which for a time seemingly estranged many of the laboring class from the Republican leader, brought a new issue into the struggle. It was seen that its almost certain effect would be to lose General Garfield the electoral votes of the Pacific States; for the settled sentiment of those States against Chinese immigration and the consequent competition of that people with American free labor, was known to be so pronounced as to make it sure that no party discipline could hold them in allegiance to a candidate who squinted at favoring the Celestials. Garfield denounced the letter written by the so-called Morey, as a bold forgery, both in its language and sentiment. The question of veracity as between Garfield and Morey was at once raised, and it did not take the American people long to decide between them. In the investigation which followed it was found that no such person lived at or near Lynn, Massachusetts, his advertised whereabouts, and that no association such as Morey pretended to represent, ever existed there. The matter was carried into court, but after the real writer of the letter was found, and the intent to libel General Garfield, and injure his prospects for election to the Presidency, were established almost beyond a peradventure, the case was dismissed. The result of the whole matter was a re-action in Garfield's favor.

As the campaign neared the time of election it was decided by the Republican leaders that every power should be centred on the tariff question. On this question, as on all others of broad statesmanship, Garfield had a splendid record. This suggestion was adopted by General Garfield, and thereafter the whole burden of the fight fell upon Protection and Free Trade. On this issue the fight was maintained to the end. In Indiana it had a particularly salutary effect, and from the moment this change was decided on, the Republican prospects brightened. It is needless to recount here how the battle waged. The Republicans won and won handsomely in both the pivotal States.

On the 2d of November was held the Presidential election. The result had been foreseen. The Democracy could not stem the tide. The "Solid South," the unfortunate plank in the platform declaring in favor of a "tariff for revenue only," and the Morey forgery which had been charged up to their account, wrought their ruin. Garfield was overwhelmingly elected. The morning of the 3d revealed the general outline of the result. For a few days it was claimed by the Republicans that they had carried two or three of the Southern States, but this idea was soon dispelled. In a like unprofitable way, the Democrats set up certain and sundry claims for some of the Northern States. One day they had carried New York; another day they had authentic information that California and Oregon were safe for Hancock. It was all in vain. The South all went Democratic, and all of the Northern States, except Nevada and one electoral vote from California, had been secured by the Republicans. The victory was unequivocal. The humble boy of Mother Garfield was elected President of the United States by 214 electoral votes against 155 for his antagonist, General Hancock. Thus under the benign institutions of our country, was conferred upon one who began his life in a log cabin the highest civic honor known among the nations of the earth.

General Garfield spent election day at home without manifest excitement. In the evening, and later in the night, news began to arrive indicative of the result. Still no agitation. To some friends he said: "I have been busying myself with a calculation to determine the rate of voting to-day. During the hours in which the election has been in progress about two thousand ballots have dropped for every tick of the pendulum." With the morning light there was no longer doubt. The title of General, won on the bloody field of Chickamauga, had given place to that of President-elect, won before the grandest bar of public opinion under the circle of the sun. On the day following the election a delegation of professors and students from Oberlin College went to Mentor to extend their congratulations. The meeting was a happy one and General Garfield, now President-elect, addressed them in an appropriate and happy manner. The closing sentence was as follows: "Whatever the significance of yesterday's event may be, it will be all the more significant for being immediately indorsed by the scholarship and culture of my State."

At this time Garfield was situated as probably no other man ever was in American history. He was United States Representative, Senator-elect of the State of Ohio, and President-elect of the United States.

Towards the latter part of November, General Garfield, accompanied by his wife and Hon. Amos Townsend, repaired to Washington, where business matters demanded his attention. In accordance with the general's request, no public demonstration was attempted, and very little conversation of a political character permitted. He remained in Washington three days, and then returned to his home. During December the Presidential electors of the State of Ohio visited the home of Garfield to pay him their respects and tender their well wishes. The remarks he made on this occasion were full of meaning and feeling:

When that omnipotent sovereign, the American people, speaks to any one man and orders him to do a duty, that man is under the most solemn obligations of obedience which can be conceived, except what the God of the universe might impose upon him. Yesterday, through your votes, and the votes of others in the various States of the Union, it is probable (the returns will show) that our great political sovereign has laid his commands upon me. If he has done so, I am as bound by his will and his great inspiration and purpose as I could be bound by any consideration that this earth can impose upon any human being. In that presence, therefore, I stand and am awed by the majesty and authority of such a command.

A general hand-shaking followed, during which General Garfield introduced his aged mother. Two days afterward there was another assembly of visitors at Mentor. These were colored Republicans from South Corolina. It was a propitious gathering, and General Garfield showed them every attention possible. Addressing them Garfield gave them every assurance that during his administration the colored man should be assisted in "building up the race from the foundation into the solidity of intelligence and industry, and upon these bases at last to see all the rights of the black man recognized." During the month of December his life was passed in comparative quiet at his home. No doubt in these December days the vision of his boyhood rose many times to view. No doubt, in the silence of the winter evening, by his glowing hearth at Lawnfield, with the wife of his youth by his side, and the children of their love around them, and the certain Presidency of the Republic just beyond, he realized in as full measure as falls to the lot of man that strange thing which is called success. As the winter wore away and premonitions of the approach of spring became more noticeable, the stream of visitors waxed greater and more virulent. The daily mail grew to an enormous size, and one private secretary was kept busy filing applications for office, which became so persistent as to be very annoying. All sorts of devices were adopted to reach the President's attention. Some of the more hungry ones appealed to the general's gentle wife, or to his mother, in a vain hope that they would interest themselves in behalf of the applicants. All applications were filed and not replied to.

On the 16th of February, Senator Conkling arrived at Mentor. In the eyes of the political world, this visit was of the greatest consequence. It was said that the haughty stalwart leader was on a mission looking to the construction of the new administration, to seek favor for his friends, and to pledge therefor the support—hitherto somewhat doubted—of himself and his partisans. A few days later the President-elect made his departure for Washington to be inaugurated. The special train which was to bear himself and family away, left Mentor on the 28th of February. Fully three thousand people were gathered at the depot. Cheer after cheer was given in honor of him who had made the name of Mentor forever famous. The journey to the capital was one prolonged ovation. Mr. Garfield's speeches at the few stopping places along the road, were all that could be desired. They were frank, unpremeditated utterances of a man who feels both the honors and responsibilities of his new place, and who responds in a candid way to the popular regard. This regard was spontaneously shown, and every one believed he was about to begin for the country a most brilliant administration, that should even astonish his friends. For his abilities were of that high order which adapt themselves easily to new situations. The man who turned from teaching to soldiering, and from soldiering to legislation, and made his mark in all these, was not likely to be at a loss when called as President.

No one who was present in the Nation's capital, March 4, 1881, can ever forget the occasion and vast assemblage. The day opened dark and gloomy. The snow that had fallen for several days previous, lay loosely on the ground. About the Capitol and all down Pennsylvania avenue as far as the White House, a surging, anxious crowd had assembled long before the hour for the party to move to the Capitol building for the inauguration ceremony. Long and loud cheers arose from every side as the long procession, escorting the President-elect, passed on to the Capitol. The buildings along the whole route were beautifully decorated, and handkerchiefs fluttered from every window. President Hayes and President-elect Garfield, rode in an open barouche, drawn by four horses. The First Cleveland Troop, splendidly equipped and drilled, marched before, as a guard of honor. Garfield looked weary. He remarked during the morning that the preceding week had been the most trying of his life. The effect of sleepless nights and deep anxiety was plainly visible on his countenance. When the Capitol was reached, President-elect Garfield took his seat on the platform, President Hayes being seated at his right, and Chief Justice Waite on his left. Mr. Wheeler and Vice President-elect Arthur were seated just behind. Prominent also among the distinguished personages on the platform, before which stood the vast audience on that bleak March day, were President Garfield's wife and little daughter and his aged and white-haired mother. At about a quarter of one o'clock General Garfield arose from the historic chair said to have been occupied by Washington at the first inauguration, and took from his pocket a roll of manuscript tied at the corners with a blue ribbon. Having been introduced by Senator Pendleton, Garfield proceeded to read his inaugural address. In a clear, strong voice he continued reading for half an hour, being frequently applauded by the audience. Before the address was completed, the clouds had completely cleared away, and the sun shone upon the glistening bayonets and gay uniforms, and sparkled upon the snow beyond. At its close Garfield turned toward the Chief Justice, who advanced and administered the oath of office, the Clerk of the Supreme Court holding a beautifully-bound Bible, upon which the oath was taken. Then occurred as impressive an episode as was ever seen in official life. After the new President had been congratulated by ex-President Hayes and Chief Justice Waite, who stood next to him, he turned around, took his aged mother by the hand and kissed her. The old lady's cup of happiness at this moment seemed full and running over. It is quite safe to say that nobody, not even Garfield himself, felt more enjoyment at the spectacle of his elevation than this woman whose mind ranged from the days of his obscure and poverty-stricken boyhood to his present elevation, and nobody witnessed the sight but rejoiced at her happiness.

Garfield next kissed his wife, and speedily found the grasp of his hand sought by everybody within reach, from Vice-President down through congressmen to the unknown strangers who could manage to push within reaching distance.

These exercises over, the Presidential party, with considerable difficulty, withdrew, and, driving to the White House, took positions on a stand erected for the purpose in front of the building, and from this point reviewed the procession. For two long hours the procession continued moving past this point. This over, the President repaired to the East Room of the Executive Mansion to receive the alumni of Williams College. About fifty of his old collegians met him, and through Mark Hopkins, ex-president of the college, they expressed the congratulations of that brotherhood.

Perhaps no better illustration of General Garfield's mighty endurance and capacity for work can be given than that contained in the history of the third and fourth of March. The third was passed in a continuous round of receptions of friends, and the important conferences relating to his Cabinet; the close of the day bringing unwonted weariness, only to be followed by a banquet at the White House, and the reunion of his classmates. Returning late to his hotel, some time after midnight he re-drafted nearly three fourths of his Inaugural address; his faithful and devoted Secretary, Mr. Brown, assisting him in his toil. The rough sheets of this important paper bear testimony to his indomitable perseverance and will, and his fastidious and scholarly tastes. These manuscripts are voluminous, and exhibit in a remarkable way his habits of thought and work, his fund of knowledge, and his versatility and reach in the handling of the great problems of statesmanship. There are no less than a half dozen separate and distinct drafts of the address in whole or in part, each profusely adorned with notes, interlineations, and marginalia. The mass of rejected material is valuable and suggestive, and, if appropriately arranged, would make a paper of no small worth and proportion. When, at the reading of one of these tentative drafts to Colonel Rockwell, in February last, he had expressed to him his desire to possess it, he exclaimed, in his characteristic and original way: "What! you would not wish the staggerings of my mind, would you?"

The festivities of March 4th ended at night with a magnificent display of fireworks, a great inaugural ball in the museum building, and numerous receptions at the houses of the most distinguished residents at the Capital.

CHAPTER XXI.

ASSASSINATION OF THE PRESIDENT.

The great Republic's foremost son
Struck foully falls; but they who mourn
Brave life cut short, good work half done,
Yet trust that from beyond death's bourne
That blameless memory's gift may be
Peace, Concord, Civic Purity.

—LONDON PUNCH.

Long before President Garfield was inaugurated, speculations of all kinds were made concerning the composition of the new Cabinet. The visit of Conkling and Grant at Lawnfield was regarded by the country as significant. It was expected that the new President would appoint such a body of advisers as that not only the sectional feelings of the country would be destroyed, but that the various factions of the Republican party itself would be harmonized. It was known that Garfield desired reconciliation in every particular, but to accomplish this in the appointment of seven principal advisers, who would be acceptable to the great mass of intelligent voters, was no easy task. Garfield listened to suggestions, and remained very reticent during the interregnum between his election and inauguration. Newspaper men could not wrest the secret from Garfield's mind. Surmises were made, and a hundred different cabinets formed for the President; but still, nothing definite with reference to Garfield's intentions could be learned. On the fifth day of March, following the inauguration, the anxious Nation read the announcement of the Cabinet as proposed for confirmation. These were unanimously confirmed; and were: Secretary of State, James G. Blaine, of Maine; Secretary of the Treasury, William Windom, of Minnesota; Secretary of War, Robert T. Lincoln, of Illinois; Secretary of the Navy, William H. Hunt, of Louisiana; Secretary of the Interior, S. J. Kirkwood, of Iowa; Attorney-General, Wayne MacVeagh, of Pennsylvania; Postmaster-General, Thomas L. James, of New York.

In the appointment of these men there was every evidence of fairness and good judgment. They were all prominent men of known honesty and integrity, and the American people began settling down to a four years' era of promised peace and prosperity. The inauguration speech was liberal in tone and sentiment, at the same time being radical in all essentials; the Cabinet was trusted, the sign of the times hopeful, and every one felt that an administration of more promise had never dawned. The intensity of the strife during the campaign seemed permanently to have estranged the people, and this estrangement continued without diminution until after the inauguration. Notwithstanding the election practically settled all questions dividing the American people, the ill-nature still lingered, but it was an ill-nature founded upon recollections of the past, and not upon any vital issue of the present. Administration began its work, and trepidation and ill-humor began to take their flight. The President grasped the reins of government with a firm hand; his capacious intellect took in the condition of the country at a glance; his great patriotic soul was impregnated with the lofty conception that he would be the president of fifty millions of people, and of each individual of those millions; his warm Christian heart yearned for the love of the whole country and of every portion thereof; and his mighty genius enabled him so to shape his acts and regulate his conduct as to make the realization of his fondest aspiration an assurance. The country immediately began to breathe freer, confidence rapidly increased, and at the end of the Senate's executive session the President had secured not only the confidence, but the affectionate love of the whole country. From ocean to ocean, from the great lakes to the southern bays, everywhere, east, west, north and south, came one united expression of confidence and good will.

Several days after the inauguration, about fifty ladies representing the National Women's Christian Temperance Union, visited the President and presented a portrait of Mrs. Lucy Webb Hayes, which had been executed by Huntington. Through the influence of Mrs. Hayes, wine had been prohibited from use in the White House during that administration; and to eulogize the spirit and draw from President Garfield an expression of opinion upon the temperance question, the visit had been planned. In responding to the ladies upon receiving the picture, Garfield gave them every assurance that he would do all in his power to abate the evils of intemperance. And he did, for there could not have been a more practical temperance man than President Garfield. Upon this subject it cannot be said that he was radical in the highest sense of that term, but he was practical; and Garfield stands to-day as the embodiment of the highest Christian and temperance sentiment.

At the very outset of his administration, Garfield was confronted with two very formidable questions. First, what should be done with the national debt so rapidly maturing? To adjust this it was first proposed to call an extra session of Congress. But the President discovered, on investigation, that the bonds falling due during the summer could be redeemed without any legislation. After a good deal of consultation and investigation, a plan was matured by Mr. Windom, on suggestions from the President, for the extending of the bonds at a lower rate of interest—three and one half per cent. The plan was acceptable in a high degree to the country, and the loans were paid when due by new bonds, issued at this lower rate, thereby saving the country many millions of dollars. The first great problem was thus most satisfactorily disposed of.

The second problem was much more difficult of adjustment. In brief it was: How could a half million of importunate office-seekers be satisfied, with only a hundred thousand offices which were at the President's power to bestow? The tremendous rush for appointments had so grown during the last twelve years as to amount, when President Garfield assumed office, to almost a revolution. That

WAYNE MCVEAGH,
Attorney-General.

THOMAS L. JAMES,
Postmaster-General.

WILLIAM WINDOM,
Secretary of the Treasury.

JAMES G. BLAINE,
Secretary of State.

WILLIAM H. HUNT,
Secretary of the Navy.

ROBERT T. LINCOLN,
Secretary of War.

S. J. KIRKWOOD,
Secretary of the Interior.

PRESIDENT GARFIELD'S CABINET.

all interests might be harmonized and the good of the country secured, President Garfield set about making such appointments as were manifestly best. Probably no administration ever opened its existence under brighter auspices than that of President Garfield, but it was not long before his great vitality showed visible signs of yielding to the dragging wear of the never ending demands and importunities for place. Each day brought its exhausting physical fatigue and intellectual weariness—the result of a continual din of selfish talk. Fairly staggering into the library at the close of a specially exhausting day, he said to Colonel Rockwell, "I cannot endure this much longer; no man who has passed his prime can succeed me here to wrestle with the people as I have done, without its killing him." Yet through it all he was cheerful. As throughout his life, so even now, his great heart held its accustomed sway; the playful, almost boyish, humor illuminating all. Leaving behind him the stress of work and the cares of his office, he would often say, "Now the fun is over, let us go to business!" referring to some proposed recreation. Colonel Rockwell says: "With two or three friends, I accompanied him to Mr. Chittenden's reception. The conversation naturally drifted to the personal relations of General Garfield to the presidency; its bearing upon his future, and the bright promises for the public good that would come from his administration. The glories of the present were brilliant and attractive enough; but to him the future brought a sobering, saddening prospect. 'Four years hence,' said he, 'I shall leave the presidency, still a young man, with no future before me, to become a political reminiscence—a squeezed lemon, to be thrown away.'"

Senator Conkling, wishing to chastise the men who were instrumental in defeating Grant at Chicago, endeavored to control as much of the Federal patronage as possible. The various prominent Grant leaders, as well as other well known politicians, became visitors at the White House. Toward the latter part of March, Garfield sent to the Senate the names of various gentlemen avowed in their adherence to Grant, for prominent positions in the State of New York. Of course, the country looked upon this as a great victory for Conkling, and it began to be believed that the New York senator would figure as one of the powers behind the throne. But such an opinion was short-lived, for on the following day President Garfield sent the name of William H. Robertson to the Senate for the office of Collector of the Port of New York. This was entirely unexpected. To the Grant forces it was a very objectional appointment; to the country it was altogether acceptable. It should be remembered that Robertson was the leader in the break of the New York delegation at Chicago. Every one predicted an immediate fight between the senator from New York and the President. There seemed to be no help for it. This emphatic declaration of independence on the part of Garfield was a matter of rejoicing all over the country. For it showed at once his determination to be the President of and for the people, untrammeled by any fetters of party or faction. Senator Conkling said that Hayes had never done a thing so terrible. He said that the nomination of Robertson, the most objectionable man possible, without consultation with the senators from New York, or without their being informed of the intention to make a change in the most important office in the State, was a grievous personal and political wrong. He said that the long dispute as to whether a small faction of New York Republicans, or four fifths of the party in the State, as represented by him, were to be treated by the administration as the Republican party of New York, had at last to be settled finally and forever.

The situation was one of intense interest. Popular opinion supported the President, though not a few took the side of Conkling. The latter, together with Platt, the junior New York Senator, resolved to fight the confirmation of Robertson. They believed that, with the Senate evenly balanced, they could, by the help of the Democrats, prevent Robertson's confirmation. It was a battle of giants. Men wondered whether, when war was declared, Garfield would strike back or not. The Stalwarts offered only one way of compromise—the withdrawal of Robertson's nomination. But the President was firm. Efforts were made to induce Robertson to ask the President to withdraw his name in the interest of harmony. But he scouted the idea. The State Senate of New York, of which Robertson was the presiding officer, passed a resolution in support of the Administration. On behalf of the President's action it was claimed, that it was his constitutional right to nominate; that the New York senators overstepped their prerogative in attacking his action; that the office of Collector of the Port was a national office, and not rightfully a part of the local patronage; that the executive should select the man through whose hands passed nine-tenths of the tariff revenues of the country.

There had been a dead-lock of the Senate over the nomination of its officers, and this still continued, and the President was, in consequence, embarrassed by the failure to act on any of the nominations. Finally the Republican Senatorial caucus sent various committees to the President to induce him to withdraw the Robertson nomination. But Garfield was firm. It was then agreed upon, being proposed by Conkling, that all the nominations not opposed by one Senator from the nominee's State were first to be acted upon. By such an arrangement almost every one except Robertson would be admitted. Such a plan could only mean the confirmation of all the unopposed. nominations, including those of Senator Conkling's friends, and then adjourn or prevent a quorum, by absentees, and thus defeat the confirmation of Robertson until the next December. Of course this would have been a Conkling victory. The President asked if certain nominations had been singled out for immediate confirmation and others for vexatious delay. He was told the result of the caucus decision. His reply is reported to have been, "Then I will take my own course. I am determined to learn who are my friends, and such as fail me will hereafter require a letter of introduction." Shortly after the Senate went into executive session, the President's private secretary arrived with a message which fell like a thunder-bolt on that body. The message withdrew the nominations of Senator Conkling's friends. It was a checkmate. The plan of the caucus was foiled. President Garfield assigned as his reason simply that the discrimination which was attempted, in acting on all the nominations from the Stalwart element and refusing to act on the solitary representative of the opposite element, was wrong and unfair. He said that the President's duty was to nominate, and that the Senate's sworn duty was to *confirm* or *reject*. To refuse to do either was surpassing their prerogative.

What would be the next move of the New York senator was eagerly anticipated. He finally announced to the Senate that he had tendered his resignation to the Governor of New York as Senator from that State. Senator T. C. Platt, Conkling's tool, did the same thing. The dead-lock was now broken, and three days afterward Robertson was confirmed almost unanimously as Collector of the New York port.

The fight was now transferred to Albany. Garfield had been vindicated and sustained. Conkling and Platt sought a re-election to rebuke the President. There was a dead-lock in the Assembly of New York; but the sequel of the whole matter is that the haughty and imperious Conkling and his follower Platt were defeated and Eldridge G. Lapham and Warner Miller were elected instead. And thus the disgraceful struggle came to an end, leaving a stain of infamy in those who brought it about and were finally and deservedly defeated.

During these exciting times the President's wife was prostrated on a bed of sickness. The fever held her in a vise-like grip. This was a calamity which no courage, no calm conservatism, no intellectual resources, no popular support, could remedy. Up to this time the President had kept heart bravely, but the mighty shadow which seemed about to darken his life forever, was too much for his great, loving soul. Hurrying away from the crowded office of State, he sought the sufferer, sat by her side hour after hour, denying himself necessary sleep, and nursed her with the most devoted care. Every day the papers told of the critical condition of the President's wife, and it seemed that her death was an assured and grievous calamity. The people's hearts swelled with sympathy for the suffering husband. Day after day the story of his silent watching at the bedside of the wife brought tears unbidden to the eye. But the calamity which seemed impending was turned aside. About the middle of May a change for the better was announced. But it was still a long time until she had sufficiently recovered to remove the care from Garfield. And during all these trials and afflictions how grandly superior had Garfield proved himself to be!

As the weeks passed, Mrs. Garfield grew steadily better. The President was wearied by the arduous duties of the past three months, and needed a vacation. A time or two, in early June, he took his children for an afternoon trip to Mount Vernon. His face grew brighter and his step more elastic. As the struggle at Albany proceeded, the Administration steadily rose in public esteem, until the admiration of the people knew no bounds. The President paid especial attention to his Departments. The Star Route cases were pushed with tremendous vigor. Irregularities in the Treasury and Naval Departments were dealt with most heroically. Altogether the sky was clear, and men looked forward to the future with confidence. Mrs. Garfield's health being still precarious, the question of where to spend the summer was carefully and thoughtfully discussed.

On the 19th of June, the President and Mrs. Garfield, accompanied by several of their children and intimate friends left the Capital for Long Branch. June 27th, Garfield returned to Washington to attend a Cabinet meeting. The session was a long and interesting one. The whole situation and administration policy was reviewed. Then the President and his advisers separated for the summer, extending to each the wishes for happiness. It had been arranged previously that Garfield should rejoin his family at Long Branch, and then go with them on a trip of pleasure, to include a visit to old Williams College, to attend the commencement exercises. "Man proposes but God disposes." Little did President Garfield, little did the Cabinet, little did the country and the world think that Garfield had presided at his last Cabinet meeting then, and that the Nation would be plunged in such overwhelming grief so soon. It was a time of general laxity not only throughout the country, but at the seat of Government. The Senate had adjourned; the exciting times at Albany were over, and everyone was seeking rest for the summer. Thus far President Garfield's life at the White House had been any thing but happy. The reason has already been learned. Office seekers had infested the Capital in hoards.

The American people will not soon forget the news carried by the telegraph on Saturday morning, July 2nd, 1881. The day had opened rather warm. People gathered at their respective places of business and labor. At the White House that morning the President was early astir. He had many matters that needed attention before he left the city, which he intended to do on an early train. His son Harry, quite a young athlete, came into his father's room and deftly turned a hand-spring across the bed. "Don't you wish you could do that?" asked the boy. "Well, I think I can," replied the President, and with a moment's consideration he was on his hands and over the bed, in a fashion almost as neat as that of his son.

Several members of the Cabinet, headed by Secretary Blaine, were to accompany him to Long Branch. A few ladies, personal friends of the President's family and one of his sons, were of the company; and as the hour for departure drew near, they gathered at the depot of the Baltimore and Potomac Railway to await the train. The President and Secretary Blaine were somewhat later than the rest. On the way to the depot the Chief Magistrate, always buoyant and hopeful, was more than usually joyous, expressing his keen gratification that the relations between himself and the members of his Cabinet were so harmonious, and that the Administration was a unit.

For sometime previous, as subsequent events have demonstrated, an assassin was dogging the President about the streets of Washington. Having decided not to kill Garfield at the church, and being deterred at the depot on the 18th of June, according to his own confession, by the sad, weak, and frail appearance of Mrs. Garfield, triumph was his at last on the fatal 2d of July. Upon arriving at the depot the President and Secretary Blaine were informed that the train was not due yet for several minutes, and they remained in the carriage, earnestly talking, until the depot official informed them that the train was ready to start. Arm in arm they passed through the broad entrance-door into the ladies' waiting-room, which gave them the readiest access to the train beyond. The room was almost empty, as most of the passengers had already taken their seats in the cars; but pacing nervously up and down the adjoining rooms, was a thin, wiry-looking man, whose peculiar appearance had once or twice been commented upon by some of the railroad officials. As the President passed through the room, this ill-favored looking man suddenly sprang up behind him, and taking a heavy revolver from his pocket, deliberately aimed and fired at the noble, commanding figure. Secretary Blaine sprang to one side, and the assassin who stood on his right re-cocked his revolver and with the deliberation of death fired at the President again. The President fell to the floor, the blood spurting profusely from a jagged wound in his side.

Almost before the echo of the report had found its way out to the open air, the President was surrounded. A terrible deed had been committed! Assassination for the second time had stricken a Chief Magistrate! For an instant those nearest to him were stupefied. Then ensued a moment of terrible agony and confusion. Secretary Blaine sprang after the assassin, who, finding his way barred in one direction, turned in another only to run into the arms of the law. Seeing he was caught, Mr. Blaine turned again to the wounded man. The assassin gave his name as Charles Jules Guiteau, and begged to be taken safely to jail. He was instantly hurried to police head-quarters and confined; and it was well for him that he was thus out of the way of the angry populace, who would not have hesitated to put an instant and tragic end to his despicable career.

By this time there had gathered about the wounded man a horror-stricken crowd. Secretary Windom, Secretary Hunt, Postmaster-General James and others of the party that had met to accompany the President north, were all in and out of the room sending hither and thither messengers and messages for doctors. The President's own carriage dashed off at a gallop to the White House, to the astonishment of the people on the avenue, who had not yet learned the direful news. A local physician, District Health Officer Dr. Townsend, was the first to arrive of those summoned. He came in breathless, in response to the awful summons, just as a mattress was brought on which to lay the wounded man. The room being uncomfortably crowded with men—in whose eyes stood tears, gathered in the first pause of their terror to offer any, every aid in their power—it was decided to remove the President to the room above. Hardly had the mattress been laid upon the floor, when the wounded man, ever thoughtful of those nearest to him, ever forgetful of self, even while his life blood was oozing from him, turned to his friend and said: "Rockwell, I want you to send a message to 'Crete' (the pet name used for his wife, Lucretia). Tell her I am seriously hurt, how seriously I cannot yet say. I am myself, and hope she will come to me soon. I send my love to her."

The dastardly deed had been done, and the bullets had found a lodgement in the President's body.

CHAPTER XXII.

THE CLOSE OF A GRAND LIFE.

"At rest at last from life's sad toil,
He's gathered in that fold
Where angels sing eternal praise,
For valiant deeds and bold.
The clinging arms that held him dear
Have loosed their loving hold;
The heart that trobb'd in gratitude
Is silent now and cold.
A Nation's hope was granted him,
A Nation's trust and care;
A martyr at his post he fell,
Lost in a cruel snare.
And now a mighty Nation mourns
All that was brave and best;
His earnest, Christian deeds will live
To sanctify his rest."

The shock communicated to the American people by the attempt upon the President's life was felt in every civilized country of the globe. Here in Christian and liberty-loving America such a deed was looked upon as an impossibility in times of peace and prosperity. True, Abraham Lincoln fell by the hands of an assassin; but that was during the exciting times of political and civil war. Then the national pulse beat at fever heat; but there was nothing of this kind to palliate the crime of Guiteau. Lincoln's assassin was a cultured, refined gentleman in the common acceptation of that term; and the bitterness of sectional strife made the deed possible. But the evidence has shown that Guiteau could have had no malice of this kind. The fanatical idea that he was entitled to position because of unimportant services rendered during the campaign which resulted in Garfield's election, only added another to the long list of office seekers that had infested Washington since the opening of the new administration. But this is not the place to moralize. We must continue the narration of the sad story.

Ere the ambulance carrying the wounded President had reached the White House, the members of the Cabinet and several of the President's family had already arrived. Troops were called from the garrison and stationed about the White House. A special train was ordered to carry Mrs. Garfield to her stricken husband. Several eminent physicians had been summoned, and every thing possible was done for the sufferer. Dr. D. W. Bliss was called to the bedside of the wounded President by a message from the Secretary of War. Upon conversing with the President he was given charge of the case, after which the following associate surgeons were engaged: Surgeon-General J. K. Barnes, Drs. J. J. Woodward and Robert Reyburn. Subsequently, Drs. Frank H. Hamilton, of New York, and D. Hayes Agnew, of Philadelphia, were secured as consulting physicians. Excitement was at fever-heat all over the country at the daring deed of assassination. All hoped that it would prove but the unaccountable deed of a madman. The assassin was found to be a mixture of fool and fanatic, who, in his previous career, had managed to build up, on a basis of total depravity, a considerable degree of scholarship. He was a lawyer by profession, and had made a pretense of practicing in several places—more particularly in Chicago. In that city and elsewhere he had made a reputation both malodorous and detestable. In the previous spring, about the time of the inauguration, he had gone to Washington to advance a claim to be consul-general at Paris. He had sought and obtained interviews with both the President and Mr. Blaine, and pretended to believe that the former was on the point of dismissing the present consul at Paris to make a place for himself!

During the first day Mrs. Garfield reached the White House, and set about as nobly as possible to prepare for the long struggle before her wounded husband. Sunday came, and what a Sabbath! Prayer after prayer, petition after petition ascended to the Ruler and Disposer of all things, for the President. The telegraph hourly informed the anxious people of the condition of the sufferer. The dastard deed became the sole topic of conversation.

The President's condition was considered imminently dangerous—so much so that his proper treatment was neglected. From the time the wound was looked at by Dr. Townsend at the depot, until eight at night, it received no effection; for ten hours and a half the surgeons only administered hypodermic injections and stimulants, and did not endeavor to ascertain the true nature of the injury. At eight o'clock in the evening, when the natural consequences of contusion had in a great degree closed the channel of the bullet, an insufficient and unskillful examination was made, from which it was concluded that the missile had entered the body about two inches to the right of the fourth lumbar vertebra, between the tenth and eleventh ribs, had passed through the liver, and could not be traced farther, and that the use of the probe would be improper. It was assumed, not ascertained, that the wound was mortal. In the course of the afternoon Dr. Bliss, the physician in charge, thought that the evidences of internal hemorrhage were distinctly recognizable, and that collapse was imminent. At about seven o'clock he believed the patient was sinking rapidly. At that time the physicians considered the case hopeless.

Messages of condolence and sympathy came from every civilized land. In that eventful hour party was forgotten, and already the dark cloud of sectionalism, which had so long been hanging over our country, and frequently giving every indication of a coming storm, was seen rising, and the rays of hope and cheer for the future took its place. But this did not come at once. The first impulse was of fear, then dread, and then daring determination. Was there a conspiracy in the land, whose tool Guiteau had become? The old Southern soldiers who had fought many a fierce battle under Lee and Johnston, as well as the legionaries who sprang up at the call of Lincoln, burst into tears at the thought of Garfield bleeding!

Three days had Garfield been lying on his bed in the White House, when the National Day of Independence was ushered in. It was a sad Fourth of July. The auspicious opening of a new administration had filled the hearts of the American people with loyalty, and extensive preparations had been made to celebrate the day all over the country with an unusual outburst of patriotism. But on that day the orators spoke only of the President and the assassination; the display and pomp was forgotten, and the day proved to be one of doubt and sorrow. Day after day wore away. From time to time there were signs of improvement, and then again of relapse; rays of hope and shadows of despair alternated. During these anxious days Vice-President Arthur became the cynosure of all eyes. In him was locked the possibilities of the Nation's future, should the assassin's deed result in death.

The summer's heat made the sufferer's condition all the more precarious. Many contrivances and machines were invented and offered to the authorities, the purpose of which was to reduce, by mechanical means, the temperature of the President's apartment. Thus the temperature was brought under control, and the possibility of a change for the better was increased.

One of the marked circumstances attending the tragic event, the course of which is outlined in these pages, was the universal desire of the American people to do something to contribute towards the President's recovery. It would be vain to attempt to enumerate the thousand and one expedients and suggestions which, out of the goodness of the popular heart, came from every direction. Each out of his own nature, added his own gift. The poet contributed his verse; the physician, his cure; the inventor, his contrivance; the gardener, his choicest cluster; and even the crazy beldam, her modicum of witchcraft. From the centre of the crowded city to the remotest corners of the prairie the slightest syllable of indifference to the President's condition would have been instantly resented—first with a look of contempt and then with a blow.

During his sickness, President Garfield was, for the most part, thoroughly conscious. His mind retained its full vigor, and the news of the day, as well as general discussion, interested him none the less than when in the full enjoyment of all his faculties.

Turning to his secretary, about half-past two in the afternoon of the day he was shot, he said, "Blaine, what motive do you think that man could have had in trying to assassinate me?" "Indeed, I do not know, Mr. President. He says he had no motive. He must be insane." "I suppose," came back the answer, with a smile, "he thought it would be a glorious thing to be a pirate king." A little later, James, his own son, sat sobbing by the bed. His father turned to him, and said, "Don't be alarmed, Jimmy, the upper story is all right; it is only the hull that is a little damaged." To Dr. Bliss, he was at times quite jocular, the vein of conversation being of a light character, and keyed so as to encourage his friends and attendants. He informed the doctor that he desired to be kept accurately posted as to his exact condition. "Conceal nothing from me, doctor; for remember, I am not afraid to die."

One of the peculiarities of the President's case was the invariable cheerfulness of the patient. He seemed to regard it as a part of his duty to keep those about him in good spirits, and to aid the physicians in the work of bringing him through. He frequently asked to see the bulletins, and sometimes made humorous remarks about their contents. His food was many times a subject of some jest, and when it did not suit him, he had his revenge by perpetrating some pleasant satire about the offending article, or the cooks who had prepared it. On one occasion the President asked for a drink, whereupon Major Swaim handed him some milk, to which the physicians had added a small quantity of old rum. The President, after drinking it, looked at Major Swaim with a dissatisfied expression, and said, "Swaim, that's a rum dose, isn't it?" On other occasions the sufferer spoke gravely, but always hopefully of his conditions and prospects, expressing the most earnest hopes for speedy and perfect recovery.

The whole Nation was being educated by the affliction. Christianity was gauged by a higher standard than ever before. The calm resignation of Garfield irresistibly drew all classes to him.

It was not long until the President's wound was in full process of suppuration. This became a heavy drain upon his constitutional and reserved forces, and his strength was rapidly depleted. He grew worse—unable to move his body or even his limbs without great exertion. At intervals, moreover, the stomach refused to perform its functions, and there was, in consequence, instant anxiety on the question of keeping life in the President until he *could* get well. The fluid food, upon which only, he was nourished, neither satisfied the longings of nature nor furnished sufficient aliment to sustain the flagging powers of life. Moreover, at this epoch began the great blunder in the President's treatment. Owing to the mistaken diagnosis of the surgeons the course of the ball had been altogether misjudged. According to the theory of the physicians the ball had gone forward and downward. As soon as the wound began to suppurate it was found desirable to insert therein a drainage tube to the end that the discharge might be perfectly free.

Several weeks after the President was shot, the sympathy of the people having taken such deep root, it was proposed that a fund be raised for the support of Mrs. Garfield and family. Cyrus W. Field, of New York, headed the subscription with twenty-five thousand dollars. It had been decided that the fund should be Mrs. Garfield's, without any contingencies. Everybody was invited to subscribe. It is a remarkable fact that, nothwithstanding the favorable indications of recovery on the part of the President, the subscription was rapidly augmented from every part of the country, until, before the President's death, the sum had reached *three hundred thousand dollars!*

When the announcement was made to her, she said, in a voice tremulous with emotion, "If it were only possible for my husband and me to go around and see all those dear people who have been so grateful in their remembrance for us here in late days, I would be so happy; I know he would, too. I want to thank them—to tell them all how kindly I feel toward them for what they have said to me. I never could understand anything about politics, and if I liked a person, it made no difference whether they were Republicans or Democrats; and now I have grown to think that there is not much difference between the two great parties, for one says just as kind words in our present affliction as the other. It makes me feel like forming an opinion as to what I would do were women permitted to vote as well as men. I believe I would get two tickets, fold them together so as to look like one, and drop both in the ballot-box."

On the twenty-second day of Garfield's illness the bulletins sent out by the surgeons in charge, indicated an unfavorable change. Blood poisoning had been feared. The bulletin read: "He had a slight rigor, in consequence of which the dressing of the wound was postponed." The consulting physicians were immediately sent for. Towards noon the President had another chill. These reports spread alarm everywhere, and the excitement of the people was only equalled on the morning when the President was shot. Drs. Hamilton and Agnew soon arrived in Washington. The President continued growing worse. In making examinations of the wound at this time, it was found that the eleventh rib had been fractured. Several operations were performed, and the beneficial effects was at once apparent on the improved condition of the sufferer. On the 29th of July a Cabinet meeting, at which all the members except Attorney-General MacVeagh were present, was held at the White House. Public matters were discussed, and certain routine official business disposed of in the usual way. All this indicated a belief, on the part of the members, that the President was on the road to recovery. There was, however, no marked change in his condition or prospects. He had passed a comfortable night—so said the attendants—and the afternoon fever was less pronounced than on the previous day.

A month and a half of suffering had now worn away, and the main feature of alarm was in the fact that his stomach could not perform its regular functions. In the main matter—that of nourishment—the case was as bad as ever. Neither the city nor the country would have been surprised to hear that the President was dying or dead. The whole question, as matters now stood, was this: How long can he live? He, himself, was conscious, in good measure, of the appalling odds against him, but his calm heroism never wavered for a moment. From the first, he only once—and that but for an instant—gave way to despondency, when he said to his wife that, considering the fact that he was already fifty years old, and that the brief remainder of his life would, perhaps, be weakened—possibly helpless—from his injury, it hardly appeared to be worth the struggle which his friends and himself were making to save it. This thought, however, found but a moment's lodgement; and even now, when his vital forces seemed to be flowing out to the last ebb of despair, he stood up manfully and faced the enemy. His will remained vigorous, and he was cheerful in spirit—this, too, when the very water which was tendered him to refresh his exhausted powers was instantly rejected by the stomach. It was clear that no human vigor could long withstand so dreadful an ordeal; and the physicians recognized and acknowledged the fact that their unnatural system of alimentation was but a makeshift, which would presently end in failure. Inflammation finally set in about the throat. And the trouble in the parotid gland became a source of profound anxiety. An operation for its relief was contemplated. Every one felt that a crisis had come, and that unless the President was promptly relieved, a fatal termination might be expected. As the days of the second month of suffering wore away, the President's condition was critical indeed. The newspapers considered the prospect of death, and the probable changes in the administration. But he still lived, and, amid hope and fear, the people waited. Finally it was decided that the President should be removed from the Capital. Garfield himself, had requested it, and so it was agreed upon that the resort at Long Branch would be the best place to take him.

The finger of hope pointed unmistakably in the direction of Long Branch, and as the morning of September 6th dawned upon the White House, all conditions appeared favorable for the removal of the beloved President beyond the malarial influences of the Capital. Preparations for this event were made. The anxiety of the President to leave Washington had been imparted to all his friends and attendants. Even the physicians were convinced that nothing would bring relief to the sufferer so effectively as the pure bracing salt breezes of the Atlantic, and their opinion increased the confidence and animated the hope of the country.

The condition of the President seemed peculiarly favorable for the journey. He had eaten well on the previous day, and retained his food. He had slept peacefully, and his wound was doing well. The parotid swelling had almost disappeared, and the general conditions were thought to be remarkably good. It was even said that a considerable increase of strength was manifest in his movements, but this was evidently a mistake. The arrangements for the President's removal were complete in every respect. He was tenderly carried from the White House, and placed in a large ambulance, prepared for that purpose. The trip to the depot was full of interesting incidents revealing the deep feeling of reverence and love of the people for the stricken man. The faithful attendants at last placed the emaciated form of Garfield upon the new bed in the car, which had been so arranged that the motion of the train could not be felt. A few sad farewells were said, and the train moved out of Washington, bearing for the last time the living Garfield.

This seven hours' journey of 233 miles is now historical, and its principal features are full of interest. The train came to a stop in a few minutes after leaving the Washington depot, to permit an approaching train to move out of the way on a siding. "What does this mean?" inquired the President. "Only a momentary detention," replied Colonel Rockwell. "But important events are often the issue of a moment," rejoined the sufferer. This is the only conversation he joined in during the trip. The train soon proceeded, gradually increasing its speed where the track was straight enough to permit, to fifty-five miles an hour, and for a few miles after leaving Philadelphia it actually attained a speed of sixty miles an hour. The President was watched very closely during the first hour of the journey, in order to detect any symptom of danger from the excitement of the occasion. To the relief and great satisfaction of the physicians, he seemed actually to enjoy the ride, and to be improving. All along the route the expressions of sadness by the people, marked their love for the fallen man. The grief of the people was too deep for other demonstration. Words failed in expressing it, and tears came unbidden. It was a time for thought and severe discipline.

The lightning train sped onward. A pilot engine preceded it, and its passage was a signal to all approaching trains to get out of the way and remain silent until the convoy had passed. Trains upon side-tracks, wherever they were encountered, were crowded with people, all desirous of obtaining a glimpse of the President, but not obtrusive or demonstrative beyond the overwhelming influence of great sorrow. Their silence was more expressive than language. It indicated the deepest sympathy and the profoundest respect. During that eventful day the prayers of the Nation rose before God that the President might find new life at Elberon. Men and women who had never prayed before, united in petitioning a merciful Providence for the restoration of the President. Business was suspended throughout a majority of the States. The day following the trip to Long Branch, the official bulletin announced no important change in the President's condition. This was discouraging. The sea-breezes did not appear to have the salutary effect so confidently expected. Everybody complained except the President. The sixty-ninth day of illness was a memorable one. The attending physicians announced positively that the President was convalescent, and within a very short time he would be sufficiently recovered to take him anywhere. The news spread over the world. It was received with the greatest joy; but alas! all the doctors were mistaken. Soon, unmistakable evidences of blood poisoning began manifesting themselves. As the last days of life were ebbing away, the President seemed to realize his condition, and once said, "I fear bringing me here will prove a roaring farce after all." His weakness was hourly becoming more apparent. He began sinking beyond the reach of the powerful arm of science and the willing hands of love. The last Sunday of life came, September 18th, and Dr. Bliss finally declared that the President could not last much longer. He had given up the last ray of hope; and the saddened people began to prepare for the inevitable. The worship of that day partook very much of sadness. From the pulpits of the churches was read the hourly bulletins, as fresh information came from Elberon. The day passed, and as the nineteenth of September was ushered in, the President was again prostrated with a hard chill. Evening came and the attendants gave themselves grounds to hope, from the fact that there was not a recurrence of a chill in the evening. During the afternoon the President rested well, and apparently enjoyed the full use of his mental powers. The physicians dressed the wound, and thought that there was a chance of the President's living a week more, even supposing that present conditions were to produce death. The country knew this, and began gradually to see the cloud of death which was hanging over Elberon. Concerning the night of death, General Swaim says:

I was hardly seated when Dr. Boynton came in and felt the President's pulse. I asked him how it seemed to him. He replied: "It is not as strong as it was this afternoon, but very good." I said: "He seems to be doing well." "Yes," he answered, and passed out. He was not in the room more than two minutes. Shortly after this the President awoke. As he turned his head on awakening, I arose and took hold of his hand. I was on the left-hand side of the bed as he lay. I remarked: "You have had a nice, comfortable sleep." He then said, "O Swaim, this terrible pain," placing his right hand on his breast about over the region of the heart. I asked him if I could do anything for him. He said, "Some water." I went to the other side of the room and poured about an ounce and a half of Poland water into a glass and gave it to him to drink. He took the glass in his hand: I raising his head as usual, and drank the water very naturally. I then handed the glass to the colored man, Daniel, who came in during the time I was getting the water. Afterward I took a napkin and wiped his forehead, as he usually perspired on awaking. He then said, "O Swaim, this terrible pain—press your hand on it." I laid my hand on his chest. He then threw both hands up to the sides and about on a line with his head, and exclaimed: "O Swaim, can't you stop this?" And again, "O Swaim!" I then saw him looking at me with a staring expression. I asked him if he was suffering much pain. Receiving no answer, I repeated the question, with like result. I then concluded that he was either dying or was having a severe spasm, and called to Daniel, who was at the door, to tell Dr. Bliss and Mrs. Garfield to come immediately, and glanced at the small clock hanging on the chandelier nearly over the foot of his bed, and saw that it was ten minutes past 10 o'clock. Dr. Bliss came in within two or three minutes. I told Daniel to bring the light. A lighted candle habitually sat behind a screen near the door. When the light shone full on the President's face I saw that he was dying. When Dr. Bliss came in a moment after, I said: "Doctor, have you any stimulants? he seems to be dying." He took hold of the President's wrist, as if feeling for his pulse, and said: "Yes, he is dying." I then said to Daniel: "Run and arouse the house." At that moment Colonel Rockwell came in, when Dr. Bliss said: "Let us rub his limbs," which we did. In a very few moments, Mrs. Garfield came in, and said: "What does this mean?" and a moment afterward exclaimed: "Oh, why am I made to suffer this cruel wrong?" At 10:30 P. M. the sacrifice was complete. He breathed his last, calmly and peaceably.

Within a very few minutes the death-knell was sounding in every city throughout the land. Lights appeared where darkness but a few moments before was seen. The telegraph and newspaper offices were besieged. Extra editions of the prominent papers were issued, and in that dark night of despair the Nation bowed its head in humble submission to the will of Providence. "The President is dead!" was heard from every lip. Ere the morning broke, the news had traveled from ocean to ocean, and from the lakes to the gulf. But it had not stopped there. The silent chambers of the sea hastened the news to the sympathizing nationalities in every part of the globe, until three hundred millions of people mourned the death. Garfield was dead, they said. But no, he still lives. The mortal man may be entombed, and his work ended, but as long as memory sits in silent watches and contemplation over the loved one, he will not be forgotten. Passing away from life only endeared Garfield, and he will ever live in blessed memory.

"No man was better prepared for death," remarked a prominent member of his Cabinet. "No, sir, nor for life, which requires infinitely superior preparation," may be safely responded. The life which he lived required the practice of all the virtues; the crucifixion of all the vices; bravery of the severest type; gentleness, trust, and clear-cut integrity. Practice had perfected in him these rules of life, and for many years he had furnished an example of purity and probity for his fellow-men. This is not taken away with the removal of the body. It can not be taken away. The pages of history will be brightened with it as long as eminent worth remains the goal of human ambition.

On the day before Garfield's death he addressed Colonel Rockwell as follows: "Old boy, do you think my name will have a place in human history?" The colonel answered, "Yes, a grand one, but a grander place in human hearts. Mr. President, you must not talk in that way. You have a great work yet to perform." After a moment's silence he said, sadly and solemnly, "No; my work is done." Numerous coincidences noticed in the life of Garfield had a peculiar influence over the late President during his life. One time when speaking to some friends concerning the similarity of his nomination with that of Lincoln, he said: "The first western man elected to the presidency was Harrison, of Indiana. Lincoln was elected in 1860, and I was elected in 1880." Thinking that they had not noticed the jumps of twenty years, he said, "'40, '60 and '80; what does that mean? Then again," said the President, "look at the part Indiana has played in it. Besides having the honor itself in Harrison's case, it was Indiana that turned the scales and made Lincoln the Republican nominee and President." Then tapping his finger on the back of his hand he repeated, "1840, 1860, 1880. Harrison died while he was President and in the White House. Lincoln was assassinated while he was President, and was nominated in Chicago. What will become of me."

During all the sad hours and days of Garfield's illness, there remained constantly by his side, ministering to his wants, cheering him into hope and confidence, the woman whom history to-day delights in honoring as a heroine of the highest order—Mrs. Lucretia Garfield—his wife. What a beautiful picture is that of this wife and companion watching by the side of one in whom her hopes were centred! And what a sad picture that of the same brave, considerate woman bereaved at the loss of her husband, weeping by his side! How well did she fulfill the vows to care for and protect her husband in sickness as well as in death! With what faithfulness, with what untiring devotion and pathetic zeal was that vow kept; and how holy must be the associations which now cluster around every act and every aspiration of the womanly faith and love which animated the noble wife in her hour of trial! "History furnishes no more prominent example of devoted affection, forgetfulness of self, sacrifice of all comfort, carelessness of every thing except the poor sufferer upon the bed of pain. He was her only object in life. And to him, she was the bright star of destiny, the ever present angel of hope, the trusty sentinel upon the ramparts of eternity, who menaced and kept at bay the arch enemy, death. Her faith and hope and love were the medicaments which sustained him through all those weary days, when the services of physicians became as naught in the process of healing. No one could perform for him the tender offices of nursing so well as she; no voice so sweet as hers; no hand so gentle nor so ready to anticipate his wants. In those other years, when they toiled together for the mental, moral, and material advancement of themselves and their children, and knew little of the gay world, he learned this; and now, when they had reached the summit of the loftiest earthly ambition, and she, by right as well as courtesy, was acknowledged the first lady in the land, he still found her the same faithful nurse, with the old devotion to her wifely duty which makes the true woman an angel of mercy, and of more worth in the chamber of sickness than any physician. She never left him in all those weary days of pain, and she it was who, on many occasions, brought him back to consciousness and life by tender care, when it seemed to others that the slender thread which bound him to earth was too weak to longer hold. The name of Lucretia Garfield will remain linked indissolubly with that of the great soul whose love she honored, so long as wifely heroism is honored of man. In his youth, in the days of his poverty, she made him rich with the countless wealth of her woman's love. She pointed the way to a great future. To her careful management and sound advice is much of his early success to be attributed. Standing beside him at the coronation of his ambition, in the hour of his glory, she looked upon him with a pride beyond language, as under such conditions what wife would not? But in the dark days, which measured the period from July 2d to September 20th, and ended so deplorably to her and the country, it was a wifely love, destitute of all vainglory, with which, in full view of Christendom, she ministered, as only angels do, to the wounded form of her dying husband. No picture could be more pathetic, more instructive, more valuable as an example to all women of this day and coming ages; and it will be so remembered. Garfield's struggle for a life that had become historic for its manly courage was brave indeed; but with the history of that struggle there must forever be associated the imperishable name of a wife as great as he in all that makes greatness worth living or dying for in the eyes of men."

All over the country, and in fact the civilized world, the mourning for the dead man was outspoken and intense. Garfield was recognized among men as the highest exponent of the better qualities of mankind. His administration had just opened, and the promising bud was frost-bitten in its earliest fruition.

A very touching incident is told of the sadness occasioned in Ireland by the death of America's President. The writer says: "I visited a cottage, and I remarked on the door-posts some mourning trappings, and expected to find inside the dead. But no. In answer to 'Who's dead?' a chubby lad said, 'The king.' 'What king?' I said. 'Why, Garfield,' he replied. And then he added, 'My father is in America, and supports me and my sisters and brothers here with aunt; so Mary and I are sorry for the king.' Touching as this was, it was not confined to one house. Garfield is a household word in every cabin and mansion."

Preparations for the funeral had begun. The cottage by the sea was darkened. Armed sentinels stood without. Great men came to Elberon to pay their respects to the honored dead. President Arthur, having taken the oath of his new office in New York, was there. The arrangements for the funeral were completed, the autopsy was finished, and many grave doubts as to the direct cause of the President's death and the course of the ball, had been settled. Officials of Cleveland, where Garfield had first gone to seek employment as a boat-hand, and where the President was so long and favorably known, requested that the body be entombed in that city. This was agreed upon.

The time had arrived for the departure of the funeral train from Elberon. A short service was held, and the cars were backed up to the cottage on the track that had been so magically laid over the lawns on the night before he was taken to Long Branch. The entire train was heavily draped in mourning. As the train moved slowly off toward the Elberon station, nearly every hat was lifted from the heads of the thousands of people. All along the route the same genuine marks of sorrow were visible. Bells tolled, flags were at half mast, and everywhere there were evidences of mourning. As the train came into the depot at Washington City there was a hush among the throng, and then every head was uncovered. The scene that followed was impressive in the extreme. Mrs. Garfield, heavily veiled and dressed in deep mourning, alighted, leaning on the arm of Secretary Blaine on the one side, and supported by her son Harry on the other. Members of the Cabinet followed, and among them towered the form of President Arthur, on whose face was written the various emotions which must have struggled within him as he was welcomed by the sad and silent thousands of the people of Washington. This party was followed by the pall-bearers, consisting of trained artillery sergeants. As the cortege reached Sixth street, where the military was massed, the Marine Band began slowly playing "Nearer, my God, to Thee." As the notes of this beautiful melody filled the air all heads were bowed in reverence, and even the rabble in the streets was awed into silence.

The scene at the east front of the Capitol was an imposing one. The wide plateau was filled with the various military organizations in bright uniforms, conspicuous among which were the marines. The general and staff officers of the army and the officers of the navy formed in two lines leading to the foot of the broad marble steps on the east front, standing upon which President Garfield had delivered his inaugural address. Directly in front was the hearse, drawn by six magnificent gray horses. At the foot of the steps stood the officers of the Senate and of the House, and the Reception Committee. When the band had played a dirge, the pall-bearers advanced, followed by the President, Cabinet, Justices of the Supreme Court, Senators and Representatives, and filed slowly and sadly up a pathway which had been kept open in the middle of the broad flight of stairs, the sides being densely packed with people who had crowded in to see this part of the pageant. On reaching the centre of the vast rotunda, the casket was placed on the catafalque which had been prepared for it, and then the President and the Cabinet, together with General Grant, the Senators and the Representatives, stood for a moment in silence. Then a panel covering the face of the dead President was removed, and they looked for the last time upon the wasted features of him who so lately was chief of the Nation, and then solemnly moved away. The sight of the face of the dead President was indeed terrible, and upon most who saw it an impression was left which time can never efface. It was pinched and haggard to the last extreme; the skin yellow and glistening; the eyes sunken, and the lips tightly drawn. The nose looked unnaturally long, sharp, and hooked; and altogether there was but the slightest resemblance to the heroic form and face of him who had been called James A. Garfield.

The arrangement made was that for two days and nights the body of the illustrious dead should lie in state in the rotunda of the Capitol. This plan was carried out. A guard of honor stood right and left, and very soon, in orderly procession past the mortal remains of their dead friend, the people began to pour in a continuous stream. It was now nightfall, and the shadows came down around the magnificent structure which for eighteen years had been the scene of the toils and triumphs of Garfield, now, alas! about to witness the last ovation in his honor.

On the morning of the 22d of September, Washington City became, at sunrise, the scene of such a pageant as had never but once been beheld within those spacious avenues. By six o'clock the crowds had assembled, and were filing through the east door of the Capitol. As the day advanced the throng increased; and, as it became absolutely necessary that each person should have his turn in the solemn procession, the latest comers were obliged to take up their stations at the end of a long line to the rear. By ten o'clock this was found to reach to the crossing of Second street and the avenue south-west—considerably more than a quarter of a mile away. All along this line policemen walked back and forth to prevent stragglers from the outside coming into line out of turn. The people forming this procession were of the highest and lowest; among the number, thousands of women and children. At one time during the day it was ascertained by actual count that sixty persons passed the coffin in one minute, or at the rate of 3,600 an hour, or more than 40,000 during the day. This is probably not above the actual number which passed through the rotunda.

There were many beautiful floral decorations at the further end of the catafalque. During the afternoon there were some indications that the decomposition of the body had set in; and, it being understood that in such event it was the wish of Mrs. Garfield that the features of her husband should be shut out from the public gaze, and so the casket was ordered closed.

The following day witnessed a renewal of the scene of the day before. About noon the doors were closed, and Mrs. Garfield went in to remain with her dead husband a few moments alone. Pen cannot picture what must have been the feelings of that hour. At two o'clock in the afternoon the funeral services commenced, Scripture lessons were read by Rev. Dr. Rankin, and prayer was offered by Elder Isaac Errett, of Cincinnati. The Rev. F. D. Powers, pastor of the Vermont Avenue Christian Church, of which President Garfield was a member, made a touching and appropriate address upon the virtues of the man, which "plead like angels, trumpet-tongued, against the deep damnation of his taking off."

These exercises over the remains were removed to the railway train, and the sad company left the Nation's capital for the city by the lake side, where the last sad funeral rites were to occur. How intensified was that sadness as memory went back to the days when Garfield's administration commenced so auspiciously! Over in that prison was the culprit that had felled the Nation's pride.

The journey from Washington to the west was made without remarkable incident. Crowds, large beyond all precedent, awaited the passage of the train at every point. In Baltimore, which was reached before dark, the whole city had apparently turned out to see the draped coaches go by. As the train reached the outer edge of the waiting throng, Mrs. Garfield was seated in her car looking out of the window. Knowing her disposition to shrink from publicity, one of her companions arose to put down the shade. But she asked that it be allowed to remain open, saying that she was glad to see the crowds which had assembled to do honor to her husband.

The reception at Cleveland upon the arrival of the train was simple, yet very expressive. When the Euclid station was reached, the citizens' committee of reception, which had met the cortege as it passed into Ohio, stepped off the train, and formed into double line. The Judges of the Supreme Court, Senators and officers of the Army and Navy followed, and took their positions in the line. The body of the dead President was carried to Monument Square, in the centre of the city, where a large pavilion had been erected, with beautifully constructed avenues of approach in four directions. The decorations of the square and the buildings, plainly gave evidence of the deep sorrow and love that a free people desired to express for their fa len Chief Executive. The structure was appropriately decorated, from base to dome, with black and white crape. Flowers and flags were displayed at various places. Early Sunday morning, the great multitudes that had congregated in Cleveland from every part of the country, began moving with slow and solemn tread through the park, into the catafalque, past the casket containing all the earthly rema ns of President Garfield. His face was not shown, and yet this liberty-loving people stood in the hot sun for hours, forgetting fatigue, that even the place where he lay might be seen. Every hour the crowd increased, and the procession became longer. It was estimated that during the day one hundred and fifty thousand human beings passed silently by the casket. The throng did not end with the night. Electric lights gave the brightness of day to the weird scene. At midnight the almost perfect silence, the bright glare of the lights, the ceaseless movements of the sentinels, the sighing of the wind through the trees, combined to create a feeling of awe in the breasts of the beholders.

The morning of September 26th at last dawned—the day of sepulture. Cleveland was overflowing with visitors. The solemn services were said, the procession moved off, and James Abram Garfield was laid away in a beautiful cemetery, by the side of Lake Erie. The Nation had paid its last tribute. England's queen and the rulers of the old world placed laurel wreaths upon America's dead son. And so ended one of the most beautiful, well rounded and glorious lives of which history can boast.

It may be of interest to know what were some of the more important features of the Garfield administration. It has been claimed, but wrongly I think, that it cannot be said that General Garfield had any policy, for he did not live to carry out any line of administration. But the policy of the Republican party, of which he was the chief exponent, may be summarized as follows: To maintain the supremacy of the Nation; to protect the citizenship of the negroes, so often and so bitterly assailed; to promote the freedom and purity of the ballot; to aid in summoning "all the constitutional powers of the nation and of the States and all the volunteer forces of the people to meet the danger of illiteracy by the saving influence of universal education;" to defend specie payments against any new revival of prejudice and ignorance, and refund the public debt at low rates of interest; to assert the right of the United States to supervise any inter-oceanic canal to cross the Isthmus; to break up polygamy in Utah by the aid of wise congressional enactments and to promote reform in the civil service by urging Congress to pass a law to fix the tenure "of the minor offices of several executive departments and prescribe the grounds for which removals shall be made."

This, in the main, Garfield had outlined as the new administration policy, and we have every reason to believe, had not the hand of an assassin deprived him of life, the administration would have been fraught with wise measures and accomplishments.

The influence of a life like that of Garfield can scarcely be estimated. His career was not only an ascending from the humblest walks of life to the most exalted position within the power of the people to give, but it was a career adorned with the loftiest patriotism and animated by the truest purposes of right. There was nothing in it of the mean or base or trifling; it was dignified and honorable. His life is an additional force among the powers for good. Here and there in our past history of a hundred years, there has come out before the people a noble soul—one that was moved by worthiest impulse—one that took a wider range of view about the public good, and the underlying principles of true national grandeur than which the thought of men commonly embrace within their reach—one that in its aspirations rose high above those of the mass of human-kind, and in its action aimed to achieve what would lift up the people into a more blessed life. A few such there have been, but they heighten our national career, they exalt the Republic, and make her to be glorious among the nations of the earth. The worth of their character, the nobleness of their deeds, the manliness of their life are imperishable. Without them the Republic would not have for itself the grand history which is now the boast of all her citizens. Her progress would have been on a lower plane, and she would, in all probability not be what she is to day, the wonder of the world. These men who tower so high above their fellows have stamped themselves upon the life of the nation. Prominent among these mighty men of other times, now stands President Garfield. Search among all our millions, and we shall hardly find another man so temperate and wise and just as James A. Garfield, with qualities so admirable for the chief magistrate of a free people. "God fulfills himself in many ways," but he accomplishes his work by means of men; and there were tokens that in this man the power that makes for righteousness had found an instrument apt to its hand. So it appears now, and it is no disloyalty to his successor to recognize that Garfield was incomparably the man for the place which shall know him no more. He, above any statesman living, knew the Americans, and rightly conceived of their destinies and duties; and all Americans, willing to leave the question of other traits to history, mingle their tears in remembrance of his goodness and truth.

His was a career which, in all its mutations, is unsullied by a single blemish. Without fear, without favor, swerving neither to the right nor to the left,

> "Like to the Pontic sea,
> Whose icy current, and compulsive course
> Ne'er feels retiring ebb, *but keeps due on.*"

A youth of labor, of penury, of struggle most intense; a manhood noble, dignified, and whether on the field or in the forum, alike admirable, beautiful and perfect. While not at all times escaping the undeserved censure of faction, and the calumny born of envy and malice, he was enabled to live it down.

In that impartial and critical balance in which we are accustomed to estimate men, we find him, in every sense, pure and good; in the various and exacting relations of life, whether as son, husband, father or citizen, we find him superlatively perfect.

In the life of Garfield there is an honest appeal for excellence and labor. He lived and died the embodiment of every Christian virtue. His name will stand in history inseparably connected with the noble and pure who have enacted a part in the world's drama. His life is proof that a man can be honest and untrammeled with vice, and still be a man of state. And if the country, society, or the state, has a crying demand for one thing more than another, it is for men of truth and nobility, to be in positions of trust and influence. The youth of the land should gather this lesson from Garfield's life. This is the highest eulogy that Christian history can bestow upon any man, that he lived and died a pure man. In American history there is not a grander life.

Garfield needs no vindication. His nobility of purpose places him above reproach, and history will ever point to him as a NOBLE MAN.

"Of such as HE was
There be few on earth;
Of such as HE is
There are many in heaven;
And life is all the sweeter
That he lived,
And all he lived
More sacred for his sake;
And death is all the brighter
That he died,
And heaven is all the happier
That he's there."

POETS' TRIBUTE TO GARFIELD.

Commend me to the friend that comes
When I am sad and lone,
And makes the anguish of my heart
The suffering of his own;
Who coldly shuns the glittering throng
At pleasure's gay levee,
And comes to gild a sombre hour
And give his heart to me.

He hears me count my sorrows o'er;
And when the task is done
He freely gives me all I ask—
A sigh for every one.
He cannot wear a smiling face
When mine is touched with gloom,
But like the violet seeks to cheer
The midnight with perfume.

Commend me to that generous heart
Which like the pine on high,
Uplifts the same unvarying brow
To every change of sky;
Whose friendship does not fade away
When wintry tempests blow,
But like the winter's icy crown
Looks greener through the snow.

He flies not with the flitting stork,
That seeks a southern sky;
But lingers where the wounded bird
Hath laid him down to die.
Oh, such a friend! He is in truth,
Whate'er his lot may be,
A rainbow on the storm of life,
An anchor on its sea.

—*Garfield's Favorite Verses.*

GEMS OF POETRY AND SONG.

In nothing more than the productions that have been contributed to current literature, in which the wealth of expression, depth and compass of the English language have been shown, is the deep love for Garfield seen. During his suffering, and after death had robbed us of our beloved, the minstrel of poesy and song gave birth to the sweetest sentiments of love and devotion. Journalism has reached a higher plane of literary excellence than ever before. With the electric bands circling the earth, joining the Orient and Occident almost in the union of brotherhood, a great national calamity becomes the interest of the world. The sorrow occasioned by Garfield's assassination sought expression in every form. But the poets' lays, more than anything else, furnished the most suitable medium for expressing the bereavement which had settled down upon the land like a great pall. The following collection has been made from a very large number of poems that have already been published.

GARFIELD.

"Dust to Dust"—September 26, 1881.

Two-score and ten! A broken life well spent,
The wise and good are glad such soul was sent—
By Him who giveth talents, one or ten,
To angels, mighty, and to mortal men!
Star of a sun-lit age in lasting luster blent!
More radiant, now, in fairer firmament.

"Dust unto dust." From hallowed lips to-day,
These farewell words fall o'er the honored clay,
As back to earth, with fitting dirge, returns
More sacred mold than sleeps in royal urns!
A stricken Nation bends with grief to lay
Upon her Noble Dead the amaranthine bay.

Of Freedom's Land a loved and laureled son,
The peer of Lincoln and of Washington
Such names to struggling man bright beacons are,
As unto mariner the true pole star!
No cloud of Time thy shining fame can mar,
But through all future gloom 'twill brighter glow afar.

—James Nesbitt Karr.

BURIAL OF GARFIELD.

I.

A Nation's head is bowed to-day,
  A world looks on in tears,
For one who passed from earth away
  In the glory of his years.
We lay his honored form in dust,
  Upon his native soil—
The great, the good, the wise, the just,
  A foul assassin's spoil.
So wondrous are the ways of God,
  So far past finding out,
We bow submissive to the rod,
  Without complaint or doubt.

II.

Through years of gloom, from years of strife,
  That found at last surcease,
Our Nation had resumed its life
  Of Union and of Peace.
From North to South, from South to North,
  Waves of new feeling rolled,
And the words on each that journey'd forth
  Were words we knew of old.
East turn'd to West, West turn'd to East,
  With looks of glad surprise,
As the bickerings of sections ceas'd,
  And we felt new hopes arise.

III.

But now the orb whose steady light
  Fell everywhere—on all—
Has passed away from mortal sight,
  And shadows 'round us fall:
Yet we have strength, if we have will,
  Those shades to drive away—
The darkness to dispel, and still
  Enjoy the perfect day.
So let us, standing by the tomb
  That holds the honored dead,
Resolve to scatter far the gloom
  That threatens overhead.

IV.

Let us be MEN, not slaves to hate;
  Look warily about;
Prejudge not any one, but bate
  Our aptitude to doubt;
Look forward more than backward; see
  What *now* lies in our way;

Work for a day that *is to be*—
  Not for a vanished day;
Afar be all our bickerings hurl'd;
  Do as *he* would have done
Whom now we mourn, and show the world
  Though MANY we are ONE.

ENGLAND TO AMERICA.

JAMES ABRAM GARFIELD.

Born November 19, 1831. *Died President of the United States, September* 19, 1881.

Silence were best, if hand in hand,
  Like friends, sea-sundered Peoples met;
But words must wing from land to land
  The utterances of the heart's regret,
Though harsh on ears that sorrow thralls
E'en Sympathy's low accent falls

Salt leagues that part us check no whit,
  What knows not bounds of time or space,
The homestead feeling that must knit
  World scattered kin in speech and race.
None like ourselves may well bemoan
Columbia's sorrow; 'tis our own.

A sorrow of the nobler sort,
  Which love and pride make pure and fair;
A grief that is not misery's sport,
  A pain that bows not to despair;
Beginning not in courtly woe
To end in pageantry and show.

The great republic's foremost son,
  Struck foully, falls; but they who mourn
Brave life cut short, good work half done,
  Yet trust that from beyond death's bourne
That blameless memory's gifts may be
Peace, concord, civic purity.

Scarce known of us till struck for death,
  He stirred us by his valiant fight
With mortal pain. With bated breath
  We waited tidings morn and night.
The hope that's nursed by strong desire,
Though shaken often, will not tire.

And now our sables, type, in truth,
  A more than ceremonial pain,
We send, Court, Cottage, Age, and Youth,
  From open hearts, across the main,
Our sympathy—it never swerved—
To Wife he loved, to Land he served

—LONDON PUNCH.

AFTER THE BURIAL.

BY OLIVER WENDELL HOLMES.

I.

Fallen with autumn's falling leaf,
  Ere yet his summer's noon was past,
Our friend, our guide, our trusted chief—
  What words can match a woe so vast?

And whose the chartered claim to speak
  The sacred grief where all have part,
When sorrow saddens every cheek,
  And broods in every aching heart?

Yet Nature prompts the burning phrase,
  That thrills the hushed and shrouded hall,
The loud lament, the sorrowing praise,
  The silent tear that love lets fall.

In loftiest verse, in lowliest rhyme,
  Shall strive unblamed the minstrel choir—
The singers of the new-born time,
  And trembling age with out-worn lyre.

No room for pride, no place for blame—
  We fling our blossoms on the grave,
Pale, scentless, faded—all we claim,
  This only—what we had we gave.

Ah, could the grief of all who mourn
  Blend in one voice its bitter cry,
The wail to heaven's high arches borne
  Would echo through the caverned sky.

II.

O happiest land whose peaceful choice
  Fills with a breath its empty throne!
God, speaking through thy people's voice,
  Has made that voice for once his own.

No angry passion shakes the State
  Whose weary servant seeks for rest—
And who could fear that scowling hate
  Would strike at that unguarded breast?

He stands, unconscious of his doom,
  In manly strength, erect, serene—
Around him summer spreads her bloom:
  He falls—what horror clothes the scene!

How swift the sudden flash of woe
  Where all was bright as childhood's dream!
As if from heaven's ethereal bow
  Had leaped the lightning's arrowy gleam.

Blot the foul deed from history's page—
  Let not the all-betraying sun
Blush for the day that stains an age
  When murder's blackest wreath was won.

III

Pale on his couch the sufferer lies,
  The weary battle-ground of pain;
Love tends his pillow, science tries
  Her every art, alas! in vain

The strife endures how long! how long!
  Life, death, seem balanced in the scale;
While round his bed a viewless throng
  Awaits each morrow's changing tale.

In realms the desert ocean parts,
  What myriads watch with tear-filled eyes,
His pulse-beats echoing in their hearts,
  His breathings counted with their sighs!

Slowly the stores of life are spent,
  Yet hope still battles with despair—
Will heaven not yield when knees are bent?
  Answer, O Thou that hearest prayer!

But silent is the brazen sky—
  On sweeps the meteor's threatening train—
Unswerving Nature's mute reply,
  Bound in her adamantine chain.

Not ours the verdict to decide
  Whom death shall claim or skill shall save:
The hero's life though Heaven denied,
  It gave our land a martyr's grave.

Nor count the teaching vainly sent
  How human hearts their griefs may share—
The lesson woman's love has lent,
  What hope may do, what faith can bear.

Farewell! the leaf-strown earth enfolds
  Our stay, our pride, our hopes, our fears;
And autumn's golden sun beholds
  A nation bowed, a world in tears.

REJOICE.

BY JOAQUIN MILLER.

"Bear me out of the battle, for lo! I am sorely wounded."

I.

From out my deep, wide-bosomed West,
Where unnamed heroes hew the way
For worlds to follow, with stern zest—
Where gnarled old maples make array,
Deep-scarred from red men gone to rest—
Where pipes the quail, where squirrels play
Through tossing trees, with nuts for toy,
A boy steps forth, clear-eyed and tall,
A bashful boy, a soulful boy,
Yet comely as the sons of Saul—
A boy, all friendless, poor, unknown,
Yet heir-apparent to a throne.

II.

Lo! Freedom's bleeding sacrifice!
So like some tall oak tempest-blown
Beside the storied stream he lies,
Now at the last, pale-browed and prone.
A nation kneels with streaming eyes,
A nation supplicates the throne,
A nation holds him by the hand,
A nation sobs aloud at this:
The only dry eyes in the land
Now at the last, I think, are his.
Why, we should pray, God knoweth best,
That this grand, patient soul should rest.

III.

The world is round. The wheel has run
Full circle. Now behold a grave
Beneath the old loved trees is done.
The druid oaks lift up, and wave
A solemn welcome back. The brave
Old maples murmur, every one,
"Receive him, Earth!" In centre land,
As in the centre of each heart,
As in the hollow of God's hand,
The coffin sinks. And with it part
All party hates! Now, not in vain
He bore his peril and hard pain.

IV.

Therefore, I say, rejoice! I say,
The lesson of his life was much—
This boy that won, as in a day,
The world's heart utterly; a touch

Of tenderness and tears. the page
Of history grows rich from such;
His name the nation's heritage—
But oh! as some sweet angel's voice
Spake this brave death that touched us all.
Therefore, I say, Rejoice! Rejoice!
Run high the flags! Put by the pall!
Lo! all is for the best for all!

SONNET—JAMES A. GARFIELD.

BY REV. H. BERNARD CARPENTER.

Lo! as a pure, white statue wrought with care
By some strong hand, which molds from Life and Death
Beauty more beautiful than blood or breath,
And straight 'tis veiled; and, whilst all men repair
To see this wonder in the workshop, there!
Behold, it gleams unveiled to curious eye
Far-seen, high-placed in Art's pale gallery,
Where all stand mute before a work so fair:
So he, our man of men, in vision stands,
With Pain and Patience crowned imperial;
Death's veil has dropped; far from this house of woe
He hears one love-chant out of many lands,
Whilst from his mystic noon-height he lets fall
His shadow o'er these hearts that bleed below.
September 26, 1881.

PRESIDENT GARFIELD.

FROM THE LONDON SPECTATOR.

The hush of the sick-room; the muffled tread;
Fond, questioning eye; mute lip, and listening ear;
Where wife and children watch, 'twixt hope and fear,
A father's, husband's living-dying bed!—
The hush of a great nation, when its head
Lies stricken! Lo! along the streets he's borne,
Pale, through ranked crowds this gray September morn,
'Mid straining eyes, sad brows unbonneted,
And reverent speechlessness!—a "people's voice!"
Nay, but a people's silence! through the soul
Of the wide world its subtler echoes roll,
O brother nation! England for her part
Is with thee: God willing, she whose heart
Throbbed with thy pain shall with thy joy rejoice.
September 6, 1881.

GOD SAVE THE PRESIDENT—GOD SAVE THE QUEEN.

BY S. S. CUTTING, D. D.

One hundred years are fled;
Victors and vanquished dead,
They sleep serene;
Kin, once asunder rent,
Lift now our banners blent—
God save the President!
God save the Queen!

One heritage of blood,
Speech, liberty and God—
With conscience clean—
Rule of the world is meant!
Lift then our banners blent—
God save the President!
God save the Queen!

When wounded lay its chief,
And prostrate in its grief,
This land was seen—
What love on lightning sent,
Lift then our banners blent;
God save the President!
God save the Queen!

New bind the severed chain,
Let love forever reign,
These lands between.
Each with its fame content,
Lift high our banners blent;
God save the President!
God save the Queen!

"HE IS DEAD, OUR PRESIDENT."

BY CHARLES TURNER DAZEY.

[THE HARVARD CLASS POET OF 1881.]

He is dead, our President; he rests in an honored grave,
He whom any one of us would gladly have died to save.
All is over at last, the long, brave struggle for life—
For a nation's sake, not his own, and for that of children and wife.
Doubt and suspense are dead; dead is the passionate thrill
Of a hope too blessed and sweet for aught but death to kill.
Do you remember yet, how, from that awful day
When the pulse of the nation stopped with a shock of wild dismay,
And voiceless horror looked from questioning eyes to eyes,
As the murmur widened and spread, "Our President murdered lies"—

How to the very last, like a star in a night of gloom,
The hope of the people burned till it sank in a hero's tomb?
We could not give him up as a mother prays for her child,
We prayed for his precious life, with a love as deep and wild.
We had known him long and well as a man of royal mind,
Who had nobly proved his birthright as a leader of mankind.
We had watched him, oh, so proudly, as in life's ranks he rose
By the fair and open warfare that endeared him to his foes:
But we never prized him rightly until he had meekly lain
Wrapped in speechless tortures of the fiery furnace of pain.
Then how we learned to love him! for all that man holds dear,
For infinite faith and patience, and courage when death drew near,
For yearning love that strove with a pitiful, mighty strife,
To shield from the sting of sorrow the hearts of mother and wife.
Then with tearful vision, purged of passion and pride,
We saw in its tender beauty that spirit glorified;
And mighty love swept o'er us with a current as deep and grand
As the Nile that swells to a sea to nourish a hungry land.
O boundless sea of love, and star of a hope that is dead,
Not vainly our President died, not vainly our loved one bled,
If still that sea shall sweep onward which at first so narrow ran
Till the hands of the nations clasp in the brotherhood of man,
Till the hate that smoulders still in hearts unreconciled
Shall change to the sweet affection that beams in the glance of a child,
And gladness shall dawn from sorrow, and glory burst from gloom,
And the flower of love fraternal shall blossom from Garfield's tomb

Cambridge, Mass., September 25, 1881.

A TOUCHING SONNET.

BY ERIC S. ROBERTSON.

The following sonnet was written in St. Paul's Cathedral, London, after the funeral anthem for President Garfield had been sung:

September 25.

Through tears to look upon a tearful crowd,
  And hear the anthem echoing
  High in the dome till angels seem to fling
The chant of England up through vault and cloud,
Making ethereal register aloud
  At heaven's own gate. It was a sorrowing
  To make a good man's death seem such a thing
As makes imperial purple of his shroud.

Some creeds there be like runes we cannot spell,
  And some like stars that flicker in their flame;
But some so clear the sun scarce shines so well;
  For when with Moses' touch a dead man's name
Finds tears within strange rocks as this name can,
We know right well that God was with the man.

—New York Herald.

J. A. G.

BY JULIA WARD HOWE.

Our sorrow sends its shadow 'round the earth.
So brave, so true! A hero from his birth!
The plumes of empire moult, in mourning draped,
The lightning's message by our tears is shaped.

Life's vanities that blossom for an hour
Heap on his funeral car their fleeting flower.
Commerce forsakes her temples, blind and dim,
And pours her tardy gold, to homage him.

The notes of grief to age familiar grow
Before the sad privations all must know;
But the majestic cadence which we hear
To-day, is new in either hemisphere.

What crown is this, high hung and hard to reach,
Whose glory so outshines our laboring speech?
The crown of honor, pure and unbetrayed;
He wins the spurs who bears the knightly aid.

While royal babes incipient empire hold,
And, for bare promise, grasp the sceptre's gold,
This man such service to his age did bring
That they who knew him servant, hailed him king.

In poverty his infant couch was spread;
His tender hands soon wrought for daily bread;
But from the cradle's bound his willing feet
The errand of the moment went to meet.

When learning's page unfolded to his view,
The quick disciple straight a teacher grew;
And, when the fight of freedom stirred the land,
Armed was his heart and resolute his hand.

Wise in the council, stalwart in the field,
Such rank supreme a workman's hut may yield.
His onward steps like measured marble show,
Climbing the height where God's great flame doth glow.

Ah! Rose of joy, that hid'st a thorn so sharp!
Ah! Golden woof that meet'st a severed warp!
Ah! Solemn comfort that the stars rain down!
The hero's garland his, the martyr's crown!

Newport, September 25, 1881.

ILLINOIS TO HER BEREAVED SISTER.

Written by a native of your State, who feels the dreadful blow.

Ohio, weep! Let tears of blood
  Fall from your eyes like rain,
And we your sister States with you
  Will mourn your martyred slain.

Aye, weep, and don your sombrest garb,
  Habiliments of woe;
For never can your troubled heart
  A keener anguish know.

Oh, weep; nor sit with clasped hands
  And eyes so full of pain,
For tears will soothe the fevered brow,
  Will ease the tortured brain

We, too, are mothers, and our hearts
  Have had, alas, to mourn
The loss of those most dearly lov'd,
  For they can ne'er return.

In vain we plead, in vain caress,
  Thou canst do naught but moan,
For from thy lips no words escape
  Save these, "No other one."

We look around in mute despair,
  We know not what to do;
Can no one break this spell, we ask,
  Nor cause the tears to flow?

A silence reigns, when from our midst
  Steps one with royal mien;
A golden crown upon her head,
  Her robe a golden sheen.

With clasped hands and bated breath
  We pray success attend,
For if she fails we dare not think
  Of what may be the end.

One glance above, as from her eye
  A tear in silence steals,
Then with her queenly, regal grace,
  Advancing, stooping, kneels.

Ohio, sister, say not so,
  Say not "No other one
Hath grief like mine so deep to bear,"
  I, too, have lost a son.

A son, indeed, beloved by all,
To me he was most dear;
But by the dark assassin's hand
I am left mourning here.

I said at first, as now say you,
This grief I cannot bear;
Turn whichsoever way I would
It all was dark despair.

But now, at last I have found peace,
I neither sigh nor moan;
For I have found the strength to say,
O Lord, thy will be done.

The years have come and gone, 'tis true,
Since he, my son, was slain,
So years will come again to you,
And Time will deaden pain.

I loved him then, I love him yet,
And I will say to you,
Love *him* not less, nor him forget,
For this you *cannot* do.

But look around, and when you e'er
Shall see another's woe,
Reach out a helping hand to her,
And sympathy bestow.

And when in grief you're tempted sore
To say, "No other one,"
Oh, think of me and try to pray,
"O Lord, thy will be done."

The spell is broken; with the tears
Fast falling down her cheeks,
Ohio clasps her sister's hand
And tremulously speaks.

I will remember your brave son,
And how he came to die;
And this to us will be a bond
Of closer sympathy.

And children now unborn will tell,
In song or eloquence,
Of those whom we so deeply mourn,
Our martyred Presidents.

—ILLINOIS.

September 22, 1881.

THE MIDNIGHT KNELL.

BY HENRY C. DANE.

I sat at the hour of midnight,
  Weary and sad and lone,
In fancy watching the lamplight
  That from the sick-room shone;
While a silence deep and solemn
  Brooded over the earth—
The silence attending the column
  Of angels—leading Death.

The heart of Nature seemed throbbing
  With pity, pain, and woe,
As it watched a nation sobbing
  With anguish deep and low,
While it waited and hoped with fear
  The tidings at the dawn—
The tidings it dreaded to hear
  From that cot at Elberon!

Once more I perused the message—
  "*It still looks very dark!*"
And thought of that noble visage
  That lay in Elberon's—Hark!
Out from the towering steeple,
  Breaking the weary spell,
Came the message to the people—
  The deep, the midnight knell!

"Gone!" "Gone!" it rang—that doleful bell,
  From spire and dome and tower,
Crushing a nation with its knell—
  That awful midnight hour!
On, on it rolled, o'er distant West,
  Through valleys broad and deep,
Waking a nation from its rest,
  To bow with grief, and weep.

Daughter heroic, and mother,
  Your tortures who dare tell—
There without son and brother,
  By him you loved so well.
A nation holds you to its heart,
  And hold you will forever:
It shares with you the bitter part;
  Its love nought e'er can sever.

Gone! gone! our hero chieftain gone!
  Struck in his hour of might,
And falling o'er his work undone,
  Because he dared the right.

O people boasting of thy power!
O nation just begun!
Learn thy lesson from this sad hour,
And see thy duty done!

Gaze on that form so tried and torn;
Gaze on that deep-scarred face:
There learn the lesson not yet won,
The duties ye must face.
O men of honor, truth and power!
O men of mighty zeal!
Step to the front in this dark hour,
And help our woes to heal!

From Vernon's deep and silent shade,
From Marshfield's solemn shore,
From Oakland's calm and peaceful glade,
And all the broad land o'er,
From those who sleep in patriot graves,
The warning voice is heard—
"This is your hour! be men, not slaves!
Redeem our plighted word!"

Boston, September 20, 1881.

AN ODE ON THE ASSASSINATION.

A prize offered by a London weekly for the best poem on the attempted assassination of President Garfield was awarded to the author of the following.

Veil now, O Liberty! thy blushing face,
At the fell deed that thrills a startled world;
While fair Columbia weeps in dire disgrace,
And bows in sorrow o'er the banner furled.

No graceless tyrant falls by vengeance here,
'Neath the wild justice of a secret knife;
No red Ambition ends its grim career,
And expiates its horrors with its life.

Not here does rash Revenge misguided burn,
To free a nation with the assassin's dart;
Or roused Despair in angry madness turn,
And tear its freedom from a despot's heart.

But where blest Liberty so widely reigns,
And Peace and Plenty mark a smiling land,
Here the mad wretch its fair white record stains
And blurs its beauties with a "bloody hand."

Here the elect of millions, and the pride
Of those who own his mild and peaceful rule—
Here virtue sinks and yields the crimson tide,
Beneath the vile unreason of a fool.

OUR DEAD PRESIDENT.

BY C. H. C.

Who has the fitting word,
When every breast is stirred
With sorrow far too deep for words to tell?
Yet as, amid death's gloom,
Friends whisper in the room,
We speak of him who lived and died so well.

Night reigned beside the sea,
When morning came to thee,
Long-waiting heart, so patient and so brave!
Light fell upon thy door,
Pain ceased forevermore,
Back to its Maker fled the life he gave.

Like messengers in quest,
Then started east and west
Two tidal waves of sorrow 'round the world:
Millions of eyes were wet
Before the tidings met
Where in the eastern seas our flags are furled.

Quickly, through throbbing wire,
Those waves of sorrow dire
Awoke across the land the mournful bells·
Men roused, and could not sleep;
For, pulsing strong and deep,
All hearts that knew were ringing funeral knells.

Wives gazed in husbands' eyes,
And tears would slowly rise
For her who fought with Death so long alone;
And children with no task
Were left themselves to ask
Why death this father took, and not their own.

On all the shadow falls,
It hushes college halls,
It consecrates the cabins of the West;
The freedmen loved him well;
Soldiers his praises tell;
The rudest boatman is too sad to jest.

Still, over hills and dells,
The beautiful sad bells
Repeat the nation's sorrow for her son;
But he doth hear the chime
Of a more peaceful clime
Than Mentor's fields or quiet Elberon.

Like him, the Crucified,
He, who so calmly died,
Has made the world the better for his pain:
Surely we now may know
Our leader was laid low
To lift the nation to a higher plane.

We say as once he said—
Our hero-ruler dead—
"The Lord still reigns, the country is secure."
There's none can fill his place:
Rule thou, O God of grace!
And guide us on to days more bright and pure.

—THE NEW YORK TRIBUNE.

THE DEAD PRESIDENT.

BY J. G. HOLLAND.

A wasp flew out upon our fairest son,
And stung him to the quick with poisoned shaft,
The while he chatted carelessly, and laughed,
And knew not of the fateful mischief done.
And so this life amid our love begun,
Envenomed by the insect's hellish craft,
Was drunk by Death in one long feverish draught,
And he was lost—our precious, priceless one.
Oh, mystery of blind, remorseless fate!
Oh, cruel end of a most causeless hate,
That life so mean should murder life so great!
What is there left to us who think and feel,
Who have no remedy and no appeal,
But damn the wasp and crush him under heel?

O Garfield! fortunate in death wast thou,
Though at the opening of a grand career!
Thou wast a meteor flashing on the brow
Of skies political, where oft appear,

And disappear, so many stars of promise. Then,
While all men watched thy high course, wondering
If thou wouldst upward sweep, or fall again,
Thee from thine orbit mad hands thought to fling;

And lo! the meteor, with its fitful light,
All on a sudden stood, and was a star—
A radiance fixed to glorify the night
There where the world's proud constellations are.

35-31
267-279

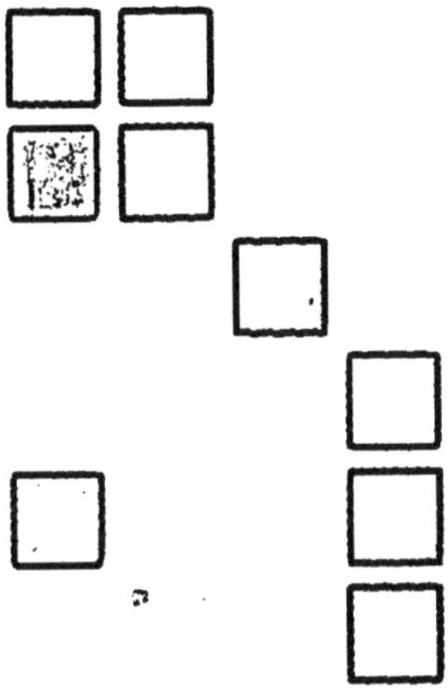

CPSIA information can be obtained
at www.ICGtesting.com
Printed in the USA
LVHW080715110422
715821LV00022B/312

9 781371 081218